Psychological Causation in Tort Law

Cícero Dantas Bisneto

Psychological Causation in Tort Law

Damage Caused by Psychological Influence and Objective Imputation

Springer

Cícero Dantas Bisneto
Tribunal de Justiça da Bahia
Salvador, Bahia, Brazil

ISBN 978-3-032-03824-1 ISBN 978-3-032-03825-8 (eBook)
https://doi.org/10.1007/978-3-032-03825-8

Translation from the Portuguese language edition: "Causalidade Psíquica" by Cícero Dantas Bisneto, © Author 2023. Published by Thomson Reuters. All Rights Reserved.

The original submitted manuscript has been translated into English. The translation was done using artificial intelligence. A subsequent revision was performed by the author(s) to further refine the work and to ensure that the translation is appropriate concerning content and scientific correctness. It may, however, read stylistically different from a conventional translation.

This Springer imprint is published by the registered company Springer Nature Switzerland AG.
The registered company address is: Gewerbestrasse 11, 6330 Cham, Switzerland

Contents

Chapter 1
Introduction

The complexity of social relations has shown that the damages arising from the exercise of daily activities do not originate exclusively from behavior that directly causes a harmful consequence. On the contrary, it can be observed that, especially in the era of information and a hyperconnected society, the actions and manifestations of certain individuals increasingly influence the conduct and way of life of other people, often resulting in compensable damages. The question is whether injuries resulting from the actions of individuals who influence or facilitate the conduct of others should be attributed to them, departing from the traditional naturalistic causal scheme.

Starting from the observation of cases where the harmful event is caused by the individual's own voluntary actions, it is questioned whether the initial perpetrator, who enabled the conduct of the latter, should be held liable for the damages suffered by the causer who acted (where the second causer and the injured party coincide) or by a third party (where the second causer and the injured party are different individuals). It is essential to determine whether this phenomenon, commonly referred to as "psychological causation," should receive autonomous legal treatment, constituting a distinct legal category with its own concept, characteristics, and solution criteria.

The primary aim of this study is to examine the need for a differentiated legal approach to these cases and assess whether current mechanisms in the Brazilian legal system address the issues arising from the specific legal particularities identified. If causal theories commonly adopted in Brazilian law are inadequate for resolving the problem, we should analyze criteria that prove effective in resolving controversies involving the theme of "psychological causation."

Initially, preliminary considerations will introduce discussions on the topic. Then, a concise historical analysis of "psychological causation" will be conducted, aiming to illustrate the evolution of the theme to the present day. It can be observed that, although the theme was not initially treated in a systematized way,

C. Dantas Bisneto, *Psychological Causation in Tort Law*,
https://doi.org/10.1007/978-3-032-03825-8_1

questions about the influence of certain behaviors on the conduct of third parties were already discussed on a case-by-case basis, using the theoretical framework available at the time.

Next, it is essential to analyze whether traditional causal theories, especially those of direct and immediate damage and adequacy, frequently used by Brazilian doctrine and jurisprudence, successfully delimit the liability of individuals who act by influencing or favoring the behavior of third parties, resulting in damages. At this stage, it is necessary to further explore the examination of these theories through a critical analysis, revealing the practical discrepancies presented by these doctrinal constructions, especially when applied to cases of damages caused by psychological influence. Far from simply deconstructing established notions, the focus will be on determining whether they can, in isolation, provide useful solutions to the problems presented or whether they should be combined with other criteria for determining liability.

At this stage, it is crucial to examine the distinction, rarely addressed in Brazilian law, between "natural causation" or "causation in fact" and the criteria for objective imputation. The former is based on the theory of the equivalence of conditions, while the latter is established through the balancing of evaluative legal parameters to demarcate and limit the scope of liability. This differentiation is highly relevant for establishing imputation criteria within the context of "psychological causation."

Additionally, this study will assess whether existing causal theories and developed imputation criteria should be applied separately or in combination when defining liability boundaries in cases of "psychological causation." This assessment will involve categorizing distinct groups of cases. If a combined approach proves viable, the research will explore the specific contribution of each criterion in establishing the limits of damage imputation.

In the second part of the work, the objective is to define and delimit the concept of "psychological causation," distinguishing it from other legal doctrines and identifying the case groups to be analyzed. Subsequently, the issue of factual causation will be explored, emphasizing its peculiarities in the context of "psychologically mediated causation," particularly as there is no physical link between the conduct and the harmful event. It will be examined whether it is possible to affirm the presence of a causal connection between the behavior of the initial perpetrator and the conduct of the one who materializes the injury.

Further on, the violation of general duties of care (*Verkehrspflichten*) in Brazilian law and its close connection with the occurrence of indirect damages, which include cases of damages caused by psychological influence, will be addressed. The investigation aims to determine whether Brazilian law allows for the establishment of duties of care as dogmatic instruments for risk prevention and elimination. If certain behavioral duties are understood to arise from the creation or maintenance of socially unacceptable dangerous situations, this would simplify the task of attributing damages to the risk creator. This approach would eliminate the need for artificial imputation techniques, such as invoking the concept of abuse of rights or implicit constitutional principles to identify an unlawful act.

The study continues with an analysis of the legal criteria applicable to cases of damages caused by psychological influence. The compatibility of certain imputational parameters used in foreign law with Brazilian law will be examined. The aim of the study is to assess which criteria for demarcating liability can prove useful in resolving cases where an initial act influences or favors the behavior of a second causer. The objective is to critically examine the criteria used by foreign doctrine and jurisprudence, particularly German, without resorting to decontextualized and uncritical legal transplants.

Finally, after establishing the criteria applicable to "psychological causation" scenarios, the theoretical models developed will be applied to concrete cases, providing practical relevance to the study and preventing the investigation from resulting in mere abstractions without any effective utility. The case groups will be analyzed individually, according to their specificities. Immediately after the description of each specific case, critical considerations will be woven regarding the judicial decision or hypothetical situation, proposing solutions and indicating the applicable criteria, while considering the specificities of Brazilian law.

Part I
Causal Theories and Psychological Causation: A First Approach

The main objective of this first part of the work is to demonstrate the insufficiency of the causation theories commonly adopted in Brazilian law to independently and universally resolve the issues related to damages caused by psychological influence.[1] This part introduces "psychological causation," explores its complexities, and presents key concepts to be developed further in the second part of the study. Subsequently, causal theories are critically analyzed, aiming to highlight the lack of effective criteria capable of addressing the diverse issues emerging from social relations, particularly in cases involving "psychological causation."

The *first part* is divided into two chapters: (1) Initial Considerations and (2) Critical Analysis of Causation Theories.

---

[1] Despite the existing terminological ambiguity, the expressions "psychological causation" and "damages caused by psychological influence" will be treated as synonyms. The issue regarding the nomenclature used will be further explored.

Chapter 2
Initial Considerations

"Psychological causation" poses a fundamental challenge to the traditional doctrine of liability, questioning the limits of imputation in cases where the causal connection extends beyond mere physical interaction. In today's hyperconnected society, where fake news, cyberbullying, and digital influencers can cause substantial harm, the psychological influence on third-party behavior requires a thorough revision of traditional causation paradigms. From Roman law to modern legal codes, the historical development reveals an ongoing effort to balance compensation needs with liability limits for indirect influences. This evolution culminates in modern German law through the development of objective imputation criteria, such as the "provocation formula" and other responsibility parameters. In the Brazilian context, the insufficiency of the theories of direct and immediate damage and adequate causation highlights the urgency of developing specific criteria for determining liability in cases of "psychological causation." This doctrinal renewal must reconcile effective victim protection with clear imputation parameters, moving beyond mere judicial case-by-case analysis and providing systematic responses to the new challenges of liability.

2.1 Introduction

Causation problems[1] are typically framed as actions or omissions by wrongdoers that directly and physically[2] cause harmful consequences. For example, when a driver hits a pedestrian, the driver's act typically constitutes the cause of the

[1] Given that the subject is generally unfamiliar to the Brazilian public, it was deemed pertinent to provide brief considerations on the issue of "psychological causation" before delving into the discussion about causal and imputation theories, in order to facilitate the understanding of the theoretical proposals related to the theme, which will only be further explored from the second part of the work.

[2] Generally, the principle of causation is invoked to explain the occurrence of natural phenomena.

C. Dantas Bisneto, *Psychological Causation in Tort Law*,
https://doi.org/10.1007/978-3-032-03825-8_2

pedestrian's injuries, unless interfered with by third parties or natural events. Similarly, science confirms that a hammer blow of sufficient force will invariably damage a glass pane. These cases represent instances where causal processes are repeatable or replicable, always leading to the same result.[3]

However, there are cases where the damage does not occur as a consequence of the direct physical effects of a person's behavior but arises indirectly through a psychological component of another individual.[4] "Psychological causation" applies to situations where injury results not from the defendant's direct act but from another individual's theoretically voluntary behavior. This other individual, whether the injured party or a third party,[5] acts in ways facilitated or encouraged by the wrongdoer's behavior.[6]

In various cases, which will be discussed in more detail below,[7] an individual causes damage to a third party or to themselves, acting under the influence of or having their actions facilitated by the behavior of a first perpetrator. Consider a young woman victimized by fake news on Instagram claiming she had a romance with a famous comedian. After suffering insults from third parties on social media, she takes her own life due to the scandal's repercussions. It is debated whether the person who disseminated the false news, failing to take due precautions, could be held civilly liable for the harmful event. Other examples include cases of revenge porn, bullying, or even environmental disasters caused by large mining companies, which may result in victims self-harming due to the distress suffered, culminating even in the suicide of those affected.

Debate exists regarding negligent drivers' liability for injuries suffered by rescuers. For instance, should a driver be liable when a rescuer suffers severe burns while saving victims, resulting in work disability? Although the rescuer's act was carried out on his own initiative, it is worth questioning whether this supposedly voluntary behavior excludes the attribution of liability between the careless driver's conduct and the injuries caused to the rescuer.[8] Similarly, it is questioned whether the fugitive who disobeys a stop order should be held liable for the damages suffered by the police officer or volunteer who undertakes the pursuit, aiming at his capture or obtaining more information about his identity.

Recently, there has been discussion about the liability of digital influencers[9] regarding the decisions made by their followers. The posts made by these new

---

Everything that happens within the realm of physical laws is due to the link of cause and effect (Nader (2016), p. 121).

[3] Ristow (2003), p. 11.

[4] Manuel Carneiro da Frada refers to "psychologically provoked harmful actions" (Frada (2010), p. 101).

[5] Lange and Schiemann (2003), p. 131.

[6] The concept of "psychological causation" and its contours will be duly explored in Sect. 4.2.

[7] The cases will be analyzed in detail from Sect. 5.2.1.

[8] Zhang (2016), pp. 46–47.

[9] Regarding the expansion of the activities of digital influencers, as well as their increased ability to reach their target audience, see Forest (2021), pp. ix–x.

professionals on social media have the power to influence the behavior of thousands of people, often leading to harmful consequences.[10] For instance, the question is whether an influencer who promotes a risky activity without any contractual relationship and is imitated may be held liable for the victim's injuries. Further examination is required regarding doctors' liability for injuries to social media followers who have no contractual relationship with the physician but follow inappropriate treatments shared online. The question arises when followers, trusting the information's accuracy, ingest the recommended drug and suffer harm.

Also, the actions and speeches of public authorities can negatively influence the behavior of the population, particularly in times of calamity. During the COVID-19 pandemic, government authorities' refusal to wear protective masks foreseeably encouraged similar behavior among the general population. The speeches of government officials also certainly contributed to the invasion of the Capitol in the USA and the National Congress in Brazil. The question of whether these individuals should be held liable presents an issue that requires careful consideration.

Equally relevant is the debate about the responsibility of a member of a group that initiates acts of vandalism or a widespread fight, followed by other members, such as an organized fan club or a certain political group. Since the Brazilian Civil Code of 2002 does not expressly recognize alternative causation theory, scholars question whether the initiator of turmoil should bear responsibility for other participants' actions, even when the initiator's direct damages have been clearly established.

There are also cases where, although psychological influence is not strictly present, the behavior of the first perpetrator favors or facilitates the action of a third party. Two main hypotheses deserve further analysis. In the first, a vehicle destroys a pasture fence that confined livestock owned by a farmer. Unknown third parties, taking advantage of the situation, steal and slaughter the animals. In the second, a car negligently collides with a cargo transport truck on the road. As a result of the vehicle's overturning, passersby appropriate the goods. Scholars debate whether injured parties can hold those first wrongdoers, who eliminated the existing safeguards, responsible for the losses suffered.

Traditional causation theories[11] prevalent in Brazilian law cannot independently resolve the diverse scenarios emerging in contemporary practice. The theories of direct and immediate damage and of adequate causation[12] should not be considered universally valid formulas,[13] as will be addressed later,[14] capable of solving all the

---

[10] Sampaio and Miranda (2021), pp. 176–177.

[11] Puppe is correct in asserting that we should abandon the illusion that a single method of determining causation can be valid for all causal processes. The distinction between the explanation of a natural process and human decision-making has been overlooked. The human decision-making process is fundamentally different from natural causation and should not be confused with it (Puppe (2017), p. 522).

[12] Barbosa (2019), p. 19.

[13] Pereira (2019), p. 242.

[14] See Sect. 3.2.7.

intricate problems of responsibility attribution, especially those resulting from damages caused by psychological influence. Through critical and doctrinal analysis,[15] we must examine why traditional causation theories need to be reconsidered when applied to these hypotheses.

2.2 Historical Notes

Before delving into the problems concerning the insufficiency of causal theories in resolving issues related to "psychological causation," it is essential to provide a brief historical analysis of the matter in order to understand the origin of imputational processes in these cases. The problem was already considered in Roman law through a case-by-case approach.

Nils Jansen cites the case of an enslaved person[16] who was persuaded by a third party to flee from his master. The question that arises is whether this enslaved person should be legally considered a fugitive (*fugitivus*), even though he had not escaped except by the advice of a third party. This question, which probably arose from a concrete case, is answered affirmatively. It is said to be irrelevant whether the advice of a third party constituted a conditio sine qua non for the enslaved person's behavior. It is sufficient that he developed the disposition to flee.

This case is discussed in the context of the seller's liability for defects in the sold item. Special rules were introduced by the edicts of the aediles curules regarding the sale of enslaved people. The seller was required to inform the buyer about any disease (*morbus*) or other latent defect (*vitium*) of the enslaved person. Defects of mere character were not covered by the term vitium. It would make no sense to label every superstitious, irascible, insolent, or melancholic enslaved person as defective, as hardly anyone could be classified as healthy or sick according to these characteristics. Among the circumstances that should be declared by the seller were the facts that the enslaved person was a fugitive (*fugitivus*), had committed some capital crime, or was prone to commit suicide.

The case presents a dual delictual dimension: The enslaver could sue the person whose negative influence prompted the enslaved person, thereby reducing the enslaved person's value. In these cases, the praetor introduced a special action of "corrupted servant", holding the person who intentionally influenced an enslaved person in a negative sense liable. This action should be understood as concerning

[15] On the cognitive core of legal dogmatics, see Aubert (2022), p. 29. About the relationship between legal models and dogmatic models, see Reale (1978), pp. 16–25; Reale (1994), pp. 63–85.

[16] It is essential to distinguish between Roman slavery, as discussed in this legal context, and modern forms of slavery. Roman slavery was a legally recognized institution within the framework of Roman law, where enslaved persons were considered property (res) subject to specific legal protections and regulations, including rules governing their sale, treatment, and the liability of owners for defects. This historical legal analysis should not be construed as legitimizing or minimizing the severity of any form of human exploitation, whether historical or contemporary.

exclusively psychological influence. Roman jurists answered negatively the question of whether external influence could legally nullify the enslaved person's autonomous decision to escape. For Roman jurists, psychological influence could be sufficient to make a man responsible for the behavior of another person.

The lex Aquilia, divided into three chapters, addressed two legally relevant damaging situations. In the first chapter, it provided for the murder of an enslaved person or the death of a quadruped belonging to someone else's domestic livestock (e.g., sheep, goats, oxen, and horses), in which case the perpetrator was obliged to pay the maximum value that the animal reached during the year prior to its death. In its third chapter, it covered the situation where damage was caused by fire, fracture, or any other deterioration (quod usserit, fregerit, ruperit) to a living or inanimate thing. In this last case, the person responsible for the injury was required to pay the amount that the item achieved in value during the last thirty days.

Iniuria[17] that the damage had been directly caused to the thing[18] through material contact (*corpore corpori*).[19] Gaius[20] stated the principle according to which only the damage directly caused by the muscular effort of the author would be within the normative forecast and, therefore, would be directly protected by the action *ex lege Aquilia*. The principle of *damnum corpore datum* was the result of jurisprudential elaboration and not a requirement by the legislator.[21] In this sense, the opinion (*placuit*) with which Gaius[22] preceded the enunciation of the criterion highlights how, with a divergence of opinion among jurists, the requirement that represented the interpretative approach of the time prevailed. The debate over the *corpore datum*[23] requirement confirms both its jurisprudential origin and its absence from the explicit language of the original legislative text.[24]

[17] The *damnum* had to be caused *iniuria*. Initially, this meant *non iure*, that is, contrary to the law, but later it came to be understood as *dolo aut culpa* (Watson (1965), p. 236). The *iniuria* is only recognized as a general dogmatic element of civil liability with the *lex Aquilia* (Jansen (2003), p. 216). Lübtow clarifies that the term "*iniuria*" consists of the feminine of the adjective "*iniurius*", assuming the meaning of illicit or contrary to the law (*sine iure*). However, already at the end of the republican period, jurisprudence inserted into the word "*iniuria*" the requirement that liability would only be established in the case of culpable damages (*dolus*, *culpa*) (Lübtow (1971), p. 83).

[18] It is pointed out that the causal requirement did not assume preponderant importance in the context of the *lex Aquilia* (Kortmann (1999), p. 95).

[19] Justo (2019), p. 136; Meira (2017), pp. 364–365; Jörs (1937), p. 365; Glissen (2001), p. 751; Cretella Jr. (2002), p. 219.

[20] Gaius, 3, 219: "*Ceterum placuit ita demum ex ista lege actionem esse, si quis corpore suo damnun dederit* [. . .]."

[21] The requirement of an injury to an external visible object, in the *damnum injuria datum*, is not a positive determination of Roman law, but rather is based on the nature of things, which is why Roman jurists always respected this boundary, despite all the freedom they allowed themselves in determining the extent of the Aquilian action (Ihering (2020), pp. 43–44).

[22] Gaius, 3, 218.

[23] Schulz (1961), p. 591; Kruse (2006), p. 7.

[24] Bignardi (2000), p. 487.

The major debate concerning bodily contact lies in the interpretation of the word "*occidere*" used in the first chapter of the *lex Aquilia*, specifically regarding when one could consider that a person killed an enslaved person or an animal. If, for example, someone raised a red flag, chasing someone else's oxen into a narrow confinement so that they perished by falling from a cliff, it is evident that the flag bearer caused the death of the animals and acted with iniuria, and should be held responsible for the damages inflicted on the owner. However, whether the act of carrying the flag could be referred to as the conduct of "killing" is a different question. Therefore, there exists a situation in which the *lex Aquilia*, when strictly interpreted, does not hold the perpetrator responsible for causing the animal's death (*mortis causam praebere or praestare*).

According to Julian's definition, the *lex Aquilia* seems to hold responsible only the one who caused someone's death by the use of force or by having almost killed them with their own hands,[25] an interpretation derived from the words "*caedere*"[26] (to kill) and "*caede*" (death).[27] Ulpian[28] appears to be more precise in stating that the term "to kill" also encompassed the employment of a sword or another similar weapon, as well as the application of the offender's bodily violence against the victim (e.g., strangulation and kicking).[29] However, Zimmermann[30] points out that Roman jurists did not always require the use of force. Thus, Labeo[31] was of the opinion that the *actio legis Aquiliae* was applicable when a midwife had administered a poisonous drug to one of her clients, provided she did so with her own hands, and the client subsequently died.[32] Nothing in the text suggests that the midwife was required to force the potion down the client's throat.

The surviving texts does not precisely indicate when or why jurists recognized the need for specific remedies in cases of the indirect killing of an enslaved person or cattle. The earliest documented evidence of how this requirement was met, although certainly not the first case, can be traced back to Ofilius, a young contemporary and friend of Caesar. Later on, about a century and a half later, Celsus attempts to formulate the principle underlying the between the two forms of action.

---

[25] However, the victim's immediate death was not required; liability arose if the offender inflicted a wound bound to prove fatal over time (Scott (2013), pp. 105–106).

[26] Winiger notes that the etymological explanation of *occidere*, which derives from *caedere*, and directly designates the violent act leading to death, emphasizes the author's mode of action (Winiger (1997), p. 47).

[27] D. 9, 2, 51 pr.

[28] D. 9, 2, 7, 1.

[29] Peter Birks argues that the term "*corpore suo*" is better translated as "with the force of his body," not necessarily meaning that the offender had physical contact with the *res* damaged. The perpetrator's body must have been the last kinetic force operating the ultimate source of movement (Birks (2014), pp. 199–200).

[30] Zimmermann (1996), p. 978.

[31] D. 9, 2, 9 pr.

[32] Valditara (2005), p. 23.

The basis for the *actio directa* is the *occidere*, while that of the *actio in factum* is the *causam mortis praestare*.

Celsus cites, as examples, the case of a doctor who, instead of medicine, gives poison (the enslaved person takes the poison himself), as well as the case of someone who hands a sword to a mentally ill enslaved person so that he can kill a foreign enslaved person. In both cases, liability is not established using the *lex Aquilia* but through an analogous action.

From the date the *lex Aquilia* was enacted until the time when the use of *actiones in factum*[33] was allowed, there was an unsatisfactory gap in legal protection in cases of *mortis causam praebere*. To avoid this dilemma, it has occasionally been suggested that the interpretation of the term "*occidere*" was, in fact, much broader in Republican times.[34] Only gradually, or at a certain specific point, was the meaning of the word restricted.[35] Zimmermann,[36] however, argues that this is not a plausible argument, as it is not supported by Roman sources. In the legal context, the term "*occidere*" seems to have always had a rather strict sense, even before the *lex Aquilia.*

Dieter Nörr[37] indicates that the requirement to remedy difficulties in resolving some cases of indirect death was addressed through the use of fictions. With this technique, cases of indirect death would be classified as *occidere,* explaining why these cases only became problematic so late. Only with the formulary procedure[38] could a distinction be made between *occidere* and *causam mortis praebere*.

---

[33] There were situations where neither the *actio directa* nor the *actio in factum* was available, but an *actio utilis* was granted. Some of the cases of indirect causation fell into this category, such as the protection granted to non-owners (Zimmermann (1996), p. 994). In some cases, where ownership was also not configured, it was possible to use the *actio in factum*, as in the case of the possessor in good faith (Biondi (1965), p. 530; Maynz (1891), p. 464). The line separating the *actio in factum* from the *actio utilis* is notoriously difficult to determine (Ebert (2004), p. 35).

[34] In the late Republic, attention was not directed to whether the injury was inflicted *corpori corpore* (according to medieval terminology), encompassing as many situations as possible. Only later, with the development of praetorian actions, could the statute be interpreted more restrictively (Watson (1965), p. 243; Honsel (2021), pp. 206–207).

[35] Barrena (2019), p. 96.

[36] Zimmermann (1996), p. 982.

[37] Nörr (1986b), p. 126.

[38] Unlike traditional legal actions with their rigid formalities, the formulary procedure offered flexibility that prevented minor procedural deviations from resulting in case dismissal. The formulas were composed of four main parts: *demonstratio*, *intentio*, *adjucatio,* and *condemnatio*. Only the *intentio* was necessarily found in all formulas (Alves (2019), pp. 219–228; Rodrigues Jr. (2006), pp. 28–29). Among the accessory parts, the *praescriptio* stands out, inserted at the beginning of the formula and which, subsequently, due to its conceptual evolution, evolved to signify the loss of the action by the lapse of its duration (Simão (2020), p. 93). In the formulary procedure, the praetor begins to play a crucial role in the judicial procedure, organizing the trial (*iudicium dare*), determining the limits of judicial power (Humbert (2023), p. 13). For a detailed definition of the phases of the formulaic process, see Savigny (1879), pp. 49–52.

In Justinian's period, the *actio in factum* had already assumed nearly the character of a general compensation action (*actio in factum generalis*).[39] During the Middle Ages,[40] there was a further expansion of the factual circumstances that authorized the use of Aquilian actions.[41] Parallel to this phenomenon, there was a significant expansion of imputation in cases of indirect damages.[42] This change reflected a fundamental transformation in the legal understanding of liability, moving away from the strict requirement of direct causation present in classical Roman law.

In cases of frequent feudal disputes, one party could be held liable for acts committed by their adversaries. Thus, someone who murdered a family member, with his son setting fire to the murderer's dwelling to avenge his father's death, thereby spreading the fire to the neighboring house, was considered responsible for the damages caused to this house, even though he did not directly cause the fire. In theory, the murderer could only be liable for the death, but in this case, it was asserted that he caused the occurrence of the damage (*occasionem damni dare*).[43] In terms of imputation, the defendant gave rise to the chain of events that ultimately resulted in the damage in question, such a circumstance being considered sufficient to establish Aquilian responsibility.[44]

The equating of *occasionem damni dare*, in these cases, to *damnum dare*, did not primarily aim to sanction the initial conduct. On the contrary, the underlying reason for this could only consist in the fact that participation in a feud was a reprehensible act and, therefore, should lead to liability for any resulting damage, even if third parties not involved were affected. This consideration, a subset of the canonical doctrine of fault, was adopted in Italian doctrine through Durantis.[45] It does not primarily aim at sanctioning misconduct but rather arises from a legitimate interest in compensation.[46]

---

[39] Bonfante (1987), p. 524; Iglesias (2019), pp. 317–318.

[40] The reception of Roman law by the School of Glossators and Commentators did not result in a profound reform of the *status quo,* as the hermeneutic rationality, based on the idea of authority dictated a strict fidelity to the text of the law. Kunkel notes that, even after the fall of the Empire, the Roman administration survived, as did Roman law, albeit in a simpler and modified configuration (Kunkel (2005), p. 223). On the importance of Roman law as a unifying factor of European rights, see Hespanha (2019), p. 117.

[41] Roman texts are interpreted, in the Middle Ages, in a way that allows the repair of various other kinds of damages, although the jurists never formulated a clear rule (Gordley (2006), p. 160).

[42] Jansen (2003), p. 276; Barbosa (2018), p. 811.

[43] Kaufmann asserts that the subject of numerous decisions is also the question, already discussed in the Middle Ages, of whether someone should compensate for the damage caused by their enemy to a third party, as a result of this enmity. This liability was generally affirmed, since the creation of the enmity was also seen as the establishment of an *occasio damni*. In the opinion of some authors, the liability should be recognized even if the defendant did not cause the enmity (*inimicitiae causam non dederit*). According to Kaufmann, in this context, *causa* functions as a synonym for *culpa* (Kaufmann (1958), pp. 69–70).

[44] Jansen (2007), p. 194.

[45] Engelmann (1965), p. 213.

[46] Jansen (2003), p. 276.

The liability of the *auctor rixae* is probably one of the oldest topics in tort law, having been regularly discussed during the time of the *ius commune*. Returning to Roman law, the influence of its discussions on the jurists of the Middle Ages can be observed. For example, Publius Mucius, one of the oldest known Roman lawyers,[47] understood that Gaius Sempronius Gracchus would be responsible for the damages caused to the dowry of Licinia during an uprising attributed to the latter. Following the death of Licinia's husband, Mucius argued that the property should return to her estate.[48]

Nils Jansen[49] asserts that it may seem surprising that the issue of psychological influence was not addressed as a more specific problem in these discussions. Apparently, it was simply assumed that the offender, who had started a riot or an uprising, was also responsible for the damages resulting from the aggressive behavior of third parties that he had provoked. In this sense, there is no deeper debate on causation by psychological influence, with a more specific doctrine of fault being decisive in resolving these cases. The difference between *causam mortis dare* and *occidere* continued to be debated but lost its importance.[50]

With the advent of codifications in the nineteenth century,[51] the legal approach to "psychological causation" entered a new phase. During this transitional period, before the formulation of more elaborate causal theories,[52] issues of harm caused by

---

[47] Wiecker (1988), p. 547.

[48] Gaius Gracchus, being a tribune of the people, attempted to introduce extensive reforms that would disadvantage the Senate, resulting in riots, as a result of which he and three thousand supporters died. The question then arose: What would happen with the dowry, quite considerable, that Gaius had acquired by marrying Licinia? According to Roman law, the property of the goods had been transferred to Gaius. Now, having the objects destroyed or confiscated by the Roman Senate, the dowry seemed to have been lost. Mucius, serving as Pontifex Maximus at the time, intervened in support of Licinia. According to his opinion, Licinia's dowry would not have been affected by the confiscation. The argument used was that the dowry passes to the husband's property, but this act should be considered a fiduciary transaction. Therefore, if the husband negligently destroys the objects transferred to him, his wife should be compensated (Zimmermann (1981), pp. 3–4).

[49] In a case from 1631, where a woman was accused of bewitching, and consequently, paralyzing a young bride, it was not the psychological influence considered a difficult problem to solve, but the bride's claim for pain and suffering (Jansen (2007), p. 195).

[50] Zimmermann emphasizes that the only requirement for liability under the *lex Aquilia* that has remained essentially unchanged is fault, with no general theory of causation being developed or applied. What mattered was whether the offender had caused the damage, but this question was always connected with the problem of fault (Zimmermann (1996), pp. 1028–1029).

[51] After its reception, the expansion, the scope of application of the Aquilian action was progressively expanded. In the practice of the *usus modernus*, it becomes a general tort action due to damages caused to material goods and free people, combining the domain of use of the previous *actio directa, actiones utiles,* and *in factum*, and, by excluding penalties, it becomes a pure reparatory demand (Kaser (2003), p. 322).

[52] This section, relating to historical notes, does not aim to descriptively present the evolution, in time and space, of causal theories, in a generic and broad way, but to specifically deal with what has been conventionally called "psychological causation." This methodological choice justifies the transition

psychological influence were often resolved through purely equitable criteria, allowing for broad discretion by the courts.

Lalou[53] reports that the Lyon Court (13 Nov. 950, D. 195) ruled that there was no direct and necessary link (*lien direct et nécessaire*) between the act of a lover, who had sexual relations with a married woman, and her suicide. The same would be true if the victim committed suicide as a result of a state of emotionality or exaltation that was inherent to her (Trib. Civ. Toulouse, July 17, 1909). A similar solution was adopted by the *Tribunal de commerce de la Seine* (June 22, 1949, D. 1950. 471) in a case where the victim of mere material damages committed suicide a few hours after the occurrence of the injury.

Within the scope of German law,[54] the issue of "psychological causation" was essentially dominated by two theories of causation. Part of the doctrine sought to address cases through the application of the theory of interruption of the chain of causation (*Theorie von der Unterbrechung des Kausalzusammenhangs*). This thesis was based on the premise that the causal course initiated by the first perpetrator would be interrupted[55] as soon as the voluntary action of a second person intervened between the conduct of the former and the injury to the protected interest.[56] However, the proposal was not well received by the prevailing doctrine, as it overly restricted the responsibility of the first perpetrator and did not equitably share the risks between the wrongdoers and the injured parties.[57]

Consequently, the *Reichsgericht*[58] adhered to the prevailing doctrine of adequacy,[59] which was not initially interpreted as a theory of imputation but as a theory of causation. The court followed the general principle that a subject

---

from medieval law directly to the era of codifications, considering that, in relation to the subject matter of analysis, no profound and significant changes are found in the treatment of the theme.

[53] Lalou (1962), p. 198.

[54] Since Josef Kohler's 1887 essay "*Die Menschenhilfe im Privatrecht*," legal scholars have typically classified acts of good Samaritans and neighborly assistance as instances of management of another person's affairs without a mandate (*negotiorum gestio*) (Nökel (1968), p. 1).

[55] According to Deutsch and Ahrens, the interruption of the chain of causation can also be characterized when the victim's voluntary decision is far removed from the situation created by the injury, moving into their own life risk area (*Lebensrisiko*). For instance, a traffic accident victim changed jobs after the incident, worked in this new occupation for 18 years, and then became self-employed, eventually suffering economic failure (Deutsch and Ahrens (2014), p. 31).

[56] Larenz (1955), p. 1009.

[57] Forst (2000), p. 46.

[58] The idea of a German Supreme Court dates back at least to the end of the fifteenth century, with the creation of the *Reichskammergericht* of the Holy Roman Empire, which was initially based in Frankfurt. The prevailing political fragmentation, however, prevented the exercise of its effective influence, especially in the area of law unification, and even the Emperor had his own court in Vienna that often competed with the *Reichskammergericht*. A true Supreme Court had to wait until the unification of Germany, which was realized in 1871, under the strong influence of Bismarck. The *Reichsgericht* was established on October 1, 1879, based in Leipzig, and survived until the end of the Second World War (1945) (Markesinis et al. (2019), pp. 1–2).

[59] Niebaum (1977), p. 25.

could only be held liable for results that, from the objective viewpoint of the individual, were foreseeable. In contrast to the theory of interruption of the chain of causation, the first perpetrator could be considered responsible, even when the harmful conduct was carried out by a second causer, provided that such an outcome was sufficiently foreseeable.[60]

A decision by the *Landgericht*[61] Düsseldorf,[62] on March 8, 1955, initiated a process of reconsideration of the application of the adequacy theory to "psychological causation." The case involved a truck driver who caused a culpable traffic accident on the *Autobahn*, blocking the passage of other vehicles. The subsequent motorists diverted onto the green strip adjacent to the roadway to circumvent the obstruction, consequently inflicting substantial damage to this emergency area. The Federal Republic of Germany, as landowner, sought compensation from the accident's responsible party. The court upheld this claim, finding adequate causation between the accident and the damage to the green strip. The decision was widely debated, with the prevailing understanding that the claim should have been rejected. According to critics, the damages caused by the cars were no longer within the scope of responsibility of the accident's perpetrator.[63]

From that point onward, the specificities of the problem were highlighted by the doctrine, and new dogmatic proposals were developed. In two decisions from 1971,[64] the BGH began to apply the "provocation formula"[65] (*Herausforderungsformel*),[66] a criterion of imputation distinct from the theory of adequate causation. In several subsequent decisions, the BGH used not only the provocation criterion but also other parameters of objective imputation,

[60] Forst (2000), pp. 46–47.

[61] In simplified terms, it can be stated that in Germany, the hierarchically inferior court in civil matters is the *Amtsgericht*. It has limited and specifically assigned jurisdiction, which includes claims up to the value of five thousand euros. Since 1977, family matters are decided by a special division of the court, the *Familiengericht*, with direct appeal to the *Oberlandesgericht*. Appeals from other decisions must be lodged at the competent *Landgericht*. The *Landgericht* (cited as LG) constitutes a court of general jurisdiction and acts as a court of first instance or a court of review of any *Amtsgericht* in its district. Appeals against its decisions are, as a rule, directed to an *Oberlandesgericht* (referred to as OLG), functioning as an appellate court. Some states, notably Bremen, Hamburg, Hessen, Saarland, and Schleswig-Holstein, have only one court of appeal. Others, like Bavaria, have more than one (Bavaria has an *Oberstes Landesgericht* (ObLG), competent for review requests related to state law). The *Bundesgerichtshof* (BGH) is at the apex of the judicial hierarchy in civil and criminal matters (Markesinis and Unberath (2002), pp. 4–6).

[62] NJW 1955, 1031.

[63] Niebaum (1977), p. 15.

[64] NJW 1971, 1980; NJW, 1971, 1982.

[65] The criterion will be further developed in Sect. 4.5.3.

[66] Zimmermann (1980), p. 10; Weitenberg (2014), p. 769.

including the theory of the scope of norm protection,[67] in order to solve cases involving the issue of "psychological causation."

2.3 Insufficiency of Traditional Causal Theories

In Brazilian law, the foundations for the construction and development of imputation criteria[68] capable of addressing the complex issues arising in contemporary society have yet to be established.[69] A significant portion of legal doctrine and national courts still adhere to a traditional causal perspective, failing to distinguish between natural causation and the various imputational parameters that, through a value-based analysis, seek to limit liability and establish the reasons why a particular individual should bear the costs of compensation.[70] Brazilian courts frequently resort to a profusion of causal theories, almost instinctively, in search of the most just outcome according to the personal standards of the judge.[71]

If the commonly adopted causal framework fails to provide clear criteria of imputation capable of defining interpretative boundaries, the problem becomes even more acute in cases of damages caused by psychological influence. In this area, controversial issues are rarely addressed by Brazilian legal doctrine and jurisprudence,[72] or theories are applied to resolve cases that are not pertinent to the subject matter.

"Psychological causation" is a topic insufficiently addressed by Brazilian doctrine. Although the problem has been extensively discussed in German law, which

---

[67] The theory of the scope of protection of the norm will be analyzed in detail in Sect. 3.2.5.

[68] Teresa Ancona Lopez states that, in Brazil, there are no known cases judged based on the objective imputation of civil liability (Lopez (2010), p. 135).

[69] Within the scope of German law, particularly in relation to environmental damage, see Haeger (1986).

[70] Distinguishing between causation and imputation removes an inappropriate burden from criminal dogmatics. Criminal law's role is not to establish whether conduct causes a result. It is up to the law to determine how, and to what extent, civil and criminal liability should be attributed to the offender (Chamon Jr. (2005), p. 47).

[71] In Brazil, Gisela Sampaio da Cruz points out that the establishment of causation is carried out in an intuitive and non-technical way, alternately shaped by different doctrinal approaches (Guedes (2005), p. 122).

[72] The Court of Justice of Paraná applied the criterion of risk increase when examining a case where a driver, proceeding normally on 08.09.1999, had their vehicle struck by a GM Vectra CD driven at high speed by two robbers, who were fleeing from the police. The injured party filed a claim for compensation for material damages against the State of Paraná. The court held the state liable, stating that the high-speed police chase, on a public road, implies an increase in the normal risk to which members of society are subject. The court decided that the state must provide compensation for damages resulting from abnormal risk situations it creates, even when third parties directly cause these damages (TJPR, ApCív 0238045-4, rel. Des. Paulo Habith, 6.ª C. Cív., j. 29.06.2004, *DJ* 06.08.2004).

has established a series of objective imputation criteria to resolve cases arising in judicial practice, Brazilian law remains anchored in the theories of direct and immediate damage, or its variant, the subtheory of "necessary causation," and in the theory of adequate causation, which have not yet been recognized as legal parameters limiting tort liability.

Brazilian legal practice, particularly in jurisprudence, often relies on theories that prove incapable of resolving the intricate and complex issues that arise from the analysis of "psychological causation." Other criteria, not addressed or only indirectly mentioned, must be developed and adapted to the Brazilian reality; otherwise, the responses to concrete cases will continue to depend on the merely equitable appreciation of the courts, without any grounding in secure theoretical parameters.

These additional imputation criteria are sometimes treated by German doctrine as criteria covered by the theory of the scope of the norm or as autonomous imputational criteria. Steffen,[73] for example, addresses the "provocation criterion" (*Kriterium der Herausforderung*) within the scope of the theory of the norm.[74] As will be seen later, the theory of adequate causation must be combined with other imputation criteria, which, although they may sometimes be confused with the parameters of the theory of the scope of the norm, will not prove to be partially or entirely identical.

It is essential, before delving into the examination of "psychological causation" and proposing criteria for addressing the issues arising from its analysis, to review the causal theories and their controversial application in Brazilian law, highlighting their insufficiency in resolving cases of "psychological causation."

2.4 Summary

The historical analysis of "psychological causation" reveals its complexity, dating back to Roman law. The treatment of this matter evolved from an initial focus on direct and physical damage (*corpore corpori*) to the gradual acknowledgment of situations where psychological influence could serve as the basis for liability.

The *lex Aquilia*, although originally limited to direct physical damages, expanded through jurisprudential interpretation and the creation of *actiones in*

[73] Steffen et al. (1989), p. 137.

[74] Another important group of cases to be treated through the doctrine of the scope of the norm are the so-called provocation cases (*Herausforderungsfälle*) (Fuchs et al. (2017), p. 87). Kötz and Wagner also insert the discussion about the provocation criterion within the topic on the doctrine of the purpose of protection of the liability norm (Kötz and Wagner (2006), p. 84). Oetker argues that, dogmatically, the "general risk of life" (*allgemeines Lebensrisiko*) is covered by the theory of the scope of the norm, not constituting an independent criterion (Oetker (2019), p. 417). This same orientation is followed, in relation to the risk criterion (Lang (1983), p. 152; Grüneberg (2020), p. 297.

factum, enabling the protection of indirect damages. In the Middle Ages, the reception of Roman law significantly expanded the instances of imputation due to psychological influence, developing concepts such as *occasionem damni dare*. Modern codifications tended to resolve these issues through equitable criteria, granting broad discretion to the courts.

It was in modern German law that the issue found a more systematic treatment, especially after the development of the "provocation formula" and other criteria for objective imputation by the BGH. This evolution demonstrates the requirement of overcoming traditional theories of causation in favor of more effective parameters to address the complexity of psychological influence on harmful conduct.

References

Aubert EH (2022) Ensaio sobre a dogmática jurídica. São Paulo, Almedina

Barbosa AMCNM (2018) Causalidade alternativa incerta: modelos de resolução da problemática e o projeto francês (2017) de reforma da responsabilidade civil. Revista de Direito Civil 3(4):807–838

Barbosa AMCNM (2019) Responsabilidade civil pelo financiamento de grupos terroristas. Revista IBERC 1:01–39

Barrena CA (2019) Causalidad y culpa en la responsabilidad civil: historia y dogmática. Grupo Editorial Ibáñez, Bogotá

Bignardi A (2000) Gai. 219 e il principio del damnum corpore datum. Archivio Giuridico CCXX(IV):487–539

Biondi B (1965) Istituzioni di Diritto Romano, 4ª edn. Dott. A. Giuffrè Editore, Milano

Birks P (2014) The Roman law of obligations. Oxford University Press, Oxford

Bonfante P (1987) Istituzioni di diritto romano, 10ª edn. A. Giuffre, Milano

Chamon JLA (2005) Imputação objetiva e risco no direito penal: do funcionalismo à teoria discursiva do delito. Mandamentos, Belo Horizonte

Cretella Júnior J (2002) Curso de direito romano: o direito romano e o direito civil brasileiro, 27ª edn. Forense, Rio de Janeiro

Deutsch E, Ahrens HJ (2014) Deliktsrecht: unerlaubte Handlungen, Schadensersatz, Schmerzensgeld, 6ª edn. Verlag Franz Vahlen, München

Ebert I (2004) Pönale Elemente im deutschen Privatrecht: von der Renaissance der Privatstrafe im deutschen Recht. Mohr Siebeck, Tübingen

Engelmann W (1965) Die Schuldlehre der Postglossatoren und ihre Fortentwicklung: eine historisch-dogmatische Darstellung der kriminellen Schuldlehre der italienischen Juristen des Mittelalters seit Accursius, 2ª edn. Scientia Verlag Aalen, Darmstadt

Forest JJF (2021) Digital influence warfare in the age of social media. Praeger, Santa Barbara

Forst SP (2000) Grenzen deliktischer Haftung bei psychisch vermittelter haftungsbegründender Kausalität. VVF, München

Frada MAC (2010) Direto civil, responsabilidade civil: o método do caso. Almedina, Coimbra

Fuchs M, Pauker W, Baumgärtner A (2017) Delikts- und Schadensersatz, 9ª edn. Springer, Berlin; Heidelberg

Glissen J (2001) Introdução histórica ao direito, 3ª edn. Trad. A. M. Hespanha e L. M. Malheiros Fundação Calouste Gulbenkian, Lisboa

Gordley J (2006) Foundations of private law: property, tort, contract, unjust enrichment. Oxford University Press, Oxford

Grüneberg C (2020) Vorb v § 249. In: Palandt O et al (eds) Palandt: bürgerliches Gesetzbuch, 79ª edn. C. H. Beck, München

Guedes GSC (2005) O problema do nexo causal na responsabilidade civil. Renovar, Rio de Janeiro
Hespanha AM (2019) Cultura jurídica europeia: a síntese de um milênio. Almedina, Coimbra
Honsell H, Fargnoli I (2021) Römisches Recht, 9ª edn. Stämpfli Verlag, Bern
Humbert M (2023) Das magistratische Edikt. In: Baldus C et al (eds) Handbuch des römischen Privatrechts. Mohr Siebeck, Tübingen
Iglesias J (2019) Derecho romano: historia e instituciones, 19ª edn. Sello Editorial, Barcelona
Jansen N (2003) Die Struktur des Haftungsrechts: Geschichte, Theorie und Dogmatik außervertraglicher Ansprüche auf Schadenersatz. Mohr Siebeck, Tübingen
Jansen N (2007) Damage caused by psychological influence: Germany. In: Winiger B et al (orgs) Digest of European Tort Law: Essential cases on natural causation. Springer, Wien, New York
Jörs P (1937) Roman private law, 2nd edn, Trans. L. Prieto Castro. Editorial Labor, Madrid
Justo AS (2019) Direito privado romano: direito das obrigações, 7ª edn. Coimbra Editora, Coimbra
Kaser M, Knütel R (2003) Römisches Privatrecht, 17ª edn. C.H. Beck, München
Kaufmann H (1958) Rezeption und usus modernus der actio legis Aquiliae, v. 5. Böhlau, Köln
Kortmann JS (1999) Ab alio ictu(s): Misconceptions about Julian's view on causation. J Legal Hist 20:95–103
Kötz H, Wagner G (2006) Deliktsrecht, 10ª edn. Wolters Kluers, München
Kruse C (2006) Alternative Kausalität im Deliktsrecht: eine historische und vergleichende Untersuchung. LIT Verlag, Berlin
Kunkel W, Schermaier M (2005) Römische Rechtsgeschichte, 14ª edn. Böhlau Verlag, Köln; Weimar, Wien
Lalou H (1962) Traité pratique de la responsabilité civile, 6ª edn (atual. por Pierre Azard). Librairie Dalloz, Paris
Lang R (1983) Normzweck und duty of care: eine Untersuchung über die Grenzen der Zurechnung im deutschen und anglo-amerikanischen Deliktsrecht. C.H. Beck'sche Verlagsbuchhandlung, München
Lange H, Schiemann G (2003) Schadensersatz, 3ª edn. Mohr Siebeck, Tübingen
Larenz K (1955) Tatzurechnung und "Unterbrechung des Kausalzusammenhanges". Neue Juristische Wochenschrift 8(28):1009–1013
Lopez TA (2010) Princípio da precaução e evolução da responsabilidade civil. Quartier Latin, São Paulo
Markesinis BS, Unberath H (2002) The German law of torts: a comparative treatise, 4ª edn. Hart Publishing, Oxford; Portland
Markesinis BS, Unberath H, Janssen A (2019) Markesinis's German law of torts: a comparative treatise, 5ª edn. Hart Publishing, Chicago
Maynz CG, (1891) Cours de droit romain: [précédé d'une introduction contenant l'histoire de la législation et des institutions politiques de Rome], 5ª edn, t. 2. Bruylant-Christophe; A. Durand, Bruxelles; Paris
Meira S (2017) Instituições de direito romano, 4ª edn. IASP, São Paulo
Moreira Alves JC (2019) Direito romano, 19ª edn. Forense, Rio de Janeiro
Nader P (2016) Curso de direito civil: responsabilidade civil, 6ª edn, vol 7. Forense, Rio de Janeiro
Niebaum G (1977) Die deliktische Haftung für fremde Willensbestätigung. Duncker & Humblot, Berlin
Nökel D (1968) Die Rechtsstellung des Nothelfers: Anglo-amerikanisches im Vergleich zum deutschen Recht. Inaugural-Dissertation zur Erlangung der juristischen Doktorwürde der Hohen Rechts- und Staatswissenschaftlichen Fakultät der Albert-Ludwigs-Universität zu Freiburg
Nörr D (1986b) Causam mortis praebere. In: MacCormick N, Birks P (eds) The legal mind: essays for Tony Honoré. Clarendon Press, Oxford
Oetker H (2019) § 249. In: Oetker H et al (orgs) Münchener Kommentar: Schuldrecht - Allgemeiner Teil I, 8ª edn, vol 2. C. H. Beck, München

Pereira RS (2019) O nexo de causalidade na responsabilidade delitual: fundamentos e limites do juízo de condicionalidade. Almedina, Coimbra
Puppe I (2017) Die psychische Kausalität und das Recht auf die eigene Entscheidung. Juristische Rundschau 10:513–522
Reale M (1978) Estudos de filosofia e ciência do direito. Saraiva, São Paulo
Reale M (1994) Fontes e modelos do direito: para um novo paradigma hermenêutico. Saraiva, São Paulo
Ristow T (2003) Die psychische Kausalität im Deliktsrecht. Peter Lang, Frankfurt am Main
Rodrigues Jr OL (2006) Função, natureza e modificação da cláusula penal no direito civil brasileiro. Tese (Doutorado)—Faculdade de Direito, Universidade de São Paulo
Sampaio MA, Miranda TB (2021) A responsabilidade civil dos influenciadores digitais diante do Código de Defesa do Consumidor. Revista de direito do consumidor 30(133):175–204
Savigny FC (1879) Sistema de Derecho Romano Actual. (Trad. M. Ch. Guenoux), t. 4. F. Gongorra, Madrid
Schulz F (1961) Classical roman law. Clarendon Press, Oxford
Schulz F (2020) Princípios do direito romano: aulas de Fritz Schulz. (Trad. Josué Modesto Passos). Filomática Sorocabana, São João de Boa Vista
Scott H (2013) Killing and causing death in roman law: Digest 9.2.51, Fairchild v. Glenhaven funeral services ltd. and contemporary tort theory. Law Q Rev 129:101–122
Simão JF (2020) Prescrição e decadência: início dos prazos, 2ª edn. Edição do autor, E-book, Amazon
Steffen E (1989) §823 BGB. In: Dunz W et al (eds) Das Bürgerliche Gesetzbuch: mit besonderer Berücksichtigung der Rechtsprechung des Reichgerichts und des Bundesgerichtshofes: §§ 812–831. 12ª edn, vol 2, t. 5. Walter de Gruyter, Berlin, New York
Valditara G (2005) Damnum iniura datum, 2ª edn. G. Giappichelli Editore, Torino
von Lübtow U (1971) Untersuchungen zur Lex Aquilia de damno iniuria dato. Duncker & Humblot, Berlin
von Ihering R (2020) Culpa in contrahendo: ou indenização em contratos nulos ou não chegados à perfeição. 2ª. Trad. Paulo Mota Pinto Gestlegal, Coimbra
Watson A (1965) The law of obligations in the later Roman Republic. Clarendon Press, Oxford
Weitenberg M (2014) Der Begriff der Kausalität in der haftungsrechtlichen Rechtsprechung der Unionsgericht: zugleich ein Beitrag zur Kohärenz der EU-Haftungssystem. Nomos, Baden-Baden
Wieacker F (1988) Römische Rechtsgeschichte: Einleitung, Quellenkunde, Frühzeit und Republik, vol 1. C. H. Beck, München
Winiger B (1997) La responsabilité aquilienne romaine: damnun iniuria datum. Helbing & Lichtenhahn, Bâle et Francfort-sur-le-Main
Zhang M (2016) Aktiv psychische Kausalität im Deliktsrecht. Duncker & Humblot, Berlin
Zimmermann R (1980) Herausforderungsformel und Haftung für fremde Willensbetätigung nach § 823 I BGB. JuristenZeitung 35(1):10–16
Zimmermann R (1981) Legal history: does it deserve its place in the curriculum?. University of Cape Town, Cape Town
Zimmermann R (1996) The law of obligations: Roman foundations of the civilian tradition. Oxford University Press, Oxford
Zimmermann R, Kleinschmidt J (2007) Damage caused by psychological influence: Germany. In: Winiger B et al (orgs) Digest of European Tort Law: essential cases on natural causation. Springer, Wien, New York

Chapter 3
Critical Analysis of Theories of Causation

Determining causation has emerged as the most intricate element of contemporary tort law. The doctrinal development of multiple causal theories, rather than establishing reliable criteria for the attribution of damages, has resulted in a scenario of profound conceptual instability. This theoretical fragility is evident in Brazilian jurisprudence, where courts apply different doctrinal constructions in an unsystematic and inconsistent manner. The theory of equivalence of conditions broadens the scope of liability, while the theory of adequate causation, by contrast, restricts it through discretionary evaluations of foreseeability. Similarly, both the theory of direct and immediate damage and the scope of norm protection serve as mere rhetorical resources to justify decisions previously established by intuitive criteria.

3.1 Introduction

Causation is one of the most complex and debated issues[1] in tort law, engaging legal doctrine in a multitude of theories aimed at explaining this prerequisite for

[1] Schreiber points out that the apparent simplicity of causal definitions contrasts with the multiple practical difficulties that arise in concrete application (Schreiber (2013), p. 55). Also, Caio Mario da Silva Pereira refers to the fact that causation is the most delicate of the elements of tort law and the most difficult to be determined (Pereira (1991), p. 84). Matozzi indicates that the delimitation of causation is not an easy task, although at first glance it may seem the opposite (Cuevillas Matozzi (2000), pp. 32–37). Zimmermann, when addressing the theme of "psychological causation," refers to the insoluble and endless problems of causation (Zimmermann (1980), p. 10), emphasizing that numerous theories have been developed aiming to solve these intricate issues, although they have rarely contributed to unravel the uncertainties and confusions that continue to surround the legal use of causal language (Zimmermann (1996), p. 988). It is also said, in a somewhat poetic tone, that causation is a formidable siren, deliberately misleading those who

C. Dantas Bisneto, *Psychological Causation in Tort Law*,
https://doi.org/10.1007/978-3-032-03825-8_3

liability.[2] Jiménez Asúa[3] indicates the existence of at least fourteen main currents and many intermediate ones seeking to elucidate the problem of causation,[4] the great protagonist of tort law. These profusion of theses[5] can be attributed to the effort made by the interpretative schools of the nineteenth century to establish general rules based on the analysis of Roman case law,[6] particularly in Germany.[7] Faced with the difficulties of achieving a definition of "legal causation" (imputation), certain authors have even questioned the relevance of a systematic search for a concept.[8]

Following the attempt to modify the traditional parameters of tort law, as articulated by Anderson Schreiber,[9] including the reduction of the fault requirement[10] through the adoption of the risk doctrine,[11] discussions in tort law have centered on the legal concept of causation. Some even assert that, in cases of strict liability, liability would be determined solely by verifying causation.[12] Causation has emerged as the final barrier to limiting responsibility, which, according to some

---

are seduced by its subtlety and who seek to penetrate its deepest mysteries (N. Dejean de la Bâtie, note under Cass. civ. 2, February 1, 1973, JCP 1974, II, no. 17,882).

[2] Martins-Costa (2003), p. 94.

[3] The author presents a comprehensive systematization of the theories of causation (Jiménez de Asúa (1951), pp. 434–445). Teresa Ancona Lopez, when citing the Spanish jurist, exiled in Argentina during the Franco dictatorship, also refers to the excess of existing theories on causation (Lopez (2008), p. 24).

[4] According to Ripert, this abundance of various theories supported by pseudoscientific language is a characteristic sign of the influence of physical and natural sciences on German sociological concepts (Ripert (1935), pp. 224).

[5] Quézel-Ambrunaz asserts that an exhaustive and rigorous classification would distinguish, within this genre, almost as many species as there are authors who have worked on the issue (Quézel-Ambrunaz (2010), p. 22).

[6] MacCormack argues that Roman texts do not reveal the use of a doctrine of causation (MacCormack (1982), p. 264). Dieter Nörr notes that, as far as Roman law is concerned, as generally accepted, classical jurists did not address an analysis of causation through the lens of theoretical assumptions, although this does not exclude the fact that these jurists, starting from a naturalistic concept of causation, have faced, in particular cases, the questions that emanated from causal problems (Nörr (1978), p. 115). Zimmermann also believes that there is no evidence of a specific theory of causation being used by Roman jurists (Zimmermann (1996), p. 991). However, there are fragments in Roman law that were used for the construction of a general doctrine, mainly formulated by Ulpian, to equate co-participants in the cause of death (Jiménez de Asúa (1951), p. 426). The topic is also addressed by Medicus (1962), p. 325.

[7] According to Markesinis, French lawyers, paraphrasing Voltaire's saying about the existence of God, state that if the theme of causation did not exist, it would have been invented, so that German lawyers would have something to exercise their minds (Markesinis et al. (2019), p. 60).

[8] Viney et al. (2013), pp. 239–240.

[9] Schreiber (2013), p. 11. Díez-Picazo mentions the erosions in the assessment of causation (Díez-Picazo (1999), p. 238).

[10] Lima (1963), p. 117; Silva (1962), p. 157.

[11] Josserand (1941), pp. 60–61.

[12] Violante (1999), p. 72.

scholars, prevents full compensation for victims' damages and has thus been intensely criticized.[13]

Even if the relativization of causation is defended or, more radically, its suppression[14] to favor the interests of the victim through an indiscriminate application of constitutional principles,[15] it seems certain to affirm, with support in vast national and foreign doctrine, that the causal prerequisite retains its importance[16] both for the purpose of affirming liability and for delimiting its extent.[17] Despite the lack of consensus on its conceptualization, causation is universally recognized as a crucial element of tort law, as Marta Infantino[18] observes.

Before examining "psychological causation," it is essential to explore various causation theories and their developments to assess whether the theoretical constructs used in Brazilian law are adequate. The analysis of causation theories is important for the resolution of various problems that arise from behaviors that influence the conduct of third parties.

3.2 Causal Theories

Several theories attempt to address the intricate issues surrounding the establishment of a causal link between an offender's conduct and the damage suffered by the victim. For a long time, however, doctrine did not consider the causal relationship an autonomous prerequisite for liability.[19] In Roman law, as previously noted, no abstract theoretical framework on causation was developed.[20] The expression

[13] Souza (2018), p. 42). Otavio Luiz Rodrigues Junior also mentions that the idea that causation has been made more flexible, or is undergoing a process of flexibilization, has been accepted by many supporters in Brazilian doctrine (Rodrigues Jr. (2016), p. 127).

[14] Fachin (2015), pp. 113–114. Pablo Frota Malheiros defends the idea of substitution of causation by the notion of "complex causation" (Frota (2014), p. 288–289).

[15] On the popularization of principles, especially in relation to the principle of human dignity, in Brazilian law, see Rodrigues Jr (2019), pp. 173–177. The widespread use of the principle of human dignity is the target of criticism from the courts: "[. . .] it is necessary to save the dignity of the human person from itself, if it is possible to make this somewhat ironic note about the excesses committed in its name [. . .]" (STF, RE 363,889/DF, rel. Dias Toffoli, j. 02.06.2011).

[16] Gisela Sampaio da Cruz asserts that causation is an indispensable element in tort law (Guedes (2005), p. 18).

[17] Bordon (2006), p. 32. In Brazilian doctrine, see Magadan (2019), pp. 22–31; Santos (2018), pp. 81–87.

[18] Infantino (2019), p. 648.

[19] At this point, the aim is not to trace a historical overview of the concept of causation, but merely to introduce the thema. For a historical analysis of causation by influence, see Sect. 3.2.2.

[20] Although it is possible to recognize a tendency of Roman law toward systematization, due to the search for continuous ordering, the idea of a system is characteristic of humanism and, essentially, of rationalism (Andrade (1997), p. 35).

"*causam mortis praestare*" was merely common terminology, not an adoption of Greek philosophical debates on causation.[21]Although the concept of *conditio sine qua non* was recognized and occasionally invoked to establish or deny liability in other contexts,[22] it rarely appears in texts concerning the *lex Aquilia*, which generally presuppose that the offender's conduct directly caused the damage.[23]

Even after the enactment of the Napoleonic Code,[24] causation was not treated as an independent element in French law. Instead, it was employed to determine damage, which had to be direct and certain, and to delimit responsibility. Part of the French doctrine considered only the damage and the *faute* as elements of tort law.[25] The exclusion of liability due to force majeure was treated by part of the doctrine within the scope of imputability (*imputabilité*).[26] The Civil Code of 1804 also did not provide any definition of causation. Unlike *faute*, neither the doctrine nor case law established a widely accepted definition of causation. Instead, French courts determined causation based on the specifics of each case, guided by principles of equity rather than theoretical or scientific reasoning.[27]

Causation remained largely unexamined until the eighteenth century, despite the general recognition of the necessity of linking conduct to damage. French jurists, drawing primarily on Charles Du Moulin's work, regarded foreseeability as a reliable criterion for limiting liability.[28] According to Cohnfeldt,[29] Du Moulin also uses the degree of fault as a benchmark for delimiting the boundaries of compensable damage. In addition to foreseeability, the proximity of damage emerges as an additional requirement. In Domat's work,[30] the criteria of foreseeability and proximity appear together, underpinning the modern French theory.[31] Like Domat, Pothier[32] also indicates the foreseeability and proximity of the damage, alluding to the degree of

---

[21] The limitation of liability, in classical law, consisted of the value of the object owed, given the ease of its determination, in line with the practical spirit of the Romans (Mommsen (1855), p. 72).

[22] In numerous texts, the *conditio sine qua non* is found as an argument for the imputation of damages (Willvonseder (1984), p. 32).

[23] Zimmermann (1996), p. 991.

[24] Roman law continued to play a very significant role in the first decades after the promulgation of the codifications, even alluding to a "third renaissance." The extraordinary degree of continuity between the tradition of the *ius commune* and the *Code Civil* allowed Roman law to become an indispensable tool in the interpretation of the new code, in resolving doctrinal disputes and in filling gaps in the law (Zimmermann (2001), p. 3).

[25] Colin and Capitant, in the part relating to tort liability, refer only to the *fault* and the damage as elements of it (Colin and Capitant (1915), p. 361).

[26] Woyciechowski (2017), p. 329.

[27] Paul Esmein already warned that it is by sentiment that judges decide whether the occurrence of damages is too unpredictable a consequence of an act for its perpetrator to be held accountable (Esmein (1964), p. 205).

[28] Wieling (1970), p. 49.

[29] Cohnfeldt (1865), p. 18.

[30] Domat (1695), p. 121.

[31] Reinig (2017), pp. 123–124.

[32] Pothier (1764), pp. 176–194.

the debtor's fault. The assumption of foreseeability is only dismissed in cases of intentional misconduct, although even in this scenario, very remote and indirect consequences should not be compensated (*suites plus éloignées & plus indirectes*).

Pandectists later addressed causation, developing the theory of difference[33] as a response to the subjective nature of damage limitation techniques. This led to the consolidation[34] of a doctrine advocating unlimited and comprehensive compensation, without incorporating restrictive criteria.[35] Cohnfeldt[36] rejects, as a rule, any limitation of liability, asserting that all damage caused must be compensated and any type of causation is sufficient. The drafters of the Bürgerliches Gesetzbuch (BGB) subscribe to this position, albeit not without opposition, dismissing the criteria of fault[37] and the distinction between direct and immediate damage.

In practice, the concept of unlimited compensation proved unfeasible due to the broad scope of liability, underscoring the need for clearer boundaries on compensable damages. The criteria for limitation were generally developed through the evolution of causal theories.

3.2.1 Theory of Equivalence of Conditions

The theory of equivalence of conditions, also known in the German legal system as *Bedingungstheorie*, *Gleichwertigkeit aller Bedingungen*, or even as *Äquivalenztheorie*[38]

[33] Friedrich Mommsen reconstructed the meaning of *id quo interest* in Roman law, defining it a synonym for compensable damage. In the difference theory (*Differenztheorie*), the damage could be identified by comparing the actual situation after the harmful event occurred with the hypothetical situation to which the victim would have been restored (Steiner (2018), p. 43). The definition of interest can be found in Mommsen (1855), p. 3. Meanwhile, San Tiago Dantas states that the *id quo interest* constituted, for the Romans, the object of liability, the amount to be paid by the wrongdoer for the benefit of the injured party, corresponding to the damage caused (Dantas (1979), p. 358).

[34] A theory of interest can already be perceived from the glossators (Lange (1955), p. 14).

[35] According to Windscheid, the debtor should compensate the creditor for the damage arising from a certain event, without it being necessary for the latter to be a direct and necessary consequence of the former. Compensation would only be excluded if the damage could have been avoided by the injured party through the adoption of necessary precautions (Windscheid (1875), pp. 37–41).

[36] Cohnfeldt (1865), p. 21–22.

[37] Hans-Peter Benöhr reports that the First Commission debated for three days on the fundamental question of whether fault should be limited to conduct and the violation of a protected right or a prohibition law, or whether it should also cover the damages incurred. The author notes that in the case of law violation (*Gesetzverstöße*), the Prussian and Dresden codifications imposed responsibility, even in the absence of damage foreseeability; on the other hand, they required such foreseeability in cases of rights violation (*Rechtsverletzung*). The First Commission decided otherwise: foreseeability in cases of law violation applies only to the existence of damage, but not to its extent, and is not required in cases of rights violations (Benöhr (1999), p. 524).

[38] Hippel (1932), p. 93.

is referred to as the oldest or first of the classical theories on causation[39] and is believed to have been developed by the German Maximilian von Buri, whose first study on the subject was titled *Zur Lehre von der Teilnahme an dem Verbrechen und der Begünstigung*,[40] dated 1860. Part of the criminal doctrine[41] and some recent studies by private law scholars[42] attribute the origin of the theory, however, to the Austrian Julius Glaser,[43] who, in 1858, suggested the use of hypothetical elimination (*hypotetisches Eliminationsverfahren*)[44] or mental suppression (*wegdenken*)[45] as a prerequisite for the formula of *conditio sine qua non,* known by the scholastics through the adage "*sublata causa, tollitur effectus*" (removed the cause, the effect is dismissed), and which would later be named the counterfactual procedure.[46] Even if the primacy of Julius Glaser's study is recognized,[47] it cannot be disregarded that von Buri, from 1860, contributed to the development and improvement of the theory of equivalence.[48]

According to Gisela Sampaio da Cruz,[49] this represents a generalizing theory of causation, as it equates causes with conditions, thereby preventing any distinction between the various elements that constitute a consequence. Influenced by authors such as Haelschner[50] and Köstlin,[51] von Buri[52] argues that each condition contributing to an event is sufficient to produce it, provided all other conditions are also present.[53] Inspired by Stuart Mill,[54] the German criminal lawyer asserts the

---

[39] Pereira (2019), p. 261.

[40] Buri (1960).

[41] Hart and Honoré (1985), p. 442.

[42] Quézel-Ambrunaz (2010), p. 32.

[43] Glaser (1858), p. 298.

[44] Rümelin (1900), p. 282; Traeger (1929), p. 60.

[45] Mota Pinto (2018), p. 719–720.

[46] Pereira (2019), p. 268.

[47] The idea of the condition theory, according to Hart and Honoré, would lie in the notion of *versari in re illicita*, applied in the past in various criminal systems and in modern times by the Spanish Supreme Court, according to which those who take part in an illegal activity are responsible for all the damage that would not have occurred without their participation (Hart and Honoré (1985), cit., p. 442).

[48] Ataíde (2019), p. 762.

[49] Cruz (2005), p. 34. Atilio Anibal Alterini differentiates theories that do not distinguish conditions, including the theory of equivalence of conditions, from individualizing theories, which make distinctions between conditions, elevating one or another to the category of efficient cause of the result (Alterini (1987), p. 143). Engisch emphasizes that individualizing theories are so named because they can separate the mere condition from the cause (Engisch (1931), p. 38). Tracing the division between individualizing and generalizing theories back to Traeger, in 1904, see (Jiménez de Asúa (1951), p. 434).

[50] Haelschner (1881), pp. 227–246.

[51] Köstlin (1845), pp. 450–454.

[52] Buri (1894), pp. 69–89; Buri (1898), pp. 7–12.

[53] Lindenmaier (1950), p. 213.

[54] Inocêncio Galvão Teles asserts that the theory of equivalence of conditions simply applies to law the philosophical or naturalistic concept defended by Stuart Mill (Telles (2010), p. 398). This

equal value of all conditions, since each of these would complete the set that produces the consequence.[55] For this reason, he faced strong opposition from Karl von Birkmeyer,[56] who pointed out a supposed contradiction in the theory, consisting of the fact that each of the conditions that produced the consequence can be considered, either individually or collectively, as the cause of the result.

The theory of equivalence of conditions quickly found acceptance in the *Reichsgericht.*[57] In a case decided as early as 1880, a defendant was convicted of murder for leaving a bottle of wine containing an arsenic solution on the windowsill, foreseeing that her alcoholic husband would eventually taste it. The German court decided that without her act of leaving the bottle with poison, the husband would not have died, so her conduct could be characterized as entirely causal.[58] The formula of the *conditio sine qua non* was also adopted in Anglo-American legal systems under the name of the "*but-for test.*"[59]

Although the theory of equivalence has been adopted by a substantial part of the doctrine and applied by courts as a valid tool in eliminating circumstances that did not contribute to the occurrence of the result, its insufficiency was noted in some scenarios, such as in cases of virtual or hypothetical causation (*hypothetische Kausalität*),[60] double causation (*Doppelkausalität*), multiple causation (Mehrfachkausalität), or cumulative[61]

---

assertion is contested by Rui Soares Pereira Soares. According to the author, the philosophical or scientific concept supported by Mill does not lead to the conclusion that every condition is a cause of the event, allowing for differentiation between conditions and circumstances necessary to produce the result. Thus, von Buri would not have derived his theory from Stuart Mill's causal conception, especially since he probably was not aware of the latter's work (Pereira (2019), p. 278). Carl Ludwig, a contemporary of von Buri, cites a long passage from Mill's work, comparing it to the theory of equivalence of conditions (Bar (1871), pp. 6–7). When the theory was adopted by continental authors and criminal courts, this was justified by the adoption of certain aspects of Mill's philosophy, to the detriment of the notion of equal causal efficiency advocated by von Buri (Hart and Honoré (1985), p. 444).

[55] Wilson Melo da Silva translated the opening page of *Über Kausalität und deren Verantwortung* into Portuguese. See SILVA (1962), pp. 206–207).

[56] Birkmeyer (1885), p. 15.

[57] RGSt 1 (1880), 373, 374.

[58] Hart and Honoré (1985), p. 444. Lindenmaier, in 1950, stated that the dominant criminal doctrine continued to apply the theory of conditions, as requirements such as illegality and fault were able to solve part of the cases. In the civil law domain, however, without the use of a corrective criterion, the equivalence theory would not be as useful (Lindenmaier (1950), pp. 214–217). Otávio Luiz Rodrigues points out that, from the 1930s, the finalist theory of action emerged as a challenge to causal explanations of human behavior based solely on results, providing an opportunity to rethink causal dogmas (Rodrigues Jr. (2006), p. 439).

[59] Pettefi da Silva (2009), p. 33. Also stating that in principle causation constitutes a two-stage approach, see Rogers et al. (2000), p. 39. The *but-for test* became part of the Restatement (Third) of Torts in 2010.

[60] About the concept of hypothetical or virtual causation, see Mota Pinto (2008), p. 652; Coelho (1998). In virtual causation, only one of the conducts is supposedly the cause of the event, the other being called a reserve cause (*Reserveursache*). Richter points out the issue of the reserve cause as problematic within the scope of the equivalence theory (Richter (2012), pp. 138–139).

[61] Regarding cumulative causation, see Serra (1959), p. 137.

not necessary[62] causation, as well as in relation to alternative causation.[63] In Anglo-American law, it is also noted that when two causes contribute to a harmful result, and one alone is sufficient to produce the same effect, an additional test is required, as the rule of equivalence, serving as an exclusion factor, does not apply in such cases.[64]

Some authors, including Traeger[65] and Tarnowski,[66] suggest that these problematic situations can be resolved using the conditio formula in its abstract form. Rather than asking whether a specific condition caused a particular concrete result, they propose starting from the observer's interest. This approach can yield significantly different answers depending on the perspective applied.[67] Thus, the conduct would be the cause of the result when, in the absence of it, the effect could still be subsumed under the abstract framing of the consequence.[68]

Thyrén[69] identifies two propositions in von Buri's theory: (a) Only those circumstances deemed relevant can be considered as causes, but not all antecedents; (b) within this circle, all causes are equivalent. He notes that von Buri himself illustratively mentioned that one who lets the contents of a drinking fountain flow until the waters surpass the destroyed dam does not contribute to the flood. Thyrén concludes that these propositions are irreconcilable after analyzing them.

Due to opposition to the theory, von Buri's followers were compelled to reformulate it. This task was primarily undertaken by von Liszt,[70] who sought to purge the irreconcilable elements of the thesis. He argued that concurrent causes become equally necessary to produce a given result, further asserting that a causal

---

[62] Reinig (2015), p. 94.

[63] About the doctrinal development of alternative causation, see Koch (2016), pp. 71–72; Bydlinski (1964), p. 86.

[64] For the resolution of these cases, the Minnesota Court applied a broader rule, which received widespread acceptance: Conduct is the cause of the event if it is a material element and a substantial factor (*substantial factor*) in its occurrence. The substantial factor test carries a stronger legal connotation than a factual one (Prosser and Keeton (1984), pp. 266–267).

[65] Traeger (1929), pp. 41–46.

[66] Tarnowski (1929), p. 38.

[67] Pereira (2019), p. 268.

[68] According to Traeger, it can be asserted that if among the antecedents of a result there coexist, in relation to each other, two or more decisive independent conditions coexist, meaning that they cannot be abstracted simultaneously without the legally relevant consequence ceasing to exist, and the elimination of any one of them would leave the result unchanged, then each of these circumstances must be considered legally relevant (Traeger (1929), pp. 47–48).

[69] Thyrén (1894), p. 27. Traeger asserts that Thyrén's objection is unfounded, as the theory of the *conditio*, according to him, does not affirm the absolute equality of all conditions, but equivalence in a legal sense. Only the antecedents, on which the analyzed legal consequence depends, are affirmed as conditions of the result (Traeger (1929), pp. 49–50). Wilson Melo da Silva explains that, for Traeger, a pile of straw that someone had thrown onto the fire of a burning house would be a legally irrelevant cause. He also notes that Thyrén differentiates relevant and irrelevant co-causes, as well as conditions that could be classified as positive, negative, or indifferent in relation to their effects (Silva (1962), p. 208).

[70] Liszt (1927), pp. 158–160. An older edition of the book can be consulted in Portuguese. See Liszt (1899).

relationship between a behavior and its effect only truly exists when it can be affirmed that this consequence would not occur without that cause. Von Liszt also eliminated any differentiation between causes and conditions, which would indifferently assume the functions of concurrent causes, given that one of the criticisms directed at the equivalence theory was von Buri's distinction between "relevant" and "irrelevant" antecedents, contradicting the supposed "equivalence" of conditions.

In contrast to Traeger, Engisch[71] proposes that the delimitation of factual material should be carried out through a legal analysis, but from a concrete point of view, this concept becoming dominant in German doctrine.[72] The author asserts that von Buri correctly defended that a circumstance or a process, which connects with others to form a causal chain, is in causal connection with a concrete result. Although aligned with von Buri's position on this point, Engisch highlights the inadequacy of the formula, suggesting an alternative construction, which came to be known as the "formula adjusted to (or in accordance with) natural laws" ("*Formel von der gesetzmäßigen Bedingung*")[73] or "theory of the condition of the result according to the laws of nature" ("*gesetzmäßige Bedingung des Erfolgs*").[74]

From Engisch's perspective, it should be ascertained, based on the rules of experience, whether the succession of initiated acts, in their entirety, would inevitably lead to that result.[75] Or, as explained by Thomas Rönnau, Florian Faust, and Michael Fehling,[76] a behavior causes a result if it is legally connected to the conduct through a series of modifications (*Dominoeffekt*), this connection being assessed by recourse to general experience or by consulting an expert.[77]

The most compelling criticism against the theory of equivalence of conditions is that it permits an endless extension of the causal chain. René Demogue[78] acknowledges that the conditio theory is scientifically accurate compared to the imprecision of other theories. Nevertheless, he questions its practical adoption since it would extend responsibility to an excessive number of individuals. The adoption of the theory of conditions, purely and simply, without any other filter, would lead to immeasurable

[71] Engisch (1931), p. 27.

[72] Samson (1972), pp. 26–31.

[73] Pereira (2019), p. 271.

[74] Reinig (2015), pp. 95–96.

[75] Ascensão (1956), pp. 141–142.

[76] The authors emphasize, as previously noted, that the "Doctrine of the Lawful Condition" was developed to address the difficulties arising from the conditio formula, particularly regarding hypothetical causation. They also highlight that Engisch's proposed formula is widely supported in German doctrine (Rönnau et al. (2004), p. 114).

[77] Regarding Engisch's theory, see Pereira (2019), p. 272.

[78] Demogue (1924), pp. 16–17. Gabriel Marty goes further, arguing that, in tort law, fault plays a fundamental role in limiting compensable damages, while causation serves as a secondary element. However, in the context of strict liability, he states that the insufficiency of the equivalence theory becomes evident (Marty (1939), pp. 703–704).

regression to preceding causes.[79] Thus, if taken to its ultimate consequences, it would result in holding the carpenter who made the bed on which the amorous couple lay as a participant in the adultery.

The application of correction filters is essential to delimit the boundaries of compensable damage. Liability is defined through causal concepts, yet the condition theory proves inadequate,[80] producing excessively broad Responsability, as previously discussed.[81] Although it can be considered, as part of the doctrine does,[82] that the theory of equivalence is a true doctrine of legal imputation,[83] it is not sufficient to delimit the types of causes and conditions that should be taken into consideration for the purpose of assessing the existence and extent of liability.[84]

Indeed, the theory of equivalence, even in cases of damage caused by psychological influence, does not manage to demarcate the limits of liability, given its wide scope, appearing only as an initial stage of causal investigation. From the multiplicity of conditions that cause the harmful event, all are initially equivalent,

[79] Attribution has been emphasized as requiring a limit; otherwise, the obligation to compensate becomes "unmanageable" (Ataíde (2019), p. 763). It has also been stated that fragments of the history of the entire universe cannot be rescued (Mendes (1986), p. 67). Savatier asserts that the indefinite weave of causation (*la trame indéfinie de la causalité*) is infinitely complex and that, as we go back in time, the number of causes increases geometrically (Savatier (1951), p. 3). It has further been argued that only those facts that are truly the causes of the event itself can be considered as causes, and not all the antecedents that contributed to the result. Therefore, the birth of a person is not the cause of the accident in which she is a victim (Demogue (1924), p. 12). Finally, attention has been drawn to the risk that the equivalence theory may regress to the causation of the universe (Viney et al. (2013), p. 247).

[80] The formula of the *conditio sine qua non* should not be confused with the theory of equivalence (Ascensão (1956), p. 114). As discussed, not all conditions are deemed relevant for producing the result, even if encompassed by the formula. Courts distinguish between negative and positive formulations of the *conditio sine qua non* (Antolisei (2000), p. 236). In this regard, aims to distinguish, among the various circumstances that contribute to the occurrence of the harmful event, those without whose contribution the damage would not have occurred and the others, which also contributed to this event, but whose absence would not have prevented its detection (Varela (2000), p. 882). Schulin emphasizes that, while the theory of condition is a causal theory, the formula of the *conditio sine qua non* serves as a practical tool for determining causal relationships within the scope of this theory (Schulin (1976), p. 105). In German doctrine, the *conditio* is regarded as "practical rule" or "general rule" ("*Faustregel*"). It does not provide an exact definition of causation but rather a description that facilitates the application of the law and suffices for most cases (Larenz (1987), p. 433). Also understanding the theory of the *conditio* as a practical rule (*Faustregel*), see Deutsch (1966), p. 556.

[81] Sourlas (1974), p. 14.

[82] Gottwald (1979), p. 96.

[83] In contrast, Antunes Varela argues that the theory of the *conditio* may be useful to the natural sciences, from which the concept was imported, but does not accommodate the peculiarities of law (Varela (1977), p. 250).

[84] Already at the end of the nineteenth century, there was a conviction that, despite the principle of full compensation, unlimited liability did not seem reasonable. The dominant doctrine at the time, which had been based solely on the *conditio sine qua non*, was perceived as increasingly problematic, requiring the establishment of limiting criteria for consequential damages (Jansen (2007), p. 576).

so the test of the *conditio sine qua non* would lead to disproportionately excessive responsibility, as the causal chains would prove to be infinite.[85] The equivalence of conditions aims to establish, in the first step, factual causation,[86] which, in psychologically mediated causation, presents certain peculiarities to be examined later,[87] followed by a stage of legal valuation (imputation) that imposes limitations.

3.2.2 Theory of Proximate Cause or Theory of the Last Condition

The theory of proximate cause[88] is regarded in doctrine as an individualizing or "selective theory"[89] ("*Auswahltheorie*"), since its purpose is to distinguish the true cause from mere conditions. It finds its foundation in the ideas of Francis Bacon,[90] especially in the maxim *in iure non remota causa sed proxima spectatur.*[91] According to this theory, the cause is the condition that appears last in the causal chain, and responsibility arises only if the unlawful human act materialized as the final condition.[92]

The theory of proximate cause derives from Binding's balance theory,[93] though the two differ profoundly. According to the German author, every change results from opposing forces clashing, some impeding and others favoring the outcome. These forces remain in balance until a condition intervenes, tipping the scale and thus becoming the cause of the result in question.

Ortmann[94] proposed a modification to the theory, replacing the idea of balance with the temporal criterion. Aware that considering only the last cause would often

---

[85] Ristow (2003), p. 29.

[86] See Section 3.2.7.

[87] See Section 5.2.

[88] Portuguese doctrine refers to this theory as the "last condition theory" (Menezes Cordeiro (2017), p. 532). The theory is embraced, with its peculiarities, in the *common law* system, where the concept of "proximate cause" refers to a causal connection between two events, which can only be legally connected when the first, as a *but-for* condition of the second event, is so closely related to it that it becomes legally significant (Infantino (2017), p. 283). Rui de Alarcão uses the last expression to refer to both the last condition theory and the efficient condition theory (Alarcão (1983), p. 237).

[89] Bordon (2006), p. 80; Antolisei (1960), p. 60. Rui Soares Pereira, however, asserts that the equivalence of the interpretation of Bacon's maxim and the theory of proximate cause is questionable, and the lineage indiccated is uncertain (Pereira (2019), p. 322). Quézel-Ambrunaz likewise describes it as an "illegitimate lineage" ("*filiation illégitime*") (Quézel-Ambrunaz (2010), pp. 48–49.

[90] Bacon (1639), p. 1.

[91] Bordon (2006), p. 80.

[92] Jorge (1999), p. 391.

[93] Binding states that an event is caused when impulsive conditions prevail over obstructive conditions (Binding (1872), pp. 42–43). He identifies the cause with the decisive condition, distinguishing it from mere "impulsive" and "obstructive" conditions (Varela (2000), p. 886).

[94] Ortmann (1876), pp. 99–100.

lead to injustices, either because a natural fact intervenes last or because an act is not characterized by faute,[95] which would exclude the liability of the last causer, he reformulated his approach, stressing that natural facts invariably precede the human act, even when the act occurs last, and that acts without *faute* are disregarded.

In France, the idea that liability can be limited from the point of view of damage was already developed by French doctrine and adopted by the *Code Napoléon*. In its Art. 1.151,[96] the code stated that only damages that are a direct and immediate (*suite immédiate et directe*) consequence of the event should be compensated. Although Art. 1.151 was intended for contractual liability, its application in the extra-contractual area has always been unequivocal. When the theory of equivalence still had proponents, there were, however, attempts to limit the application of the legal provision. Currently, its acceptance is widespread.[97]

A point discussed in French doctrine is whether this provision contains a causal rule. The doctrine was initially skeptical about the possibility of establishing useful criteria, with some even arguing the unnecessary or even dangerous nature of a causation theory, since in many countries the courts have refused to commit to any theory.[98] Carbonnier[99] even goes so far as to renounce any kind of systematization,[100] arguing that the limitation of causation should be determined empirically by judicial discretion.

Currently, it is understood that the direct cause, originally provided for in Art. 1.151 of the French Civil Code, is distinct from the proximate cause. Although the requirement of a direct causal link, established by the indicated

[95] Quézel-Ambrunaz (2010), pp. 50–51.

[96] In 2016, a comprehensive legislative reform of obligations law (*Ordonnance* n. 2016–131) renumbered the relevant statutory provision (Art. 1231–4) and revised its language, without introducing substantive modifications to its content. The preparatory work of the French Civil Code consisted of three Cambacérès projects and the project of the year VIII (August 13, 1800), whose commission was composed of Portalis, Bigot, Maleville, and Tronchet, all magistrates (Foignet (1946), p. 28). The first three drafts were unsuccessful, with only the last one prevailing, representing a definitive change in the way the other projects regulated the theme of compensable damage, and consolidating the influence of Pothier's *Traité des obligations* on the emerging codification (Dias (2020), p. 76).

[97] Motulsky (1960), p. 248.

[98] Honoré (1983), p. 23.

[99] Carbonnier (1962), pp. 593–595. The Mazeaud corroborates this thesis, stating that the *Cour de Cassation* does not hesitate to annul decisions when causation has not been established, but is less decisive when it comes to verifying whether causation has fulfilled the necessary prerequisites or, conversely, whether the appellate court correctly refused to recognize the existence of causation (Mazeaud and Mazeaud (1931), p. 5).

[100] French jurists of the late nineteenth and early twentieth centuries treated the causal issue as a matter of fact, with the idea prevailing that the cause should be unique (Reinig (2017), pp. 127–128). Treating causation as a matter of fact, see Josserand (1933), p. 239; Planiol and Ripert (1909), p. 285.

legal provision, may seem similar to the proximate cause, such an interpretation should be avoided. Thus, what the codifiers expressed as "*suite immédiate et directe*" is, therefore, just a simple requirement of causation distinct from the idea of proximate cause.[101]

The theory of the proximate cause, or the last condition, was not well received in jurisdictions belonging to the civil law tradition. This causal conception focuses its attention entirely on the chronological order of events, without paying attention to their relevance. It is certain, however, that the last condition identified can, considering the complexity of the causal chain as a whole, assume little or no relevance to the result,[102] besides being highly detrimental to the victim.[103] Finally, in cases where there is a significant time lapse[104] between the conduct and the harmful result, the theory of the proximate cause cannot be taken into account for liability purposes.[105]

In cases of "psychological causation," the chronological order of events cannot be said to play a determining role in setting the limits of legal imputation, which reveals the theory's insufficiency at this point. As this group of cases[106] is characterized by the intervention of a second causer, who is not the perpetrator of the initial act, it is not possible to simply assert that this second individual is solely responsible for the damages caused to third parties. On the contrary, the main discussion revolves around the responsibility of the first perpetrator, to whom the claim for damages is directed and who, in theory, facilitated or influenced the action of the second causer. The central issue becomes whether a causal link exists between the first wrongdoer's conduct and the second person's subsequent behavior.[107]

[101] Quézel-Ambrunaz (2010), pp. 54–55. The theory, which received some recognition, at least in formal terms, in English case law, seems to have been almost unanimously rejected (Viney et al. (2013) p. 245). In Italian doctrine, some state that the theory was adopted by Art. 1229 of the *Civil Code* of 1865 and by Art. 1223 of the current codification. Pietro Trimachi asserts that this formula evokes the rules of *common law*, which limit liability to "proximate" consequences, excluding those that are "too remote." The author notes that it is clear this is a metaphorical formula, which cannot be interpreted literally (Trimarchi (2019), p. 489).

[102] Coelho (1951), p. 196.

[103] The criterion of proximity should not be measured in terms of space or time, but rather through the verification of the absence of elements that would allow the conclusion that the link between the fact and the damage is broken or excessively attenuated (Infantino (2012), p. 94).

[104] Morsello (2007), p. 216.

[105] Quézel-Ambrunaz (2010), pp. 55.

[106] The importance of establishing case groups will be further analyzed in Sect. 3.2.7. Recognizing that one of the main characteristics of current legal science is the consideration of the elaboration of case groups, see Canaris (1995), p. 44.

[107] Ristow (2003), p. 28.

3.2.3 Theory of Direct and Immediate Damage or Theory of Interruption of the Chain of Causation

As previously discussed, the Code Napoléon, influenced by Pothier's doctrine,[108] expressly stated in its former Art. 1.151 that compensation must cover only losses that are a direct and immediate consequence of contractual non-performance. This principle applied even in cases of debtor fraud, limiting recovery to the creditor's actual losses and lost profits.[109] This legislative provision generates numerous doctrinal and jurisprudential controversies due to its lack of clarity and precision. Some even argue that it is not a true theory of causation but merely an attribute of compensable damage.[110]

Therefore, it is always difficult, within the scope of French law, to identify the factors that led the courts to a particular solution.[111] French courts generally issue very brief and enigmatic decisions, in which neither the analysis of causation nor the underlying political reasons are mentioned. Furthermore, although the matter of causation is considered a question of law and, as such, subject to the control of the *Cour de Cassation*, the assessment of facts related to the verification of causation is left to the discretion of the lower courts.[112] This discretion[113] is expanded by the fact that judges can declare themselves satisfied with the proof of causation simply by excluding any other possible explanation of the events.[114]

Italian law follows the French tradition based on the doctrine of Pothier, adopting the distinction between direct and indirect damages in Art. 1.223 of the *Codice Civile*,[115] which states that only damages that directly and immediately

---

[108] To illustrate his considerations, Pothier uses the example of Ulpiano (D. 19, 1,13, pr.), in his well-known passage regarding the case of the pestilent cow (Pothier (1764), pp. 190–191).

[109] "Art. 1.151. Even in the case where the non-performance of the contract results from the debtor's fraud, damages should include, regarding the loss suffered by the creditor and the profit of which he has been deprived, only what is an immediate and direct consequence of the non-performance of the contract."

[110] Malaurie and Aynès (2016), p. 55.

[111] André Tunc emphasizes that long before Bacon's writings and before Pothier speculated about the damages that a pestilent cow could cause, jurists were already attempting to determine the damages for which a person who acted with *faute* should held responsible. He asserts that, being a somewhat philosophical matter of causation, and relating more to "finesse" than to "geometry," it will always escape very precise rules (Tunc (1953), p. 6).

[112] The authority of Belgian judges to decide on factual issues is discussed in Ommmeslaghe (2013).

[113] Zimmermann, referring to the case presented by Pothier, points out that the reason why the causal chain should be interrupted at a certain point, and why the ultimate consequences should be considered indirect, is not immediately apparent (Zimmermann (2014), p. 201).

[114] Infantino and Zervogianni (2017), pp. 92–93.

[115] "Art. 1.223. The compensation for damage. The compensation for damage due to non-performance or delay must include both the loss suffered by the creditor and the missed profit, provided they are a direct and immediate consequence."

result from the offender's activity are compensable.[116] Giovanna Visintini[117] underlines that the causal issue is not usually addressed, and judges tend to rely on presumptive techniques, framing the respective investigation within the scope of application of Art. 1.223, thereby overlapping the various aspects of causation.

In practice, it can be observed that indirect damages[118] can also be compensated. Other criteria have been developed in Italian doctrine to limit the imputation of compensable damages, such as the existence of an organic connection (*connessione organica*) between the fact and the consequences. This connection is considered interrupted when a particular circumstance is introduced during the course of events, leading to an unexpected influence on the causal course itself, resulting in an unforeseeable result. Reference is also made to the criteria developed by German doctrine, such as the "sphere of risk" and the "general risk of life."[119]

De Cupis, when analyzing Art. 1.223, concludes that it does not exclude indirect or mediate damages, meaning that direct and immediate damages are always compensable, while the latter may be compensable depending on the case, according to the criterion of regularity (*regolarità*) applied in the latter instance.[120] Guido Alpa and Zeno Zencovich[121] state that if the events can be reconstructed, starting with the damage and tracing back to the preceding events linked to it, this constitutes an operation known as "seeking the material cause." From a legal perspective, however, it would not be necessary to trace events back so far in time. By applying the principle of regularity, it would suffice to identify the act that was sufficiently the cause of the event that led to the damage (the so-called legal causation).

Vincenzo Roppo also[122] resorts to the idea of regularity to explain the establishment of causation. Distinguishing material causation (*causalità materiale*) from legal causation (*causalità giuridica*), he notes that the latter is characterized by a reasonable probability that a certain event has produced the particular damage, adding that it is not necessary to form a judgment of "absolute certainty," only a relative probability, expressed in the formula "more likely than not"

[116] The Italian Civil Code retained, in the Art. 1.223, the expressions of the previous code. The ministerial draft addressed compensation for emergent damage and lost profits "*in quanto siano conseguenze necessarie del fato lesivo.*" However, the Legislative Assembly Commission proposed replacing the expression "necessary consequence," with a formulation that would also encompass indirect damages (Alvim (1980), p. 354).

[117] Visintini (2005), p. 715.

[118] The term "indirect damage" may lead to confusion, as it does not provide a decisive basis for establishing causation (Pirson (1964), p. 22).

[119] Busnelli and Patti (2013), pp. 30–32.

[120] Also referring to the idea of *regolarità*, see Franzoni (2010), pp. 67–68; Cendon (2009), p. 1.223; Sella (2007), p. 74; Rajneri (2017), pp. 381–383. In Italian jurisprudence, see Cass. civ., Sez. U., 11 January 2008, n. 581, *RCP*, 827; Cass. civ., Sez. III., 24 March 2000, n. 3536, *DResp*, 2000, 6, 599.

[121] Alpa and Zeno-Zencovich, p. 257.

[122] Roppo (2016), pp. 584–585.

(“*più probabile che non*”). This pertains to the circumstance wherein, to express the identical concept, jurists refer to causal adequacy,[123] denoting that a fact should be evaluated, according to reasonable criteria of statistical frequency, as potentially capable of producing the harmful outcome.

In Brazilian law, the rule of Art. 1.060[124] of the Beviláqua Code,[125] clearly inspired by French[126] and Italian law, was transposed to Art. 403[127] of the Civil Code of 2002, initially appearing to adopt the theory of direct and immediate damage. However, many scholars contend that the codification embraced the theory of adequacy. Notwithstanding, a significant doctrinal and jurisprudential disagreement persists regarding the applicable theory, highlighting the lack of technical criteria in determining causation. In practice, interpreters are often guided more by a sense of justice than by a consistent application of legal principles.

Various variants of the theory have emerged due to the difficulty in establishing a satisfactory general theory of causation that could guide determinations about the proximity of consequences. These variants share a common principle: Causation is “interrupted” when a creditor or third party commits a violation, releasing the initial perpetrator from liability. The primary disagreement concerns whether natural events similarly “interrupt” the causal chain.[128]

Tomaso Mosca[129] supports the first theory, known as the “theory of legal causation.” He argues that while every event without which the result would not have occurred constitutes a concause in the physical or logical order, different rules apply at the juridical level. Legal analysis focuses on identifying the legally relevant cause. When the damage results from a natural fact or from a non-imputable person, liability continues to rest with the original causer of the injury.

---

[123] Supporting the application of the adequacy criterion in Italian law, see Scognamiglio (2010), p. 78.

[124] “Art. 1.060. Even if the non-performance results from the debtor’s fraud, losses and damages only include actual losses and lost profits as a direct and immediate effect thereof.” The draft presented by Coelho Rodrigues already provided for a similar rule: “Art. 1234. Even in the case where the non-performance of the obligation results from the debtor’s fraud, losses and damages only include actual losses and lost profits, directly and immediately resulting from the same non-performance.”

[125] Beviláqua indicates, as references in foreign law, Art. 1.151 of the French Civil Code, Art. 1.223 of the Italian Civil Code, Art. 707 of the Portuguese Civil Code, Art. 521 of the Argentine Civil Code, Art. 1.295 of the Venezuelan codification and Art. 1.295 of the Mexican Civil Code, also referring to the rule of Roman law found the Code, 7, 47, 1 only (Beviláqua (1955), p. 177). Thus provided the Portuguese Civil Code of 1867, in its Art. 707: “Only losses and damages that necessarily result from the non-compliance of the contract can be taken into account.”

[126] Recognizing that Art. 1.060 of the CC/16 is derived from the *Code Civil* French, see Pontes de Miranda (1981), p. 249.

[127] “Art. 403. Even if the non-performance results from the debtor’s fraud, losses and damages only include actual losses and lost profits as a direct and immediate effect thereof, without prejudice to the provisions of procedural law.”

[128] Alvim (1980), p. 348.

[129] Mosca (1896), pp. 18–21.

The causal chain is deemed "interrupted" only if the second act is attributable to an imputable person, which excludes the liability of the first.[130] Mosca's thesis fails by eliminating force majeure as a cause "interrupting" the causal chain.[131]

By contrast, Coviello[132] relies on Art. 1.298 of the Italian Civil Code of 1865[133] (with wording similar to Art. 957 of the CC/16 and to Art. 399 of the CC/02), which provides that, assuming the debtor's default, he is responsible for fortuitous events unless he demonstrates that such events would have occurred even if there had been no default. Coviello then deduces that the event, which together with the debtor's fault contributed to the damage, must be such that it would have produced the damage even if the previous culpable act had not occurred.[134] According to the thesis proposed, it should be verified whether the cause that generated the new damage would have caused it regardless of the act of the debtor. If so, the causal chain would be interrupted.[135]

Agostinho Alvim,[136] responsible for drafting the preliminary project of the law of obligations, which resulted in the Civil Code of 2002, argues that the doctrine that most effectively explains the theory of direct and immediate damage[137] is that of "necessary causation."[138] Defended, according to the author, by Chironi,[139] Giorgi,[140] and Polacco,[141] it would be the thesis that most comprehensively interprets the doctrine of Pothier, as well as that of his predecessor, Du Moulin.

---

[130] Polacco, citing Pessina, questions Mosca's theory, giving the example of a person who, through fault, causes another person a mental disturbance, and this mentally disturbed person, not being in control of himself (*compos sui*), perpetrates, on himself or on others, while unconscious, a damage (Polacco (1915), p. 594). A detailed presentation of the criticisms formulated by Polacco can be found in Alvim (1980), pp. 350–353.

[131] Cruz (2005), p. 98.

[132] Coviello (1897), pp. 211–216.

[133] Art. 1.298 "[. . .] Even if the debtor is in default and has not assumed the risk of force majeure, the obligation is extinguished if the thing would have perished equally with the creditor if it had been delivered to him [. . .]."

[134] Alvim (1980), p. 353.

[135] The criticisms formulated by Formica can be found in Scialoja (1899), pp. 542.

[136] Alvim (1980), p. 356.

[137] Jorge Ferreira da Silva notes that Agostinho Alvim's inspiration may come from a passage from Eduardo Espínola's work, in which he analyzes the explanatory theories of causation (Ferreira (2007), pp. 183–184).

[138] It has been argued that the limitation of liability cannot be derived from the mere notion of causation; instead, the analysis must verify whether the act was necessary for the damage to occur (Planiol and Ripert (1930) p. 740). In tort law, it is also maintained that a sine qua non fact cannot, by itself, be regarded as the cause of the damage, since "causation" extends to every necessary factual antecedent. The theory of adequate causation is further acknowledged by many French scholars (Aubry and Rau (1952), p. 486).

[139] Chironi (1884), pp. 271–272.

[140] According to Giorgi, damage can never be considered as an indirect or mediate consequence, when it was or should have been within the author of the illicit act's field of foreseeability (Giorgi (1926), p. 268).

[141] Polacco, (1915), p. 590.

According to the "subtheory of necessary causation," the causal chain is "interrupted" not only when the creditor or a third party is the author of the proximate cause of the subsequent damage, as Mosca argues, but also when the proximate cause constitutes a natural fact (the theory of Coviello, according to which the natural fact "interrupts" the causal chain).

The author bases his argument on a supposedly historical foundation, since the "subtheory of necessary causation," according to Agostinho Alvim,[142] would be a creation of Pothier and Du Moulin and would have been adopted by the expositors of the *Code Napoléon.*[143] He argues, after concluding the synonymy between the expressions "direct" and "immediate," that the damage, despite being remote, can be a necessary consequence of the conduct, since there is no intervention of any other cause. The required proximity would not be understood as immediacy but rather as necessariness;[144] the Brazilian jurist thereby reconstructs the literal meaning of the expression employed in the codification.[145] It is, therefore, related to the idea of necessariness in the absence of concurrent causes.

A substantial part of Brazilian legal doctrine supports the "subtheory of necessary causation."[146] The Supreme Federal Court's (STF) decision in RE 130.764–1/PR[147] on May 12, 1992 stands as the paradigmatic jurisprudential ruling on this

---

[142] Alvim (1980), p. 359.

[143] In Brazilian law, this position is also adopted by Mulholland (2009, p. 168) and Gisela Sampaio da Cruz. The latter even transcribes an excerpt from Pothier's work, in his *Treatise on Obligations,* where the author cites the expressions "necessary relation" ("*relation nécessaire*") and "necessary consequence" ("*suite nécessaire*") (Cruz (2005), p. 100). In French law, Fromageot defends that the damage must be the necessary consequence of the fault, asserting that this was the theory adopted in Roman law and accepted by French law, influenced by Pothier (Fromageot (1891), pp. 42–45).

[144] Given a certain damage, the cause is identified as either the nearest or most distant, but in the case of the latter, it must be directly linked to the damage. It is the necessary cause of this damage, because it necessarily follows from it; it is the sole cause, because it operates by itself, other causes being unnecessary. Thus, all damage that follows from a cause, even if remote, is compensable, provided that it is a necessary cause, as there is no other that explains the same damage (Alvim (1980), p. 356).

[145] Reinig (2017), p. 131.

[146] The theory is adopted, for example, by Tepedino (2011), p. 110; Souza (2018), pp. 62–63; Cruz (2005), p. 107; Lopez (2008), p. 26; Silva (1962), p. 230; Miragem (2021), p. 126; Gomes (2002), p. 275; Benjamin (1998), p. 46; Scavone et al. Jr (2006), p. 403; Pereira (1991), pp. 88–89; Zanetti (2021), pp. 272–274; Nanni (2021), p. 288. Sanseverino asserts that the theories of equivalence, adequacy, and of the necessary causa should be combined and applied in successive stages (Sanseverino (2010), p. 163). Judith Martins-Costa indicates the path of "complementarity and synthesis," considering the theory of direct and immediate damage a "hermeneutic tool" for a better understanding of the theory of adequate causation (Martins-Costa (2009), pp. 214–215). In the first edition of the same work, she identified the theory of adequacy as the one derived from the interpretation of Art. 403 of the CC/02. This reference was omitted in the second edition (Martins-Costa (2003), p. 138). Limongi França asserts that Art 1.060 of the CC/16 enshrines the theory of immediate effect, without engaging in the discussion regarding the necessariness of the cause (França (1976), p. 234).

[147] Judge Sepúlveda Pertence acknowledged the emergence of a relatively independent cause, in an analogous application of Art. 40 of the Criminal Code, grounding his vote on the circumstance

matter. In this decision, the STF expressly admitted that, still under the scope of Art. 1.060 of the CC/16, the theory adopted regarding causation would have been that of direct and immediate damage, also known as the "theory of the interruption of causal chain." It was also affirmed that the application of this theory would avoid the inconveniences of the other two existing theoretical constructions: that of the equivalence of conditions and that of adequate causation.

The appeal concerned a compensation claim filed against the State of Paraná, motivated by the fact that the plaintiffs, on 21/06/85, had their residence and commercial establishment robbed by a group composed of eight criminals, one of whom had escaped from the state penitentiary 21 months earlier, on 13/09/83. Although he was a highly dangerous prisoner, he was not properly monitored when transferred to the hospital of Guarapuava/PR for medical treatment. The state was held liable in the first instance, and the Court of Justice of Paraná upheld the initial decision on this point, based on the full responsibility of the state entity. The STF[148] upheld the extraordinary appeal filed by the state and, citing Agostinho Alvim and Wilson de Melo da Silva, decided that the damage resulting from the crime was not the necessary effect of the public authority's omission, resulting, instead, from concurrent causes, such as the formation of a gang and the robbery that occurred.[149]

---

of the occurrence of another causal chain, as well as the fact that the damage indicated had exceeded the normal consequences of the omission or negligence of the administration. Judge Celso de Mello observed that the temporal extension of causal antecedents functions as an impediment to establishing the necessary and immediate etiological connection between state officials' conduct and the resultant harm suffered by third parties (STF, RE 130.764–1/PR, rel. Moreira Alves, j. 12.05.1992).

[148] In RE 172.025–5/RJ, decided on 08/10/96, the STF, referring to the decision in RE 130.764–1/PR, held that the Public Power's responsibility was not substantiated, in a case related to robbery committed by a prison escapee, almost three months after the escape, due to the lack of a causal link between the harmful event and the performance of state tasks (STF, RE 172.025–5/RJ, rel. Min. Ilmar Galvão, j. 08.10.1996). The same reasoning was later applied in RE 369.820/RS, decided on November 4, 2003. This time, however, it was decided that the state is not responsible for robbery committed by a fugitive, after four months of his evasion, in co-authorship with three other non-fugitive people (STF, RE 369.820/RS, rel. Carlos Velloso, j. 04.11.2003). However, in RE 409.203–4/RS, in a decision rendered on March 7, 2005, the STF held that the State should be held liable for the rape of a 12-year-old minor, given that the convicted individual, under an open prison regime, had evaded custody on seven occasions, without the authorities responsible for enforcing the sentence applying the measure of regime regression. It is interesting to note that Judge Carlos Velloso adhered to the STF's settled jurisprudence, according to which liability, even in the presence of faute du service, requires proof of causation assessed under the theory of direct and immediate damage. However, in a concurring opinion, Judge Joaquim Barbosa asserted that the case under analysis would depart from the established precedents, since, in the cases where liability is excluded, there is always a subtle element to mischaracterize the direct causation: either the time element, or the circumstance of the crime having been committed by a fugitive convict in partnership with other fugitive delinquents (STF, RE 409.203–4/RS, rel. Min. Carlos Velloso, j. 07.03.2006).

[149] According to Tepedino, the adoption by the STF of the theory of direct and immediate damage excludes the application of the theory of equivalence of conditions and of adequate causation (Tepedino (2002), p. 9).

More recently, the STF, in RE 608.880[150] (Theme 362), stated that the escape of a prisoner and the perpetration of a crime, without any logical relation to his evasion, eliminate the normative element. In these hypotheses, there is no direct causation for the purpose of attributing liability. In the case now analyzed, the convict escaped on November 10, 1999 and, on February 28, 2000, committed the crime of homicide. Although Justice Marco Aurélio[151] argued that the remote cause of the damage was the state's omission, supporting the dismissal of the appeal, Justice Alexandre de Moraes disagreed. He held that the interval between the administrative act and the typical act (chronological criterion), along with the emergence of independent supervening causes (specifically, the formation of a gang), would "interrupt" the causal chain. The latter position prevailed, and the appeal was upheld.

Despite the efforts of those supporting the application of the "subtheory of necessary causation," a more detailed analysis of this doctrinal elaboration reveals its theoretical inconsistency and its lack of technical refinement.[152]

As a starting point, the unconvincing argument that the expression "direct and immediate," in the view of Pothier and Du Moulin, refers to a necessary causal link should be rejected. Such a conclusion cannot be deduced from the studies of the indicated authors, since they were far from intending to develop an abstract and systematic causal theoretical construction but were merely seeking solutions to practical problems involving the limitation of liability.[153] According to Quézel-Ambrunaz,[154] the tradition of French law has hardly been tempted to develop a general theory of causation,[155] in contrast to German doctrine. Domat and

[150] In the mentioned decision, the following thesis was established for general repercussion: "In accordance with Art. 37, § 6º, of the Constitution, the State's strict liability for damages arising from a crime committed by a person who has escaped from the prison system is not characterised, when the direct causal link between the moment of escape and the conduct practiced is not demonstrated" (STF, RE 608.880/MT, rel. Marco Aurélio, j. 08.09.2020).

[151] Judge Marco Aurélio advanced the following thesis: "The State bears liability for material and non-pecuniary damages in cases of robbery resulting in death when the offender was serving a sentence in a closed regime and subsequently escaped, taking into account the detention facility." Notably, this formulation makes no reference to any causal theory. Judge Luiz Edson Fachin similarly aligned himself with the position favoring the acceptance of the appeal.

[152] Guilherme Calmon and Rafael Viola propose the application of the "subtheory of necessary causation," although it differs from the models proposed by Agostinho Alvim. In this context, the use of the NESS test could serve as an aid to the application of the "subtheory of necessary causation" (Gama and Viola (2021), pp. 226–227).

[153] According to Clóvis do Couto e Silva, French doctrine and jurisprudence traditionally show a preference for the theory of adequate causation (*causalité adéquate*) (Couto e silva (2022), p. 191).

[154] Quézel-Ambrunaz (2010), p. 6. Daniel Dias takes a similar position, asserting that Pothier was not rigorous in the use of terms to set the limits of liability (Dias (2020), p. 73).

[155] The causal requirement did not stand out in the *travaux préparatoires* of the Civil Code and in the doctrinal discussions that followed the enactment of the codification. The specificities of causation were not discussed during the drafting of Art. 1.382 of the *Code Civil* (Fairgrieve and G'sell-Macrez (2011), p. 112).

Pothier merely argued that causation should not be maintained if it appeared that the damage could have had other causes.

When reproducing the expression "direct and immediate" in Art. 1.060 of the CC/16, the Brazilian legislator clearly aimed to limit liability, not to adopt the "subtheory of necessary causation,"[156] which had not yet been discussed within the national legal framework.[157] The rule, inspired by the ancient Art. 1.151 of the Code Napoléon, reflects late nineteenth-century French doctrine that treated causation as a mere factual question.[158] The norm was virtually reproduced by the CC/02; however, the doctrine did not engage in further theoretical digressions. This position was also followed by part of the jurisprudence, including the STF.[159]

The "subtheory of necessary causation," however, is problematic due to its ambiguity and lack of precision.[160] It fails to establish clear criteria for limiting liability. Agostinho Alvim, in conceiving the proximate cause of the damage as that which "necessarily follows" it because it "operates by itself, dispensing other causes," or even when he states that a cause is said to be necessary "because there is no other that explains the same damage,"[161] allows for the use of subjective and even arbitrary decision-making parameters, as it presents a circular definition of causation.[162] For Alvim, establishing the cause involves excluding alternative causes, yet the meaning of this proposition remains unexplained.

It should also be noted that the use of the criterion of "interruption of causal chain," as defended, refers to a physical sense of causation, ignoring the various criteria for

---

[156] Against the doctrine of adequate causation, it is not refuted, either closely or remotely, the fact that Art. 1.060, concerning contractual liability, even if resulting from the debtor's fraud, has limited the compensable profits to those that constitute a direct and immediate effect of non-performance. It also does not persuade, in any way, the doctrine that identifies the requirement of direct and immediate cause (to which Art. 1.060 refers) with the necessary character of the damage, as apparently did the Portuguese Civil Code of 1867 (Art. 707) (Varela (1977), p. 252–253).

[157] Reinig (2015), pp. 134–135.

[158] Such reasoning is consistent with the fact that, as previously stated, a similar rule was already expressed in the draft presented by Coelho Rodrigues in 1893. Clóvis Beviláqua also mentioned Art. 1.151 of the French Civil Code, further defending the idea that Art. 1.060 of the CC/16 establishes a limit for compensation. In addressing direct and immediate consequences while distancing himself from the so-called "remote damage", he concludes that such a circumstance is "a matter of fact to be verified." What emerges is not a coherent doctrinal elaboration but merely the reproduction of Pothier's practical and concrete analysis (Beviláqua (1955), p. 177).

[159] The STJ has also established the understanding in favor of the application of the theory. In this regard, see STJ, Ag. in REsp 1,408,660/SP, rel. Gurgel de Faria, j. 16.08.2022; STJ, REsp 1,557,978/DF, rel. Moura Ribeiro, j. 03.11.2015; STJ, REsp 1,154,737/MT, rel. Luis Felipe Salomão, j. 21.10.2010.

[160] Henri de Page argues that the characteristic of the "necessary causation" is the one that prevails, stating that the expression "dommage indirect" (indirect damage), which generates confusion, should disappear from our language (De Page (1934), p. 818).

[161] Alvim (1980), p. 356.

[162] According to René Rodière, the distinction between direct and indirect damages adds nothing to the requirements of causation (Rodière (1952), p. 239).

attributing liability. Helmut Koziol[163] even states that, in any case, the "theory of interruption of the causal chain" cannot present a coherent justification for the irrelevance of the condition, establishing only a result.[164] According to the author, this pseudo-justification to exclude liability should be avoided.[165] Part of the doctrine, therefore, considers that the interruption of the causal course by the intervention of external factors places the debate in a context of extraordinary ambiguity.[166] It would be necessary to explain why a causal course is interrupted and why the additional cause should be regarded as unrelated to the causal chain in which it was introduced.[167]

Fernando Noronha[168] further argues that, according to terms formulated by Agostinho Alvim, the cause of the damage is both a necessary and sufficient condition,[169] as without it, no damage would have occurred, and it alone was capable of producing the result. The author concludes that this understanding

---

[163] Koziol (2012), p. 271. Asúa, emphasizes that, even within the theory of equivalence of conditions, the interruption of causation chain should not be discussed. According to the author, under the conditio theory, the concause is treated as any other condition and does not prevail over the others, as all are equally causal, meaning it does not exclude causation. Therefore, it is possible to refer to a new causal chain and does not prevail over the others, meaning it does not exclude causation. Therefore, it is possible to refer to a new causal chain (*novus actus interveniens*), but not of interruption of the causal chain (Jiménez de Asúa (1951), pp. 505–508).

[164] Traeger states that very causal theory, which uses this concept, expresses the result itself (Traeger (1929), p. 177). According to Oftinger, authors who discuss causation rarely miss the opportunity to assert that the expression "interruption of the causal connection" is incorrect. He further argues that if one claims that the causal connection was interrupted by a new cause, it simply indicates that the original cause may be inadequate (Oftinger and Stark (1995), pp. 154–156).

[165] Enneccerus initially contends that the theory originally developed for criminal law seems inadequate, suggesting that causation should be interrupted by every free act of an individual. However, he later states that, as a rule, the causal connection can be interrupted by the intervention of an independent act of a person, based on their own voluntary decision (Enneccerus (1932), pp. 68–71). This inconsistency did not go unnoticed by Hart and Honoré, who highlighted that Enneccerus contradicts himself by both condemning and, shortly thereafter, affirming the same notion (Hart and Honoré (1985), p. 496). Esser and Schmidt, when addressing the responsibility of the original perpetrator in the case of subsequent and voluntary interventions by third parties, reject the idea of interruption of causal chain as a criterion for liability (Esser und Schmidt (1993), p. 220).

[166] It is preferable to refer to an interruption of the attribution of liability, according to Deutsch (Deutsch (1996), p. 105). Daniel against confusing the interruption of the attribution with the "interruption of causation," as the latter notion corresponds to the situation of interruption of the link of causal chain itself (Dias (2020), p. 242).

[167] Díez-Picazo (1999), p. 337–338.

[168] Noronha (2013), p. 624.

[169] The requirement of sufficiency should not be confused with the theory of efficient causation. According to this theory, the law is concerned with causal connection that has established the highest degree of efficiency in the result. Birkmeyer used the quantitative criterion in determining the most active condition. Max Ernst Mayer and J. Köhler highlighted the qualitative issue of efficient cause, considering as such the one with the highest efficacy according to the intrinsic quality of the causal process (Cuevillas Matozzi (2000), p. 90). Roger Pirson and Albert de Ville assert that the theory of equivalence of conditions and the theory of adequate causation do not

overly restricts liability, making it more difficult to identify the necessary cause, especially when multiple causes contribute to the damage.[170] Noronha observes that, even if the test were limited to necessariness, damages falling outside this condition would still need to be recognized as compensable.[171]

Also, in the case of "psychological causation," the theory of direct and immediate damage and the "subtheory of necessary causation" do not offer reliable criteria for the resolution of practical cases. In addition to attributing factual sense to the expression "direct and immediate," diverging from the modern legal dogmatics of liability as imputation, they disregard other relevant criteria in identifying the individual responsible for compensating the damages.

The absence of a precise and consistent definition[172] has led these theories to rely on intuitive solutions, such as declaring the "interruption" of the causal chain[173] whenever an intervening act stands between the initial behavior and the damage, as in "psychological causation." However, they fail to explain why, in certain cases, the act of the second causer does not exclude the liability of the first, despite the fact that, under the theory of direct and immediate damage, the subsequent conduct would normally "interrupt" the chain.

3.2.4 Theory of Adequate Causation

The theory of adequate causation (*Adäquanztheorie*) arose from the requirement to set limits on the theory of equivalence of conditions. This theory, without a correction factor, cannot constitute the only decisive criterion of imputation, especially in relation to subsequent damages, as it would lead to an excessively broad scope of liability.[174]

---

present satisfactory conclusions. They argue that the notion of efficient cause can provide more appropriate results (Pirson and De Ville (1935), pp. 35–36).

[170] Although acknowledging that the criticism raised by Fernando de Noronha is valid, Gisela Sampaio da Cruz explains that the necessary cause does not need to be the one that, alone, could produce the result. She thus admits, within the theory of interruption of causation, the concurrence of causes. When two necessary concurrent causes exist, and not complementary, it is stated that each of them is capable, by itself, of causing the damage. In addition, each one of them, according to the author, can explain the phenomenon exclusively (Guedes (2011), p. 109–110).

[171] Noronha (2013), p. 625–626.

[172] This is also the understanding of Renato Moraes, who asserts that the notion of necessary causation is as imprecise as the requirement of direct and immediate damage, as stated in Art. 403 of the Civil Code (Moraes (2017), p. 45).

[173] According to Zimmermann, not only the expression, but also the practical result achieved by this concept, has been increasingly rejected over time, as it is understood as a very comprehensive limitation of responsibility (Zimmermann (1980), p. 14).

[174] Paul Sourlas reminds that most of the limiting solutions proposed have not been successful, either because they were artificial constructions, such as the differentiation between cause

Like the theory of equivalence of conditions, the origin of the adequacy theory is controversial. Some authors suggest that it emerged as a way to justify and provide a more precise formulation for von Bar's[175] reference to the normal course of events[176] and for Zitelman's inquiries.[177] The Italian legal doctrine invokes, as a precursor of the theory, the name of Gian Domenico Romagnosi.[178] Some claim[179] that it originated from the ideas of Heinrich Luden[180] or even find echoes in the teachings of Saint Thomas Aquinas, identifying elements that anticipated the formulation of the theory.[181]

The theory of adequacy,[182] according to the prevailing opinion, was developed by the physiologist Johannes von Kries from the University of Freiburg, and, although rejected by criminal jurisprudence, it was accepted by German civil courts, which applied this theoretical concept primarily in determining the extent of liability (*haftungsausfüllende Kausalität*).[183]

Von Kries[184] created a counterpoint to individualizing or discriminatory theories[185] by assuming that a cause's adequacy relates to the possibility and probability of a result occurring according to common experience (the so-called *id quod plerumque accidit*). His doctrine has a subjective character because the probability calculation

(*Verursachung*), occasion (*Veranlassung*), and facilitation (*Ermöglichung*), or because they led to unacceptable outcomes (Sourlas (1974), p. 14).

[175] A person is, in a legal sense, the cause of an event to the extent that it is conceived as the condition by which the course of events, which would otherwise be regular, becomes different, as asserted by (Bar (1871), p. 11). Günther Bernert states that the theory of adequacy was established by Ludwig von Bar in 1871, especially in criminal law (Bernert (1969), p. 422).

[176] Pontes de Miranda (1984), p. 223.

[177] The theory of adequacy was initially defended as the theory of the "rule of life" ("*Regel des Lebens*") by von Bar and referred to as "adequacy" by von Kries. Zitelman also uses the expression "rule of life," but in a different sense (Zitelman (1879), p. 240).

[178] Costa Jr. (2007), pp. 96–97.

[179] Jiménez de Asúa (1951), pp. 455–456.

[180] Luden (1840), p. 288.

[181] Müller (1912), p. 29.

[182] Many variants of the adequacy theory have been developed, some focusing on the reasonable foreseeability of the damage, others on whether the cause was adequate to produce the injury and others on the increased chance of the damage occurring (Dam (2006), p. 1103).

[183] In German law, the distinction between causation that establishes liability (*haftungsbegründende Kausalität*) and the one that determines the extent of liability (*haftungsausfüllende Kausalität*) is widely accepted in the doctrine. The former links the defendant's behavior to the infringement of the protected legal interest, while the latter establishes the connection between the initial violation and the subsequent damages (Gotzler (1977), p. 101). Part of the German doctrine defends that the concept of adequacy only makes sense if related to causation that determines the extent of liability (*haftungsausfüllende Kausalität*). See Lorenz (1964), p. 179; Deutsch (1967), p. 641; Roussos (1992), pp. 68–70; Jakobs (1983), p. 164. In contrast, some argue for its application also in causation that establishes liability (*haftungsbegründende Kausalität*). See Grüneberg (2020), p 291; Schiemann (2017), p. 79; Weitnauer (1969), p. 326.

[184] Kries (1888), p. 230.

[185] Also addressing the adequate causal theory as generalizing, see Moore (2009), pp. 469–495.

must consider the acting subject's point of view. Moving away from the theory of equivalence, von Kries argued that only some of the conditions should be selected through the formulation of an *ex ante,* or prospective judgment, tied to a criterion of predictability (*Berechenbarkeit*) or foreseeability.[186] The author distinguishes, in this sense, the adequate consequences from the merely casual or accidental.[187]

According to Kries, the judgment on possibility, as it is based on ontological knowledge—that is, grounded in the understanding of individual facts—should be carried out from the perspective of the offender. Regarding the nomological basis of judgment on possibility, all empirical knowledge of humanity (*Erfahrungswissen der Menschheit*) should be assumed. In that case, the specific situation should be generalized in all instances where there was a lack of knowledge or where the knowledge was unclear. This solution would lead to the inadequate result that the perpetrator would only be held liable for an intentional action. Kries,[188] however, modifies his conception of the generalization of conditions in his subsequent elaborations, also assuming the conditions that would be cognizable by the causer at the time he acted.[189]

Kries's theory, which considers conditions the perpetrator knew or should have known, faces criticism[190] for conflating the distinct concepts of causation and fault.[191] Even scholars who acknowledge these as separate legal concepts highlight the practical difficulty in distinguishing between them in application.[192] Regarding nomological knowledge, all empirical knowledge is assumed, while in the formation of the probabilistic judgment necessary to determine negligence, only the empirical knowledge of the individual can be assumed.[193]

Although von Kries laid the foundations for the recognition of a theory of adequacy,[194] his excessive subjectivist bias[195] did not prove useful in private law,

---

[186] Huerta Ferrer (1948), pp. 126–127.

[187] Sourlas (1974), p. 15; Goeckenjan (2017), p. 78.

[188] Kries considered that it was already evident, based on the "general legal feeling" ("*allgemeines Rechtsgefühl*"), that the concrete cause, in any case, still did not provide sufficient grounds for attribution (Kries (1888), p. 532).

[189] Adequacy should not be determined based on objective criteria, but rather on "purely psychological" ("*rein psychologisch*") parameters, that is, according to the knowledge of the individual, as his action represents a "volitional behaviour" ("*Verhalten des Willens*") occurring "under certain intellectual conditions" ("*unter gewissen intellektuellen Bedingungen*") (Kries (1888), p. 228).

[190] Pereira (2019), p. 336.

[191] Jiménez de Asúa (1951), p. 458.

[192] Reinig (2015), p. 106.

[193] Reinig (2019), p. 230.

[194] Liepmann, drawing on von Kries' considerations, argues that, in the context of criminal law, a result can only be attributed to an action if it maintains a calculable connection (*berechenbarer Zusammenhang*) with the event (Liepmann (1900), p. 72). For criticisms directed at Liepmann's formula, see Traeger (1929), pp. 154–157.

[195] Pereira (2019), p. 336.

especially in relation to cases of strict[196] and contractual liability.[197] Within criminal law, the doctrine that favored the adoption of the theory did not address the issue of identifying the ontological judgment, relying on overly indeterminate formulations.[198]

This insufficiency[199] was soon recognized by Max Rümelin. In his inaugural lecture "*Der Zufall im Recht*"[200] delivered at Tübingen in 1896, and later in his 1900 monograph "*Die Verwendung der Causalbegriffe in Straf- und Civilrecht,*" he presented a modified formulation, which he called—using von Liszt's expression[201] - the "objective and retrospective prognosis theory" ("*Theorie der objektiven nachträglichen Prognose*").

According to Rümelin,[202] for the formation of judgment about the possibility, based on all empirical knowledge of humanity, not only the circumstances known or knowable by the individual, as von Kries argued, but all the circumstances existing at the time of the occurrence of the condition examined for its causation,[203] even those unknown to the perpetrator,[204] must be considered. Also to be considered are the subsequent conditions, which could have been foreseen at the time of the harmful conduct, according to general human experience.[205] Thus, even though conditions that were only discovered after the factual unfolding are included, the determination of their adequacy should be made through a judgment *ex post.*[206]

Rümelin's formulation leads, in some cases, to results similar to, or even broader and therefore unsatisfactory than, those achieved by the condition theory.[207] Traeger[208] exemplifies the insufficiency of the criterion with the *Lloyd dampfer's* or *Thomas* case: workers of the steamship Lloyd Mosel negligently dropped a barrel while loading the ship, which had supposedly been filled with

---

[196] Schilcher notes that Larenz and Heinrich Lange do not consider the theory of adequacy applicable to cases of strict liability (*Gefährdungshaftung*) (Schilcher (1977), p. 35).

[197] Lindenmaier (1950), p. 224; Rumpf (1905), p. 224.

[198] Ordeig (2007), p. 13–14.

[199] One of the critics of the theory, August Thon, asserts that an action is adequate when, according to the judge's assessment, it can be considered as creating a risk (Thon (1895), p. 37). Lüer argues that the adequacy formula does not allow for a proper evaluation of the degree of increased risk, which is necessary, however, to define risk areas (Lüer (1969), p. 127).

[200] Rümelin (1896).

[201] Lindenmaier (1950), p. 224.

[202] Rümelin (1900), p. 189.

[203] Lindenmaier (1950), p. 224.

[204] Pereira (2019), p. 336.

[205] Traeger (1929), pp. 137–138.

[206] The Rümelin formula, as presented, does not fully adhere to the *ex post* perspective. It is a prognosis, in which the *ex ante* criterion (circumstances existing at the time of the fact) is combined with the *ex post* (subsequent circumstances that were, however, "foreseeable" at the time of the event) (Reinig (2015), of causation in liability civil . . ., cit., p. 107).

[207] Lindenmaier (1950), p. 225.

[208] Traeger (1929), p. 144. Also referencing the case, see Lindenmaier (1950), p. 217; Reinig (2015), p. 77. Heinrich Lange refers to the well-known case when discussing the concept of the "ideal observer" (*optimal observer*) (Lange (1958), pp. 118–119).

caviar but was instead packed with explosives by the serial killer Thomas (pseudonym Keith), causing a large explosion. As a result of the incident, more than a hundred people were killed or injured, and several ships were damaged.

Starting from the premise that the workers were negligent in causing the barrel to fall, they would be liable for the damages resulting from the negligent conduct, that is, for all the consequences adequately caused. Following Rümelin's theory, however, the adequate consequences in this case would also include the death and injuries of the people and the damages caused to the ships. This is because, given the subsequently known condition of the fact that the barrel contained dynamite instead of caviar, the judgment of possibility would take into account the circumstance that, if the barrel fell on the ground, especially on a cold day, as it was on December 5, 1875, the explosion would not only be highly possible but would be considered almost certain.[209]

In the early twentieth century, the proponents of the theory of adequate causation were divided between those who harbored the subjective conception of von Kries, with the inherent difficulties in attempting to overcome the dilemma of differentiating between fault and causation, and those who adopted the objective *ex post* thesis proposed by Rümelin, which fell short by timidly limiting liability.[210]

The theory of causal adequacy is definitively consolidated through the formula of Traeger, considered an intermediate doctrine[211] between those of von Kries and Rümelin. According to the author, an action or other event proven as *conditio sine qua non* is considered an adequate condition of the result if it consists of a "generically favourable circumstance"[212] ("*generell begünstigender Umstand*") of a result of the same kind as occurred, that is, if it generally increases the objective possibility of a result (*objektive Möglichkeit*) in a not irrelevant way.[213]

Focused on determining the conditions characterizing the judgment of adequacy, Traeger's thesis[214] became known as the "theory of the generally favourable circumstance" ("*Theorie des generell begünstigenden Umstands*"),[215] attempting to avoid the criticisms leveled against previous formulations.[216] To assess the adequacy of the cause, the judge should mentally revert to the moment of the conduct's execution,[217] adopting a prognostic judgment,[218] determining whether, *ex ante*, the

---

[209] Traeger (1929), pp. 144–145.

[210] Radbruch (1902), pp. 26–27.

[211] Mota Pinto (2008), p. 931; Lindenmaier (1950), p. 227.

[212] Serra (1959), pp. 27–28.

[213] Traeger (1929), p. 159.

[214] Concerning the distinction between the theories of von Kries and Traeger, see Barbosa (2013), p. 102.

[215] Lange und Schiemann (2003), p. 83.

[216] Pereira (2019), p. 339.

[217] The adequacy should not only be assessed between the action and the damage, but also among the various intermediate links that connect the former to the latter, that is, the entire causal process (Orgaz (1952), p. 73).

[218] Hedemann (1949), p. 69.

behavior constituted, or not, a favorable circumstance for the occurrence of the result, taking into account the circumstances actually known by the individual and those that would be recognizable by an ideally observant observer,[219] or, in the words of Traeger,[220] the "most experienced and reasonable human being" ("*erfahrenster und einsichtigster Mensch*").

In some cases, however, such as the mentioned *Moselfall*, the criterion adopted by Traeger for ontological knowledge would prove unfair by absolving the wrongdoer's responsibility when their knowledge surpassed the ideal observer model. In this case, however, according to the author, the perpetrator's viewpoint should be assumed when they had greater knowledge.[221] Nomological knowledge, by contrast, would not require the exhaustion of experimental knowledge, thus dispensing with the knowledge of "natural laws" ("*Naturgesetz*"), requiring only the "empirical laws" ("*empirische Gesetze*") or even the regular succession of the events in question.[222]

Traeger's formulation also faced harsh criticism. Scholars argued that considering a condition as a cause merely because the individual knew it would inappropriately validate atypical factual courses. Traeger refuted this by emphasizing that "adequate cause" should not be equated with "typical or normal cause." According to him, a condition's adequacy is not determined by whether it "generally" or "normally" produces the result in question. He illustrates his argument by stating that death is not a typical or normal consequence of a fever caused by a wound but can, however, be qualified as adequate.[223]

Another criticism directed at Traeger's theory concerns an alleged subjectivization of the judgment of possibility.[224] This censure is challenged by the author, who argues that the key issue is whether the individual was aware of the condition, since

---

[219] Mota Pinto (2008), p. 931. The formula proposed by Traeger, by requiring an extremely perceptive person, seems to have exceeded all the requirements of the possibility judgment (Ferrer (1948), pp. 128–129), to the point of demanding the presence of a true superman (Florian (1934), p. 607). Antunes Varela refers to an "experienced observer" (Varela (2000), p. 891). Rui Soares Pereira notes that subsequent authors, such as Larenz, Welzel, Engisch, and Enneccerus, referred to the knowledge that a "moderately experienced and sagacious person," a "prudent man," a "careful and interested man," an "intelligent and careful person," an "experienced observer," or more simply, only "capable person" could have (Pereira (2019, p. 362). In contrast, see Branda Proença (1997), p. 192.

[220] Traeger (1929), p. 160–161.

[221] Coelho (1998), p. 207.

[222] Traeger (1929), pp. 162–163. For a detailed explanation of nomological and ontological knowledge in the various variants of causal theories, see Reinig (2019), pp. 229–234.

[223] Reinig (2019), p. 233.

[224] Leitão (2020), pp. 346–347. Rui Soares Pereira stresses the dual character of Traeger's theory, stating that he resorted to both an objective and another subjective criterion. The first consists of conditions that could be known by a perceptive or sagacious individual, while the second refers to the conditions actually known by the subject (Pereira (2019), p. 340). The theory of von Kries is noted for making a subjective assessment of adequacy, while Thon and Traeger provide a diagnosis of an objective nature, although the diversity of nuances is acknowledged by Goldenberg (1998, p. 129).

such awareness increases the objective possibility of an outcome of the same nature as the one that ultimately realized.[225]

Subsequently, Enneccerus[226] developed an alternative formulation to that of Traeger, said to be negative, considering that the proposition of the latter was quite restrictive in many hypotheses. According to this negative formulation, which greatly influenced the doctrine[227] and jurisprudence in various countries,[228] the perpetrator's conduct would only be excluded when, having caused the damage, it was concluded that it had been done due to abnormal or extraordinary circumstances (*nur infolge anderer außergewönlicher Umstände zu einer Bedingung des Schadens wurde*).[229] Thus, the condition ceases to be the cause of the injury whenever, according to its general nature, it was entirely indifferent (*gleichgültig*) to the production of the damage and only became a condition of it due to other extraordinary circumstances, meaning it was adequate to cause the damage.

Accepting the theory of adequacy in its negative form facilitates the injured party's proof of causation. Once the plaintiff demonstrates that the damage would not have occurred without the event that gave rise to liability, the burden then shifts to the defendant to prove that the loss was the result of an extraordinary or anomalous circumstance. The adoption of the negative aspect of the theory of adequacy also presents clearer parameters of application compared to other formulations, functioning as an initial filter of imputation and permitting the later application of additional limiting criteria.

[225] Traeger (1929), p. 161–162.

[226] Enneccerus (1932), p. 66.

[227] Varela affirms that Enneccerus's negative conception was adopted by the Portuguese codification, noting that the formula was clearly imported from Pereira Coelho's work (Varela (2000) pp. 900–901). In Portuguese law, the theory of adequate causation is adopted, for example, in its negative variant. In this sense, see Almeida Costa (2009), p. 764; Coelho (1998), p. 208; Alarcão (1983), p. 239; Jorge (1999), p. 394. Menezes Leitão and Calvão da Silva defend the application of the theory of adequate causation, not indicating, however, a preference among its various aspects (Menezes Leitão (2020), p. 347; Calvão da Silva (1990), p. 711). Also asserting that the adverb "probably," contained in Art. 563 of the Portuguese Civil Code, refers to the adequacy test, but without taking a position on one of the variants of the theory, see Dias Pereira and Oliveira (2020), p. 173. Paulo Mota Pinto supports that the attribution should initially be based on the criterion of adequate causation in its negative formulation, and, if necessary, adjusted by reference to the purpose of the liability rule (Mota Pinto (2008), p. 947). Massimo Bianca indicates that the theory of adequacy is widely accepted by Italian jurisprudence, in its variant of causal regularity (Bianca (2012), p. 144). In France, Viney and Philippe le Tourneau state that the theory of adequate causation is used to establish causation (Viney et al. (2013), p. 252; Torneau (1976), p. 191). Art. 1,239 of the Tort Law Draft, presented on March 13, 2017, provides: "Liability assumes the existence of a causal link between the act attributed to the defendant and the damage."

[228] Regarding Chinese law, see Yang (2018), p. 70; Binding (2012), pp. 37–38. In Japanese law, see Kihara (2015), p. 75; Yamamoto (2019), p. 93.

[229] Pereira (2019), p. 340.

In Germany,[230] the theory of causal adequacy has long dominated decisions in higher courts.[231] The *Reichsgericht*[232] first recognized this theoretical elaboration in 1902, and despite initial hesitation, it became the absolutely dominant doctrine in German civil jurisprudence within a decade.[233] The formulations, however, are not uniform. In some decisions, the Enneccerus formula was applied, although the *Reichsgericht* more consistently followed the perspective of Traeger. In a paradigmatic judgment from 1913,[234] the requirement was that the preceding conduct must have facilitated or favored the objective possibility of a result of the same kind as the one that eventually materialized, thereby establishing the basis for liability.[235] Many subsequent decisions adopted this criterion.[236] Even in the jurisprudence of the BGH,[237] completely uniform parameters do not emerge, since the theory of adequacy continues to compete with the theory of the scope of protection of the norm.[238]

The adequacy theory has been subjected to extensive criticism in legal doctrine.[239] The refutations are based both on the theoretical structure of thought and on the practical implications.[240] Initially, the proponents of the theory of the scope of protection of the norm argue that it is not appropriate to determine the extent of the damage without considering the objective of the liability norm and the duties

[230] In Austria, the theory of adequacy did not acquire the importance it had in Germany. According to the prevailing doctrine, it is sufficient, in relation to subsequent damages, to apply the "common conditional connection" (*gewöhnlicher Bedingungszusammenhang*) (Bydlinski (1985), p. 3). It is also pointed out that there are differences between Portuguese law, which would have adopted the "experienced observer" parameter (*erfahrener Beobachter*), and German law, which would use the "excellent observer" criterion (*optimaler Beobachter*). In this respect, see Oliveira (2009), pp. 99–100.

[231] Lange und Schiemann (2003), p. 86.

[232] RG 20.2.1902 RGZ 50, 219.

[233] Sourlas (1974), p. 18.

[234] RGZ 81, 359, 361.

[235] Lange und Schiemann (2003), p. 86.

[236] The *Reichsgericht,* at the end of the nineteenth century, and the beginning of the twentieth century, started to avoid the use of the expression "interruption of the causal chain," since it adopts the theory of adequate causation (Knoche (1959), p. 294).

[237] In 1952 (BGHZ 3, 261, 266f), detailed criteria were established, following the Traeger's guidance: An event is deemed an adequate cause of the result if it has increased the possibility of the occurrence of an event of the same nature (Lange und Schiemann (2003), p. 87).

[238] Teichmann (2014), p. 234.

[239] In a BGH ruling dated June 6, 1968, it was even declared the end of the adequacy theory (*Das Ende der Lehre vom adäquaten Kausalzusammenhang*) (Huber (1969), p. 677). Pontes de Miranda criticizes the formula that states the cause of damage is what generally favors it stressing that harm may arise from acts that ordinarily do not, and that causation may exceptionally fail even when it would normally be expected (Pontes de Miranda (1984), p. 188).

[240] Lange und Schiemann (2003), p. 90.

arising from it. Furthermore, it is defended that the theory is problematic because it measures the dangerousness of the conduct based on life experience, rather than evaluating the concrete course of events in comparison to the culpable violation of the risk prohibition.[241]

Critics also contend that the theory of adequacy fails to significantly limit liability,[242] as nothing could escape the "ideal observer" ("*optimaler Beobachter*"[243]). Whether judging possibility *ex ante* or *ex post*, this idealized observer possesses all available empirical knowledge when forming judgments. It is also asserted that, in practice, in the few decisions where adequacy was rejected,[244] other points of view were, in fact, decisive.[245]

The various perspectives presented by the formulas of von Kries, Rümelin, Traeger, and Enneccerus, although they allow a margin of freedom of decision to the judge, also bring legal uncertainty.[246] According to Bernert,[247] it is an "empty formula"[248] ("*Leerformel*"), as, even though it has been defended by various authors for over a century, its content and basis have not yet been determined.[249] The result would be that the judgment of possibility would oscillate between the criterion of the ideal observer's perspective and the arbitrariness[250] of an equity judgment made by the judge.[251]

---

[241] Stoll (1968), p. 20.

[242] Schack (1986), p. 314. Concerning the criticisms directed at causal adequacy in environmental law, see Oliveira (2007), pp. 58–59.

[243] Larenz also maintains that if the idea of an "optimal observer" is taken seriously, the theory of adequacy loses its capacity to limit the scope of the offender's liability (Larenz (1987), p. 436). This view is also shared by Vicente (2017, p 448).

[244] Dunz even states that, after a judicial career dedicated exclusively to the practice of tort law, he cannot remember a single case in which the adequacy formula has been useful in solving a practical problem of attribution (Dunz (1984), p. 601). Caemmerer observes that, among fifty decisions of the *Reichsgericht* addressing the theory of adequacy, only four rejected adequacy (Caemmerer (1956), p. 12).

[245] Lange und Schiemann (2003), p. 91.

[246] Lange (1976), pp. 198–207.

[247] Bernert (1969), p. 422.

[248] The adequate cause may vary depending on the circumstances, functioning as a convenient expression to delineate the causal process. In this regard, he references the "empty formula" discussed by Bernert (Menezes Cordeiro (2004), pp. 533–534).

[249] Regarding the criticisms about the theory of causation within the scope of Brazilian criminal law, see Garcia (2008), p. 294.

[250] Another challenging question, as noted by Acciari, concerns the extent to which the antecedent must increase the probability of the consequence occurring to be regarded as a cause (Acciari (2009), pp. 112–117).

[251] Xynapolou (2013), p. 134. Regarding the analysis of a supposed insufficiency of the adequacy theory, see Schünemann (1979).

Brazilian legal doctrine has widely adopted the theory of adequacy.[252] Otavio Luiz Rodrigues Junior[253] notes that, despite various innovations in causation theory, the theory of adequate causation remains foundational and has not been completely supplanted. According to the author, the transition from the theory of equivalence to the theory of adequacy was precisely to establish filters at the level of imputation and liability of individuals in relation to certain behaviors, this notion still being valid in the twenty-first century. This thesis was established in Proposition No. 47 of the First Civil Law Conference (I Jornada de Direito Civil), noting that Art. 945 of the CC/02 does not exclude the application of the theory of adequate causation.[254]

Pontes de Miranda,[255] seemingly aligning with the theory of adequacy, states that if the fact is not causally adequate to the production of damage, one should not consider the causer liable, whether by a positive or negative act. The author further contends that losses and damages do not extend to what lies outside the causal relationship. For instance, if a building is on the verge of collapse and a flood ultimately brings down the local structures, including the one in danger, the individual who feared the consequences of the collapse cannot claim damages, as the proximate cause was the flood, not the building's ruin.

In Brazilian case law, there are decisions mentioning and applying the theory of adequacy, although not always with technical precision. Indeed, the Superior Court of Justice (STJ),[256] in various decisions, indicates the theory of adequate cause as one of the grounds for liability. However, it is not uncommon to find overlapping theoretical conceptions or insufficient attention to the conceptual framework adopted in establishing the result.[257]

The theory of adequacy fails to resolve "psychological causation" issues. By expanding the scope of recognizable circumstances present at the time of the initial

[252] Rodrigues Jr. (2016), p. 132; Couto e Silva (2014), pp. 186–187; Dias (2006), p. 946.; Cavalieri Filho (2012), p. 52); Simão and Dantas (2020); Rosenvald and Braga (2020), p. 404; Azevedo (1997); Aguiar Jr. (1995), pp. 537–538. This is the position endorsed by Judith Martins-Costa, in the first edition of Comments on the Civil Code. In a subsequent edition, the author defends the path of "complementarity and synthesis" between the theories of adequate causation and direct and immediate damage (Martins-Costa (2009), pp. 214–215). Fernando Noronha understands that the negative formulation of adequate causation is preferable (Noronha (2013), p. 630).

[253] Rodrigues Jr. (2016), p. 132.

[254] Statement no. 47 of National Justice Council (CJF): "Article 945 of the new Civil Code, which does not find a correspondent in the Civil Code of 1916, does not exclude the application of the theory of adequate causation."

[255] Pontes de Miranda (1984), pp. 185–186. In another passage of the same work, this time, on p. 189, Pontes de Miranda warns, apparently in a contradictory way, that not always the occurrence of another fact "interrupts" causation.

[256] STJ, REsp 169,872/RJ, rel. Ricardo Villas Bôas Cueva, j. 01.06.2021.

[257] The theoretical confusion operated by Brazilian jurisprudence will be better addressed in Sect. 3.2.6.

conduct, the adequacy criterion substantially reduces its effectiveness in limiting compensable damages. Mafalda Miranda Barbosa[258] correctly observes that adequacy criteria alone cannot provide satisfactory solutions to "psychological causation" cases. This inadequacy stems partially from the theory's assumption that events follow an objective regularity, a premise that psychological influence cases frequently challenge.

The sole reliance on the theory of adequate causation in cases of damages caused by psychological influence would excessively broaden the scope of liability, as in many cases—which will be investigated later,[259] the adequacy of the cause is affirmed, but ultimately the imputation is excluded by the application of another complementary criterion, such as the non-realization of a specific risk created by the first perpetrator.

3.2.5 Theory of the Scope of Protection of the Norm

Already in the nineteenth century, German jurists expressed the necessity of limiting liability.[260] Although the theory of adequacy was developed to restrict responsibility, von Kries' view that adequacy would coincide with a "trained sense of justice" was considered too vague and uncertain. Such criticisms did not lead to the abandonment of the theory of adequate causation but to the development of a new criterion. Tarnowski and Grispigni, among others, argued that private and criminal legislation involve normative judgments, since the law decides whether a person's conduct, on a given occasion, is to be regarded as having taken a particular form.[261]

According to Tarnowski,[262] adequacy would belong to the factual dimension, constituting, autonomously and prior to culpability,[263] a prerequisite for normative consideration. For Grispigni,[264] adequacy would pertain to the legal stage of the attribution process, as the notion of cause is interpreted in a normative sense. The

[258] Barbosa (2019), p. 19. Also understanding that the adequacy theory is not sufficient for the delimitation of liability, cf. Niebaum (1977), p. 54.

[259] From Sect. 5.2.1.

[260] For damage to be compensable, directness is not required; it is sufficient that negligence caused it through intervening events. Yet, as Dernburg notes with reference to von Bar, this reasoning cannot result in boundless liability. In such cases, fault is no longer seen as a cause (*Ursache*) but merely as a remote occasion for the harm (*entfernte Veranlassung der Beschädigung*), which rules out liability. He concludes by stating that it is more justifiable to extend liability in cases of intentional misconduct or gross negligence than in cases of slight negligence (Dernburg (1892) pp. 122–123).

[261] Hart and Honoré (1985), p. 472–473.

[262] Tarnowski (1927), p. 33.

[263] Jiménez de Asúa (1951), p. 502.

[264] Grispigni (1950), p. 95.

latter revised the theory of adequate causation so that it would be understood as a "theory of the condition qualified by danger" (*'la teoria della condizione qualificata dal pericolo'*), giving the cause a normative meaning (*concetto normativo della causa*).

In Germany, Larenz[265] was already explicitly arguing in his doctoral thesis that the theory of adequate causation could not be understood in purely naturalistic terms, but rather as a true theory of imputation.[266] According to the author, the act is not assessed merely in terms of causation but in terms of its teleological connection. This connection is considered an attribution of the conduct, reflecting the relationship between an event and the will.[267] He argues that the purpose of objective imputation, interpreted as the possibility of foreseeability (not in a subjective sense), is to distinguish action from fortuitous events,[268] so that objectively foreseeable consequences can be attributed to the individual as a rational being.[269]

Larenz[270] highlights the fact that causation, in its naturalistic sense (*reine natürliche Kausalität*), performs only an auxiliary function (*Hilfsfunktion*) and does not serve as the basis for any liability. He acknowledges that, in addition to adequacy, other attribution criteria have been developed, all aimed at limiting responsibility for subsequent damages[271] to a reasonable level.[272] Larenz[273] paves the way for the creation of new criteria to limit liability, emphasizing their role in promoting coherence and order. These criteria may also, in connection with the grounds for liability already recognized by jurisprudence, contribute to the development of law through analogy.[274]

In jurisprudential terms, the BGH,[275] in 1955, held that the question of adequacy between the condition and the result cannot be answered in a purely logical and

---

[265] Instead of requiring an "adequate" causation, legal science should demand an "objectively imputable" causation, one whose dominant principle lies in the will (Larenz (1927), p. 84).

[266] Briz (1963), p. 217.

[267] It is emphasized that, according to Larenz, fortuity is not encompassed within the will or purpose. Furthermore, based on his interpretation of Hegel's work, imputation would only apply to intentional acts, never to negligent actions, as these fall outside the subject's will (Roxin (2002), pp. 16–17).

[268] Larenz (1927), p. 76.

[269] Larenz was the first to place imputation in terms of determining what should be attributed to a subject as their action, in order to hold them liable for it (Rodrigues Jr. (2006), p. 441).

[270] Larenz (1955), p. 1011.

[271] The theory of objective imputation is not a theory for attributing, but for limiting the incidence of prohibition or typical determination on a certain subject (Tavares (2019), p. 290).

[272] On the occasion of Honig's 80th birthday, Larenz asserts that Honig developed his doctrine with a focus on the issues of criminal law, while Larenz's interest, since his doctoral work in 1927, had been dedicated to the study of private law. Thus, Larenz believed it was possible to maintain the adequacy parameter unchanged but understood as a criterion of imputation. Honig, in contrast, distanced himself more significantly from the adequacy theory (Larenz (1970), pp. 79–80).

[273] Larenz (1959), pp. 10–11.

[274] Larenz (1965), p. 374.

[275] BGHZ 18, 286; NJW 1955, 1876.

abstract way, based solely on the numerical frequency of events. Rather, a value-based assessment in the scientific–philosophical sense must be applied. Conditions that, upon reasonable evaluation, cannot be considered circumstances establishing liability should be disregarded.[276]

The idea that causal inquiry can be divided into two stages of investigation—one eminently factual and another of a legal nature[277]—is currently recognized by all European jurisdictions, according to Marta Infantino.[278] In many legal systems, the division coincides with the distinction between issues of fact and law,[279] thereby permitting the review of judicial decisions. However, their distinction lies especially in the various frameworks of theories that are used at each stage. While the establishment of factual causation is determined by the theory of *conditio/but-for* (with occasional modifications), the second stage of investigation is usually governed by a wide range of tests, from adequacy to proximity, and from risk to the interruption of the causation chain.[280]

In this context of normative development, initially framed within the theory of adequacy, other parameters of legal imputation emerge.[281] This concept, well-established in common law, was later transposed into modern private law doctrine through Larenz,[282] who reintroduces the concepts of *imputatio facti* and *imputatio juris.*[283] Due to part of the doctrine's dissatisfaction with the possibility/probability criterion, which is considered insufficient on its own to address a wide range of practical situations, the theory of the scope of the norm emerges as a legal means of delimiting compensable damages.

---

[276] Thomas Raiser notes that the BGH deviates from the inflexibility of the judgment of possibility, using the adequacy criterion only to determine the reasonable limits of the individual's liability (Raiser (1963), p. 463).

[277] Mello (2007), p. 43. Also following the understanding that only legal criteria can delimit liability, see Frada (2010), p. 100.

[278] Infantino (2019), p. 649.

[279] Some authors argue that the distinction between "cause-in-fact," "factual causation," and "but-for-cause," on one side, and "scope of liability," "legal causation," and "truncation of responsibility," on the other, should be clearly demarcated, so that the causal investigation is carried out in two clearly distinct moments. This group includes, albeit for different reasons, Jane Stapleton (Stapleton (2001), p. 945) and Richard W. Wright, who proposed replacing the "but-for-test" with the "NESS test," according to which the conduct should be considered a "Necessary Element of a Sufficient Set of circumstances that led to the plaintiff's loss" (WRIGHT (1985), p. 1788).

[280] Infantino (2019), p. 650. Gerald Spindler believes that systems based on broad liability norms, such as general tort law clauses, focus more on causation issues, which in other systems are addressed in different categories, such as the distinction between pure economic losses (*Vermögensschäden*) and subsequent damages resulting from property infringement (*Folgeschäden bei Eigentumsverletzungen*) (Spindler (2008), p. 289).

[281] Cantzler (1957), p. 39.

[282] Larenz (1927), pp. 60–61.

[283] Deutch (1963), p. 65. Regarding the concepts of *imputato facti* and *imputatio juris*, see Reinhold (2009), pp. 72–85.

The theory of the scope of the norm (*Normzwecktheorie*) or of the scope of protection of the violated norm (*Schutzbereichtheorie*) also originates in Germany. It emerged as a criterion opposed to the generalizing theory of adequate causation and was fundamentally inspired by previous investigations in Austrian legal doctrine.[284] Armin Ehrenzweig[285] criticized the doctrinal reliance on adequate causation as a tool for restricting liability, arguing that this theory should either be rejected or used merely as a complementary criterion. He proposed, in contrast, that law or legal transactions should be interpreted in accordance with their scope (*zweckentsprechende Auslegung*). Ehrenzweig also argued that the scope or the remote purpose (*entfernter Nebenzweck*) of the norm could also justify liability.

In Germany, the theory of the scope of the norm was initially adopted by Ernst Rabel in the context of contractual non-performance, later developed by Walter Wilburg[286] and widely disseminated by Ernst von Caemmerer in 1956. Since then, it has achieved wide acceptance, influencing doctrines in both Portuguese[287] and Italian[288] law. However, it remains relatively underexplored in Brazilian legal scholarship.

In 1936, influenced by the Anglo-American model, Rabel[289] conducted an analysis of sales contracts to explore the limits of contractual liability. He concluded that every legal or contractual obligation serves specific interests, and debtors should be liable only for damages to these protected interests. His theory allocates liability according to the criterion of contractual purpose (*Theorie der Schadensverurteilung nach Maßgabe des Forderungszwecks*).[290] Although initially referred to, in terms of application, § 823 (2) BGB, he argues that in countries

---

[284] Reinig (2018), p. 241.

[285] Ehrenzweig (1920), p. 40.

[286] Liability presupposes that the norm violated by the conduct is intended to protect against the damages incurred. For the adequacy theory, an imagined foreseeability from the perpetrator's perspective would be relevant, while in a legal context, on the contrary, only the provision established in the rule would matter (Wilburg (1941), p. 244).

[287] Menezes Cordeiro (2004), p. 550; Menezes Leitão (2020), p. 347; Menezes Leitão (2005), p. 281. The adequacy theory is not applied when establishing the connection between the conduct and the infringement of protected legal interests. At this stage, the prevailing approach is the verification of a typical risk capable of affecting these interests within the scope of the norm's protection (*Normsschutzzweck*) (Almeida Costa (2009), p. 765). Also, Sinde Monteiro limits its operability to causation that establishes liability (Sinde Monteiro (1989), p. 270). The doctrine of the scope of the norm in Portugal finds its origin in the causation theory adopted by da Silva (2020, p. 148–149).

[288] Barcellona (1973). Conversely, Mauro Sella warns that there was no shortage of criticism from the doctrine arguing that the theory was conceived in an environment different from Italian law (Sella (2007), p. 90).

[289] Rabel (1936), p. 497.

[290] Rabel (1936), p. 502.

where there is a general tort clause, like France and Austria, or a generic provision, like § 823 (1) BGB, the scope of protection of the norm[291] should be observed.[292]

Ernst von Caemmerer[293] objects to efforts aimed at formulating an abstract formula, which often leads to unsatisfactory results. He suggests that the most appropriate criterion for solving practical problems would be the one proposed by Rabel, which involves investigating the scope and extent of the protection provided by the norm that establishes liability for damages. The issue of the extension of liability should be addressed by developing the meaning and scope of this specific norm,[294] rather than through general causal formulas.

Caemmerer gives the example of a person who drives a well-known pianist to a concert hall and, due to a serious violation of the right of way, negligently causes an accident. The pianist fractures his arm, and the concert has to be canceled. The author questions to what extent the driver's liability would extend. Would he be responsible, in addition to medical costs and lost profits, for the losses of the concert management and cloakroom attendants, and even for the losses experienced by the electricity company, which supplied less power due to the lack of lighting in the hall?

From a foreign law perspective, Caemmerer argues[295] that French law practice leads to very broad understandings in tort matters. In German law, decisive criteria would be political–legal limitations of compensable damages, not parameters of causal connection distance. According to the author, it is a matter of knowing

---

[291] Closely related to the theory of the scope of the norm is the doctrine of the "normative connection of unlawfulnes" ("*Rechtswidrigkeitszusammenhang*"). Its concept is not unanimous in the doctrine. In one context, the meaning of "normative connection of unlawfulnes" closely resembles that used to define the theory of the scope of protection. In this sense, Larenz asserts that the connection exists when the damage corresponds to the that the violated norm of conduct was intended to prevent (Larenz (1987), p. 446). Alternatively, the term is used to designate the "lawful alternative behaviour" (*rechtsmäßiges Alternativverhalten*), meaning the possibility for the injured party to argue that they would have caused the damage, even while acting lawfully (Münzberg (1966), p. 128). The issue of *rechtsmäßiges Alternativverhalten* is illustrated, for instance, when a patient dies following negligent medical treatment, but would have died in the same manner had the doctor exercised reasonable care, as the doctor arrived at the scene of care too late (Bar (1999), p. 466). Puppe argues that establishing a hypothetical decision of the victim amounts to mere speculation. Instead, the decision-making process should serve as the basis (Puppe (2017), p. 517). The doctrine of the "normative connection of unlawfulnes" ("*Rechtswidrigkeitszusammenhang*") does not differ, as the BGH mentions, from the theory of the scope of the norm, with respect to the results (Schickedanz (1971), p. 917).

[292] Rabel (1936), pp. 505–506.

[293] Caemmerer (1956), p. 12.

[294] Unlike the theory of adequacy, the doctrine of the scope of the norm has the advantage of remaining open to the task of limiting liability. In this latter theoretical framework, the issue is clearly recognized as a teleological question and is no longer obscured behind a predefined causation. According to the author, decisions about the adequacy and inadequacy of certain causes are nothing more than mere appeals to fairness (Schack (1986), p. 307).

[295] The limitation of liability, expressed in the formula of proximate causation, constitutes a legal–political problem (question of policy), as emphasized by Caemmerer, even in Anglo-American law (Caemmerer (1970, p. 285).

whom certain standards of conduct, established by the legal system, are intended to protect, as American courts repeatedly emphasize.[296]

In January 1953, the BGH, in applying the scope-of-protection doctrine (§ 823 (2) BGB[297]), addressed a case where a son claimed compensation for the death of his father, referring the solution to the scope of the compensatory norm.[298] In June of the same year,[299] in a work accident case, the same scope was applied, following the same reasoning that would later reappear in a BGH ruling from 1956[300] concerning "neurotic damages."[301]

The jurisprudential recognition of the doctrine of the scope of the norm, beyond the domain of protection norms, was materialized through the decision of the *Bundesgerichtshof* on April 22, 1958.[302] In this case, the issue of who should bear the costs of a criminal trial resulting from a vehicular accident, in which the defendant was acquitted, was discussed. The BGH made it clear that the formula of adequate causation would not be sufficient to solve the problem of limiting liability (BGHZ 8, 325, 329; 10, 107, 108; 20, 137, 142, 143). The German court, citing von Caemmerer, stated that the decisive question lay within the scope of protection of the violated norm. It acknowledged that this test is commonly used to determine liability for the violation of a protection norm (§ 823(2) BGB),[303] but there are no barriers to its application in the context of § 823(1) BGB.

The application of the theory of the scope of the norm to violations of § 823 (1) BGB is closely linked to the concept of general duties of care[304] (*Verkehrssicherungspflichten*).[305] In this context, the analysis focuses on the meaning and scope of the specific rule of conduct rather than the general provision in § 823 (1) BGB, although the former indirectly reflects the latter.[306]

Hermann Lange[307] was responsible for systematizing the doctrine of the scope of the norm. By analyzing BGH jurisprudence on the application of § 823 (2) BGB,

[296] Caemmerer (1956), p. 14.

[297] Concerning the origin of the norm and its legislative history, see Schmiedel (1974), pp. 12–28.

[298] BGHZ 8 (1953), 325–331.

[299] BGHZ 10 (1953), 107–111.

[300] BGHZ 20 (1956), 137–144.

[301] Expression used by Menezes Cordeiro (2004), p. 538.

[302] BGHZ 27 (1958), 137, 143. In this decision, the VI Senate of the BGH denied a compensation claim based on § 823 (1) BGB, on the grounds that the damage, which the claimant demanded to be compensated, was not within the protective scope of that paragraph (Wolf (1962), p. 13).

[303] Violates a protection law in the sense of § 823 (2) BGB every person who does not observe the general duties of care (*Verkehrspflichten*) (at least also intended to protect the individual) (Dörner (1987), p. 522).

[304] In relation to violations of general duties of care (*Verkehrspflichten*), see Sect. 4.4.

[305] Also relating to the application of the theory of the scope of the norm in the context of § 823 (1) BGB to the violation of general duties of care (*Verkehrspflichten*), see Kötz und Wagner (2006), p. 82; Lange und Schiemann (2003), p. 114.

[306] Reinig (2018), p. 279.

[307] Lange (1960), p. 38.

which had already considered the protective purpose of the norm for compensation purposes,[308] he identified three developed elements according to which the scope of protection is determined.[309]

Firstly, the injured party must belong to the group of people protected by the norm (*geschützter Personenkreis*). Lange asserts[310] that the violated law should primarily aim to protect the victim and not just protect another. The author cites the example of the issue faced in RGZ 102, 223: an executive order required all animal owners in a certain district to allocate all meat from dead or slaughtered animals, declared inappropriate for consumption, to the district's slaughterhouse. However, a farm owner violated the prohibition and was sued by the slaughterhouse manager, as he was deprived of the meat that was rightfully his. The claim was rejected, as the order served only sanitary purposes and was not intended to ensure the economic viability of slaughterhouses.[311]

In addition to the personal element, Lange refers to a material criterion,[312] according to which it is not sufficient for the injured party to belong to the group of individuals protected by the norm; there must also have been a legal interest protected (*geschütztes Rechtsgut*), whose protection is intended by the violated norm.[313] He illustrates this with the example of § 367 Ziff. 12 StGB,[314] which penalized the insufficient and inadequate guarding of wells, ditches, and similar risks. Since this legal provision was intended solely to protect human beings, it could not serve as a basis for compensating damages caused to an animal.

---

[308] The Austrian OGH (*Supreme Court*) has firmly maintained that the scope of the norm should be assessed according to the respective normative regulation, since the will or motives of the authority that established the norm are not decisive (Karollus (1992), p. 367). In the same vein, cf. Puppe (2019), p. 119.

[309] According to Wolf, the three criteria had already been theoretically covered by Endemann's work in 1903 (Wolf (1962), pp. 16–17).

[310] Lange (1955), p. 39.

[311] Deutsch mentions another interesting case, which was decided by the BGH (NJW 1965, 28). The State of Bavaria conducted an inspection of a cable car, but the inspection was not carried out satisfactorily. Shortly thereafter, the cable car malfunctioned, prompting the operator to seek compensation for losses and damages from the state. The BGH dismissed the claim, ruling that the inspection's purpose was to protect the users, not the transport service provider (Deutsch (1999), p. 81).

[312] The personal element can be understood as directly deriving from the material component of protection. An example is the defendant who allegedly influenced a colleague to use, without authorization, the company car from his workplace to drive him to his girlfriend's house, but, on the way. However, on the way, the driver negligently ran over the claimant's son. The BGH (BGHZ 22, 293) held that the scope of protection of the norm set out in § 248b of the StGB, which provides for the crime of "unauthorised use of another's vehicle" covers only the holder of the right to use the vehicle. Thus, only the person whose car was damaged would be entitled to compensation, excluding third parties who suffered other forms of loss (Reinig (2015), p. 148).

[313] Lange (1960), p. 39.

[314] The German Criminal Code (*Strafgesetzbuch*—StGB) once prescribed under § 367 a fine or imprisonment for individuals who abandoned objects or hazards in squares, paths, or public streets, especially in areas with pedestrian traffic such as sources, pits, or uncovered openings, thereby creating a danger to others.

Finally, Lange[315] refers to the theory of the scope of the norm as a modal element (*bestimmte Schädigungsart*). He argues that most protection laws do not aim to prevent all kinds of damage but only those resulting from a specific manner of execution. Only if there is a coincidence with the scope of the norm should liability be affirmed. Thus, for example, there is no correspondence between the nature of the damage and the scope of the norm when a bus driver carries too many people, contrary to police regulations, and a thief steals a wallet in the crowd.

The theory of the scope of the norm also faced doctrinal objections.[316] First, the thesis proposes identifying protected interests in each contract or injurious situation. As a result, imputational issues should not be resolved through general causal theories but through concrete analysis of general duties of care (*Verkehrspflichten*).[317] However, as Rui Ataíde rightly observes, it is a significant paradox that the theory of the scope of the norm has evolved into a dense dogmatic framework detached from the norms applied in concrete cases.[318]

The question remains open as to whether the theory of the scope of the norm should be applied in conjunction with or independently[319] from the theory of adequacy, given the significant methodological indeterminacy that surrounds the content of both theories.[320] As Hans Stoll observes,[321] there is no consensus on whether, and to what extent, the doctrine of the scope of the norm is useful for imputation when the infringement of legal rights forms the basis of liability, or whether it can replace the theory of adequacy at this stage. The BGH has not yet adopted a definitive position on this question.

Excessive reliance on the theory of the scope of the norm may lead to an almost boundless confidence in the capacity of teleological interpretation to identify the specific purposes pursued by each normative provision,[322] while overlooking other objective imputation factors that, depending on the peculiarities of the case, may be

---

[315] Lange (1960), p. 40.

[316] It is worth noting that the framing within the scope of protection of the violated norm is of limited significance (Noronha (2003), pp. 734–735).

[317] Rabel (1936), p. 508; Caemmerer (1956), p. 12.

[318] Ataíde (2019), p. 770. This is also the understanding shared by Spickhoff (2005, p. 126).

[319] In 1968, Huber asserted that the most radical solution of applying the theory of the scope of the norm in isolation was defended by von Caemmerer, Hermann Lange, and Joseph Georg Wolf. The alternative approach, which considers the theory as a corrective measure to the adequacy formula, is predominant in doctrine and is supported by authors such as Larenz and Esser (Huber (1969), p. 678). According to Fikentscher and Heinemann, the theory of the scope of the norm does not serve as a substitute or complement to the theory of causation; instead, it represents a self-standing theory of imputation (Fikentscher und Heinemann (2006), p. 300).

[320] Spickhoff (2008), p. 20.

[321] Stoll (1976), p. 10. In 1993, although acknowledging the issue as controversial in Germany, he continued to defend the thesis that the adequacy theory needs a value-based corrective. Furthermore, he mentions that in Switzerland, where the theory of adequacy has become more firmly established, the requirement for normative control of the adequacy formula is recognized (Stoll (1993), p. 398).

[322] Ataíde (2019), p. 771.

more useful in addressing the complex issues arising from the imputation process.[323] However, when combined with other criteria of objective imputation, including that of causal adequacy, the theory of the scope of the norm can prove functional in resolving various practical cases.

The application of the theory of the scope of the violated norm is considered incompatible with tort law systems that adopt the model of a general clause,[324] making its use impractical, for example, in Brazilian law. A significant part of French doctrine refers to it pejoratively[325] as the "theory of Aquilian relativity"[326] (relativité aquilienne[327]). Generally, the criterion of the scope of the norm is rejected in France, as it is considered incompatible with French legal doctrine.[328] It is argued that the theory originates in Roman law, which, like German law, did not provide for a general clause, such as the one found in Art. 1382 of the *Code Civil.*[329] Thus, it has been contended that the "Aquilian relativity" (relativité aquilienne) can only be applicable in specific legal systems,[330] like the German one.

However, the idea that the application of the theory of the scope of the violated norm is conditioned on the existence of a rigid system of legal typification of protected legal interests cannot be accepted. Initially, it should be noted that § 823 (1) of the BGB provides, alongside certain specified interests such as life, body, and freedom, the protection of "other legal rights" ("*sonstiges Recht*"), characterizing what some authors call a "small general clause" ("*kleine Generalklausel*"[331]), although the legal safeguard is restricted to absolute rights (*absolute Rechte*).[332]

---

[323] Critically, Carneiro da Frada asserts that the potentials of this doctrine are much more apparent than real, readily converting into a circular discourse (Frada (2015), pp. 312–313).

[324] Quézel-Ambrunaz (2010), p. 153.

[325] Wagner (2003), p. 226.

[326] The nomenclature "Aquilan relativity" is criticized for implying that the theory applies solely in the context of negligent liability, which is the only context that can be appropriately designated as "Aquilan." However, as some scholars argue, the theory also applies to cases of strict liability. Therefore, it is suggested that a more fitting designation would focus on the "scope of the violated norm" (Noronha (2013), p. 624).

[327] Quézel-Ambrunaz (2010), p. 141–153; Lacroix (2013), p. 431; Limpens (1965), pp. 559–581; Viney (2008), p. 248; Philippe (1994), p. 472. Bar (1999), p. 496; Bar (2009), p. 596.

[328] In Belgian law, the expression "*illégalité relative*" is mentioned (Ommmeslaghe (2013), p. 831. According to Bernard Dubuisson, Art. 5.148 of the Belgian Civil Code draft does not address both the group of individuals protected by the rule and the nature of the damage that should be prevented (Dubuisson (2019), p. 414).

[329] The Art. 1382 of the French Civil Code stated before the reform promoted by the *Ordonnance* n. 2016–131: "Art. 1382. *Tout fait quelconque de l'homme, qui cause à autrui un dommage, oblige celui par la faute duquel il est arrivé, à le réparer.*" Free translation: "Art. 1382. Any act of a person that causes damage to another obliges the one who was the cause of the event to compensate this damage." After the reform, Art. 1382 was renumbered, with its content reproduced unchanged in Art. 1240. (Borghetti and Whittakar (2019), p. 7).

[330] Quézel-Ambrunaz (2010), p. 145; Kaczmarek (2012), p. 468; Bussani und Palmer (2005), p. 205.

[331] Markesinis et al. (2019), p. 104.

[332] Looschelders (2019), p. 298.

This is the reason why purely economic damages (*reine Vermögensschaden*) are not compensable under German law.[333]

A general right of personality (*allgemeines Persönlichkeitsrecht*) came to be recognized after some hesitation. This development stemmed from the relative hermeneutic openness provided by the indeterminate legal concept of "*sonstiges Recht*" ("other legal rights") in § 823 (1) BGB.[334] The BGH, seeking to ensure full protection, did not wait for legislative intervention[335] but instead addressed the normative gap by referencing Arts. 1 and 2 of the Basic Law for the Federal Republic of Germany (*Grundgesetz*), which emphasize human dignity and the development of personality as superior legal values.[336]

Also, the provision of § 826 of the BGB,[337] which provides protection against intentional acts that offend common decency, was, even at the beginning of the twentieth century, converted into a powerful tool by German courts[338] as a way to escape the limitations brought by the German tort system. This provision was applied in various groups of cases, notably in relation to the liability of third parties who instigate contractual default.[339] This opening provided by the legal provision also contributed to mitigating the rigors of the German tort law system.

The structure of the tort law system, with three general clauses[340] (§§ 823 (1), 823 (2), and 826 BGB), and the subsequent flexibility developed by doctrine and jurisprudence, brought the German tort regime closer to the general clause model of liability,[341] while preserving distinct characteristics.

The jurists who first examined the theory of the scope of the violated norm argued for the usefulness of the criterion for tort regimes of the general clause.[342] According

---

[333] Keuk (1972), p. 229; Schmidt (2011), p. 732. Von Bar proposed, within the reform of the Germanic system of obligations, liability for primarily financial damage, in cases of providing incorrect information or inadequate advice, due to the professional position (*Berufsstellung*) of the declarant. The intended legislative change was not successful (Frada (2010), p. 234).

[334] The drafters of the Bürgerliches Gesetzbuch (BGB) refused, despite strong criticism, to extend § 823 (1) BGB to cover the protection of the person's personality. The right to honor had been mentioned after freedom in the First Draft but was subsequently removed from the legal enumeration. The Imperial Court never came to recognize a general right of personality, although it safeguarded relative rights, insofar as possible, based on existing legal norms (Zimmermann (2001), pp. 66–69).

[335] Wieacker (2015), p. 607.

[336] Larenz (1989), pp. 28–129.

[337] "§ 826. Intentional damage offending common decency. A person who, in a manner offending common decency, intentionally inflicts damage on another person is liable to the other person to provide compensation for the damage."

[338] Schmidt (2011), pp. 732–733.

[339] Reinig (2015), pp. 30–31.

[340] For a critique of the excessive use of general clauses in German law, see Hedemann (1933), p. 11.

[341] Caemmerer (1968), p. 488.

[342] Reinig (2015), cit., p. 238.

to Rabel,[343] in countries such as France and Austria, the primary focus is placed on the protected interest—that is, the legal right whose negligent and unlawful infringement gives rise to compensation in accordance with the applicable norm. Von Caemmerer[344] asserts that French courts use the criterion of "non-hypothetical damage" (*dommage certain*[345]) to limit liability. Nevertheless, the decisive question lies elsewhere, as the attributtion of liability must be based on legal and political considerations.

Wagner[346] emphasizes that, contrary to initial impressions, French tort law does not have an unlimited scope. On the contrary, French law restricts liability for immaterial damages and purely economic losses in two ways, especially by varying the concept of *faute*[347] and defining the concept of damage. He concludes that French law, through its own mechanisms, delimits liability while also considering the requirement to protect certain legal interests. For this reason, these legally protected interests are subject to limited protection under German, English, Swiss, and Dutch laws.

The theory of the scope of the violated norm has developed even in countries that adopt a general clause model of liability, such as the Netherlands, where this criterion of imputation was applied based on provisions that, before 1992,[348] were identical to those of the Napoleonic Code.[349] In Austria, § 1295 (1) of the ABGB,[350] which lays down a general rule, closely resembles Art. 1382 of the French Civil Code.[351] Despite this, the theory of the scope of the violated norm is frequently used by the Supreme Court (*Oberster Gerichtshof*—OGH)[352] and has also been supported in Spanish law.[353]

[343] Rabel (1936), p. 505.

[344] Caemmerer (1956), p. 14.

[345] Steel (2015), p. 60.

[346] Wagner (2003), pp. 226–227.

[347] Recognizing that the Napoleonic model of *faute* encompasses various realities, see Leitão (2009), p. 52.

[348] Contrary to the previous civil codification, which followed the pattern of the *Code Napoléon*, the Dutch Civil Code of 1992 approached the German model (Infantino und Zervogianni 119).

[349] Quézel-Ambrunaz (2010), p. 141.

[350] Art. 1295 (1). "*Jedermann ist berechtigt, von dem Beschädiger den Ersatz des Schadens, welchen dieser ihm aus Verschulden zugefügt hat, zu fordern* [.]." Free translation: "Anyone has the right to claim compensation from the injurer for the damages that he has negligently caused." Section 1295 (1) of the ABGB generally establishes liability for negligently caused damages. Additional requirements are also stipulated, including causation and unlawfulness (§ 1294) (Gschnitzer (1963), p. 169).

[351] In Chile, the criterion of the scope of the norm is recognized in traffic regulations (Art. 171), as well as in Law no. 18.287, which governs with procedures before local police courts (Art. 14). According to Guilherme Bourie, it can be considered that these rules express a general principle of causal imputation of damages, considering the purpose of the norm (Bourie (2007), p. 389).

[352] Koziol (2000), p. 12.

[353] Pantaleon Prieto (1990), pp. 1562–1563; García-Ripoll Montijano (2008), pp. 33–35; Yágüez (2014), p. 47. The doctrine of the purpose of protection of the contract has been gradually incorporated into the jurisprudence of the Spanish Supreme Court (Arranz (2016), pp. 421–431).

The European Group of Tort Law[354] established the scope of protection of the violated norm as a criterion for imputation to limit liability. Markesinis and Lawson[355] argue that, even in France, it cannot be stated that there is a complete and total rejection of the approach of the "scope of the norm," as several decisions can be better explained by the theory of so-called "Aquilian relativity."

From this perspective, there is no obstacle to applying the theory of the scope of the violated norm within Brazilian law as well.[356] This does not mean that this limiting criterion can be indiscriminately used in all tort law cases as a solution to every issue regarding the attribution of damages.[357] However, the parameters developed for its use, particularly those related to the materialization of the risk created, can prove useful in specific groups of cases, including some involving damages caused by psychological influence, as will be discussed later.[358]

3.2.6 The Problematic Application of Causal Theories in Brazilian Law

The multiplicity of causal theories has always made the establishment of the link between conduct and result, as well as the limitation of compensable damages, an extremely complex problem, reaching, in Brazilian law,[359] however, a very concerning level. Jurisprudential inconsistency is evident, and national courts have applied whichever theory appears most convenient, often relying on equitable considerations rather than coherent legal criteria.[360] Given the vast range of criteria at their disposal,

---

[354] On the criteria adopted in the *Principles of European Tort Law (*PETL), see Sect. 3.2.7.

[355] Lawson und Markesinis (1982), p. 137.

[356] The theory of the scope of the norm is adopted by Guilherme Reinig, limited to the investigation of the foundation, that is, directed at the primary injury (Reinig (2015), p. 294). Patricia Iglecias, emphasizing the principles of prevention and precaution, argues that the theory, applied in the context of environmental law, is also relevant (Lemos (2012), p. 165). Renata Steiner recognizes the utility of the theory but asserts that its applicability does not need further argumentation in Brazilian law. However, in a later part of her work, when discussing forms of compensation, she argues that the "scope of the norm" of protection against contractual noncompliance must be respected (Steiner (2018), p. 180). Rafael Viola affirms the theory of the scope of the violated norm is applicable in Brazilian law, as long as the protected interest can be clearly identified (Viola (2023), pp. 152–153).

[357] In defense of the non-existence of a universally valid legal imputation rule, see Sect. 3.2.7.

[358] In Section 5.2.2.2, the theory is applied to cases where a negligent traffic accident causes a cargo vehicle to overturn, which then allows third parties to steal the transported goods.

[359] José Fernando Simão mentions the significant controversy surrounding the causal theory adopted in Brazilian extra-contractual liability (Simão (2021), p. 267).

[360] According to Giovanni Ettore Nanni, since no single doctrine can resolve all real-life situations, the criterion of common sense should be applied, enabling the judge to decide based on their free conviction (Nanni (2018), p. 657).

courts often select the causal conception that intuitively aligns with the outcome already determined. In the absence of the constraints imposed by a systematic legal analysis, judges adopt the definition of causation that best reflects their own perception of justice,[361] resulting in a fragmented and untechnical treatment of the matter.

Although the theories of direct and immediate damage and adequate causation are based on distinct conceptual frameworks—the first focusing on the interruption of the causal link and the second, in its various formulations, on the probability or possibility of damage occurrence—Brazilian legal scholarship has generally not undertaken a clear effort to distinguish them,[362] often arguing that both theories lead to similar outcomes.[363]

An emblematic illustration of this conceptual imprecision is found in the position adopted by Sérgio Cavalieri Filho.[364] While addressing adequate causation, the author asserts that, under this theory, the cause must be not only necessary but also adequate for the production of the result.[365] Similarly, Aguiar Dias[366] states that the direct cause is considered the necessary and adequate cause, even if indirect, meaning that, without its intervention, the damage would not have occurred.

Although the theories of adequate causation and the so-called subtheory of necessary causation may lead to similar outcomes, they should not be treated as equivalent, as they arose in distinct historical and conceptual contexts. The resemblance in legal consequences stems primarily from jurisprudence reproducing the vagueness and imprecision present in doctrinal discussions on the topic,[367] gradually eroding the dogmatic boundaries that once separated the two theories. Two legal constructs grounded in distinct theoretical frameworks cannot be treated as corresponding merely because they often lead to analogous results.

---

[361] Before the widespread use of objective imputation criteria by Spanish courts, the application of the appropriate theory was subject to the personal judgment of each judge, as reported by Yágüez (2014, p. 10).

[362] Peteffi da Silva (2009), p. 42.

[363] Tepedino (2002), p. 10. Arguing that criticisms of jurisprudence, for failing to make clear use of various theories on causation, are unfounded, Paulo de Tarso Sanseverino claims that such criticisms only hold when the legal operator is unaware of the existence of these theories. He further states that the occasional use of one or more theoretical frameworks, or even their combination, can be helpful in resolving a specific case (Sanseverino (2010), pp. 162–163).

[364] Cavalieri Filho (2012), p. 51.

[365] Judith Martins Costa holds that no substantial difference exists between the theory of adequate causation, referred to as "rational causation," and the theory of direct and immediate damage, referred to as "necessary causation," stating that the cause must always be "necessary" and the cause is necessary precisely because it is adequate (Martins-COSTA (2009), pp. 214–215). According to Marcelo Benacchio, the theory of direct and immediate damage conveys the same content as the theory of adequate causation, differing only in its focus on the same issue (Benacchio (2015), p. 222). Lastly, Fábio Podestá maintains that the theory of direct and immediate damage emerged as a refinement of the adequate causal theory (Podestá (2018), p. 383).

[366] Dias (1983), p. 178.

[367] Peteffi da Silva (2009), p. 45.

In Brazilian case law, courts frequently treat the two theories as synonymous.[368] The Superior Court of Justice (STJ),[369] almost literally echoing the words of Sérgio Cavalieri Filho, has held that the prevailing private law doctrine adopts the theory of adequate causation or direct and immediate damage, whereby causation is recognized only when the harm is a necessary and adequate consequence of a given cause. In a notable case, a child, after watching a television program featuring a magic trick, attempted to reproduce it at home and set his younger brother on fire, causing severe burns. The STJ rejected liability, reasoning that despite the duality of theories, they are almost entirely identical. As such, the act committed by the child could not be regarded as a foreseeable, possible, or necessary consequence of broadcasting the television program.[370]

In another case concerning the liability of the state and the notary for registering a non-existent property, the court emphasized that the attribution of extra-contractual liability depends on two factual elements (the perpetrator's conduct and the resulting harm) and one logical-normative element (causation). When assessing this normative element, the court reaffirmed that the principle of adequate causation (or direct and immediate damage) prevails in Brazilian law.[371]

Both the STF and the STJ, in various precedents, demonstrate that the distinction between adequate causation and the so-called subtheory of necessary causation is regarded as irrelevant for resolving certain cases. Without properly analyzing the theoretical foundations of each approach and their practical implications, these courts tend to affirm the existence of causation based on the fact that, under either construction, the outcome would be the same.[372]

The STJ has also invoked the theory of efficient cause in certain decisions concerning causation. In a claim for non-pecuniary damages filed against the Sanitation Company of Minas Gerais (COPASA), due to the discovery of

---

[368] An analysis of jurisprudence reveals that courts have applied either theory without identifying a consistent standard of judgment (Schreiber (2013), p. 63). In a decision reported by Min. Paulo de Tarso Sanseverino, it was affirmed that jurisprudence oscillates between the theories of adequate causation and direct and immediate damage (theory of interruption of causal chain) (STJ, REsp 1,787,026/RJ, rel. Paulo de Tarso Sanseverino, 3rd T, j. 26.10.2021, *DJe* 05.11.2021).

[369] STJ, REsp 1,307,032/PR, rel. Raul Araújo, j. 18.06.2013.

[370] STJ, REsp 1,067,332/RJ, rel. Marco Buzzi, j. 05.11.2013.

[371] STJ, REsp 1,198,829/MS, rel. Teori Albino Zavascki, j. 05.10.2010.

[372] "[. . .] Adoption by doctrine and jurisprudence of the theories of adequate causation and direct and immediate damage. Regardless of the theory chosen, it is essential that the relationship between the act and the harm is direct and immediate [. . .]" (STF, ACO 1853, rel. Gilmar Mendes, j. 17.08.2018). Also in this sense: "Regardless of the theory adopted, whether direct and immediate causation or adequate causation, it is not possible to affirm that the publication of the journalistic articles offensive to the appellant's reputation, mentioned in the initial petition, results from the termination of the contract signed with the respondent" (STJ, REsp 1,630,665/BA, rel. Moura Ribeiro, j. 23.05.2017). More recently, it was stated that "the dominant doctrine of private law adopts the theory of adequate causation or direct and immediate damage, so that causation is only considered to exist when the harm is a necessary and adequate effect of the cause considered (action or omission)" (STJ, AgInt in REsp 1,401,555/MG, rel. Raul Araújo, j. 03.10.2022).

a decomposing human body in a water reservoir, the court concluded that the public service was not the efficient cause of the damage, since the criminal act that led to the presence of the body excluded liability.[373] The theory of efficient cause was also cited in a case involving compensation for an unlawful act, in which working conditions experienced by the employee were deemed to have caused his permanent disability.[374]

In the latter decision, no explanation was offered regarding the application of the theory of efficient causation, a rarely employed doctrinal construct[375] due to the inherent difficulty in concretely identifying which among multiple contributing conditions was most capable of producing the result. This leads to the use of an empty formula, lacking any systematic foundation, that merely serves to justify an outcome previously chosen by the judge based on equity. Although the outcome may be perceived as equitable in the particular case, the reference to largely marginal theories, along with the indiscriminate use of causal concepts without delineating their theoretical premises, generates legal uncertainty and allows courts to reach any conclusion according to their subjective sense of correctness.

Some state court decisions, albeit in a limited manner, suggest the application of the theory regarding the scope of the violated norm in specific factual scenarios.

In a case decided by the Court of Justice of Goiás,[376] the plaintiff claimed to have had a romantic relationship with the defendant, who was married. The defendant had allegedly made promises of financial support that were never fulfilled, resulting in psychological harm and a diagnosis of depression. The trial court awarded R$ 25,000.00 in non-pecuniary damages. On appeal, the court upheld the decision, reasoning that, in order for damage to be compensable, it must result from a violation of a legally protected interest, meaning it must fall within the protective scope of the norm.

Although the decision refers to the theory of the scope of the norm, it fails to identify the specific provision or rule of conduct allegedly violated.[377] At that stage, the reasoning is reduced to a citation of Fernando Noronha's work, without clarifying the protective scope of the rule or specifying the theoretical components involved.

In another case decided by the São Paulo Court of Justice,[378] the plaintiff was driving on a São Paulo highway when, due to the wet road, he skidded and collided

---

[373] STJ, REsp 1,643,846/MG, rel. Herman Benjamin, j. 07.03.2017.

[374] STJ, REsp 246,596/MG, rel. Fernando Gonçalves, j. 16.09.2004.

[375] According to Jorge Facio, the thesis of efficient causation almost coincides, in its results, with the criterion of adequate causation (Facio (1981), p. 426).

[376] TJGO, ApCív 5,188,124.60.2018.8.09.0021, rel. Sandra Regina Teodoro Reis, j. 10.07.2020. Also using the scope of the violated norm as a basis for decision, see TJMA, ApCív 3652–54.2016.8.10.0052, rel. Paulo Sérgio Velten Pereira, j. 03.03.2020; TJSC, ApCív 2000.003966–7, rel. Anselmo Cerello, j. 29.05.2002.

[377] In the absence of a specific rule of conduct, the judge must assess the concrete situation to determine the applicable normative behavior, deciding on its existence and scope as an expression of the general framework of legal traffic (Kupisch and Kruger (1983), p. 53).

[378] TJSP, ApCív 10,032,812–59.2018.8.26.0533, rel. Percival Nogueira, j. 25.05.2021.

with another car, which was parked on the highway's channelization markings.[379] The plaintiff sought to hold both the highway concessionaire and the owner of the improperly parked vehicle liable. The appellate court dismissed the claim, reasoning that liability applies only to harmful events resulting from the kind of risk that the prohibited conduct was intended to prevent. In the present case, the court emphasized that the violated rule was not designed to prevent accidents of the kind that occurred.[380] This conclusion was drawn from a contextual interpretation of similar prohibitions, such as those relating to parking in cycle lanes, traffic islands, lawns, or gardens. According to the decision, the rule's primary purpose was to ensure the proper flow of traffic, not to prevent collisions under adverse weather conditions.[381]

Brazilian courts, in their efforts to ensure compensation for victims, frequently rely on measures lacking a solid dogmatic foundation or invoke legal concepts without proper normative support.[382] The use of presumptions of causation remains common, even in the absence of statutory authorization.[383] In cases where causation cannot be clearly established under classical frameworks, generic arguments such as the principles of full compensation, human dignity, and social solidarity are frequently invoked, suggesting a supposed distributive function of liability.[384]

Theories such as probabilistic and alternative causation have also been applied, often without deeper theoretical elaboration.[385] Although developed in foreign legal systems, these constructs have received limited systematic treatment in Brazilian legal scholarship and deserve greater attention. Few academic works have sought to examine these doctrines methodically, without resorting to interpretative shortcuts such as the now commonplace appeal to human dignity.

---

[379] Channelization markings, commonly referred to as "zebra stripes," are guidelines painted on the ground of vehicle circulation lanes. Their primary purpose is to direct the flow of traffic.

[380] The doctrine suggests that the violated norm should be intended to prevent the occurrence of a danger, which may materialize at a later time (Michalski (1996), p. 394).

[381] The judgment refers to an example provided by Marco Capecchi, where a vehicle parked in a spot reserved for the disabled, and thus prohibited, is involved in a collision. In this case, liability cannot be attributed to the offending driver, as the norm's purpose was not to prevent the accident but to benefit the person with a disability (Capecchi (2012), p. 90–91).

[382] Acknowledging the trend in civil law to ensure that damages are not left unrepaired, see Hironaka (2005), p. 350. Although recognizing the importance of personal protection, Marco Fábio Morsello asserts that the practical ineffectiveness of a broad and exclusive system of risk socialization is evident, and contends that this system should coexist with both strict liability and liability for negligence (Morsello (2006), 20).

[383] The difficulty of identifying causation is noted. However, this circumstance should not lead to the idea of that one can dispense with or even relax the causation link (Gama and Viola (2021), p. 234).

[384] Bonna (2020), p. 253.

[385] Analyzing alternative causation, from a perspective of Brazilian law, see Moraes (2017), pp. 148–190; Giustina (1991); Giustina (2012), pp. 362–379.

A critical analysis of the compatibility of these recent theoretical developments with Brazilian law is urgent.[386] Any transplant of foreign theories must be contextually grounded. The attenuation of the causal requirement,[387] rather than serving as a mechanism for income redistribution, should be admitted only in exceptional cases and must be supported by a solid normative basis within Brazilian law. Arguments grounded solely in the victim's vulnerability are insufficient to justify the mitigation or suppression of the causation requirement.

Driven by the perceived requirement to compensate for all forms of harm experienced in modern life,[388] as an expression of a broader culture of social victimization or blame,[389] some judicial decisions attempt to relax the causation requirement, allowing mere statistical probability, rather than causation grounded in empirical reasoning or common experience, to justify compensation.[390] Under this view, "probabilistic causation" is admitted, permitting the use of statistical data as an indication that a particular activity was likely the cause of the damage, with probability or plausibility becoming the evidentiary threshold. These statistics, although derived from specific events, are then applied analogously to other cases.[391]

It has been argued that the statistical probability of a harmful outcome becomes legally relevant when it reaches a degree of seriousness sufficient to justify a judgment of social disapproval. Some authors even suggest fixed thresholds for establishing liability.[392] For instance, Caitlin Mulholland,[393] by analogy with Italian law regarding loss-of-chance cases, adopts a 50% probability threshold for attributing responsibility, presuming that causation is established when this level is met.[394]

---

[386] The recurring translation of "*Deliktsrecht*" as "*Derecho de Daños*" and its adaptation in Brazil as "law of damages" exemplifies the improper importation of legal concepts, as if this expression could adequately replace the notion of "tort law" (Rodrigues Jr. (2016), cit., p. 128).

[387] The Germanic legal system, as an exception, does not completely disregard the causation requirement but allows for its attenuation. In strict liability rules, causation is presumed, whereas, in cases of alternative or cumulative causation, mere potential causation is considered sufficient (Koziol (2012), p. 139).

[388] Tiago Bitencourt attributes the unlimited expansion of liability to the mistaken premise that all damage must be compensate. According to the author, this belief reflects an "infantile illusion" that there is always someone "to blame to pay the bill" (David (2018), p. 97).

[389] Atiyah (1997), p. 138.

[390] Mulholland (2009), p. 303.

[391] Rodrigues Jr. (2016), pp. 116–117.

[392] A high correlation between two variables does not necessarily imply a causal relationship between them. Or in this instance, a strong statistical correlation could be observed over the past twenty-five years between the average annual price of wheat in Armenia and the number of students who drop out of high school in Lufkin, Texas. (Schum (2001), p. 147). Statistical evidence, as a general principle, is insufficient to prove a specific causal connection (Carpes (2016), p. 161).

[393] Mulholland (2009), p. 303.

[394] In German law, as previously stated, adequate causation is not solely determined by the criterion of mathematical probability (BGHZ, 18, 286).

Anchored in such premises, part of the doctrine has argued that the model requiring absolute certainty for a claim to be accepted is gradually being abandoned. In its place, probability is being embraced, with plausibility replacing the unattainable ideal of truth as the guiding criterion, based on statistical parameters established by science.[395] This shift reflects an effort to align the concept of causation with the notion of greater probability rather than with the standard of inexorable certainty.[396]

The reasoning presented should be considered incorrect, as it rests on a false premise. Natural causation does not presuppose a judgment of unequivocal certainty regarding the facts.[397] There is no requirement to irrefutably prove that a specific act caused the harm. As Otavio Luiz Rodrigues Junior[398] points out, the concept of causation is already embedded in probability theory, which makes the term "probabilistic causation" a contradiction. It constitutes a misguided appropriation of mathematical reasoning and, for that reason alone, should not be adopted.

Although mathematical probability may assist the judge in the factual evaluation of the case,[399] it cannot serve as the sole basis for a finding of liability or for dismissing a claim. Abstract statistical data,[400] disconnected from the specific circumstances under analysis, are insufficient. For example, if the consumption of nicotine over a certain period, as found in a particular brand of cigarette, carries a 50% risk of causing lung cancer, this fact alone is not enough to justify a judgment in favor of the claimant.[401] The court should consider other

[395] The prevailing opinion is that pure statistics do not provide valid evidential support for a statement about a specific fact, as they can only determine the relative frequency of classes of events (Taruffo (2014), p. 98).

[396] Bezerra et al. (2011), p. 43. Facchini Neto, when addressing the liability of the tobacco industry, argues that the mere difficulty of obtaining compelling evidence to support the facts alleged by the author should not lead to an "easy dismissal of the claim" (Facchini Neto (2016), pp. 16–17).

[397] Causation between fact and damage is probabilistic. It should not be assumed that there is absolute determinism between the fact and the damage (Pontes de Miranda 1984), p. 184). In contrast, Domingos Novaes states for the need for definitive proof of the causation, opposing the attribution of liability based solely on probabilistic criteria (Novaes (2017), p. 117).

[398] Rodrigues Jr. (2016), p. 122.

[399] Costa (2016), p. 36. In Brazilian doctrine, Marcos de Souza Paula highlights that statistics is a science with its own limitations and contradictions, and thus should be subject to discussion in the process (Paula (2018), p. 140).

[400] Inferences linking evidence and facts are not based on quantitative probability calculations, but on logical argumentation patterns. While statistical probabilities may serve as evidence in certain cases, they cannot be accepted as a general standard of judicial proof (Taruffo (2014), p. 32).

[401] Statistics are not appropriate for verifying the truth of factual allegations in process, unless the statistical frequency itself constitutes an allegation and the object of proof (Mitidiero (2013), p. 99).

relevant elements in resolving the case,[402] such as the existence of other previous comorbidities, the lifestyle of the claimant, the occurrence of similar diseases in the family, among various other factors subject to consideration.[403]

The STJ has consistently held that, under the principle of free judicial evaluation of evidence, the judge may depart from an expert opinion when there is other evidence in the record supporting such a conclusion.[404]

It is also important to avoid confusing the expansion of strict liability with the relaxation of the requirement of causation.[405] The development of a risky activity, by itself, does not eliminate the requirement of proving the existence of causation.[406] Fernando Noronha[407] distinguishes between ordinary strict liability and aggravated liability. The latter, which is of an extremely exceptional nature, would dispense with the proof of causation. Judith Martins-Costa[408] correctly affirms that causation is an indispensable element of tort law; without it, liability would become a blind lottery.

The classifications that suggest disregarding causation prove artificial, as they seek to suppress an elementary condition of tort liability. Not even in exceptional cases,[409] as highlighted by Noronha, can the exclusion of the causal requirement be justified, even when invoking arguments based on social solidarity or the claimant's need for compensation.

---

[402] In England, unlike the United States, there is no consistent doctrinal study on the issue of pure statistics (*naked statistics*). Some scholars argue that introducing the rule allowing only evidence based on group statistics would so radically transform the nature of proof that it should be subject to legislative review. They point out that it is possible, in a particular case, such evidence may be so reliable, and align so well with the facts of the case that it forms the necessary degree of conviction about what happened (Stapleton (2016), pp. 103–104). In the USA, in the case of *Sindell v. Abbot*, regarding the damages caused by the ingestion of the drug *Diethylstilbestrol* (DES), the Supreme Court of California, in 1980, applied the doctrine of *market share liability* (Dam (2006), p. 334).

[403] "Art. 375, CPC/2015. The judge will apply the rules of common experience supplied by the observation of what ordinarily happens and, also, the rules of technical experience, except, as to these, the expert examination." Recognizing the importance of applying the common rules of experience, see Schreiber (2013), p. 67.

[404] STJ, REsp 1,651,073, rel. Herman Benjamin, j. 14.03.2017.

[405] Rodrigues Jr. (2016), p. 133.

[406] Discussing the acts committed by the legally incapacitated, José Fernando Simão bases the strict liability of parents and representatives on the so-called dependency-based risk, without, however, eliminating the need to prove causation (Simão (2008), pp. 62–75).

[407] Noronha (1998), p. 28. Also defending the existence of an aggravated liability, see Venturi (2014), pp. 315–316.

[408] Martins-Costa (2009), p. 196. To include lost profits or emergent damage in the provision of losses and damages, it is essential to observe certain fundamental aspects, such as causation, as the injury may lead to other damages from different causes, making it necessary to ascertain whether that particular damage arises from the injury (Dantas (1978), v. 2, p. 46).

[409] Statement no. 659 of National Justice Council (CJF): "Acknowledging the difficulty in identifying causation does not eliminate the obligation to examine it."

3.2.7 Adopted Position: Imputation Criteria by Group of Cases

The first challenge concerning causation is to establish the distinction between its factual aspect,[410] governed by the theory of equivalence of conditions,[411] and imputation, understood as the normative limitation of liability.[412] Once the existence of factual causation is determined according to the ordinary means of proof allowed by civil procedural law, it becomes relevant, as a second step, to apply normative criteria for attributing liability based on value considerations.

Although part of Brazilian legal scholarship occasionally acknowledges the necessity of a normative evaluation stage[413] following the investigation of natural causation, prevailing civil doctrine largely disregards the distinction between factual causation and the autonomous legal question of whether the harmful result, although causally linked to the conduct, may be attributed to the wrongdoer. This doctrinal gap prevents a proper limitation of liability and risks holding the tortfeasor responsible for all ensuing consequences. The matter is strictly legal and must be addressed through the application of normative liability criteria.[414]

Brazilian doctrine and case law continue to approach issues of imputation as if they were merely questions of factual causation. Elements such as the "interruption" of the causal chain and the assessment of force majeure are often treated as criteria for delimiting liability. Confusion also persists regarding the distinction between fault and objective imputation, which are frequently conflated despite their normative divergence.[415]

An illustrative example is the state's liability for an act committed by a fugitive,[416] in which the STF, as previously noted, has repeatedly invoked the

[410] The terms "factual causation" and "natural causation" are used synonymously in this study.

[411] Many courts in European countries do not explicitly address the *conditio sine qua non* test, not because they reject it, but because they consider it uncontroversial in various claims.

[412] In defining the scope of liability, Paulo Queiroz states that the theory of objective imputation is more a theory of "non-imputation" than a theory of "imputation" (Queiroz (2020), pp. 247–248).

[413] Adalberto Pasqualotto distinguishes between "causation" and "imputation," asserting that the latter refers to the legal basis that determines the person liable for the obligation to compensate the damage (Pasqualoto (2016), p. 186). Judith Martins-Costa refers to the fact that the law may assign liability to those who did not directly cause the damage but are held, through an "imputation link," responsible for safety, guarantee, or risk (Martins-Costa (2009), p. 196).

[414] The expression "imputation" primarily refers to attributing or, conferring (to someone or something), as well as qualifying or designating in legal language a link of attribution established by the norm set by the legal authority (Martins-Costa (2007), p. 520).

[415] It is reported that, with the practical application of various criteria of objective imputation, the burred boundary between the imputational criteria, fault, and fortuitous event has also been highlighted in Spanish jurisprudence (Peña (2011), p. 15–16).

[416] The cases were discussed in Sect. 3.2.3.

theory of direct and immediate damage. However, the case does not concern the interruption of the causal chain,[417] but rather an issue of normative imputation, which involves judicial policy considerations. It is a matter that could be more appropriately resolved through the application of attribution criteria such as risk increase (*Risikoerhöhung*), materialization of the risk, the scope of the violated norm, and the recognition of general life risk (*allgemeines Lebensrisiko*).[418]

Accordingly, when a significant period of time has passed between the prisoner's escape and the perpetration of the crime, the exclusion of liability is justified by the fact that the specific risk inherent in the escape did not materialize. The danger of falling victim to a crime after a certain period constitutes a general risk to which all individuals are exposed and thus cannot be directly linked to the state's omission that enabled the prisoner's evasion. In such cases, the basis for holding the public administration liable does not rest on whether the harm is classified as direct or indirect, necessary or unnecessary, but rather on a broader assessment of the nature and scope of the risk involved.[419]

Similarly, issues related to so-called presumptions of causation, such as alternative causation and the flexibilization of the causal requirement, are frequently analyzed using the conceptual tools provided by the subtheory of necessary causation. As foreign scholarship correctly points out, these are in fact problems of factual causation, constituting exceptions to the application of the theory of equivalence of conditions.[420] What is often disregarded, however, is that causation may only be relaxed in exceptional cases[421] and cannot be entirely set aside merely because its proof presents evidentiary difficulties.[422]

---

[417] It is urged that the courts abandon once and for all the erroneously called "subtheory of necessary causation," as it fails to offer any dogmatic guidance and contributes nothing to the resolution of the problem (Reinig (2015), p. 134).

[418] The criteria for imputation will be analyzed in more detail from Sect. 4.5.

[419] Reinig (2015), p. 153.

[420] When discussing causation in its naturalistic sense, Larenz points out that, exceptionally, in the cases of § 830 I (2) of the BGB (alternative causation), the possibility of causation is sufficient for determining liability (Larenz (1987), p. 434). Jens Ekkenga and Thilo Kuntz assert that alternative causation constitutes an exception to the theory of equivalence, as it proves problematic in addressing with these cases (Ekkenga und Kuntz (2014), p. 73).

[421] Despite the criticisms directed at it, it can be asserted that the conditional directive is appropriate, at least in most cases, for establishing the causal link between the conduct and the damage, and for excluding liability those facts that did not establish an essential condition for the occurrence of the event; however, it requires the support of other criteria, which circumscribe its sphere of action (Infantino (2012), p. 87).

[422] The norm can attenuate causation in certain hypotheses, being satisfied with a mere possibility, or even dispensing with the establishment of direct causation between the fact and the damage, as is the case with indirect liability (e.g., for the act of the thing or of third parties), provided there is a certain connection between the attributed liability and the activity carried out (liability for safety, guarantee or risk (Martins-Costa (2009), p. 196). The broader the gap between legally attributed liability and the factual situation that actually occurred, the greater the argumentative burden required to justify such attribution, lest it violate the principles of proportionality and

In the evaluative stage,[423] which aims to impose stricter limits on liability, many legal formulations aspiring to provide a single and uniform solution for complex scenarios increasingly struggle to prevail.[424] It is not coincidental that the theory of adequacy has been the object of recurrent criticism, even though its practical utility in addressing a wide variety of case-specific nuances is acknowledged.[425] The more abstract a legal proposition becomes, the greater the number of cases it can potentially encompass, thereby expanding its applicability. However, at a certain level of abstraction, the legal concept loses its normative force, reducing the act of subsumption to a form of arbitrariness.[426]

Despite the criticisms directed at the adequacy theory, its complete replacement or displacement by the theory of the scope of the norm or by other imputation parameters does not seem justified.[427] The adequacy test remains valid as an initial filter for attributing liability, excluding conditions that are entirely indifferent to the production of the result (negative formulation), according to the perspective of an experienced observer. Nevertheless, given that this initial legal evaluation does not satisfactorily restrict the scope of liability, it should be supplemented by additional normative attribution criteria,[428] especially those related to risk allocation. The application of adequate causation, when combined with other attribution parameters, makes the process of assigning liability more precise and manageable.

For the same reason, the theory of the scope of the violated norm should not be elevated to the status of a general and universally applicable model for all cases,[429] as some scholars appear to suggest. Its usefulness should not be disregarded, as it has proven to be valuable in many scenarios, including those involving damages

---

reasonableness. Liability imposed inappropriately, unnecessarily, or in any manner that proves arbitrary, capricious, or irrational finds no support in law (David (2018) p. 95).

[423] Causal series, from a naturalistic point of view, are uninterrupted. It is the legal system that, in the words of Lourival Vilanova, "interrupts" them, reputing a cause as initial (Vilanova (2015), p. 34).

[424] Niebaum (1977), p. 26). As pointed out by Von Caemmerer in 1970, no general uniform formula has been established anywhere. According to the author, the task is to develop case categories and, under the guidance of jurisprudence, address and refine the case law reasoning (Caemmerer (1956), p. 287). Similarly, Menezes Cordeiro argues that, in the current state of legal science, regarding causation, no universally valid formulas exist regarding causation. According to the author, such formulas can be attempted; however, they are attainable at high levels of abstraction. The relevant causation must be constructed, on a case-by-case basis, guided by the principles of legal science (Menezes Cordeiro (2004), pp. 548–549).

[425] Rodrigues Jr. (2016), p. 132.

[426] Forst (2000), p. 208.

[427] Mota Pinto (2008), p. 940.

[428] The Austrian draft reform project, in its Art. 1.310 (1), combines adequate causation with the theory of the scope of protection (Rodrigues Jr. (2016), p. 132).

[429] Paulo Mota Pinto and Sinde Monteiro argue against the treatment of the scope of protection as a general requirement of liability (Mota Pinto (2008), pp. 943–949; Sinde Monteiro (2005), p. 384). The theory of the scope of the norm is not capable of consolidating into a fixed criterion the various aspects that may be applied in a specific case (Lüer (1969), pp. 133–134; Santolim (2014), p. 85).

caused by psychological influence. However, it is misguided to assume that this theory, on its own, would be sufficient to address the full range of practical situations without allowing the interpreter to resort to other objective attribution criteria, such as adequate causation.

The possibility of combining imputation criteria has been defended,[430] according to the practical and theoretical peculiarities of each group of cases.[431] The establishment of attribution criteria by group of cases does not imply, in any way, what has been described as a flexibilization of causation. It does not involve mitigating or eliminating the requirement of causation but rather identifying which criteria are most appropriate, based on legal and policy considerations, to resolve specific disputes.[432]

Menezes Cordeiro,[433] in this regard, argues that causation, as a prerequisite for tort law, develops in four stages: (a) *conditio sine qua non*; (b) adequacy, assessed in terms of social normality; (c) causation by the wrongdoer to achieve their purpose; and (d) consistency with the values protected by the violated norm. The theory of adequacy, when combined with another corrective element of objective imputation, proves sufficient and appropriate for resolving a significant number of practical cases.

It is entirely possible that, after applying the theory of equivalence of conditions, with its possible refinements, different attribution criteria may be employed. This approach is acknowledged by Larenz,[434] who argues that the theory of the scope of protection of the norm can satisfactorily resolve the issue of limiting consequential damages in certain cases, but not in all. According to the author, this is because there is often no clear indication of the extent to which the norm's protective scope covers subsequent harm. As a result, the adequacy criterion remains essential as an initial limiting criterion for assigning liability, beyond which other criteria may be applied to further restrict it.

Larenz,[435] however, maintains that liability may still be attributed under the theory of the scope of the norm even when the causal link between the initial event and the resulting harm is inadequate. He refers to cases of strict liability (*Gefährdungshaftung*) and compensation for vaccine-related injuries as illustrative

[430] Attention is drawn to the fact that there is no consensus in the doctrine regarding the arrangement of the various theories of causation, nor regarding the importance to be attributed to each of them. This circumstance reveals the impropriety of defending universally valid formulas, making it necessary to combine various attribution criteria (Pereira (2019), p. 242). Recognized as a successor to a universally valid theory, the catalogue of evaluative aspects is obtained by considering groups of individual case (Niebaum (1977), p. 26).

[431] Also in the law of obligations, the importance of the matter has been emphasized based on a group of cases (Pires (2021), p. 19).

[432] A favorable position is adopted regarding the identification of groups of cases. This perspective, however, does not mean casuistry. Courts must safeguard the legal and dogmatic foundations of judicial legitimacy, overcoming the subjectivities that frequently stem from the arbitrariness of the criteria employed in establishing liability (Reinig (2015), p. 279).

[433] Menezes Cordeiro (2004), p. 550.

[434] Larenz (1987), pp. 444–445.

[435] Larenz (1987), p. 445.

examples.[436] In the latter, compensation must be awarded for subsequent harm whose occurrence is not generally foreseeable, as it results from extremely rare events that would not ordinarily be taken into account.

Beyond traditional approaches, such as the theory of adequacy and the theory of the scope of the norm, additional imputation criteria can be found in the legal systems of European Union Member States. The Principles of European Tort Law (PETL) explicitly provides the combination of various criteria. In Article 3:201 PETL,[437] the European Group of Tort Law established a principle that explicitly requires the consideration of multiple attribution criteria to limit liability. According to the non-exhaustive list of relevant factors, the interpreter should consider the following parameters: (a) foreseeability of damage; (b) nature and value of the protected interests; (c) basis of liability; (d) normal life risks; and (e) scope of the violated norm.[438]

Unlike German law, which specifies certain absolute rights in § 823 (1) BGB but, in relation to subsequent damages, allows comprehensive protection,[439]

[436] There is a great discussion in the German doctrine regarding the basis for compensating damages arising from vaccination. Huber states that, if vaccination leads to a fatal complication, the claim for compensation of the surviving claimants does not depend on the existence of a statistical regularity of the event (BGHZ 18, 286). He argues, thus, that the theory of adequacy is not applicable combined with the "theory of the risk area" (*Gefahrbereichstheorie*). The subsequent adequate damages that do not fit into the specific danger area created by the violation of a legal protected interest, but that only involve a general "risk of life," should not be compensated. In contrast, the subsequent inadequate damages, which are still attributable to this danger zone, should be compensated (Huber (1969), p. 682). Kramer states that the exclusion of liability for subsequent inadequate damages can only occur when it is properly demonstrated that the legislator intended to exempt the injured party from any risk, including uncommon or extraordinary causal courses, as is the case with damages caused by vaccination (Kramer (1976), p. 343). This is not an issue of attribution, but rather a justification for liability in cases of sacrifice (*Aufopferung*), which aligns with the state's obligation to compensate individuals whose rights were sacrificed for the greater benefit of the community (Reinig (2015), p. 118).

[437] "Art. 3:201. Scope of liability. Where an activity is a cause within the meaning of Sect. 3.1 of this Chapter, whether and to what extent damage may be attributed to an individual depends on factors such as (a) the foreseeability of the damage to a reasonable person at the time of the activity, taking into account in particular the closeness in time or space between the damaging activity and its consequence, or the magnitude of the damage in relation to the normal consequences of such an activity; (b) the nature and the value of the protected interest (Article 2:102); (c) the basis of liability (Article 1:101); (d) the extent of the ordinary risks of life; and (e) the protective purpose of the rule that has been violated."

[438] Weitenberg (2014), pp. 771–772.

[439] Larenz (1987), p. 444. The assertion that liability for negligently caused damages in the BGB is unlimited means that it is limited only by the causal connection between the harmful act and the damage occurred (Werner (1960), p. 283). According to § 249 of the BGB, the obligation to compensate, once established, includes all consequences that are in connection with the basis of liability, regardless of how temporally distant they are from the initial event (Lange und Schiemann (2003), p. 59–60). For example, in the case of physical injury, the victim has the right to undergo all necessary surgeries and treatments and can even demand the amount spent by the closest relatives for visits during the period in which they were hospitalized (Jauernig (1994), p. 227).

Brazilian law adopts a general clause (Arts. 186 and 927 of the CC/02), seeking to restrict the compensation for such damages through Art. 403. Therefore, despite the broad scope in terms of primary injuries, it cannot be inferred that Brazilian law endorses unrestricted compensation for consequential losses. The rule of Art. 403, which—as discussed—far from adopting the "subtheory of necessary causation" imposes limits on damage compensation, should serve as a hermeneutic guide when applying attribution criteria.

Accordingly, the analysis of causation and imputation under Brazilian law commences with the application of the theory of equivalence of conditions (*conditio sine qua non*), in the absence of which liability cannot be imposed, unless exceptional circumstances are present. The determination of factual causation, particularly in cases involving psychological causation, entails distinctive features that will be addressed in subsequent sections.[440]

In a subsequent stage, the theory of adequate causation should be applied in its negative formulation. As Paulo Mota Pinto rightly observes,[441] this approach rarely leads to the attribution of results outside all probability, serving as a prima facie filter in delimiting liability. The adequacy theory has not been entirely supplanted by doctrinal or jurisprudential developments[442] and remains embedded in the Brazilian legal tradition, serving to prevent abrupt dogmatic shifts in the application of causal theories. Its negative formulation functions primarily as an initial filter, offering broader interpretative flexibility at this stage[443] and allowing for the later application of complementary attribution criteria.

Despite its utility as a first legal limiting barrier, the adequacy theory should be combined with other objective attribution criteria[444] to determine whether the initial wrongdoer can be held liable. Adequacy operates as a preliminary, non-decisive test, subject to adjustment through additional normative parameters, especially in cases involving damages resulting from psychological influence. In such cases, the subsequent conduct rarely falls entirely outside all probability from the perspective of an experienced observer, particularly when the influence of the initial act is taken into account. For instance, as discussed in Sect. 3.2.2, in cases involving damage to the green strip, the causal adequacy of the roadway obstruction is generally acknowledged, yet responsibility should not be attributed to the

[440] See Section 4.3.

[441] The author emphasizes that the idea of adequacy conveys a generic line of concretization, understandable by the layperson, based on an idea of probability (Mota Pinto (2008), p. 947–948).

[442] Rodrigues Jr. (2016), p. 132.

[443] This is the position adopted by Almeida Costa, who advocates a broader definition of adequate causation, according to which a fact acting as a condition ceases to qualify as the cause of damage only when it is wholly inadequate and has given rise to the result exclusively through abnormal or exceptional circumstances (Martins Costa (2009), p. 764).

[444] The theory of "objective imputation" is the most widely accepted currently, and it considers that the most appropriate way to carry out this imputation is through the theory of adequate causation (Aguiar Jr. (2003), p. 113).

initial accident. The use of lateral access routes represents a general traffic risk and falls within the liability scope of the adjacent property owner.[445]

Finally, other attribution criteria, addressed later,[446] should be applied independently of adequacy to refine and limit liability. This approach permits the application of diverse normative parameters[447] depending on the group of cases analyzed. The indiscriminate and generalized use of a single attribution theory is not appropriate.[448]

3.3 Summary

The study of causal theories reveals the insufficiency of traditional doctrinal constructions to delimit the scope of tort law. Rather than offering clear criteria for damage attribution, the proliferation of theories has deepened legal uncertainty, as evidenced by the unsystematic and inconsistent application of various theoretical constructs in Brazilian jurisprudence. The pursuit of a single, all-encompassing theory to resolve causal issues has proven ineffective given the complexity of contemporary legal relations.

The theory of equivalence of conditions, also known as the sine qua non condition theory, posits that any event contributing to an outcome must be regarded as its cause. It relies on the hypothetical elimination method, which asserts that if a factor is removed and the event no longer occurs, that factor is a necessary condition for the outcome. This approach, despite its logical precision, does not offer criteria for limiting liability, potentially resulting in infinite regressions and an excessive expansion of liability. A striking example of this shortcoming would be attributing liability to the manufacturer of the paint used for a pedestrian crossing in an accident occurring at that location. Thus, this theory must be supplemented by additional criteria to delimit responsibility attribution.

The theory of direct and immediate damage, especially its "subtheory of necessary causation," seeks to restrict liability by asserting that only damages that are direct effects of conduct can be attributed to the causer. This theory, adopted by the

[445] Hart and Honoré, commenting on the "green strip case," assert that, in this hypothesis, other factors, besides adequacy, establish limits to liability. The court bases its decision on the circumstance that impatient drivers, not the defendant, had control of the situation (*master of situation*) (Hart and Honoré (1985), p. 475).

[446] See Section 4.5.

[447] As an example, Fernando Pantaleón Prieto indicates some attribution criteria applied by Spanish courts: (a) general life risk (*allgemeines Lebensrisiko*); (b) prohibition of return (*Regressverbot*); (c) provocation (*Herausforderung*); (d) increase of risk (*Risikoerhöhung*); and (e) purpose of protection of the norm establishing liability (*Schutzzweck der Haftungsbegründenen Norm*) (Pantaleón Prieto (1990), pp. 1566–1590).

[448] Wagner Mota Alves de Souza critiques the "fallacy of unitarism" in causation theories (Souza (2021), p. 137).

STF in relevant precedents such as RE 130.764–1/PR and RE 608.880, is based on the idea that the causal chain should be considered interrupted when the damage stems from independent intervening causes. The central problem with this approach is its lack of conceptual precision and its reliance on intuition, often leading to arbitrary solutions. Moreover, by adopting a purely physical criterion for causal interruption, this theory ignores other normative and evaluative considerations that are essential to the attribution of liability.

The theory of adequate causation emerges as a refinement of the theory of equivalence of conditions, aiming to delimit attribution based on the foreseeability of the result. Created by Johannes von Kries, it proposes that only conditions that, in the normal course of events, are likely to cause harm should be considered legally relevant. However, the application of this theory faces challenges. The definition of foreseeability can vary depending on the perspective adopted for analysis, making it subjective. Additionally, courts often apply this theory indiscriminately, mixing it with other attribution criteria without a clear definition of its limits.

The theory of the scope of the norm (or the theory of the purpose of the norm's protection) presents itself as one of the complementary objective attribution criteria used to limit liability. This theory posits that liability should only arise when the damage suffered falls within the protective scope of the violated norm. Initially developed by Ernst Rabel and further disseminated by Ernst von Caemmerer, this approach asserts that the attribution of damage must be contingent upon the protection of legally recognized interests by the violated norm. However, this theory has not been immune to criticism. Although it can be applied in general clause systems, such as the Brazilian legal system, it cannot stand as the sole theory of objective imputation, as it is alone insufficient to resolve all the complex issues of liability, especially in cases of psychologically mediated causation.

The current state of doctrine points to the requirement for a clear distinction between two stages of analysis: natural causation, governed by the theory of equivalence of conditions, and legal attribution, guided by normative evaluative criteria. This separation allows for overcoming the confusion between purely causal issues and attribution problems, which are often treated indistinctly by the courts. The attempt to solve attribution problems based on alleged causal criteria has generated poorly founded and technically inconsistent decisions.

The most appropriate solution for Brazilian law involves the establishment of different attribution filters, applied in successive stages: first, the determination of natural causation through the theory of equivalence of conditions; then, the use of the theory of adequate causation in its negative formulation as an initial criterion for legal evaluation; and finally, the application of other objective attribution parameters according to the peculiarities of each group of cases.

This multi-level approach allows for greater consistency in the analysis of causal connection, overcoming the subjectivity and randomness that characterize the current jurisprudential practice. Recognizing that different groups of cases may require specific attribution criteria does not mean abandoning dogmatic rigor but adapting it to the complexities of contemporary tort law. The identification of groups of cases and the development of specific attribution criteria contribute to greater legal certainty, without rigidifying the system of tort law.

References

Acciari HH (2009) La relación de causalidade y las funciones del derecho de daños: reparación, prevención, minimización de costos sociales. AbeledoPerrot, Buenos Aires

Aguiar Júnior RR (2003) Extinção dos contratos por incumprimento do devedor: resolução, 2ª edn. Aide, Rio de Janeiro

Alarcão R (1983) Direito das obrigações. Coimbra

Almeida Costa MJ (2009) Direito das obrigações, 12ª edn. Almedina, Coimbra

Alpa G, Zeno-Zencovich V (2007) Italian private law. Routledge-Cavendish, New York

Alterini AA (1987) Responsabilidad civil: Límites de la reparación civil, 3ª edn. Abeledo-Perrot, Buenos Aires

Alvim AN (1980) Da inexecução das obrigações e suas consequências, 5ª edn. Saraiva, São Paulo

Andrade FS (1997) Da codificação: crônica de um conceito. Livraria do Advogado, Porto Alegre

Antolsei F (1960) Il rapporto di causalità nel diritto penale. Giappacheli, Torino

Antolsei F (2000) Manuale di Diritto Penale: Parte Generale (a cura di Luigi Conti), 15ª edn. Giuffrè Editore, Milano

Arranz AI Ruiz (2016) La doctrina del fin de protección del contrato como vía de delimitación del daño indemnizable en derecho alemán y español. Un análisis comparado. RJUAM 34:409–440

Ascensão JO (1956) Acção finalista e nexo causal. Dissertation, Faculdade de Direito, Universidade de Lisboa

Ataíde RPCM (2019) Responsabilidade civil por violação de deveres no tráfego. Almedina, Coimbra

Atiyah P (1997) The damages lottery. Hart, Oxford

Aubry C, Rau C (1952) Droit civil français. In: (atual. por Paul Esmein), 6ª edn. Librairies Techniques, Paris, 6

Bacon F (1639) The elements of the Common Laves of England. In: Printed by the assignes of ion more esquire. London

Bar von C (1999) Gemeineuropäisches Deliktsrecht, vol 2. Beck, München

Bar von C (2009) Non-contractual liability arising out of damage caused to another. Sellier, European law publishers, Munich

Bar von CL (1871) Die Lehre vom Kausalzusammenhang im Recht, besonders im Strafrecht. Verlag von Bernhard Tauchnitz, Leipzig

Barbosa AMCNM (2013) Do nexo de causalidade ao nexo de imputação: contributo para a compreensão da natureza binária e personalística do requisito causal ao nível da responsabilidade civil extracontratual, vol 1. Principia, Cascais

Barbosa AMCNM (2019) Responsabilidade civil pelo financiamento de grupos terroristas. Revista IBERC 1:01–39

Barcellona M (1973) Scopo della norma violata: interpretazioni teleologica e tecniche di attribuzione della tutela aquiliana. Rivista di Diritto Civile 19(1):311–371

Benacchio M (2015) Algumas considerações acerca da relação de causalidade na responsabilidade civil. In: Benacchio M, Guerra ADM (eds) (orgs) Responsabilidade civil. Escola Paulista da Magistratura, São Paulo

Benjamin AHV (1998) Responsabilidade civil pelo dano ambiental. Revista de Direito Ambiental 3(9):5–52

Benöhr HP (1999) Die Redaktion der Paragraphen 23 und 826 BGB. In: Zimmermann R Rechtsgeschichte und Privatrechtsdogmatik. C.F. Muller Verlag, Heidelberg

Bernert G (1969) Die Leerformel von der "Adaequanz". Archiv für die civilistische Praxis 169:421–442
Beviláqua C (1955) Código dos Estados Unidos do Brasil Comentado, 10ª edn. (atual. por Achilles Bevilaqua e Isaias Bevilaqua). Paulo de Azevedo, Rio de Janeiro
Bezerra de Menezes J, Coelho JMA, Bugarim MCC (2011) A expansão da responsabilidade civil na sociedade de riscos. Scientia Iuris 15(1):29–50
Bianca MC (2012) Civil Law: liability, 2ª edn. Giuffrè Francis Lefebvre, Milan
Binding J (2012) Das Gesetz der VR China über die deliktische Haftung. Walter de Gruyter, Berlin
Binding K (1872) Die Normen und ihre Übertretung. Verlag von Wilhelm Engelmann, Leipzig
Birkmeyer von K (1885) Über Ursachenbegriff und Causalzusammenhang im Strafrecht. Universitäts—Buchdruckerei von Adler's Erben, Rostock
Bonna AP (2020) Direito de danos, políticas públicas e a Covid-19: a pandemia que exige um novo conceito de responsabilidade civil. In: Monteiro Filho CER, Rosenvald N, Densa R. (eds) Coronavírus e responsabilidade civil: impactos contratuais e extracontratuais. Foco, Indaiatuba
Bordon R (2006) Il nesso di causalità. UTET, Torino
Borghetti JS, Whittaker S (2019) Introduction. In: Borghetti JS, Whittaker S (eds) French civil liability in comparative perspective. Hart Publishing, Chicago
Bourie EB (2007) Tratado de responsabilidad extracontractual. In: Editorial Jurídica de Chile, Santiago
Brandão Proença JC (1997) A conduta do lesado como pressuposto e critério de imputação do dano extracontratual. Almedina, Coimbra
Briz JS (1963) Derecho de daños. Editorial Revista de Derecho Privado, Madrid
Buri von M (1894) Beiträge zur Theorie des Strafrechts und zum Strafgesetzbuche: gesammelte Abhandlungen. Verlag von Veit & Comp., Leipzig
Buri von M (1898) Questioni d'Imputabilità. Estratto dalla Rivista Penale, vol XLVII, fascicolo V. Unione Tipografico-Editrice, Torino
Buri von M (1960) Zur Lehre von der Teilnahme an dem Verbrechen und der Begünstigung. Ferber'sche Universitäts-Buchhandlung (Emil Roth), Gieβen
Busnelli FD, Patti S (2013) Danno e responsabilità civile, 3ª edn. G. Giappichelli Editore, Torino
Bussani M, Palmer VV (2005) Between contract and tort: pure economic loss in Europe. In: Cohen N, Mckendrick E. (eds) Comparative remedies for breach of contract. Hart Publishing, Oxford; Portland; Oregon
Bydlinski F (1964) Probleme der Schadensverursachung nach deutschem und österreichischem Recht. Ferdinand Enke Verlag, Stuttgart
Bydlinski F (1985) Zum gegenwärtigen Stand der Kausalitätstheorie im Schadensersatz. Juristische Blätter 80(1):1–8
Caemmerer von E (1956) Das Problem des Kausalzusammenhangs im Privatrecht. Hans Ferdinand Schulz Verlag, Freiburg
Caemmerer von E (1968) Wandlungen des Deliktsrechts. In: Leser HG (ed) Ernst von Caemmerer - Gesammelte Schriften: Rechtsvergleichung und Schuldrecht, vol 1. J.C.B. Mohr (Paul Siebeck), Tübingen
Caemmerer von E (1970) Die Bedeutung des Schutzbereichs einer Rechtsnorm für die Geltendmachung von Schadensersatzansprüchen aus Verkehrsunfällen. Deutsches Autorecht:283–292
Calvão da Silva J (1990) Responsabilidade civil do produtor. Almedina, Coimbra
Canaris CW (1995) Función, estructura y falsación de las teorías jurídicas. (Trad. Daniela Brückner e José Luis de Castro). Civitas, Madrid
Cantzler K (1957) Die Vorteilungsgleichung beim Schadensersatzanspruch. Archiv für die civilistische Praxis 156:29–59
Capecchi M (2012) Il nesso di causalità: da elemento della fattispecie "fato illecito" a criterio di limitazioni di risarcimento del danno, 3ª edn. CEDAM, Padova

Carbonnier J (1962) Droit Civil: les biens et les obligations, 4ª edn. Presses Universitaires de France, Paris
Carpes AT (2016) A prova do nexo de causalidade na responsabilidade civil. Ed. RT, São Paulo
Cavalieri Filho S (2012) Programa de responsabilidade civil, 10ª edn. Atlas, São Paulo
Cendon P (2009) Commentario al Codice civile: artt. 1173-1320. Giuffrè, Milano
Chironi GP (1884) La colpa nel diritto civile odierno: colpa contrattuale. F. Bocca, Roma; Torino; Firenze
Coelho FP (1951) O nexo de causalidade na responsabilidade civil. Boletim da Faculdade de Direito da Universidade de Coimbra, Suplemento IX:65–242
Coelho FP (1998) O problema da causa virtual na responsabilidade civil. Almedina, Coimbra
Cohnfeldt R (1865) Die Lehre vom Interesse nach römischem Recht: mit Rücksicht auf neuere Gesetzgebung. Verlag von Bernhard Tauchniz, Leipzig
Colin A, Capitant H (1915) Cours Élémentaire de Droit civil français, t. 2. Librairie Dalloz, Paris
Costa Jr PJ da (2007) Nexo causal, 4th edn. Revista dos Tribunais, São Paulo
Costa PC (2016) Causalidade, dano e prova: a incerteza na responsabilidade civil. Almedina, Coimbra
Couto E Silva C (2014) O dever de indenizar. In: Fradera VMJ (ed) (org) O direito privado na visão de Clóvis do Couto e Silva, 2ª edn. Livraria do Advogado, Porto Alegre
Couto e Silva C (2022) Princípios fundamentais da responsabilidade civil em direito brasileiro e comparado (Portuguese translation by Fernanda Escobar Bins). Sergio Antonio Fabris, Porto Alegre
Coviello N (1895) Del caso fortuito in rapporto alla estinzione delle obbligazioni. Rocco Carabba, Lanciano
Coviello N (1897) La responsabilità senza colpa. Rivista italiana per le scienze giuridiche 23 (1):188–216
Cruz GSC (2005) O problema do nexo causal na responsabilidade civil. Renovar, Rio de Janeiro
Cuevillas Matozzi I (2000) La relación de causalidad em la órbita del derecho de daños. Tirant lo Blanch, Valencia
Dam van C (2006) European tort law. Oxford University Press, New York
Dantas ST (1978) Programa e Direito Civil: aulas proferidas na Faculdade Nacional de Direito [fim de 1943–1945]: os contratos, vol 2. Editora Rio, Rio de Janeiro
Dantas ST (1979) Programa e Direito Civil: aulas proferidas na Faculdade Nacional de Direito [1942–1945]: parte geral, vol 1. Editora Rio, Rio de Janeiro
David TB (2018) Da culpa ao nexo causal: o caráter valorativo do juízo de causalidade e as (de) limitações da responsabilidade objetiva. Revista de Direito Civil Contemporâneo 17(5):87–104
De Cupis A (1946) Il danno: teoria generale della responsabilità civile. Giuffrè, Milano
De Page H (1934) Traité élémentaire de droit civil belge, vol 2. Bruylant-Sirey, Bruxelles, Paris
Demogue R (1924) Traité des obligations en général: source des obligations, t. 4. Librairie Arthur Rousseau, Paris
Dernburg H (1892) Pandkten: Obligationenrecht, 3ª edn. Verlag von H. W. Müller, Berlin
Deutsch E (1963) Fahrlässigkeit und erforderliche Sorgfalt: eine privatrechtliche Untersuchung. Carl Heymanns Verlag KG, Köln; Berlin; Bonn; München
Deutsch E (1966) Begrenzung der Haftung aus abstrakter Gefährdung wegen fehlender adäquater Kausalität?. JuristenZeitung 21(17):556–559
Deutsch E (1967) Zivilrecht. JuristenZeitung 22(20):639–643
Deutsch E (1996) Allgemeines Haftungsrecht, 2ª edn. Carl Heymanns Verlag KG, Köln, Berlin; Bonn, München
Deutsch E (1999) Zurechnungszusammenhang, Rechtswidrigkeit und Verschulden. In: Beuthien V et al (eds) (orgs) Festschrift für Dieter Medicus: zum 70. Geburtstag. Heymanns, Köln; Berlin; Bonn, München, pp. 77–88
Dias D (2020) Mitigação de danos na responsabilidade civil. Thomson Reuters Brasil, São Paulo
Dias JA (1983) Responsabilidade civil em debate. Forense, Rio de Janeiro
Dias JA (2006) Da responsabilidade civil, 11ª edn. Renovar, Rio de Janeiro

Dias Pereira AG, Oliveira P (2020) Tort law in Portugal. Wolters Kluwer, The Netherlands
Diaz-Picazo L (1999) Derecho de daños. Civitas, Madrid
Domat J (1695) Les loix civiles dans leur ordre naturel, 2ª edn, t. 1. Paris
Dörner H (1987) Zur Dogmatik der Schutzgesetzverletzung - BGH, NJW 1982, 1037 und NJW 1985, 134. Juristische Schulung 7:522–528
Dubuisson B (2019) The projet de réforme du Code Civil belge and the reform of the French Civil Code: a comparison of selected topics. In: Borghetti JS, Whittaker S (eds) French civil liability in comparative perspective. Hart Publishing, Chicago
Dunz W (1984) Gefährdungshaftung und Adäquanz in der neueren Rechtsprechung des BGH. Versicherungsrecht 25:600–602
Ehrenzweig A (1920) System des österreichischen allgemeinen Privatrechts: das Recht der Schuldverhältnisse, vol 2, t. 1. Manz'sche Verlags- und Universitäts-Buchhandlung, Wien
Ekkenga J, Kuntz T (2014) Vor §249. In: Soergel HT, Siebert W (eds) (orgs) Soergel: Kommentar zum Bürgerlichen Gesetzbuch: Schuldrecht 1/2: §243–304, 13ª edn, vol 3/2. W. Kohlhammer, Stuttgart
Engisch K (1931) Die Kausalität als Merkmal der strafrechtlichen Tatbestände. Verlag von J. C. B Mohr (Paul Siebeck), Tübingen
Enneccerus L (1932) Lehrbuch des bürgerlichen Rechts: Recht der Schuldverhältnisse, 12. Bearbeitung (völlige Neubearbeitung) von Heinrich Lehmann, vol 2. Elwert'sche Verlagsbuchhandlung, Marburg
Esmein P (1964) Le nez de Cléopâtre ou les affres de la causalité. Recue Dalloz:205–216
Esmer J, Schmidt E (1993) Schuldrecht: Allgemeiner Teil, 7ªedn, vol 1, t. 2. C. F. Müller Juristischer Verlag, Heidelberg
Facchini Neto E (2016) A relativização do nexo de causalidade e a responsabilização da indústria do fumo - a aceitação da lógica da probabilidade. Civilistica.com 5(1):1–41
Fachin LE (2015) Direito Civil: sentidos, transformações e fim. Renovar, Rio de Janeiro
Facio JP (1981) Responsabilidad extracontractual, 3ª edn. Editorial Temis Librería, Bogotá
Fairgrieve D, G'sell-Macrez F (2011) Causation in French Law: Pragmatism and Policy. In: Goldberg R (ed) Perspectives on causation. Hart Publishing, Oxford; Portland
Ferreira da Silva JC (2007) Inadimplemento das obrigações. Ed. RT, São Paulo
Fikentscher W, Heinemann A (2006) Schuldrecht, 10ª edn. Walter de Gruyter Recht, Berlin
Florian E (1934) Parte generale del diritto penale, 4ª ed. F Vallardi, Milano
Foignet R (1946) Manuel Elémentaire de Droit Civil, 19ª edn, t. 1. Librairie Arthur Rousseau, Paris
Forst SP (2000) Grenzen deliktischer Haftung bei psychisch vermittelter haftungsbegründender Kausalität. VVF, München
Frada MAC (2010) Direto civil, responsabilidade civil: o método do caso. Almedina, Coimbra
Franzoni M (2010) Trattato della responsabilità civile: l'illecito, 2ª edn, t. 1 edn. Giuffrè, Milano
Fromageot H (1891) De la faute comme source de la responsabilité en droit privé. Librairie Nouvelle de Droit et de Jurisprudence, Paris
Frota PMC (2014) Responsabilidade por danos: imputação e nexo de causalidade. Juruá, Curitiba
Fuchs M, Pauker W, Baumgärtner A (2017) Delikts- und Schadensersatz, 9ª edn. Springer, Berlin; Heidelberg
Gama GCN, Viola R (2021) Perspectivas sobre o nexo de causalidade: passado, presente e futuro. Revista de Direito Civil Contemporâneo 29(8):207–240
Garcia B (2008) Instituições de Direito Penal, 7ª edn, vols 1, t. 1. (coord. Maíra Rocha Machado e Denise Garcia). Saraiva, São Paulo
García-Ripoll Montijano M (2008) Imputación objetiva, causa próxima, y alcance de los daños indemnizables. Editorial Comares, Granada
Giorgi G (1926) Teoria delle obbligazioni nel diritto moderno italiano, 7ª edn. Casa Editrice Libraria "Fratelli Cammelli", Firenze
Giustina VD (1991) Responsabilidade civil dos grupos: inclusive no Código do Consumidor. Aide, Rio de Janeiro

Glaser J (1858) Abhandlungen aus dem österreichischen Strafrechte. Tendler & Comp, Wien

Goeckenjan I (2017) Revision der Lehre von der objektiven Zurechnung: eine Analyse zurechnungsausschließender Topoi beim vorsätzlichen Erfolgsdelikt. Mohr Siebeck, Tübingen

Goldenberg IH (1998) Causalidad. In: Alterini AA, Cabana RM (orgs) Enciclopedia de la responsabilidad civil. Abeledo-Perrot, Buenos Aires

Gomes O (2002) Obrigações, 15ª edn. (rev. e atual. por Humberto Theodor Júnior). Forense, Rio de Janeiro

Gottwald P (1979) Schadenszurechnung und Schadensschätzung. C. H. Beck'sche Verlags Buchhandlung, München

Gotzler M (1977) Rechtsmäßiges Alternativverhalten im haftungsbegründenden Zurechnungszusammenhang. Beck, München

Grispigni F (1950) Diritto penale italiano: la struttura della fattispecie legale oggettiva, 2ª edn, vol 2 edn. Giuffrè, Milano

Grüneberg C (2020) Vorb v § 249. In: Palandt O et al (eds) Palandt: bürgerliches Gesetzbuch, 79ª edn. C.H. Beck, München

Gschnitzer F (1963) Schuldrecht: besonderer Teil und Schadenersatz. Springer-Verlag, Wien

Guedes GSC (2005) O problema do nexo causal na responsabilidade civil. Renovar, Rio de Janeiro

Guedes GSC (2011) Lucros cessantes: do bom-senso ao postulado normativo da razoabilidade. Ed. RT, São Paulo.

Haelschner HPE (1881) Das gemeine deutsche Strafrecht: Die allgemeinen strafrechtlichen Lehren, vol 1. Verlag von Adolph Marcus, Bonn

Hedemann JW (1933) Die Flucht in die Generalklauseln: eine Gefahr für Recht und Staat. Mohr Siebeck, Tübingen

Hedemann JW (1949) Lehrbücher und Grundrisse der Rechtswissenschaft: Schuldrecht des Bürgerlichen Gesetzbuches, vol 2. Walter de Gruyter, Berlin.

Hart HLA, Honoré T (1985) Causation in the law, 2ª edn. Oxford University Press, Oxford

Hippel von R (1932) Lehrbuch des Strafrechts. Verlag von Julius Springer, Berlin

Hironaka GMFN (2005) Responsabilidade pressuposta. Del Rey, Belo Horizonte

Honoré AM (1983) Causation and remoteness of damage. In: Tunc A (ed) International encyclopedia of comparative law: torts, vol 11. J. C. B. Mohr Siebeck, Tübingen

Huber U (1969) Normzwecktheorie und Adäquanztheorie: Zugleich eine Besprechung des Urteils des BGH v. 7.6.1968. Juristenzeitung 24(21):677–683

Huerta Ferrer A (1948) La relación de causalidad em la Teoría del Delito. Gráficas Gonzales, Madrid

Infantino M (2012) La causalità nella responsabilità extracontrattuale: studio di diritto comparato. Stämpfli Editore, Berna

Infantino M (2017) Causation theories and causation rules. In: Bussani M, Sebok AJ (eds) Comparative tort law: global perspectives. Edgar Elgar Publishing, Northampton

Infantino M (2019) Unravelling Causation in European Tort Law. Rabels Zeitschrift für ausländisches und internationales Privatrecht 83:647–673

Infantino M, Zervogianni E (2017) The European ways to causation. In: Infantino M, Zervogianni E (eds) Causation in European tort law. Cambridge University Press, New York

Jakobs G (1983) Strafrecht, Allgemeiner Teil: die Grundlagen und die Zurechnungslehre Lehrbuch. Walter de Gruyter, Berlin; New York

Jansen N et al (2007) "Haftungsbegründende und Haftungsausfüllend Kausalität". In: Winiger B (ed) (orgs) Digest of European tort law: essential cases on natural causation. Springer, Wien; New York

Jauernig O (1994) Bürgerliches Gesetzbuch: mit Gesetz zur Regelung des Rechts der Allgemeinen Geschäftsbedingungen. Beck, München

Jiménez de Asúa L (1951) Tratado de Derecho Penal: el delicto, t. 3. Editorial Losada, Buenos Aires

Jorge FSP (1999) Ensaio sobre os pressupostos da responsabilidade civil. Almedina, Coimbra

Josserand L (1933) Cours de Droit civil positif français: théorie générale des obligations les principaux contrats du droit civil les suretés, 2ª edn, t. 2. Recueil Sirey, Paris

Josserand L (1941) Evolução da responsabilidade civil. (Trad. Raul Lima). Revista Forense 86 (454):52–63

Junqueira de Azevedo A (1997) Estacionamento gratuito como caso de "relação contratual de fato". Admissão da prova de não culpa. Estupro tentado fora do estacionamento, seguido de morte. Falta da relação de causalidade adequada. Revista dos Tribunais 735:121–128

Kaczmarek L (2012) La responsabilité pour fait normal: étude critique sur son originalité en matière civile extracontractuelle. Publibook, Paris

Karollus M (1992) Funktion und Dogmatik der Haftung aus Schutzgesetzverletzung: zugleich ein Beitrag zum Deliktssystem des ABGB und zur Haftung für casus mixtus. Springer, Wien; New York

Keuk B (1972) Vermögensschaden und Interesse. Ludwig Röhrscheid Verlag, Bonn

Kihara H (2015) Tort law in Japan. Wolters Kluwer, The Netherlands

Kleinschmidt J (2012). Causation. In: Basedow J et al (eds) The Max Planck encyclopedia of European private law, vol 1. Oxford University Press, Oxford

Knoche W (1959) Die Entwicklung der Lehre vom Kausalzusammenhang im Zivil- und Strafrecht. Inaugural-Dissertation zur Erlangung der juristischen Doktorwürde der Rechts- und Staatswissenschaftlichen Fakultät der Philipps-Universität zu Marburg. Druck von Gg. Nolte, Marburg

Koch BA (2016) Proportional liability for causal uncertainty: How it works on the basis of a 200-year-old code. In: Papayannis DM, Martín-Casals M (eds) Uncertain causation in tort law. Cambridge University Press, Cambridge

Köstlin CR (1845) Neue Revision der Grundbegriffe der Criminalrechts, vol 2. Verlag der H. Laupp'schen Buchhandlung, Tübingen

Kötz H, Wagner G (2006) Deliktsrecht, 10ª edn. Wolters Kluers, München

Koziol H (2000) Austria: causation under Austrian Law. In: Koziol H et al (eds) (orgs) Unification of tort law: causation. Kluwer Law International, The Hague

Koziol H (2012) Basic questions of tort law from a Germanic perspective. (Trad. Fiona Salter Townshend). Jan Sramek Verlag, Wien

Kramer EA (1976) Schutzgesetze und adäquate Kausalität. JuristenZeitung 31(11/12):338–346

Kries von J (1888) Über den Begriff der objectiven Möglichkeit und einige Anwendungen desselben. Vierteljahrsschrift für wissenschaftliche Philosophie 12:179–240, 287–323e393–428

Kupisch B, Krüger W (1983) Deliktsrecht. C.H.Beck'sche Verlagsbuchhandlung, München

Lacroix M (2013) La relativité aquilienne en droit de la responsabilité civile - analyse comparée des systèmes germanique, canadien et québécois. McGill Law Journal - Revue de droit de McGill 59(2):425–474

Lange H (1955) Schadensersatz und Privatstrafe in der mittelalterlichen Rechtstheorie. Böhlau, Münster

Lange H (1958) Herrschaft und Verfall der Lehre vom adäquaten Kausalzusammenhang. Archiv für die civilistische Praxis 156:114–136

Lange H. (1960). Gutachten für den Verhandlungen des dreiundvierzigsten deutschen Juristentages deutschen Juristentag. In: Ständigen Deputation des deutschen Juristentages. Verhandlungen des dreiundvierzigsten Deutschen Juristentages. vol 1 J.C.B.Mohr (Paul Siebeck), Tübingen

Lange H (1976) Adäquanztheorie, Rechtswidrigkeitszusammenhang, Schutzzwecklehre und selbständige Zurechnungsmomente. JuristenZeitung 31(7):198–207

Lange H, Schiemann G (2003) Schadensersatz, 3ª edn. Mohr Siebeck, Tübingen

Larenz K (1927) Hegels Zurechnungslehre und der Begriff der objektiven Zurechnung: ein Beitrag zur Rechtsphilosophie des kritischen Idealismus und zur Lehre von der "juristischen Kausalität. In: Inaugural-Dissertation zur Erlangung der Doktorwürde der Hohen Rechts- und Staatswissenschaftlichen Fakultät der Georg August-Universität zu Göttingen. Druck von Reinhold Berger, Lucka

Larenz K (1955) Tatzurechnung und "Unterbrechung des Kausalzusammenhanges". Neue Juristische Wochenschrift 8(28):1009–1013
Larenz K (1959) Möglichkeiten einer Begrenzung der Haftung über Kausalität, Rechtswidrigkeit, Verschulden. Karlsruher Forum 1959: Haftung und Verschulden. Versicherungsrecht:10–15
Larenz K (1965) Die Prinzipien der Schadenszurechnung: ihr Zusammenspiel im modernen Schuldrecht. Juristische Schulung 5(10):373–379
Larenz K (1970) Zum heutigen Stand der Lehre von der objektiven Zurechnung im Schadensersatzrecht. In: Festschrift für Richard M. Honig: zum 80. Geburtstag. Verlag Otto Schwartz & Co, Göttingen
Larenz K (1987) Lehrbuch des Schuldrechts: Allgemeiner Teil, 14ª edn, vol 1. C. H. Beck'sche Verlagsbuchhandlung, München
Larenz K (1989) Allgemeiner Teil des deutschen bürgerlichen Rechts, 7ª edn. C.H.Beck'sche Verlagsbuchhandlung, München
Lawson FH, Markesinis BS (1982) Tortious liability for unintentional harm in the common law and the civil law, vol 1. Cambridge University Press, New York
Le TP (1976) La responsabilité civile, 2ª edn. Dalloz, Paris
Leitão AM (2009) Normas de proteção de danos puramente patrimoniais. Almedina, Coimbra
Lemos PFI (2012) Meio ambiente e responsabilidade civil do proprietário: análise do nexo casual, 2ª edn. Ed. São Paulo
Liepmann M (1900) Einleitung in das Strafrecht: eine Kritik der kriminalistischen Grundbegriff. Dogma Verlags, Bremen
Lima A (1963) Culpa e risco. Ed. RT, São Paulo
Limongi França R (1976) Manual de Direito Civil: doutrina geral dos direitos obrigacionais, 2ª edn. RT, São Paulo
Limpens J (1965) La théorie de la "relativité aquilienne" en droit comparé. In: Mélanges offerts à René Savatier. Dalloz, Paris
Lindenmaier (1950) Adäquate Ursache und nächste Ursache. Zeitschrift für das Gesamte Handelsrecht und Konkursrecht 113:205–280
Liszt von F (1899) Tratado de Direito Penal Allemão. (Trad. José Hygino Duarte Pereira). F. Briguiet, Rio de Janeiro
Liszt von F (1927) Lehrbuch des Deutschen Strafrechts, 25ª edn. (rev. e atual. por Eberhard Schmidt). Walter de Gruyter, Berlin; Leipzig
Looschelders D (2019) Die Mitverantwortlichkeit des Geschädigten im Privatrecht. Mohr Siebeck, Tübingen
Lopez TA (2008) Nexo causal e produtos potencialmente nocivos: a experiência brasileira do tabaco. Quartier Latin, São Paulo
Lorenz W (1964) Zivil- und Zivilprozeβrecht. JuristenZeitung 19(5/6):178–183
Luden H (1840) Abhandlungen aus dem gemeinen teutschen Strafrechte, vol 2. Vandenhoeck u. Ruprecht, Göttingen
Lüer HJ (1969) Die Begrenzung der Haftung bei fahrlässig begangen unerlaubten Handlungen: eine rechtvergleichende Studie zum deutschen, englischen und amerikanischen Zivilrecht. Verlag C. F. Müller, Karlsruhe
MacCormack G (1982) Juristic interpretation of the lex aquilia. In: Sanfilippo C (ed) (org) Studi in onore di Cesare Sanfilippo. Giuffré, Milano
Magadan GFM (2019) Responsabilidade civil extracontratual: causalidade jurídica: seleção das consequências do dano. Editora dos Editores, São Paulo
Magnus U (2000) Causation in German tort law. In: Koziol H et al (eds) (orgs) Unification of tort law: causation. Kluwer Law International, The Hague
Malaurie P, Aynès L (2016) Droit des obligations. LGDJ, Paris
Markesinis BS, Unberath H (2002) The German law of torts: a comparative treatise, 4ª edn. Hart Publishing, Oxford; Portland
Markesinis BS, Unberath H, Janssen A (2019) Markesinis's German law of torts: a comparative treatise, 5ª edn. Hart Publishing, Chicago

Martins-Costa J (2003) Ação indenizatória. Dever de informar do fabricante sobre os riscos do tabagismo. Revista dos Tribunais 812:75–99

Martins-Costa J (2007) Os avatares do abuso do direito e o rumo indicado pela boa-fé. In: Delgado ML, Alves JF (eds) (coords) Novo Código Civil—Questões controvertidas: Parte Geral do Código Civil. Método, São Paulo

Martins-Costa J (2009) Comentários ao novo Código civil: do inadimplemento das obrigações, 2ª edn, vol 5, t. 2. Forense, Rio de Janeiro

Marty GM (1939) La relation de cause a effet comme condition de la responsabilité civile: etude comparative des conceptions allemande, anglaise et française. Revue Trimestrielle de Droit Civil 38:685–712

Mazeaud H, Mazeaud L (1931) Traité théorique et pratique de la responsabilité civile délictuelle et contractuelle, t. 2. Librairie du Recueil Sirey, Paris

Medicus D (1962) Id quod interest: Studien zum römischen Recht des Schadensersatzes. Böhlau, Köln

Mello MB (2007) Teoria do fato jurídico: plano da existência, 13ª edn. Saraiva, São Paulo

Mendes PS (1986) Raciocínios hipotéticos e processos causais virtuais em direito penal. Dissertação (Mestrado)—Faculdade de Direito, Universidade de Lisboa

Menezes Cordeiro A (2004) Da modernização do Direito Civil: aspectos gerais, vol 1. Almedina, Coimbra

Menezes Cordeiro A (2017) Tratado de Direito Civil: direito das obrigações: gestão de negócios, enriquecimento sem causa, responsabilidade civil, vol 8. Almedina, Coimbra

Menezes Leitão LMT (2005) A responsabilidade do gestor perante o dono do negócio no Direito Civil português. Almedina, Coimbra

Menezes Leitão LMT (2020) Direito das obrigações: introdução da constituição das obrigações, 15ª edn, vol 1. Almedina, Coimbra

Michalski L (1996) Haftungsbeschränkung durch den Schutzzweck der Norm. Juristische Ausbildung 18:393–396

Miragem B (2021) Responsabilidade civil, 2ª edn. Forense, Rio de Janeiro

Mitidiero D (2013) Antecipação de tutela. Ed. RT, São Paulo

Mommsen F (1855) Beiträge zum Obligationenrecht, Zweite Abtheilung - zur Lehre von dem Interesse. Braunschweig

Moore MS (2009) Causation and responsibility: an essay in law, morals and metaphysics. Oxford University Press, New York

Moraes RDFD (2017) A causalidade alternativa e a responsabilidade civil dos múltiplos ofensores. LiberArs, São Paulo

Morsello MF (2006) A responsabilidade civil e a socialização dos riscos: o sistema neozelandês e a experiência escandinava. Revista da Escola Paulista da Magistratura 7(2):13–22

Morsello MF (2007) O nexo causal e suas distintas teorias: apreciações críticas. Revista do Instituto dos Advogados de São Paulo 19:211–218

Mosca T (1896) Nuovi studi e nuove dottrine sulla colpa nel diritto civile, penale ed amministrativo. G. Bertero, Roma

Mota Pinto P (2008) Interesse contratual negativo e interesse contratual positivo, vol 2. Coimbra Editora, Coimbra

Mota Pinto P (2018) Direito civil: estudos. Gestlegal, Coimbra

Motulsky H (1960) Die Zurechenbarkeit des Kausalzusammenhanges im französischen Schadenersatzrecht. Rabels Zeitschrift für ausländisches und internationales Privatrecht 25:242–260

Mulholland CS (2009) A responsabilidade civil por presunção de causalidade. GZ, Rio de Janeiro

Müller ML (1912) Die Bedeutung des Kausalzusammenhangs im Straf- uns Schadensersatzrecht. Verlag von J. C. B. Mohr (Paul Siebeck), Tübingen

Münzberg W (1966) Verhalten und Erfolg als Grundlagen der Rechtswidrigkeit und Haftung. Vittorio Klostermann, Frankfurt

Nanni GE (2018) Art. 403. In: Nanni GE (ed) (coord) Comentários ao Código Civil: direito privado contemporâneo. Saraiva Educação, São Paulo

Nanni GE (2021) Inadimplemento absoluto e resolução contratual: requisitos e efeitos. Thomson Reuters Brasil, São Paulo

Niebaum G (1977) Die deliktische Haftung für fremde Willensbestätigung. Duncker & Humblot, Berlin

Noronha F (1998) Desenvolvimentos contemporâneos da responsabilidade civil. Revista Sequência 19(37):21–37

Noronha F (2003) O nexo de causalidade na responsabilidade civil. Revista dos Tribunais 92 (816):733–752

Noronha F (2013) Direito das obrigações, 4ª edn. Saraiva, São Paulo

Nörr D et al (1978) Kausalitätsprobleme im klassischen römischen Recht: ein theoretischer Versuch Labeos. In: Behrends O et al (eds) Festschrift für Franz Wieacker zum 70. Geburstag. Vandenhoeck und Ruprecht, Göttingen

Novaes DR (2017) Nexo causal como realidade normativa e presunção de causalidade na responsabilidade civil. Lumen Juris, Rio de Janeiro

Oftinger K, Stark EW (1995) Schweizerisches Haftpflichtrecht: Allgemeiner Teil. 5ª edn. (rev. e atual. por Emil W. Stark), vol 1. Schulthess Polygraphischer Verlag, Zürich

Oliveira AP (2007) Causalidade e imputação na responsabilidade civil ambiental. Almedina, Coimbra

Oliveira NMP (2009) Estudos sobre o não cumprimento das obrigações, 2ª edn. Almedina, Coimbra

Ommmeslaghe P Van (2013) De Page: Traité de droit civil belge: Les obligations. Bruylant, E-book, Bruxelles

Ordeig EG (2007) Delitos cualificados por el resultado y causalidad, 2ª edn. B de F, Buenos Aires

Orgaz A (1952) El daño resarcible. Editorial Bibliografica Argentina, Buenos Aires

Ortmann R (1876) Von dem Begriffe der Verursachung in Lehre und Rechtsprechung: das Zusammentreffen einer Handlung mit einem Maturereignis zur Herbeiführung eines verletzenden Erfolges. Goltdammer's Archiv für Strafrecht 24:93–103

Pantaleón Prieto AF (1990) Causalidad e imputación objetiva: criterios de imputácion. In: Centenario del Código Civil (1889–1989). Editorial Centro de Estudios Ramon Areces, Madrid

Pasqualoto A (2016) Causalidade e imputação na responsabilidade civil objetiva: uma reflexão sobre os assaltos em estacionamentos. Revista de Direito Civil Contemporâneo 7:185–206

Paula MS (2018) A questão do nexo causal probabilístico no direito brasileiro. In: Souza EN, Silva RG (eds) Controvérsias atuais em responsabilidade civil: estudos de direito civil-constitucional. Almedina, São Paulo

Peña López F (2011) Dogma y realidad del derecho de daños: imputación objetiva, causalidad y culpa en el sistema español en los PETL. Editorial Aranzadi, Navarra

Pereira CM (1991) Responsabilidade civil, 2ª edn. Forense, Rio de Janeiro

Pereira ML (2022) Direito da responsabilidade civil: A obrigação de indemnizar. Imprensa FDUL, Lisboa

Pereira RS (2019) O nexo de causalidade na responsabilidade delitual: fundamentos e limites do juízo de condicionalidade. Almedina, Coimbra

Peteffi da Silva RP (2009) Responsabilidade civil pela perda de uma chance, 2ª edn. Atlas, São Paulo

Philippe DM (1994) La théorie de la relativité aquilienne. In: Mélanges R.O. Dalcq: responsabilité et assurances. Larcier, Bruxelles

Pires CM (2021) Direito das obrigações em tempos de calamidade: reflexões durante um ano de pandemia. Almedina, Coimbra

Pirson R (1964) Droit belge de la responsabilité civile, 6ª edn. Librairie Dalloz, Paris

Pirson R, De Ville A (1935) Traité de la responsabilité civile extra-contractuelle, t 2. E. Bruylant, Bruxelles

Planiol M, Ripert G (1909) Traité élémentaire de droit civil, 5ª edn, t. 2. Librairie Générale de Droit & Jurisprudence, Paris
Planiol M, Ripert G (1930) Traité pratique de droit civil français: obligations, t. 6. Librairie Générale de Droit & Jurisprudence, Paris
Podestá FH (2018) Direito das obrigações: teoria geral e responsabilidade civil, 7ª edn. Almedina, Coimbra
Polacco V (1915) Le obbligazioni nel diritto civile italiano, 2ª edn. Athenaeum, Roma
Pontes de Miranda FC (1981) Fontes e evolução do direito civil brasileiro, 2nd edn. Forense, Rio de Janeiro
Pontes de Miranda Fc (1984) Tratado de direito privado, 3ª edn, 2ª reimp, t. 22 edn. RT, São Paulo
Pothier RJ (1764) Traité des obligations: selon les règles tant du for de la conscience, que du for extérieur, 2ª edn, t. 1. J. Rouzeaud-Montaut, Paris
Prosser W, Keeton W (1984) On Torts, 5ª edn. West Publishing Company, St. Paul
Puppe I (2017) Die psychische Kausalität und das Recht auf die eigene Entscheidung. Juristische Rundschau 10:513–522
Puppe I (2019) A imputação objetiva do resultado a uma ação contrária ao dever de cuidado. (Trad. Beatriz Corrêa Camargo). Revista Brasileira de Ciências Criminais 155(27):103–123
Queiroz P (2020) Direito Penal: Parte Geral, 14ª edn, vol 1. JusPodivm, Salvador
Quézel-Ambrunaz C (2010) Définition de la causalité en droit français: la causalité dans le droit de la responsabilité civile européenne. La causalité dans le droit de la responsabilité civile européenne, Groupe de recherche européen sur la responsabilité civile et l'assurance (GRERCA), Mar 2010, Genève, Suisse, pp. 341–368
Rabel E (1936) Das Recht des Warenkaufs: eine vergleichende Darstellung, vol 1. Walter de Gruyter, Berlin
Radbruch G (1902) Die Lehre von der adäquaten Verursachung. Inaugural-Dissertation zur Erlangung der Doktorwürde der hohen Juristischen Fakultät der Königlichen Friedrich-Wilhelms-Universität. Druck von Georg Reimer, Berlin
Raiser T (1963) Adäquanztheorie und Haftung nach dem Schutzzweck der verletzten Norm. JuristenZeitung 18(15):462–466
Rajneri E (2017) An Epidemic in town. In: Infantino M, Zervogianni E (eds) Causation in European tort law. Cambridge University Press, New York
Reinhold J (2009) Unrechtszurechnung und der Abbruch rettender Verläufe. Mohr Siebeck, Tübingen
Reinig GHL (2015) O problema da causalidade na responsabilidade civil: a teoria do escopo da proteção da norma (Schutzzwecktheorie) e sua aplicabilidade no Direito Civil brasileiro. Tese (Doutorado) -Faculdade de Direito, Universidade de São Paulo
Reinig GHL (2017) A teoria do dano direto e imediato no Direito Civil brasileiro: análise crítica da doutrina e comentários à jurisprudência do STF sobre a responsabilidade civil do Estado por crime praticado por fugitivo. Revista de Direito Civil Contemporâneo 12:109–163
Reinig GHL (2018) O escopo de proteção da norma como critério limitativo da responsabilidade civil por ato ilícito: algumas contribuições ao Direito Civil brasileiro a partir do Direito Civil alemão. Revista de Direito Civil Contemporâneo 14:237–309
Reinig GHL (2019) A teoria da causalidade adequada no Direito Civil alemão. Revista de Direito Civil Contemporâneo 18(6):215–248
Renzikowski J (2011) Ist psychische Kausalität dem Begriff nach möglich?. In: Paeffgen HU et al (eds) (orgs) Festschrift für Ingeborg Puppe zum 70. Geburtstag. Duncker & Humblot, Berlin
Richter S (2012) Schadenszurechnung bei deliktischer Haftung für fehlerhafte Sekundärmarktinformation. Mohr Siebeck, Tübingen
Ripert G (1935) La règle morale dans les obligations civiles, 3ª edn. Librairie Genérale de Droit & de Jurisprudence, Paris
Ristow T (2003) Die psychische Kausalität im Deliktsrecht. Peter Lang, Frankfurt am Main
Rodière R (1952) La responsabilité civile. Rousseau, Paris

Rodrigues Jr OL (2006) Causalidade, imputação objetiva e novos paradigmas da dogmática penal. Revista dos Tribunais 95(849):435–444
Rodrigues Jr OL (2016) Nexo causal probabilístico: elementos para a crítica de um conceito. Revista de Direito Civil Contemporâneo 8(3):115–137
Rodrigues Jr OL (2019) Direito civil contemporâneo: estatuto epistemológico, Constituição e direitos fundamentais. Forense Universitária, Rio de Janeiro
Rogers WVH et al (2000) England: causation under English Law. In: Koziol H et al (eds) Unification of tort law: causation. Kluwer Law International, The Hague
Rönnau T, Faust F, Fehling M (2004) Durchblick: Kausalität um objektive Zurechnung. Juristische Schulung:113–118
Roppo V (2016) Diritto privato, 5ª edn. G. Giappichelli Editore, Torino
Rosenvald N, Braga Netto F (2020) Código civil comentado. JusPodivm, Salvador
Roussos K (1992) Schaden und Folgenschaden: die systematischen und die Wertungsgrundlagen der Schadenszurechnung. Heymanns, Köln; Berlin; Bonn; München
Roxin C (2002) Funcionalismo e imputação objetiva no direito penal, 3ª edn. (Trad. Luís Greco). Renovar, Rio de Janeiro
Roxin C (2011) Probleme psychisch vermittelter Kausalität. In: Hellmann U, Schröder C (eds) (orgs) Festschrift für Hans Achenbach. C.F. Müller, Heidelberg
Rümelin M (1896) Der Zufall im Recht. Akademische Verlagsbuchhandlung von J. C. B. Mohr, Freiburg i. B. und Leizpig
Rümelin M (1900) Die Verwendung der Causalbegriffe in Straf- und Civilrecht. Archiv für die civilistische Praxis 90:171–344
Rumpf M (1905) Zum jetzigen Stand der Lehre von der adäquaten Verursachung im Zivil Recht. Jherings Jahrbücher für die Dogmatik des bürgerlichen Rechts 49:333–406
Samson E (1972) Hypothetische Kausaulverläufe im Strafrecht: zugleich ein Beitrag zur Kausalität der Beihilfe. Alfred Metzner Verlag, Frankfurt am Main
Sanseverino PTV (2010) Princípio da reparação integral: indenização no Código Civil. Saraiva, São Paulo
Santolim C (2014) Nexo de causalidade e prevenção na responsabilidade civil. Revista da AJURIS 41(136):79–100
Santos MR (2018) Responsabilidade civil dos grupos: responsabilidade civil por dano de autoria anônima e responsabilidade civil por dano de autoria coletiva. Tese (Doutorado) -Faculdade de Direito, Universidade de São Paulo
Savatier R (1951) Traité de la responsabilité civile en droit français, 2ª edn, t. 2. Librairie Générale de Droit et de Jurisprudence, Paris
Scavone Jr LA et al (2006) Art. 404. In: Scavone Jr LA et al (eds) (coords) Comentários ao Código civil. Ed. RT, São Paulo
Schack H (1986) Der Schutzzweck als Mittel der Haftungsbegrenzung im Vertragsrecht. JuristenZeitung 41(7):305–314
Schickedanz E (1971) Schutzzwecklehre und Adäquanztheorie. Neue Juristische Wochenschrift 21:916–920
Schiemann G (2017) § 249. In: J. von Staudingers Kommentar zum Bürgerlichen Gesetzbuch mit Einführungsgesetz und Nebengesetzen: §§ 249–254 (Schadensersatzrecht). Walter de Gruyter, Berlin
Schilcher B (1977) Theorie der sozialen Schadensverteilung. Duncker & Humblot, Berlin
Schmidt E (1970) Kompensation der Pflichtwidrigkeit durch nachfolgendes pflichtgemäßes Verhalten?. Versicherungsrecht 17(A)
Schmidt JP (2011) Responsabilidade civil no direito alemão e método funcional no direito comparado. In: Rodrigues Jr OL, Mamede G, Vital da Rocha M (eds) Responsabilidade civil contemporânea: em homenagem a Sílvio de Salvo Venosa (coord.), Atlas, São Paulo
Schmiedel B (1974) Deliktsobligationen nach deutschem Kartellrecht, vol 1. J. C.B. Mohr (Paul Siebeck), Tübingen

Schreiber A (2013) Novos paradigmas da responsabilidade civil: da erosão dos filtros da reparação à diluição dos danos, 5ª edn. Atlas, São Paulo

Schulin B (1976) Der natürliche, vorrechtliche, Kausalitätsbegriff im zivilen Schadensersatzrecht. J. Schweitzer Verlag, Berlin

Schum DA (2001) The evidential foundations of probabilistic reasoning. Northwestern University Press, Evanston

Schünemann WB (1979) Unzulänglichkeit der Adäquanztheorie? - AG und LG Regensburg. JuristenZeitung:19–24

Schwartz VE, Kelly K, Partlett DF (2010) Prosser, Wade and Schwartz's torts: cases and materials, 12ª edn. Foundation Press, New York

Scialoja V (1899) Dizionario pratico del Diritto privato. Dottor Francesco Vallardi, Milano

Scognamiglio R (2010) Responsabilità civile e danno. G. Giappichelli Editore, Torino

Sella M (2007) La responsabilità civile nei nuovi orientamenti giurisprudenziali. Giuffrè, Milano

Serra APS (1959) Obrigação de indemnização (Colocação. Fontes. Conceito e espécies de dano. Nexo causal. Extensão do dever de indemnizar. Espécies de indenização). Direito de abstenção e de remoção. Boletim do Ministério da Justiça 84:5–301

Silva MG (2020) O dever de prestar e o dever de indenizar. Imprensa FDUL, Lisboa

Silva WM (1962) Responsabilidade sem culpa e socialização do risco. Bernardo Álvares, Belo Horizonte

Simão JF (2008) Responsabilidade civil do incapaz. Atlas, São Paulo

Simão JF (2021) Art. 403. In: Schreiber A et al (eds) Código Civil Comentado: doutrina e jurisprudência, 3ª edn. Forense, Rio de Janeiro

Simão JF, Dantas Bisneto C (2020) Responsabilidade civil nos casos de transmissão coletiva do coronavírus. Revista Eletrônica Conjur. Direito Civil atual, São Paulo, 6 abr 2020

Sinde Monteiro JF (1989) Responsabilidade por conselhos, recomendações ou informações. Almedina, Coimbra

Sinde Monteiro JF (2005) Rudimentos da responsabilidade civil. Revista da Faculdade de Direito da Universidade do, vol 2. Porto, Coimbra, 2:349–390

Sourlas P (1974) Adäquanztheorie und Normzwecklehre bei der Begründung der Haftung nach § 823 Abs. 1 BGB. Duncker & Humblot, Berlin

Souza EN (2018) Em defesa do nexo causal: culpa, imputação e causalidade na responsabilidade civil. In: Souza EN, Silva RG (eds) Controvérsias atuais em responsabilidade civil: estudos de direito civil-constitucional. Almedina, São Paulo

Souza WMA (2021) Causalidade e imputação na responsabilidade civil extracontratual. Tese (Doutorado) - Faculdade de Direito, Universidade de São Paulo

Spickhoff A (2005) §823. In: Soergel HT, Siebert W (eds) (orgs) Soergel: Kommentar zum Bürgerlichen Gesetzbuch: Schuldrecht 10: §823–853, 13ª edn, vol 12. W. Kohlhammer, Stuttgart

Spickhoff A (2008) Folgenzurechnung im Schadensersatzrecht: Gründe und Grenzen. In: Lorenz E (eds) (org) Karlsruher Forum 2007: Folgenzurechnung im Schadenersatzrecht. Verlag Versicherungswirtschaft, Karlsruhe

Spindler G (2008) Kausalität im Zivil- und Wirtschaftsrecht. Archiv für die civilistische Praxis 208:283–344

Stapleton J (2001) Legal cause: cause-in-fact and the scope of liability for consequences. Vanderbilt Law Review 54:941–1009

Stapleton J (2016) Uncertain causes: Asbestos in UK courts. In: Papayannis DM, Martín-Casals M (eds) Uncertain causation in tort law. Cambridge University Press, Cambridge

Steel S (2015) Proof of causation in tort law. Cambridge University Press, Cambridge

Steiner RC (2018) Reparação de danos: interesse positivo e interesse negativo. Quartier Latin, São Paulo

Stoll H (1968) Kausalzusammenhang und Normzweck im Deliktsrecht. J.C.B. Mohr (Paul Siebeck), Tübingen

Stoll H (1976) Neuere Entwicklungen auf dem Gebiete des deutschen Schadensrechtes. Juridiska Föreningen, Lund

Stoll H (1993) Haftungsfolgen im bürgerlichen Recht: eine Darstellung auf rechtsvergleichender Grundlage. C.F. Müller Juristischer Verlag, Heidelberg
Tarnowski H (1927) The systematic significance of the adequate causation theory for the structure of the concept of crime. Walter de Gruyter, Berlin
Tavares J (2019) Teoria do injusto penal, 4th edn. Tirant lo Blanch, São Paulo
Taruffo M (2014) A prova. (Trad. João Gabriel Couto). Marcial Pons, São Paulo
Teichmann A (2014) Vor §§249–253. In: Stürner R, Jauernig O (ed) Bürgerliches Gesetzbuch Kommentar: mit allgemeinem Gleichbehandlungsgesetz, 15ª edn. C.H.Beck, München
Telles IG (2010) Direito das obrigações, 7ª edn. Coimbra Editora, Coimbra
Tepedino G (2002) Notas sobre o nexo de causalidade. Revista Jurídica 50(296):7–18
Tepedino G (2011) Nexo de causalidade: conceito, teorias e aplicação na jurisprudência brasileira. In: Rodrigues Jr OL, Mamede G, Vital da Rocha M (eds) Responsabilidade civil contemporânea: em homenagem a Sílvio de Salvo Venosa (coord.). Atlas, São Paulo
Thon A (1895) Von dem Begriffe der Verursachung in Lehre und Rechtsprechung. Blätter für Rechtspflege in Tübingen und Anhalt 42:20–43
Thyrén JCW (1894) Abhandlungen aus dem Strafrechte und der Rechtsphilosophie. Gleerupska Univ.-Bokhandeln, Lund
Traeger L (1929) Der Kausalbegriff im Straf- und Zivilrecht: Zugleich ein Beitrag zur Auslegung des BGB. N. G. Elwert'sche Verlagsbuchhandlung, Marburg
Trimachi P (2019) La responsabilità civile: atti illeciti, rischio, danno, 2ª edn. Giuffrè Francis Lefebvre, Milano
Tunc A (1953) Les récents développements des droits anglais et américain sur la relation de causalité entre la faute et le dommage dont on doit réparation. Revue internationale de droit comparé 5(1):5–54
Varela JMA (1977) Das obrigações em geral: conceito, estrutura e função da relação obrigacional, fontes das obrigações, modalidades das obrigações. Forense, Rio de Janeiro
Varela JMA (2000) Das obrigações em geral, 10ª edn. Almedina, Coimbra
Venturi TGP (2014) Responsabilidade civil preventiva: a proteção contra a violação dos direitos e a tutela inibitória material. Malheiros, São Paulo
Vicente DM (2017) Direito comparado: obrigações, vol 2. Almedina, Coimbra
Vilanova L (2015) Causalidade e relação no direito, 5ª edn. Noeses, São Paulo
Viney G (2008) Tort liability. In: Bermann GA, Picard E (eds) Introduction to French law. Kluwer Law International, The Netherlands
Viney G, Jourdain P, Carval S (2013) Les conditions de la responsabilité, 4ª edn. LGDJ, Paris
Viola R (2023) Risco e causalidade. Foco, Indaiatuba
Violante A (1999) Responsabilità oggettiva e causalità flessibile. ESI, Napoli
Visintini G (2005) Trattato breve della responsabilità civile: fatti illeciti, inadempimento, danno risarcibile, 3ª edn. Cedam, Padova
Wagner G (2003) Grundstrukturen des Europäischen Deliktsrechts. In: Zimmermann R (Hrsg) Grundstrukturen des Europäischen Deliktsrechts. Nomos Verlagsgesellschaft, Baden-Baden
Waldkirch C (2018) Zufall und Zurechnung im Haftungsrecht. Mohr Siebeck, Tübingen
Weitenberg M (2014) Der Begriff der Kausalität in der haftungsrechtlichen Rechtsprechung der Unionsgericht: Zugleich ein Beitrag zur Kohärenz der EU-Haftungssystem. Nomos, Baden-Baden
Weitnauer H (1969) Zur Lehre von adäquaten Kausalzusammenhang: Versuch einer Ehrenrettung. In: Keller M (ed) Revolution der Technik, Evolution des Rechts: Festgabe zum 60. Geburtstag von Karl Oftinger. Schulthess & Co. AG, Zürich
Werner A (1960) Zum Problem der Begrenzung der Haftung für schuldhaft verursachte Schäden. Juristische Rundschau 8:282–285
Wieacker F (2015) História do direito privado moderno, 5th edn. (Portuguese translation by A.M. Botelho Hespanha). Fundação Calouste Gulbenkian, Lisboa
Wieling HJ (1970) Interesse und Privatstrafe vom Mittelalter bis zum Bürgerlichen Gesetzbuch. Böhlau, Köln

Wilburg W (1941) Die Elemente des Schadensrechts. N. G. Elwert'sche Verlagsbuchhandlung, Marburg
Willvonseder R (1984) Die Verwendung der Denkfigur der "conditio sine qua non" bei den römischen Juristen. Böhlau, Wien
Windscheid B (1875) Lehrbuch des Pandektenrechts, 4 edn. Verlagsbuchhandlung von Julius Buddeus, Aufl. Düsseldorf
Wolf JG (1962) Der Normzweck im Deliktsrecht: ein Diskussionsbeitrag. Verlag Otto Schwartz & Co, Göttingen
Woyciechowski S (2017) Haftungen im französischen Deliktsrecht. Mohr Siebeck, Tübingen
Wright RW (1985) Causation in tort law. California Law Review 73:1735–1828
Xynapolou A (2013) Die Voraussehbarkeit als Voraussetzung des Schadensersatzes in der Vertragshaftung. Mohr Siebeck, Tübingen
Yágüez R de Ángel (2014) Causalidad en la responsabilidad extracontractual: sobre el arbitrio judicial, la imputación objetiva y otros extremos. Civitas, Pamplona
Yamamoto K (2019) Basic features of Japanese tort law. Jan Sramek Verlag, Wien
Yang L (2018) Tort liability law of China. (Trad. Zhu Wang e Chunhua Dong). Jan Sramek Verlag, Wien
Zanetti AC (2021) Reflexões sobre o dano indireto indenizável e sua expansão na responsabilidade civil extracontratual. In: Rosenvald N et al (eds) (coords) Da estrutura à função da responsabilidade civil: uma homenagem do IBERC ao Professor Renan Lotufo. Foco, Indaiatuba
Zimmermann R (1980) Herausforderungsformel und Haftung für fremde Willensbetätigung nach § 823 I BGB. JuristenZeitung 35(1):10–16
Zimmermann R (1996) The law of obligations: Roman foundations of the civilian tradition. Oxford University Press, Oxford
Zimmermann R (2001) Roman law, contemporary law, European law: the civilian tradition today. Oxford University Press, New York
Zimmermann R (2014) Limitation of liability for damages in European contract law. The Edinburgh Law Review 18:193–224
Zitelman E (1879) Irrtum und Rechtsgeschäft: eine psychologisch-juristische Untersuchung. Verlag von Duncker und Humblot, Leipzig

Part II
Psychological Causation: Case Studies and Legal Dogmatics

The first part demonstrated that the theories of causation typically adopted in Brazilian law are, by themselves, insufficient to address the complex issues involved in legal imputation within the framework of liability. As shown, liability may be determined through the integration of the theory of adequate causation with other normative imputation criteria, which diverge from traditional causal approaches commonly employed in Brazilian jurisprudence. This combined method becomes necessary given the limitations of applying universally accepted parameters across diverse categories of cases.

The *second part* aims to introduce the concept of "psychological causation" and to establish, based on Brazilian law, the criteria for legal imputation applicable in such contexts.

Building on this foundation, this section analyzes practical cases that address the difficulty of attributing liability to perpetrators who influence or facilitate harm through third-party conduct, despite not directly causing it. The second and final part of this work is organized into two chapters: (1) Psychological Causation and (2) The Application of Theoretical Models to Practical Cases.

Chapter 4
Psychological Causation

Psychological causation is a legal phenomenon characterized by the interference of a voluntary decision by a second causer in the causal chain initiated by a first perpetrator. This complex concept raises fundamental questions in private law, ranging from the very structure of causation to the establishment of objective imputation criteria. Although widely developed in German legal doctrine, the theme also applies to various legal systems and requires careful analysis of the foundations of liability. The different imputation criteria, such as self-responsibility, controllability, the "provocation formula," and the models of indirect and negligent causation, demand rigorous critical examination. The notion of general duties of care (*Verkehrspflichten*) and its relationship to the creation of legally relevant risk situations assumes particular importance. Traditional causal theories prove insufficient to resolve such complex cases, making it necessary to develop objective imputation criteria to ensure proper liability attribution.

4.1 Introduction

The distinctive feature of the so-called "psychological causation"[1] ("*psychische Kausalität*"), also referred to as "psychologically mediated causation"[2] ("*psychisch vermittelte Kausalität*"), "psychologically provoked harmful actions,"[3] and

[1] Although this is not only a matter of causation, but also of imputation, the established expressions will be used throughout this work.

[2] Forst refers to the phenomenon as "psychologically mediated causation establishing liability" ("*psychisch vermittelte haftungsbegründende Kausalität*") (Forst (2000), p. 1). Ahrens and Deutsch prefer to use the expression "psychologically mediated cause" ("*psychisch vermittelte Ursächlichkeit*") (Deutsch and Ahrens (2014), p. 22).

[3] Frada (2010), p. 101. Furthermore, in Portuguese law, Mafalda Miranda uses the term "psychological causation" (Barbosa (2020), p. 983).

C. Dantas Bisneto, *Psychological Causation in Tort Law*,
https://doi.org/10.1007/978-3-032-03825-8_4

"damages caused by psychological influence,"[4] is that the causal chain initiated by the primary perpetrator does not lead to the harmful event by means of purely physical processes characteristic of the natural sciences. Instead, at least one intermediate component of the causal chain is formed by a voluntary action or omission of a second person. The harmful result is only achieved through this second cause.[5] The intervention of a second individual is what makes this group of cases so particular, so the question arises as to who should be held liable for the damage.[6]

Some legal scholars[7] argue that the expression "psychological causation" ("*psychische Kausalität*"; "*causalità psichica*") is, in some aspects, imprecise and, in others, excessively generic.[8] The term "causal" is applied to a phenomenon that is unrepeatable, internal, and therefore not reducible to scientific criteria of definition. It must also be admitted that the psychological element is not present in all groups of cases. In certain instances, such as in rescue cases,[9] failure to take safety precautions,[10] and interference with preexisting safety measures,[11] the first perpetrator's behavior does not psychologically influence the wrongdoer but merely facilitates or enables their action.[12] However, given the established use of these expressions,[13] they are applied in the present study as synonyms.

Thus, despite its designation, "psychological causation" does not necessarily involve a psychological component. These cases are characterized and acquire theoretical and practical coherence because someone other than the initial perpetrator, whether the injured party or a third individual, engages in their own

[4] The expression "damage caused by psychological influence" is used in the compilation of cases brought in the work organized by Winiger, Koziol, Koch, and Zimmermann, entitled *Digest of European Tort Law: essential cases on natural causation*. See Winiger (2007), pp. 193–263).

[5] Hart and Honoré address these hypotheses within the context of "interpersonal transactions," focusing more on "*causes of events*" (Hart and Honoré (1985), p. 51).

[6] Ristow (2003), p. 11.

[7] Risicato (2007), p. 7; Cornacchia (2011), p. 187.

[8] Joachim Renzikowski argues that the term "psychological causation" cannot be considered, as it would be contradictory to assert that an event arises from a free action and, simultaneously, constitutes a necessary occurrence (Renzikowski (2011), pp. 201–216). This text was translated into Portuguese by Lucas Montenegro. See Renzikowski (2020). Koriath maintains that the problem of "psychological causation" does not exist. The author defends there are various themes that are connected with this expression (Koriath (1988), p. 196).

[9] See Sect. 5.2.1.1.

[10] See Sect. 5.2.2.1.

[11] See Sect. 5.2.2.2.

[12] Barbosa (2019), p. 20.

[13] The term "psychological causation" has already been used in the STJ, in the following terms: "The explanation for such a conclusion is the existence of a psychological causation between the harmful conduct of the defendants (broadcasting of news and the administrative inquiry) the damage to the plaintiff's health (stroke) that directly reflected on the plaintiff's assets (leave and salary reduction), this link being immediate" (STJ, Ag. in REsp 1,661,791/CE, rel. Antônio Carlos Ferreira, j. 28.05.2021).

voluntary act that causes harm.[14] The first actor, from whom compensation is claimed, does not directly cause the event, as the injury occurs only through the intervention of another individual,[15] whose behavior is either influenced or facilitated by the act of the first perpetrator.[16]

This matter raises several questions[17] and has attracted only limited attention in Brazilian legal literature.[18] From the recognition of the existence of a factual causal link between the act of the first perpetrator and the conduct of the second one, to the formulation of guiding principles aimed to resolving such cases, numerous challenges persit in attempts to elucidate the problem of psychologically mediated causal processes, for which no doctrinal consensus has emerged.[19]

It is important to note that "psychological causation" is not a matter confined to German law, although in that country the topic has received greater attention, leading to the development of various theories and in-depth analyses on the subject. Winiger[20] highlights that damages caused by psychological influence are widely recognized within the European tort law system. The author, after presenting a series of cases faced by European courts, concludes that, even in countries where no specific decisions on the issue have been identified, this particular form of causation has not been excluded by jurisprudence.[21]

---

[14] Barbosa (2020), p. 983.

[15] Niebaum (1976), p. 1673.

[16] Ristow (2003), p. 11.

[17] Winiger (2007), p. 252.

[18] The term "psychological causation" is addressed by Guilherme Reinig, emphasizing the necessity of an independent investigation (Reinig (2015), p. 185).

[19] Roxin asserts that the issues related to "psychologically mediated causation" have not yet found a consensual solution, neither in cases of commission acts, nor in hypotheses of omission. According to the author, although the transgressor's decision may be causally conditioned, its precise determination remains unclear. He also indicates that there are cases of "psychological causation" where the causal link is doubtful and controversial (Roxin (2011), p. 409). The vernacular version of the text can be found in Roxin (2013). Geigel notes that the physical or emotional consequences of a harmful event cannot always be attributed to clearly identifiable physical causes. Causation can thus be psychologically mediated in various ways (Geigel (2020), p. 10).

[20] In addition to addressing the theme in Roman law, the author analyzes the issues related to damages caused by psychological influence, in countries such as Austria, Switzerland, Greece, France, Belgium, Netherlands, Italy, Spain, Portugal, England, Scotland, Ireland, Denmark, Norway, Sweden, Finland, Estonia, Poland, Slovakia, Hungary, and Slovenia. In the end, he analyzes the cases in accordance with the Principles of European Tort Law (PETL) (Winiger (2007), pp. 193–264). In Serbian law, Mihajlo Cvetković highlights the importance of studying "psychological causation," in order to better explain the causal link between the influencer and the influenced (Cvetković (2021), p. 58).

[21] In Spain, Fernando Pantaleón cites the case decided by the Sala Segunda del Tribunal Supremo on January 27, 1984. The defendant, Don Manuel, due to his inexperience and lack of attention, drove his vehicle onto the pedestrian lane, hitting Don Santiago, who died instantly. Two other pedestrians, Don Pascual and Doña Victoria, managed to avoid the collision. The latter, terrified by the sight of Don Santiago's body on the ground, fled in panic to call his wife, who had just separated from the group. Doña Victoria was then run over by a car traveling in the opposite direction, with no fault on the part of the driver. The Supreme Court upheld the objective

In Portuguese-language doctrine, the topic was addressed by Mafalda Miranda Barbosa[22] in a journal article dedicated to the investigation of liability for misinformation. She contends that the mere requirement of unlawfulness is insufficient to resolve these cases and that the causal issue must be examined. According to Mafalda Miranda Barbosa, it is essential to juxtapose the sphere of risk/liability of the first wrongdoer with the general sphere of life risk, as well as the spheres of risk of both the injured party and any third party involved.[23]

Brazilian legal doctrine has insufficiently addressed problems concerning damages caused by psychological influence. This has resulted in a lack of criteria for resolving intricate and complex cases that do not fit within traditional natural causation frameworks. Due to this lack of assessment parameters,[24] cases are decided and grounded in mere equity considerations, leading to the imprecise application of direct and immediate damage theories, adequate causation, or concepts unrelated to private law. For example, in cases concerning digital influencers' liability, discussions have been conducted solely around the concept of the consumer by equivalence (bystander), as provided in Art. 29 of the CDC.[25]

This work examines the most controversial issues regarding "psychological causation" and the criteria developed by foreign legal scholars to resolve the various challenging cases that courts face. Rather than seeking answers that merely import legal concepts without context,[26] this study aims to establish effective criteria for resolving concrete cases frequently arising in judicial practice by comparing Brazilian normative provisions with constructions developed in foreign legal systems.[27]

---

imputation of the first driver, Don Manuel, arguing that the victim's desperate reaction was a direct result of the initial action of the driver, who created the dangerous situation and caused the terror and astonishment, which in turn prevented the injured party from taking appropriate precautions (Prieto, p. 1990).

[22] Barbosa (2020), pp. 1005–1006.

[23] Barbosa (2019), p. 20.

[24] While the category of objective imputation resolves the question of whether an event constitutes an act of an individual, subjective imputation seeks to solve the problem of whether the act is legally or morally reprehensible, that is, whether it can be attributed to the individual's fault (Safferling (2008), p. 21).

[25] Brito et al. (2021), pp. 349–350.

[26] Judith Martins-Costa, in addressing compensation for non-patrimonial damages, notes that the "displaced transplant" of notions originating from other legal traditions, or even the use of these concepts as instruments of legitimization, as in the case of punitive and social exemplarity functions of punitive damages, undermines judicial credibility and fosters legal uncertainty (Martins-Costa (2014), p. 7105).

[27] Although this work does not employ methods specific to comparative law, the importance of studying foreign legal models and the critical analysis of their use in other countries is recognized, thus avoiding the decontextualized adoption of legal concepts.

4.2 Concept

The term “psychological causation” (“psychische Kausalität”),[28] also referred to as “damages caused by psychological influence” or “psychologically mediated causation” (“psychisch vermittelte Kausalität”), refers to situations where a first wrongdoer creates the conditions for the voluntary conduct of another to cause harm.[29] It can be described as occurring in cases where the voluntary action[30] of a second causer is interposed between the causal connection of the first wrongdoer’s action and the harmful result. According to Alessandra Galluccio,[31] “psychological causation” in practice loses much of the “aura of mystery” (“*aura di mistero*”) typically attributed to it, becoming instead characterized by a well-defined causal chain. In a typical succession of three events, the first and last are physical in nature, while only the intermediate event—which links the two—is characterized by an individual’s voluntary decision.

What distinguishes cases of “damages caused by psychological influence” is that the intervening event is not determined by natural laws.[32] The damage for which compensation is sought arises only because an individual who is not the defendant, whether the injured party[33] or a third party, voluntarily acts in a way that results in harm. The first perpetrator from whom compensation is claimed does not directly cause the damage by his own act. The injury occurs only because another individual feels compelled to act or has their actions facilitated[34] by the first wrongdoer’s conduct.[35]

---

[28] In the context of criminal law, the term “subjective or psychological causation” is used in cases where the accused individual acts with intent or negligence (Marrey (1968), p. 56; Munhoz (1943), pp. 24–25; Garcia (1941), p. 596; Mello (2010), p. 263; Brandão (2004), p. 179). In the STJ, the expression is also used as a synonym for the subjective element (intent or negligence) that motivates the perpetrator’s conduct (STJ, RHC 80,142/SP, rel. Maria Thereza de Assis Moura, j. 28.03.2017). Paulo Freire Teotônio and Aline Bezerra argue that “psychological causation” is a requirement for the characterization of joint participation, corresponding to the consciousness of one’s role in the crime (Teotônio (2015), p. 14).

[29] Koziol (2020), p. 200.

[30] Schiemann (2017), pp. 90–91; Luckey (2019), p. 391.

[31] Galluccio (2014), p. 196.

[32] Forst (2000), p. 18.

[33] Lange and Schiemann (2003), p. 131.

[34] What has been conventionally referred to as psychological causation holds broader conceptual relevance than cases of liability for information and is not limited to this specific group of problematic cases. The definition of this concept depends on the circumstance in which a free decision intervenes between the initial cause and the result, identified as the second cause. The issue, therefore, lies in the uncertainty raised regarding the qualification of the first cause as a cause tout court, due to the psychological influence exerted on the second causer, affecting their will (Barbosa (2020), p. 983). It is also important to note that, although the issue is based on the idea of psychological influence, its scope seems to be broader, encompassing cases where one individual’s behavior facilitates the action of a second (Barbosa (2019), p. 20).

[35] Ristow (2003), p. 11.

For "psychological causation" to be established, both the second causer's act and their underlying voluntary decision[36] must be involved in the causal process.[37] Consequently, this case group excludes situations where, although a second causer mediates the causal link between the first wrongdoer's conduct and the result, the causal sequence follows natural laws rather than expressing a voluntary decision. A typical example of this is found in "chain reaction accidents" ("*Fallgruppe des Kettenunfalls*"): driver A causes an accident by colliding with driver B's vehicle, so that driver C, who is coming right behind, cannot brake in time and collides with A's car. Only C's car is damaged.[38]

It is still necessary to distinguish between "psychological causation" and the category recognized in German law as "nervous shock"[39] ("Schockschaden"),[40] which some scholars subsume under the broader concept of the former.[41] The "nervous shock"[42] should not be confused with "psychologically mediated causation," as, in this case, the violation of legally protected interests results from the fact that the first wrongdoer's conduct affects the psyche of the injured person. However, the internal process that gives rise to the violation of personality rights is not grounded in a voluntary decision, nor can it be interpreted as conduct. Thus, for example, the claim for compensation was accepted in the case of the husband who suffered a nervous shock when witnessing the death of his wife in an accident, as well as in the case of the mother who, upon arriving at the place where her daughter, hit by a train, lay dead, suffered a nervous breakdown.[43]

On July 22, 2017, the legislative amendment that introduced a third part into § 844 of the BGB came into force. According to the legal text, the person responsible for the damage must compensate survivors who had a particularly

---

[36] One of the challenges in cases of damage caused by psychological influence is assessing whether the person exposed to such influence could, and ought to, have resisted the interference (Winiger (2007), p. 253).

[37] Grüneberg et al. (2020), p. 295.

[38] Forst (2000), p. 19.

[39] The expression "nervous shock" is used by Peteffi and Reinig (2017), p. 6; Barreto (2022).

[40] Mia Zhang classifies the cases of "chain reaction accidents"("*Fallgruppe des Kettenunfalls*") and "shock damage" or "nervous shock" ("*Schockschaden*") as examples of "passive psychological causation" ("*passiv psychische Kausalität*"). The "passive psychological causation" has all the characteristics of "psychologically mediated causation." The peculiarity of this first legal concept lies in the reflexive behavior of the second causer. It is characterized by the fact that the intervention of the second subject results from a non-volitional action (Zhang (2016), p. 38).

[41] Oetker (2019), p. 1313; Ekkenga and Kuntz (2014), p. 85; Peteffi and Reinig (2017), p. 13.

[42] Regarding the concept of "shock damage," in German law, see (Karczewski (1992), p. 10). Unlike Germany, where jurisprudence frequently addresses these types of cases, in Switzerland, the Federal Court (*Schweizerisches Bundesgerichts*) took almost 60 years to decide this issue. The compensation claim of a father, who suffered severe nervous shock upon hearing the news of the death of his two children, was accepted by the Swiss court not as reflex damage, but as a direct injury (Fischer (1988), pp. 3–5).

[43] Herldermann (2004), pp. 20–25.

close relationship with the deceased at the time of the injury, due to the emotional suffering caused. The law presumes this close relationship if the survivor is the spouse, the civil partner (*Lebenspartner*), the parent, or the child of the deceased.[44]

In Brazilian law, the term "reflex or ricochet damage" is used when the damage suffered by the victim reverberates in a third person.[45] According to Fernando Noronha,[46] "ricochet damage" affects other people linked to the one who is the immediate victim of a certain harmful event. These other people are considered indirect victims. The matter is addressed in Art. 948 of the Brazilian Civil Code[47] which determines that the compensation must include the amount of expenses for medical and hospital treatment, funeral and mourning expenses, in addition to alimony, without excluding other compensations. Unlike the German system, Brazilian law adopted the French solution, failing to specify those entitled to claim compensation, tending to use the notion of causation to determine the compensatory standards, and relegating to the courts a wide margin of interpretation.[48]

Given the historical, conceptual, and practical differences, it is not appropriate to import the German idea of the so-called "shock damage".[49] It is sufficient to affirm, for the purposes of this work, that "reflex or ricochet damage" does not fall within the scope of damages caused by psychological influence, deserving separate study, as there is no voluntary conduct by the one who is indirectly affected by the damage.

Also, it does not integrate the notion of "psychological causation," for the purposes of this study, the so-called "intentionally mediated causation" ("absichtlich vermittelte Kausalität"), characterized by the intentional, malicious act of the first perpetrator who, through their conduct, intends to bring about the final harmful result. This includes cases of deception *(Täuschung)*,[50] where the wrongdoer deliberately seeks, through their behavior, to create or maintain an error in another individual. Also included in this categorization is the threat *(Drohung)*, where the second causer is morally compelled to carry out a harmful activity against

[44] The Portuguese Civil Code also stipulates, in Art. 496, that in the event of the victim's death, "the right to compensation for non-pecuniary damages belongs jointly to the spouse not judicially separated from persons and goods, and to the children or other descendants; in their absence, to the parents or other ascendants; and, lastly, to the siblings or nephews who represent them."

[45] Stoco (2007), p. 1244.

[46] Noronha (2013), p. 603.

[47] "Art. 948. In the case of homicide, the compensation consists, without excluding other reparations: I—the payment of expenses with the treatment of the victim, their funeral and the grief of the family; II—the provision of alimony to the people to whom the deceased owed them, considering the probable duration of the victim's life."

[48] Rodrigues Jr. and Peteffi (2017), p. 223.

[49] On the peculiarities of German law on the matter, see Fischer (2016).

[50] According to Engisch, the phenomena referred to as "psychological causation" occur not only in cases of fraud, but also in many other situations within criminal law theory (Engisch, p. 269).

a third party. Finally, reference may be made to instigation or incitement *(Anstiftung)*[51] of a dangerous or unlawful act, as in the case of a friend who persuades[52] another individual without a a driving license to drive a vehicle, resulting in an accident.

In cases of intentional mediation, issues related to causation and imputation generally present themselves as less controversial, though cases situated in conceptual border zones admittedly pose greater difficulties for resolution.[53] The actions of the first perpetrator are deemed to exert a significant psychological influence on the course of events and, therefore, sufficient for determining causation according to general empirical principles.[54] From a foreign law perspective, a significant number of countries recognize the evidentiary sufficiency of the first wrongdoer's voluntary act, as it is causally indisputable that the requisite degree of psychological influence has been attained.[55] Under Brazilian law, the instigator can be considered a co-author and is generally jointly responsible for all damages, in accordance with Art. 942, sole paragraph, of the Brazilian Civil Code (CC/02).[56] Therefore, the application of the "psychological causation" criteria is dismissed in these cases.[57]

This problem is distinctive because two individuals may be held liable for the harmful event. The central issue is why the first party, whose conduct is more remote from the harmful outcome, ought still to bear liability for compensation. In cases where the second perpetrator is the injured party themselves, that is, when

51 Zhang (2016), p. 35.

52 An instigator motivates another person to commit an unlawful act. According to the prevailing view, both the instigator and the instigated must act intentionally (*double intent*). If the instigated person acts merely negligently, the instigator is considered an indirect perpetrator (*mittelbarer Täter*), who uses the instigated as an instrument to pursue his own wrongdoing (Magnus (2020), p. 1633). Therefore, cases based on a defective formation of tortfeasor's will, such as in cases involving individuals with intellectual disabilities, do not fit within the categorization of "psychologically mediated causation," as the person with the pathology does not act according to their own will (Forst (2000), p. 21).

53 The episode of collective suicide that occurred in Jonestown, a community located in Guyana, on November 18, 1978, is well known. Under the influence of religious leader Jim Jones, 918 people belonging to the so-called People's Temple sect died after performing a ritual in which they ingested fruit punch with cyanide. The testimonies about the event are conflicting, with some people claiming that the victims were forced to take the poison, while others stated that the drink was consumed voluntarily (Moore (2009), pp. 1–3; Chidester (2003), pp. 15–16).

54 Zhang (2016), p. 36.

55 Winiger (2007), p. 261.

56 "Art. 942. The patrimony of the person responsible for the offense or violation of the rights of another is subject to the compensation for the damage caused; and, if the offense has more than one author, all will be jointly liable for the compensation. Sole paragraph. Co-authors and persons designated in Art. 932 are jointly liable with the authors."

57 This is a methodological choice adopted in this work. This does not definitively mean that the existence of intent on the part of the first perpetrator dispenses with the proof of establishing the causal link. The approach to these hypotheses, given their breadth, exceeds the limits of this study.

they suffer damage due to their own conduct, the answer is obvious, as it is only possible to discuss liability if the first causer is held responsible. Otherwise, the injured party would have to bear the damages incurred.

Where the second perpetrator coincides with the injured party—that is, when the harm arises from their own conduct—the conclusion is evident: liability is only at issue if the first wrongdoer is held responsible. Even if the second causer's liability is recognized, the injured party could sue directly against the first causer, as in the case where the second perpetrator is unknown or where the former appears to be more solvent than the latter,[58] especially if they have insurance coverage for the damage.[59]

4.3 The Problem of Factual Causation

As previously noted,[60] mere factual causation is insufficient for determining the wrongdoer's liability.[61] Although Brazilian doctrine rarely mentions the differentiation between factual causation and legal imputation,[62] this distinction proves essential. In this regard, after establishing factual causation through the application of the theory of equivalence of conditions, it is indispensable, in a subsequent

---

[58] Forst (2000), pp. 19–20.

[59] Already in the 1980s, Carlos Alberto da Mota Pinto emphasized that the establishment of mandatory insurance and guarantee funds contributes to greater victim protection. According to the author, it has been proposed that the coverage of damages resulting from an accident should not be made through tort law, but through the use of social security schemes (Pinto (1992), p. 122).

[60] See Sect. 3.2.7.

[61] Despite the importance of ascertaining causation in a naturalistic sense, the attribution of liability requires further refinement (Bydlinski (2007), p. 16). Kleinschmidt asserts that, even in Belgium, where it is often argued that the *conditio sine qua non* test constitutes the only element of causal inquiry, the courts do not dispense with the second stage of evaluation (Kleinschmidt (2012), p. 159).

[62] According to Gisela Sampaio, the discussion around objective imputation has influenced theories of causation within private law, especially by highlighting the difference between naturalistic causation and imputation (Guedes (2005), p. 122). Guilherme Reinig, in defending the applicability of the scope of the norm theory in the Brazilian legal system, emphasizes that the investigation of the purpose of the norm requires the interpreter to recognize the normative nature of the imputation criterion (Reinig (2015), p. 278). Daniel Dias, debating the mitigation of damages in tort law, adopts the position that the criteria for delimiting the offender's liability constitute criteria for objective imputation (Dias (2020a, b), p. 218). Otavio Luiz Rodrigues Júnior indicates that the transition from the theory of equivalence of conditions to the theory of adequate causation occurred precisely to establish filters at the level of imputation and liability (Rodrigues Jr. (2016), p. 132). Finally, Gabriel Magadan argues that "legal causation" acquires relevance in establishing a regime of imputation of consequences resulting from damage (Magadan (2019), p. 32).

evaluative stage, to establish limits to liability using imputation criteria based on the analysis of case groups.

Regarding factual causation and its relationship with "psychologically mediated causation," a first issue arises. Considering the peculiarities of damages caused by psychological influence, the question emerges as to whether it is possible to affirm the existence of a causal connection between the behavior of the first perpetrator and the conduct of the following one.[63] Winiger[64] argues that determining when an individual acted under psychological influence is often difficult. This challenge stems from psychological causation's purely immaterial nature and its immeasurable phenomena, unlike physical or natural causation. As a result, a judge confronted with such questions must evaluate indicators rather than relying on clear-cut facts.

The ways of addressing cases of "psychological causation" vary enormously from one country to another. While certain jurisdictions simply accept or reject psychological influence as a cause without entering further legal discussions, others establish theoretical systems with specific conditions. The supreme courts of France, Belgium, and Denmark, which make only limited use of consistent theoretical argumentation, have drawn criticism from legal scholarship[65] due to the lack of reasoning in their decisions. By contrast, the doctrine and jurisprudence of countries like Germany, England, and Ireland engage in complex debates on the matter, requiring the recognition of psychological influence to meet various conditions.[66]

In Germany, judges examine the existence of the *conditio sine qua non* as a basic prerequisite of "psychological causation," although a positive response to the test does not necessarily entail that the damages suffered by the victim should be attributed to the offender. Applying the theory of equivalence of conditions in isolation provides no basis for determining which party bears liability for damages, as it treats the first and second causer's acts as equivalent.[67]

Analyzing "psychological causation" through the theory of equivalence of conditions presents difficulties not commonly found in causal connections established by physical laws.[68] Given the freedom of action (*Handlungsfreiheit*)

---

[63] It is alluded to the fact that, as the result is only achieved through the behavior of a second causer, the affirmation of the existence of the causal chain is less certain. It cannot be stated with absolute certainty that the second causer would have caused the event without the occurrence of the original cause (Ristow (2003), p. 28).

[64] Winiger (2007), p. 252.

[65] Many doctrinal works do not address "psychologically mediated causation," because, apparently, they take its possibility for granted. Roxin questions why a verbal instigation should establish causation, when the predominant position is that causation requires a real source of energy, capable of generating a force expenditure. He points out that the understanding of causation as an effective force fails to explain "psychological causation" (Roxin (2011), p. 411).

[66] Winiger (2007), pp. 256–257.

[67] Forst (2000), p. 121.

[68] Dencker observes that, even within the domain of physical causation, causal connections are generally difficult to visualize, as in the case of Thalidomide. In this case, however, it is widely accepted that a connection, in accordance with natural laws, likely exists and, in principle, be

of the second causer, it becomes more complex to assert with certainty the causal link between the behavior of the first perpetrator and the actions of the second. Universally valid scientific rules are not applicable here.[69] Deutsch and Ahrens[70] argue that the psychological element leads to a peculiar causal process, as in the psychological domain it is not possible to resort to the laws of nature,[71] meaning that the repeatability of the outcome under identical conditions cannot be guaranteed. In the case of a traffic accident, although it is likely that the rescuer will attempt to save the victim, it cannot be asserted, according to general laws of nature, that such an act will indeed occur.[72]

Assessing "psychological causation" through statistical methods, instead of using deterministic natural laws, also appears inadequate to resolve the issue. Hilgendorf's suggestion[73] in this regard should be rejected, as previously mentioned. When analyzing "probabilistic causation," mathematical probability may assist the judge in forming a conviction but is not a decisive factor in establishing causation.[74] The complexity of human decisions does not allow any statistically measurable prediction.[75] Hilgendorf himself[76] points to the enormous difficulties posed for an exact quantification of legal statistical hypotheses.

---

proven, even if science has not yet been able to provide rigorous proof (Dencker (1996), pp. 36–37). Thalidomide was discovered in 1953 by Wilhelm Kunz and launched on the market in 1956 as an anti-flu drug. Between ten and fifteen thousand children worldwide were born with typical malformations associated with its use, and 40% of them died within their first year of life (Moro and Invernizzi (2017), p. 607).

[69] According to Min Zhang, "psychologically mediated causation" can hardly be explained using traditional natural sciences. Thus, "psychological causation" could be regarded as an independent type of causation, distinct from natural causation (Zhang (2016), p. 31).

[70] Deutsch and Ahrens (2014), p. 22.

[71] The concept of causation, not as a transfer of forces or energies, but as the determination of a natural law, can be traced back to Engisch. The author acknowledges that the definition of causal connection between behavior and event was initially focused on processes in the external physical world. However, he asserts that the *Formel der gesetzmäßigen Bedingung* can also be applied to cases of "psychologically mediated causation." According to Engisch, at least from a deterministic perspective, a connection according to laws can be affirmed between, for example, the behavior of the instigator and the psychological processes of the main perpetrator. He concluded that judges often convince themselves of the existence of "psychological causation" based on psychological laws acquired through experience (Engisch (1931), p. 28).

[72] Roxin (2011), p. 411.

[73] Hilgendorf (1995), pp. 514–517.

[74] Law has largely adopted the model of the natural sciences, but has not done so satisfactorily, relying on a logical–hypothetical criterion in its determination, or incorporating, in some cases, a probabilistic or even statistical criterion (Tavares (2009), p. 290).

[75] It is underlined that even extreme improbability does not exclude the existence of "psychologically mediated causation" (Roxin (2011), p. 415).

[76] Hilgendorf (1995), p. 520.

The failure of all attempts to find statistical or deterministic regularities[77] for "psychologically mediated causal" processes led other authors to abandon causal explanations through conditions. This is the case of Bernsmann,[78] who advocated a "non-causal approach" ("non-kausale Betrachtungsweise"), according to which a psychologically induced event can be attributed to the initial wrongdoer if it was rational for the second perpetrator, from a teleological perspective, to act in that particular way. Koriath[79] concludes that the expression "psychological causation" ("psychischer Kausalität") represents a mistaken concept. He supports the development of non-causal attribution principles. This theoretical conception is criticized by Roxin,[80] who argues that such a model is not convincing, as it does not present attribution standards that can solve the problem.

Deutsch[81] argues that the *conditio sine qua non* formula only provides an uncertain result in cases of "psychologically mediated causation." Due to the impossibility of proving psychological causal chains in the same way as natural causation, he suggests resorting to empirical values and probabilities (*Erfahrungswerte und Wahrscheinlichkeiten*).[82] Leitermeier[83] criticizes this approach, asserting that it inappropriately aligns the examination of natural causation with adequacy theory. Niebaum[84] adds that demonstrating causation through general laws is irrelevant for the purpose of determining causation, according to the theory of equivalence. According to the author, the focus should not be on whether the result could have been predicted with certainty at the time of the action but on assessing whether the event occurred as a result of the offender's conduct.

Roxin seems correct[85] in supporting the application of the theory of equivalence of conditions also in the domain of "psychological causation,"[86] yet he does not rely[87] on

[77] In cases of "psychological causation," it is necessary to establish another kind of link between cause and effect, other than that provided by physical laws or statistical rules. Conscious reasons (*bewusste Gründe*) lead to another category of connection between cause and consequence, which can also be called causation, although it represents a completely different form of natural causation (Puppe (2016), p. 44). Roxin argues, however, that what matters is the cause of the decision and not its motive (Roxin (2011), p. 417).

[78] Bernsmann (1982), p. 549.

[79] Koriath (1988), p. 249.

[80] Roxin (2011), p. 416.

[81] Deutsch (1996), p. 83.

[82] Other German authors also support this understanding. See Ristow (2003), p. 28; Spickhoff (1998), p. 238; Steffen (1989), p. 124.

[83] Leitermeier (1968), p. 26.

[84] Niebaum (1977), pp. 45–46.

[85] Roxin (2011), pp. 416–419.

[86] According to the theory of equivalence, the causal link between the actions of the first and second perpetrators and the harmful event constitutes a necessary condition for liability to be established (Forst (2000), p. 121).

[87] Puppe (2016), p. 516.

any deterministic, statistical,[88] or probabilistic law to substantiate it. The author asserts that there are necessary conditions for the occurrence of an event, which are not based on natural laws but can still be proven with a certain degree of certainty.[89]

Therefore, it is possible to establish the occurrence of "psychologically mediated causation," although in a somewhat different manner from that of physical connections, which further supports the notion that these are not structurally identical causations. While physical causes can generally be determined by natural laws, involving expert examinations and inspections, the proof of "psychological causation" primarily relies on convincing conclusions about the situation, empirical rules and principles,[90] or practical experience.[91]

Despite differences between the first stage of "psychological causation" analysis and physical causal processes—particularly regarding the absence or unrecognizability of connections determined by natural law—it remains necessary to examine whether an act qualifies as causal for the outcome using the theory of equivalence of conditions (*the conditio sine qua non formula*). Although proving this causal link is not entirely unattainable, its demonstration follows rules that differ in part from those applied to physical causal processes.[92] Its greater indeterminacy highlights the importance of legal criteria as factors in delimiting liability.

4.4 Violations of General Duties of Care in Brazilian Law

"Psychological causation" is closely related to "general duties of care"[93] ("*Verkehrspflichten*"), since these duties also apply to cases of indirect damages (*mittelbare Verletzungen*).[94] Accordingly, psychological influence is generally

---

[88] Strict causation cannot be maintained within the framework of human free will. For a legally relevant causal connection, it would suffice to rely on statistical rules, rational reasons devoid of legal character, or even personal motivations, which would make the occurrence of the result foreseeable based on life experience (*Lebenserfahrung*) (Gottwald (1979), pp. 94–95).

[89] Staffler (2017), p. 138.

[90] Roxin (2011), p. 419.

[91] In discussing the L'Aquila case (see Sect. 5.2.1.2), Alessandra Galluccio asserts that the identification of reliable maxims of experience, supported by clear evidence in the specific case, and the elimination of potential alternative causal courses make the evaluation conducted by the judge perfectly capable of achieving a high degree of logical probability and procedural certainty (Galluccio (2014), p. 205).

[92] Roxin (2011), pp. 419–421.

[93] In Portuguese law, the notion of general duties of care is traced back to Vaz Serra (Serra (1959), p. 126), under the nomenclature of "duty of danger prevention," a term also advocated by Menezes Cordeiro ((2017), pp. 831–832).

[94] Although the differentiation between direct and indirect damage is not settled in German doctrine, the criterion adopted by Larenz seems to prevail, in the sense that direct damage constitutes interventions in someone else's right or interest that are placed in the scope of the one who acts (*im Rahmen der Handlung*) (Larenz (1963), p. 195). Indirect offenses are

assessed in terms of whether it constitutes a breach of these duties.[95] According to von Bar,[96] comparing the decisions and reasoning in these cases with tools developed in the context of general duties of care reveals intense similarities. The question about the scope of the norm that establishes liability ("*haftungsbegründende Kausalität*") can only be interpreted as a duty of care problem.

German jurisprudence played a pioneering role, starting from the second half of the nineteenth century in addressing legal issues arising from the creation of new risk factors due to technical developments, specifically concerning the legal treatment of danger. The German courts had already demonstrated a comprehensive command of the criteria for imputation applicable to this category of cases. Liability was imposed on those who negligently created the risk of harm (*causam sive occasionem praestit*). In 1885, a farmer left his house without properly securing a loaded shotgun. One of his employees removed the gun from two nails under the ceiling, injuring another employee in the arm. The owner was held liable for the damage caused. The *Oberlandesgericht* Kiel[97] held that, for the purposes of compensation, it was irrelevant whether a labor relationship existed. Regardless of whether the immediate perpetrator was an employee or another individual, liability would remain, as the basis for imputation lay in the unlawful creation of a risk.[98]

German jurisprudence was also firm in affirming liability for omissions arising from the failure to take necessary measures to eliminate a preexisting danger created by a prior or concurrent act. Thus, for example, the person who failed to eliminate the formation of ice on the river during winter should be held for the flooding of neighboring lands, as well as woodcutters who let felled tree trunks roll without warning passersby of the danger they were facing.[99]

---

characterized by the fact that the injurious result is produced outside the temporal framework of the action (Ataíde (2019), p. 1002). Indirect damage occurs outside the confines of the offender's behavior, presupposing the interposition of circumstances not controllable by the perpetrator (Stoll (1963), p. 227).

[95] Ristow (2003), pp. 126–127.

[96] Bar (1980), p. 195.

[97] OLG Kiel, 20.03.1885, SeuffArch, 41, n. 15.

[98] Ataíde (2019), p. 180.

[99] The reasoning was based on properly theorized Roman sources, so that anyone who took advantage of or unleashed natural forces for their own benefit should assume responsibility for their control, to the extent that they proved to be controllable, if they presented dangers to third parties (Ataíde (2019), p. 181). Mere omission could not justify an action under the *lex Aquilia*. The boundary between unsanctioned omission and that which gave rise to liability was, however, questionable. In both cases, the responsible parties failed to eliminate a preexisting risk source or triggered natural forces. The principles of liability developed from Roman sources made it possible to take into account the risks of damage from modern technology (Kleindiek (1997), pp. 56–57).

Two decisions of the *Reichsgericht* (RG) are considered fundamental in the development of the so-called general "duties of care" ("*Verkehrssicherungspflichten*").[100] Just two years after the BGB's enactment, in 1902, the German court was tasked with determining whether the owner of a decayed tree that fell onto a neighboring property should be held liable for the damages caused. The *Oberlandesgericht* Marienwerder rejected the plaintiff's claim, reasoning that § 836 of the BGB[101] did not apply, as it solely covered the collapse of buildings or other ground-connected structures. Similarly, § 823 (2) of the BGB would not apply in this instance, as no legal obligation existed for the tree owner to inspect the tree for the risk of it falling.[102]

The Reich Court[103] had to address the question of whether the owner or possessor had a duty to take precautions to prevent the tree from causing damage, or whether individuals were entitled to leave their property in its prior condition, without their intervention, even if it had become dangerous to others.[104] Dissenting from the solution that would be adopted according to Roman law,[105] the RG established the foundations of the doctrine of general duties of care, stating that everyone should be held liable for the damages caused by their property, to the extent that they should have reasonably considered the interests of others in avoiding the harmful event.[106]

A few months later, the RG articulated its reasoning more fully in a 1903 decision,[107] where the term "Pflichten zur Verkehrssicherung" was mentioned for the first time.[108] In this case, the *Oberlandesgericht* Rostock failed to hold the defendant liable for the damages suffered by the victim, who had fallen on a staircase that was in a poor condition, as well as poorly lit and slippery. The

---

[100] The term "*Verkehrssicherungspflicht*" is not easily translated. According to Markesinis, its meaning could be summarized by stating that whoever, through their activity or through their assets, establishes a potential source of danger that can affect the interests and rights of others, is obliged to ensure their protection against the risks created by them (Markesinis and Unberath (2002), p. 86).

[101] "§ 836. Liability of the owner of a plot of land. If a human being suffers injury to life, limb or health, or if a thing is damaged, by the collapse of a building or any other work attached to a plot of land or by parts of the building or work separating therefrom, then the possessor of the plot of land is liable to provide compensation to the injured person for damage resulting from this, to the extent that the collapse or separation is a consequence of defective construction or inadequate upkeep. Liability in damages does not apply if the possessor has exercised the care required in business dealings for the purpose of averting danger."

[102] Ataíde (2019), p. 13.

[103] RGZ 52, 373.

[104] Voss (2007), p. 49.

[105] After the enactment of the BGB, the legal situation changed; it is no longer possible to argue that no one is obliged to take positive action to reduce the harmful influence of their thing on other people or things (Ataíde (2019), p. 13). Zimmermann points out that the matter would have to be resolved differently if one followed the authority of Roman law, as it would have been necessary for a *cautio damni infecti* to have been granted, or at least requested, in order to demand compensation for the loss caused by the defective state of a part of the property, since this kind of damage had not been foreseen in the *actio legis Aquilia* (Zimmermann (2010), pp. 94–95).

[106] Hartmann (2009), p. 66.

[107] RGZ 54, 53.

[108] Voss (2007), p. 50.

court decided that the accident had occurred as a result of the ice not being removed, and that the defendant could not be held responsible, given the absence of a legal obligation to do so, whether under the BGB or under administrative law. The RG, however, applied § 823 (1) of the BGB, stating that, regardless of whether one is qualified as an owner, anyone who has a legal or factual relationship with an object must exercise reasonable precautions when interacting with the public domain.[109]

In a third decision dating from 1921, also by the RG,[110] the scope of these duties was expanded to situations where the damage did not result from the condition of an object[111] but from an activity carried out by the liable party. In this case, the butcher, called by the owner to slaughter a cow with anthrax, contracted the disease, claiming that the vet was negligent in two respects: First, he failed to take precautions to protect the butcher against the risk of contamination, even though the butcher had a visible wound on his hand; second, the vet did not warn him to cease the task, even after the butcher had been injured.[112]

The RG's decision stated the growing expansion[113] of the concept of "general duties of care," initially limited to cases of liability for omission, to numerous areas of social interaction.[114] The understanding that those who create or maintain a source of danger must take all necessary measures to safeguard the interests of third parties[115] extends beyond mere omission, also encompassing the issue of indirect injuries (mittelbare Verletzungen), due to the investigations of von Caemmerer.[116]

---

[109] Ataíde (2019), p. 14.

[110] RGZ 102, 372.

[111] In the 1921 decision, the expression "*Verkehrspflichten*" was used for the first time, so that the use of the terminology "*Verkehrssicherungspflichten*" was restricted to dangers originating from or related to real estate (Bar (1988), p. 170).

[112] The reasoning was based on the attribution of liability arising from the ordinary course of events to which service providers interacting with the public are subject. This liability materializes in specific legal duties which are referred to, in a broader sense, as "duties of care" (Ataíde (2019), p. 988).

[113] According to Adelaide Menezes Leitão, that concept has undergone significant expansion, applying to nearly all areas of life (Leitão (2009), p. 577). Deutsch notes that sport also contributed to the consolidation of jurisprudence on general duties of care. He cites the case where an aviation club must take the necessary precautions with its members who act as landing assistants (BGHZ 137, 89), as the pilot must ensure that the flaps are in the correct position before takeoff (Deutsch (2005), p. 991).

[114] Kindermann (1984), p. 12.

[115] Varela (2000), p. 552.

[116] Von Caemmerer observes that § 823 (1) of the BGB presents an open factual basis. When someone's actions put at risk the life, health, or rights of others, leading to the violation of these interests, or when damage occurs due to inadequate defensive measures, then an "unlawful" ("*widerrechtliche*") violation is characterized. This happens when a duty of care, implied by the legal system but not explicitly written, has been breached (Caemmerer (1968), p. 488).

Von Bar[117] exemplifies the importance of studying indirect interventions and their distinct criteria for imputation by citing the case of industrial product manufacturing. The production of these goods significantly increases the probability of health damage. Accepting that any causally adequate violation of a protected interest constitutes an unlawful act leads to the conclusion that the production of goods itself would be considered illegal. According to the author, in these cases, a legal violation is only characterized when there is a breach of a duty. However, not every remote act constitutes prohibited dangerous conduct.

In German law, Larenz's prevailing thesis[118] holds that violating an objective duty of care constitutes the unlawful element in indirect legal violations, whereas direct interventions considered presumptively contrary to the legal order.[119] Therefore, in order to prove the unlawfulness of such interferences, it is not necessary to provide evidence of the conduct contrary to law.[120] Indirect legal violations accordingly derive from the breach of general duties of care. They can be understood as a partial general clause in German tort law and, structurally, are similar to cases of liability for omission.[121]

Canaris[122] acknowledges that general duties of care were originally developed to address problems related to omissions. Subsequently, they were used in cases of indirect interventions affecting interests protected by § 823 (1) BGB. He argues that separating a "legislative" from a "judicial" conception—associating direct interventions only with the former and general duties of care solely with the latter—leads to a problematic approach. According to the author, general duties of care also play a role in the context of direct damages, for instance, someone who drops a hammer on a passerby's head while working on a roof.[123]

---

[117] Bar (1980), pp. 154–157.

[118] Larenz (1963), pp. 183–184.

[119] The intervention in the affected legal interests provides evidence of the unlawfulness of the harmful conduct, which can only be dismissed by exclusions of unlawfulness (self-defense, necessity, etc.). If the perpetrator fails to prove a legitimating cause, and the harmful event was foreseeable and avoidable, they are liable for the damages inflicted, according to § 823 (1) of the BGB (Reinig (2015), p. 11).

[120] Stoll (1963), pp. 229–230.

[121] Bar (1980), p. 191.

[122] The author acknowledges that the boundary between action and omission and between direct and indirect injuries is difficult and fluid. This conceptual uncertainty would inevitably affect the distinction between § 823 (1) and § 823 (2) of the BGB (Canaris (1983), pp. 77–81).

[123] Manuel Carneiro da Frada distinguishes between liability for breach of behavioral duties and liability from reliance, but argues that certain issues can be addressed from both perspectives, such as in the case of liability for information provided (Frada (2015), p. 245). In contrary, von Bar argues that the frustration of expectations is one of the central criteria for the emergence of duties of care, for determining the liable party, and for the type and scope of the duty (Bar (1980), p. 117). Canaris, similarly, notes that the concept of reliance is related to the existence of duties of care, citing the case of the architect who, contracted to carry out a project, places the client's trust in him and assumes the risks, including those related to third parties, of carrying out a defective work (Larenz and Canaris (1994), p. 410).

General duties of care do not derive from explicit legal rules but instead represent standards of conduct developed judicially.[124] Judges specify the expected concrete behavior and compare it with the actual behavior of the liable party.[125] They thus constitute a theoretical arsenal for the judicial concretization of the general rule that prohibits the negligent violation of legal interests. Leser[126] asserts that the application of the concept of general duties of care is a tool that provides flexibility to German tort law,[127] comparable to negligence in Anglo-American law.

The Brazilian legal debate on unlawful acts[128] and general duties of care is influenced by an often uncritical adoption of the Italian concept of *danno ingiusto.*[129] Since the introduction of the term "*ingiustizia del danno*"[130] in Art. 2.043 of the 1942 Italian Civil Code,[131] the use of this expression has become commonplace in Brazilian doctrine,[132] grounded in a supposed interpretation of tort law from the perspective of "constitutional legality."[133] In 1989, Orlando Gomes[134] proposed a conceptual shift from the notion of an unlawful act to the broader category of "unjust damage."[135] He observes that the concept of "unjust damage" enables the

[124] Violation in traffic occurs in cases where the source of danger was not inspected by the authorities, based on a public law license or compliance with safety regulations, as emphasized by Larenz. These measures are intended solely to protect third parties from potential risks, not to absolve the perpetrator of their own responsibility (Larenz and Canaris (1994), p. 416).

[125] Ataíde (2019), p. 990.

[126] Leser and Klippel (1983), p. 585.

[127] According to von Bar, liability has become more flexible with the development of judicial rules for danger control (Bar (1980), p. 157).

[128] Miranda (1983), pp. 204–205.

[129] The uncritical adoption of the Italian concept of unjust damage leads to presenting as new solutions that are already settled in our legal tradition, which makes use of various developments of unlawfulness (Peteffi (2019), p. 449).

[130] According to Giovanna Visintini, the leading doctrine states that the expression constitutes a general clause, as the legislative choice was to entrust the judge with the valuation and selection of interests deserving protection. The author explains that the aim was to avoid a typification of the wrongful act through jurisprudence. Thus, what characterizes the Italian system is the reference to the qualification of injustice applied to the damage and not to the act itself (Visintini (2005), pp. 426–427). Massimo Bianca conceptualizes unjust damage as the injury of a legally protected interest in relational life (Bianca, p. 584). Mario Barcelona emphasizes that, by adding the adjective "unjust," the legislator of 1942 intended only to ratify the *communis opinio* according to which only damage *contra jus* and *sine jure* would be compensable (Barcelona (2011), p. 55).

[131] "Art. 2.043. Any willful or negligent act that causes unjust damage to another obliges the author of the act to compensate the damage."

[132] Among others, see Guedes (2011), p. 76; Steiner (2018), pp. 156–157; Martins-Costa (2017), p. 616.

[133] Moraes (2003), p. 179. Also, Karinne Ansiliero notes that the liability will only arise when an unjust damage is characterized, which may or may not result from a wrongful act (Angelin (2012), p. 25).

[134] Gomes (1989), pp. 293–295.

[135] On the subject, see Cunha (2022), pp. 193–196.

interpreter to identify the interests worthy of protection,[136] in line with constitutional values such as social solidarity and human dignity, thereby expanding the scope of compensable damages.[137]

The "unjust damage" concept extends liability boundaries, allowing unlawfulness to be identified based on the importance of the legally protected interest, as assessed at the judge's discretion. Such practice, in addition to not allowing a theoretical densification of the concept of unlawfulness, slips into the arbitrary use of indeterminate legal concepts. In practice, no control of unlawfulness is effectively carried out; instead, the judge decides based on equity criteria.[138] The equivocal use of the concepts of fault,[139] unlawfulness, and causation,[140] resulting from the adoption of the notion of *faute* from French law, obscures a precise and independent understanding of these elements.

The wording and systematic placement of Art. 159 of the CC/16, followed by Art. 186 of the CC/02, led to the conflation of unlawfulness with fault, preventing it from developing its own operational scope. However, a new perspective emerges with the "reconstruction of the idea of unlawfulness," giving rise to a dual meaning of this legal concept, which is divided into "subjective unlawfulness" and "objective unlawfulness." The first is defined by an attribution link based on fault, requiring an assessment of intent, negligence, or recklessness. In contrast, objective unlawfulness is determined solely by the deviation from or opposition to the legal norm.[141]

The term "unlawfulness" derives from the Latin word "*iniuria*," which was translated by German scholars as "*Unrecht*," "*Rechtswidrigkeit*," or "*Widerrechtlichkeit*," referring to conduct violating the law.[142] In the Latin-German dictionary, the words "*Unrecht*" and "*iniuria*" are treated as synonyms.[143] Nils Jansen[144] explains that the words "*iniuria*," "*Unrecht*," and "*Rechtswidrigkeit*" originate from the idea that something occurred outside the legal sphere (*non iure*).

---

[136] Roppo (2016), p. 582.

[137] Tepedino (2019), p. 11.

[138] In discussing the application of indeterminate legal concepts and general clauses in Brazilian law, Schmidt asserts that their main drawback lies in the risk of arbitrariness and legal uncertainty in individual cases, which in turn weakens the law's function of control and predictability. According to the author, even in higher courts, judgments are made in the sense of a "sentimental jurisprudence" (sentimentale Rechtsprechung), based more on equity than on law (Schmidt (2009), p. 398).

[139] Regarding the division of fault into gross, ordinary and slight, see Ribas (1905), p. 451.

[140] It has been noted that, for many authors, the causal link between the wrongdoer and the damage means fault (Beviláqua (1953), p. 352).

[141] Martins-Costa (2007), pp. 518–520.

[142] Peteffi (2019), p. 450.

[143] Scheller (1805), p. 3021.

[144] Jansen (2002, 2003), p. 201.

The notion of unlawfulness, frequently regarded as synonymous with "illegality," has been maintained as an independent element[145] of tort law by a significant part of Brazilian doctrine.[146] It has been rightly emphasized that unlawfulness does not always manifest itself in the violation of a specific normative provision,[147] but is characterized by a conflict with rules of the legal system,[148] understood as a dynamic and complex totality of norms, principles, and legal models.[149]

It makes little sense to condition the determination of unlawfulness on the existence of a violation of a mandatory or prohibitive legal norm. This criterion is insufficient, as there are numerous harmful acts that give rise to liability without any specific norm regulating them.[150] At this stage, emphasis is placed on the importance of defining and substantiating unlawfulness through reference to the specific duty of care that has been breached. Pontes de Miranda contends that certain moral duties migrate into the legal sphere, becoming legal duties through the prevailing understanding in legal transactions and thus acquiring normative force as legal rule.[151]

Given the general liability clauses in Brazilian civil law (Arts. 186 and 927 of the CC/02), courts can develop standards of conduct that effectively protect legal interests by ensuring compliance with the general prohibition against negligent conduct. This approach eliminates the need for artificial imputation techniques,

[145] In the procedural context, the distinction between wrongful conduct and damage is emphasized by legal scholars, corresponding to the difference between restorative and compensatory remedies. Restorative remedies seek to eliminate a situation of illegality, whereas compensatory remedies aim to redress the harm caused by the unlawful act. Notably, such redress may take the form of specific remedies rather than the monetary equivalent of the damage (Marinoni (2011), p. 133).

[146] Pontes Miranda affirms the independence of unlawfulness from fault, noting that it is possible to have unlawfulness without fault (Miranda (1983), p. 197). In Volume 53, it is stated that unlawfulness does not constitute an element of fault, but rather an element of the act's illegality (Miranda (1984a, b, c), p. 48). Fernando Noronha also points out unlawfulness as one of the autonomous elements of liability (Noronha (2013), p. 493). At the IX Civil Law Conferences in Brazilian, Statement 661 was approved, with the following content: "The application of art. 931 of the Civil Code for the liability of individual entrepreneurs and companies for damages caused by products put into circulation does not dispense with the verification of the unlawfulness of the act."

[147] Peteffi distinguishes between "formal unlawfulness" and "material unlawfulness." The former, according to the author, refers to the direct violation of a norm, mandate or prohibition, expressly provided for in the legal system. The latter, in turn, concerns the violation of the legal system understood in its entirety, encompassing legal principles and customary norms (Peteffi (2019), p. 462).

[148] Recognizing the influence of the BGB on Brazilian law, San Tiago Dantas asserts that the wrongful act is a creation of the nineteenth-century Pandectist doctrine, which can be defined as a human act that transgresses a legal duty imposed by law (Dantas (1979), p. 352).

[149] Martins-Costa (2007), p. 518.

[150] Tolsada (1993), p. 131.

[151] The author asserts that liability is not limited to the state for damages caused by unmarked road excavations; it also extends to individuals who, upon noticing a severed electrical wire on the road, fail to report it to the competent authorities, thereby contributing to the harmful event (Miranda (1984a, b, c), pp. 194–195).

including the recurrent reliance on abuse of rights[152] or implicit constitutional principles.

The duty of care[153] arising from creating or maintaining socially unacceptable dangerous situations demonstrates how the legal system values conduct rules that safeguard interests against potential harm.[154] While engaging in risky or dangerous activities is not prohibited,[155] general duties of care serve as instrumental obligations imposed on individuals to ensure responsible participation in social coexistence.[156] Mertens[157] emphasizes that, through these duties, courts define the permissible scope of anyone's behavior. Duties of care, thus, function like a scale, weighing, on one side, the exercise of self-responsibility and, on the other, the need to hold liable all those who behave in disregard of others' legal spheres.[158]

It should not be asserted that the general duties of care are a peculiarity of German law,[159] due to the typification of the interests protected by § 823 (1) of the BGB. On the contrary, these duties of care bring the German tort system closer to the general clause model,[160] in the sense that everyone should take the precautions that can be reasonably expected in a given situation in order to avoid harming others. According to von Caemmerer,[161] in practice, German courts have not proceeded differently from French and Anglo-American courts regarding the fulfillment of the factual support of *faute* and *negligence.*

Unlike legal systems where protected interests are typified by the law and where the concept of duties of care often serves as a safety valve to rigid legal typification,

---

[152] Carnaúba and Reinig (2016), p. 91.

[153] Larenz asserts that a more recent doctrine qualifies as "unlawful" only the conduct that fails to meet the standard of care required by the legal norm. This understanding ultimately aligns the concept of unlawfulness with the objective criterion of negligence, as set forth in § 276 of the BGB, according to the dominant doctrine (Larenz (2019), p. 688).

[154] The importance of establishing rules of conduct as a prerequisite for unlawfulness is emphasized by Guilherme Reinig (Reinig (2015), p. 264).

[155] General duties of care constitute a boundary line in the tension between integrity and freedom of action (Steffen (1980), p. 410).

[156] When acting, a person assumes responsibility, being required to fulfill a series of duties of care, either by performing a specific function or by integrating into a general community of risk (Rocha (2016), p. 233).

[157] Mertens (1980), p. 399.

[158] Lima (2019), p. 382.

[159] In practice, Brazilian doctrine and jurisprudence achieve results very similar to those of German law, as courts establish rules of conduct based on legally protected goods and interests (Reinig (2015), p. 267).

[160] It is argued that, as § 823 (1) of the BGB represents an open factual basis (*offener Tatbestand*), the determination of duties of care, the decision on which risks should be tolerated, and the protective measures to be required constitute a problem of balancing interests (*Interessenabwägung*) (Caemmerer (1968), pp. 557–559). Bruno Carrá identifies in § 823 (1) of the BGB, due to the use of the expression "other rights" ("*sonstiges Recht*"), the gateway for situations not expressly provided for (Carrá (2015), pp. 156–157).

[161] Caemmerer (1968), pp. 488–489.

in regimes based on general clauses, as Carneiro da Frada pointed out,[162] the specification of the required conduct in the concrete case allows for a balanced approach to the protection needs of individuals and the safeguarding of freedom of action. There is no risk, as in the German system, of distorting the legislative tort model or expanding the scope of liability.[163] On the contrary, in tort law systems based on general clauses, the treatment of specific conduct enables a clearer and more precise delineation of the boundaries of liability.

The adoption of the notion of general duties of care in Brazilian law enables the development of objective criteria for imputation that are highly effective in resolving various cases of "psychological causation." These duties of care serve as a doctrinal tool for the prevention and elimination of dangers.[164] The central criterion of the doctrine of general duties of care, which provides it with internal coherence and theoretical foundation, lies in the protection against sources of danger.[165] Its usefulness can be indicated mainly in groups of cases that involve the creation or maintenance of a dangerous situation, as will be seen later.

4.5 Guiding Criteria for Case Resolution

As "psychological causation" revolves around the voluntary intervention of a second tortfeasor, either influenced or facilitated by the first wrongdoer's conduct,[166] it is essential to establish the exceptional nature of the first perpetrator's liability.[167] Given

---

[162] Frada (2015), p. 247.

[163] Critically, Voss refers to this movement as the starting point for the so-called "corrosion of the legislative tort system" ("*Korrosion des legislativen Deliktsrechts System*") (Voss (2007), p. 48).

[164] The role that the distinction between concrete and abstract dangers plays in the context of the doctrine of general duties of care is questioned. It is partially acknowledged that these duties primarily aim to prevent concrete dangers, while it is also suggested that abstract dangers fall within their functional scope (Larenz and Canaris (1994), p. 402). Concrete danger threatens protected interests that are individualized in specific persons or objects. By contrast, abstractly dangerous behaviors are prohibited because their general potential to cause harm, regardless of any concrete risk to a particular legal interest (Ataíde (2019), p. 640).

[165] The standard of due care can only be defined concretely, on a case-by-case basis, through the assessment of relevant circumstances. Normative criteria are the measures established as necessary and required to prevent the corresponding danger. All known risks, or at least those that are recognizable, should be prevented as far as possible and as required (Leitão (2009), pp. 573–574).

[166] Barbosa (2019), p. 20.

[167] The law should preserve claims against different debtors as distinct as possible, in accordance with their respective liabilities. Creditors, however, consistently seek joint and several liability from all debtors, allowing them to choose the economically strongest party. This tendency is particularly pronounced when only the original debtor is known. However, the legal system cannot submit to these demands without restrictions, so that the first perpetrator is not unreasonably burdened (Rother (1965), p. 28). Ristow also argues that, as a general principle, the individual who directly caused the damage is held liable for it (Ristow (2003), p. 200).

that, in principle, the voluntary act is based on the free decision of the second offender, the damages resulting from their own conduct should, as a rule, be attributed to them.

The legal criteria proposed by doctrine and widely applied in German jurisprudence indicate the cases in which, through the application of objective imputation parameters, the harmful consequences should be attributed to the first wrongdoer who initiated the causal chain. The matter is not fully settled in German doctrine,[168] although certain criteria prevail in judicial practice, guiding interpreters in addressing the intricate problems that emerge from its analysis.

In the context of Brazilian law, given the lack of development of objective imputation criteria,[169] at least in the domain of private law,[170] conflicts tend to be resolved based on the use of traditional causal theories, often without strict technical rigor, which frequently results in arbitrary responses to practical problems. Although many of the attribution criteria already mentioned and further developed below originate in the context of German law, their application, even if partial, is possible in Brazilian law as long as the peculiarities of the two legal systems are respected.[171]

Expanding the liability of the first perpetrator based on abstract constitutional principles, such as human dignity, finds no support in law. While victim protection serves as an important interpretative guide in tort law, it cannot transform this framework into a tool of distributive justice.[172] The logic and methods of

---

[168] Zhang acknowledges that cases of "psychological causation" are problematic (Zhang (2016), p. 14). Ristow states that, in legal doctrine, the topic has rarely been addressed in a comprehensive manner, with discussions often limited to specific individual cases. He emphasizes that, although numerous criteria have been developed, particularly the "provocation formula," inconsistencies persist in jurisprudence (Ristow (2003), p. 12).

[169] Discussing criminal law, and specifically referring to the prohibited conduct, Cezar Roberto Bitencourt argues that, under the theory of objective imputation, the result of a human action can only be objectively imputed to its author when it has created a situation of legally prohibited risk to a legal interest. The author summarizes by stating that a particular result can only be imputed to someone as their action, not as a mere consequence of chance (Bitencourt (2021), p. 349).

[170] The doctrine of objective imputation, developed in criminal law, cannot be mechanically or uncritically applied to private law (Martins-Costa, Judith. Moral damage à la Brazilian ..., cit., p. 7.109). Although the criminal legal system cannot be simply adopted, it is argued that the imputation model helps reduce the differences between civil and criminal liability regimes (Cándano-Pérez and Guerra-Espinosa (2017), p. 139).

[171] The distinction between causation that establishes liability (*haftungsbegründende Kausalität*) and the one that determines the extent of liability (*haftungsausfüllende Kausalität*) does not have practical relevance in Brazilian law. In Germany, liability for the violation of an absolute right is provided for in § 823 of the BGB. This distinction is also followed by Portuguese law due to the typification of absolute rights (Leitão (2009), p. 569). In Brazilian law, Bruno Miragem argues that this bipartition was not adopted, although this distinction may have a didactic purpose, helping to define and apply standards for the determining causation (Miragem (2021), p. 118). Guilherme Reinig proposes a reinterpretation of the dichotomy, suggesting that the basis of liability is not solely defined by the breach of a duty of conduct. Instead, it presupposes the violation of a legal right or legally protected interest. Any subsequent injuries and their harmful effects would then fall within the scope of liability (Reinig (2015), p. 231.

[172] Rodrigues Jr. (2016), p. 117.

distribution mechanisms and social policy objectives do not align with the principles governing private law interpretation.[173]

Considering the central role of the voluntary interference of the second tortfeasor, some important considerations must be made regarding this aspect, which is crucial for the attribution of damages suffered by the victim. As the issues of "psychologically mediated causation" should be addressed regarding the free will of the wrongdoer, it is necessary to question, from a legal standpoint, which criteria and parameters can be derived from this understanding for purposes of legal attribution.[174]

4.5.1 *Criterion of Self-Responsibility*

Human freedom's limits[175] are closely related to individual responsibility for wrongful acts.[176] This raises the issue of whether wrongdoers should be held liable because, as autonomous individuals, they could have acted differently to prevent the harmful outcome. The damaging event arises from the wrongdoer's intentional act, precisely because the individual made one specific decision instead of another. The intervention of the second perpetrator is then considered the act of an individual who, following the initial conduct of the first wrongdoer, chooses to act in a way that causally contributes to the resulting harm.

Forst[177] argues that the "responsibility connection" ("*Verantwortungszusammenhang*") between the act and the damaging event is "interrupted"[178] when a second perpetrator intervenes in the course of events

[173] Michelon (2023), p. 170.

[174] Forst (2000), p. 124.

[175] At this point, no philosophical considerations about human freedom will be discussed, as they fall outside the scope of this work. The analysis will be restricted to legal aspects, specifically regarding the theme of damages caused by "psychological influence."

[176] The delimitation of individual freedoms within the scope of liability is essential. For example, consider the case of a homeowner who inadvertently fails to comply with the police regulation to remove ice accumulating in front of his house. A passerby, avoiding the sidewalk because of the ice, is run over, even though no negligence was involved in their actions. In this situation, it can be assumed that the injured party made the decision with full awareness of the danger. However, the homeowner should be held liable for the risks they created by neglecting their duty, leaving pedestrians with no alternative but to navigate those dangers (Mertens (1980), p. 744). It is argued by Larenz and Canaris that, contrary to the common belief, private residents are not obligated, under § 823 (1) of the BGB, to spread ice on the ground, even if they could easily do so and thereby mitigate the danger, as they are not responsible for opening or tolerating traffic on sidewalks and road (Larenz and Canaris (1994), p. 413).

[177] Forst (2000), p. 125.

[178] According to Deutsch, only when intentional conduct is not entirely free should the causal link be traced back to previous negligent acts. Therefore, the intentional intervention of a third party could interrupt the causal chain (Deutsch (1972), p. 553).

after the first, based on an equally autonomous decision, and establishes another necessary condition for the result. The damaging result would then be regarded solely as the act of the second party's will, falling within their responsibility. This delineation of liability between various perpetrators, whose decisions follow one another in a causal process, would be based on the criterion of self-responsibility. The author concludes that, in terms of objective imputation, the violation of protected interests appears exclusively as an act of will of the second tortfeasor and, in principle, should be attributed solely to him.[179]

Niebaum[180] also refers to the "legal value of self-determination or self-responsibility" ("*die Rechtswerte der Selbstbestimmung bzw. -verantwortung*")[181] as a fundamental principle of the legal community. He illustrates its importance with an example: a sick office worker who is invited to participate in the company's sports activities. According to the author, if he accepts the proposal and suffers damage to his health due to excessive physical effort, he cannot, under any circumstances, demand compensation from his colleagues.[182]

Such a conclusion, according to Niebaum,[183] could superficially rely on the idea that the individuals acted in a socially appropriate manner or that a "general risk of life" ("*allgemeines Lebensrisiko*") materialized. However, these statements merely describe the outcome, while the underlying reasoning is more complex. The decision to participate in the company's sports activities was self-determined, meaning no external influence was involved, and, consequently, no third-party liability should apply. Niebaum concludes that the values of self-determination and self-responsibility limit "external liability".

The legal values of self-determination and self-responsibility, according to Leitermeier,[184] have not yet been widely discussed in private law, so Niebaum could only be supported by vague and philosophical considerations from authors

179 Objective imputation leads to the notion of self-responsibility for the victim. Pablo Malheiros exemplifies this by citing a person who knowingly uses a syringe with heroin or transmits contagious venereal diseases to a partner, fully aware of the associated risks (Frota (2014), p. 197).

180 Niebaum (1977), pp. 70–71.

181 The criterion of self-responsibility is applied when a compensation claim cannot be legally sustained. According to Haberhausen, this parameter is only used when there are two acts of the same nature (Haberhausen (1973), p. 1309).

182 A frequently cited illustration is the case of patient B, who, after accepting A's invitation to a banquet, eats and drinks excessively and suffers a stroke, later attempting to hold A liable for the resulting damages (Thalheim (1964), pp. 90–91).

183 Niebaum (1977), pp. 70–71.

184 Leitermeier (1968), p. 61.

like Reinecke[185] and Haberhausen.[186] Other jurists would merely refer to these parameters in passing, often as *obiter dictum.*

In Brazilian law, self-responsibility is a fundamental principle derived from the model of the Democratic State of Law[187] and is grounded in the inviolability of the rights to freedom, privacy, and private life.[188] As Juarez Tavares[189] explains, under the criterion of self-responsibility, the consequences of an individual's voluntary actions must be attributed solely to that individual, rather than to the person whose actions initially motivated them.[190]

Although self-responsibility is recognized as a relevant criterion in the delimitation of damage attribution, particularly in cases of "psychologically mediated causation," adopting the arguments of Forst[191] and Niebaum is not entirely convincing, as they tend to overestimate its significance. These authors define self-determination as a decisive criterion for objective attribution in such cases. However, other factors, independent of the individual's voluntariness, must also be considered, including the materialization of a risk source created by the initial perpetrator and the violation of general duties of care.

Forst himself[192] admits that self-responsibility does not have categorical application in all cases of "psychological causation." He refers to the case of the flight demonstration event (*Flugveranstaltungsfall*),[193] where the BGH[194] decided that the association that organized the air show and the participants who trespassed on the neighboring land should be held jointly liable, even though

---

[185] Reinecke posits that the implementation of responsibility is a more fundamental value than the freedom of will, understood in its philosophical sense of indeterminacy. However, this responsibility is grounded in the natural and legal freedom of individuals. According to the author, self-responsibility begins when individuals, through the phenomenon of freedom and their connection to their "personal self" ("personales Selbst"), acquire control over what they have experienced (*personales Selbst*), assume control over their actions and their consequences (Reinecke (1960), p. 72).

[186] Haberhausen (1973), p. 1309.

[187] Tavares (2009), p. 370.

[188] Marinho (2013), pp. 48–49.

[189] Tavares (2009), p. 300.

[190] In obligation law, Judith Martins-Costa emphasizes that self-responsibility is the essential counterpart to the recognition of private autonomy (Martins-Costa (2018), p. 257).

[191] Forst's theory is grounded in the principle of human freedom, particularly in the rejection of determinism. However, this notion, initially introduced, is later subjected to closer scrutiny by the author, as noted by Mafalda Miranda (Barbosa (2020), p. 986).

[192] Even so, Forst argues that self-responsibility provides a fundamental assessment that guide the search for criteria by which risk can be adequately distributed between the first and second perpetrators (Forst (2000), pp. 125–126).

[193] This case concerns an association that organized an air show demonstration. However, some spectators trespassed onto a neighboring property, damaging the fence that separated the two areas. The BGH (NJW 1980, 223) held the association liable for compensating the neighboring owner for the damages caused by the spectators. A detailed analysis of this case will be provided in Sect. 5.2.2.1.

[194] NJW 1980, 223.

the trespassers acted based on autonomous will. Indeed, the third party's liability, even if derived from free conduct, does not, by itself, exclude the liability of the first perpetrator.[195]

The perspective that self-responsibility has only limited relevance in damage attribution should not prevail. Depending on the specific group of cases analyzed, the fact that the decision to act was made voluntarily may have a significant impact on the attribution of liability.[196] For instance, in cases of suicide,[197] the assessment of the victim's self-determination becomes more relevant, as it is not possible to attribute the consequences of this act to the first tortfeasor if the deceased took their own life for reasons deemed insufficiently serious. Even while recognizing the relevance of the causes that led to the fatal act, co-responsibility must be recognized when the victim failed to offer the minimum expected resistance.[198]

4.5.2 Controllability Criterion

Liability is generally recognized when the harm results from a causal process that remains within the individual's sphere of control.[199] Thalheim[200] asserts that liability arises in two circumstances: when a person deliberately directs events to cause harm (intentional offenses) or when the course of events, under their control, leads to damages that a reasonable person could have anticipated, yet they failed to act accordingly to prevent the result (negligent offenses).

The concept of controllability goes beyond the mere ability of the perpetrator to initiate the causal chain, as this is a fundamental requirement for any form of liability.[201] Rather, it asserts that the harmful event, which the duty of care imposed on the perpetrator sought to prevent, and for which they are held responsible, must

---

[195] Greger (2013), p. 46.

[196] Emphasizing the relevance of self-responsibility and individuals' freedom of action in structuring tort liability, see Frada (2015), p. 293.

[197] Cases of self-harm arise when an individual, influenced by prior conduct, deliberately causes harm to themselves or their interests. Examples include individuals who took their own lives following the Fukushima nuclear disaster and the dam failures in Brumadinho. These cases will be examined in Sect. 5.2.1.4.

[198] Lange and Schiemann (2003), p. 139.

[199] According to Larenz, human action is not just a link in the infinite chain of causes and effects but is the expression of a determinable will. It is attributable, as action to the extent that it is controllable, even if it constitutes an unconscious act, as it is understood as the expression of a being capable of free determination. The judgment of objective imputation indicates that an individual's action is his act of will, for which he can be held responsible, as he had the opportunity to behave one way or another (Larenz (1955), p. 1011).

[200] Thalheim (1964), p. 92.

[201] In contractual obligations, risks should be borne by the party who controls their respective source or origin (Koller (1979), p. 78).

fall within their sphere of influence.[202] Referring to the case of the *Bundesbahn* inspector who chased the passenger for not paying the ticket, Reinhold Weber[203] states that the pursuer became the "master of events" ("*Herr des Geschehens*").

According to this guideline, a person can, through their will, control natural causal events and, in this way, direct them. Only at this moment do they transform the natural event into their own act, leading to the objective imputation of the harmful consequences. From this connection between will[204] and controllability, it follows that liability for negligence would only be justified if the perpetrator had the possibility of controlling the course of events they initiated[205] and preventing the violation of protected interests.[206]

Niebaum[207] argues that the "principle of controllability" ("*Beherrschbarkeitsprinzip*") justifies the exclusion of liability. The voluntary actions of third parties would be excluded, as they lie outside the sphere of influence of the initial perpetrator. The author questions the extent to which causal factors could be considered within the control of the first wrongdoer.

In contrast, Forst[208] states that, unlike self-responsibility, which in principle excludes the liability of the initial tortfeasor, no general rule for or against attribution can be derived from the controllability criterion. The specific circumstances of each case determine whether and to what extent a causal course is considered controllable by either perpetrator. Such circumstances, however, do not change the fact that this criterion is of fundamental importance in the attribution of liability in the context of "psychologically mediated causation."

The application of the controllability criterion leads to significant consequences in specific groups of cases involving damages caused by psychological influence. This results from the fact that certain consequences would no longer fall within the control of the initial perpetrator and, therefore, could not be attributed to them.[209] This principle suggests that the sphere of influence corresponds to the scope of responsibility. In this context, the general duties of care focus solely on preventing events within the control of the original wrongdoer, as the decision-making rests not with the initial tortfeasor but with the second, determining the violation of protected interests.[210]

---

202 Niebaum (1977), p. 68.

203 Weber (1995), p. 513.

204 Larenz (1927), p. 76.

205 Ataíde (2019), p. 643.

206 It is not necessary for the perpetrator to have been actually capable of controlling the causal process up to the occurrence of the violation of the legal interest; it is enough that the harmful event was controllable by him in case of socially appropriate behavior (Forst (2000), p. 126).

207 Niebaum (1977), p. 68.

208 Forst (2000), pp. 127–128.

209 Schwarz (1966), p. 164.

210 The second causer determines whether the action leads to the result, occupying the central position and "pushing" the others to the periphery, who can only contribute to the success of the event through him (Roxin (2015), p. 48).

In situations involving two parties, such as in cases of rescue and pursuit,[211] the controllability criterion does not play an important role. Indeed, in these situations, the decisive criteria, as will be discussed, are the materialization of a created risk and the proportionality of the conduct adopted. The mere act of putting oneself in danger does not inherently constitute a wrongful act. However, a duty of care (*Verhaltenspflicht*) may be established to prevent the creation of inappropriate emergency situations from a social perspective.[212] This includes the duty for other parties not to act in a dangerous manner.[213]

In cases involving a third party, although their importance cannot be disregarded, the criterion of controllability should not be treated as decisive, as a significant part of German doctrine does.[214] It is not the fact that the causal course can no longer be controlled by the initial perpetrator that completely exonerates their responsibility for the acts committed,[215] as in the case of a driver who causes an accident and others, bypassing the location, invade and damage the adjacent land. The determining criterion for attribution is the realization of the risk created or increased by the first perpetrator for failing to adopt the required behavioral norms in each situation. As Zimmermann notes,[216] the act controllable by their will consists in creating an impermissible dangerous situation.[217] The creation of a dangerous situation results from their voluntary act. If this risk materializes, there is no reason to question the attribution of liability.

Brazilian doctrine, as discussed by Juarez Tavares, although focusing on criminal law, utilizes the criterion of "capacity to control the causal process." He provides the example of a nephew who sends his uncle on a train trip, during

---

[211] See Sect. 5.2.1.1.

[212] Zimmermann (1980), p. 15.

[213] Lange and Schiemann (2003), p. 132.

[214] Among others, Hans Stoll asserts that the decisive factor is whether the risk of the intentional intervention of third parties can still be seen as controllable by the initial tortfeasor (Stoll (1993), p. 406).

[215] According to Leitermeier, the "controllability of the event" ("*Beherrschbarkeit des Geschehens*"), in its everyday meaning, cannot be considered a requirement of objective imputation. In many cases of indirect causation, where the harmful event only occurs after the interference of other causes, the first perpetrator has no influence over subsequent events (Leitermeier (1968), p. 54).

[216] It is considered that perhaps the actions of the second causer are no longer controllable by the first perpetrator from a certain point. However, the first perpetrator is not responsible for the acts of the second causer, but for his own acts, since he created a socially inappropriate danger (Zimmermann (1980), p. 15).

[217] It is necessary to assess whether the author's conduct increased the probability of producing the result in comparison to the permitted risk (Martins-Costa (2014), p. 7108). Miguel Reale Júnior adopts a similar position, asserting that for the perpetrator's liability to arise, there must be an increase in the risk beyond the permissible limits, with the disapproved conduct representing a failure to exercise the necessary diligence (Reale Jr. (2013), p. 238).

which an accident occurs and the uncle dies.[218] According to the author, the harmful result cannot be attributed to the nephew, considering that the event was completely beyond his control. However, as previously stated, it is not the fact that the causal process is outside the control of the initial perpetrator that excludes liability, but rather the fact that a "general risk of life" has materialized.

4.5.3 Provocation Formula

In 1927, Larenz[219] developed his theory of imputation, according to which every consequence must be objectively attributed to the perpetrator's will. For many years, this reasoning provided the philosophical legal foundation for adequacy theory: improbable causal courses would not be seriously expected and, therefore, were not attributable to the perpetrator's will.[220] The decision of the *Landgericht* Düsseldorf[221] on March 8, 1955 led Larenz[222] to assert that not all consequences could be attributed to the first tortfeasor, especially when they had been caused by an intentional act of will by a third party. In such cases, the "sphere of will" ("*die Willenssphäre*") of the first wrongdoer would be regarded as concluded with the behavior of the second tortfeasor.

Three years later, Larenz[223] partially distanced himself from this thesis: It is not the mere intentional act of another that excludes attribution. However, attribution is excluded when a third party's action causing the result lacks an internal connection with the event establishing the first perpetrator's liability. This "internal connection" ("*innerer Zusammenhang*") is now defined by Larenz through the concept of

[218] Although the nephew's conduct was causally linked to the result, in terms of "psychological causation," based on the hypothetical elimination criterion, the consequences should not be attributed to him, as the result was entirely beyond his control (Tavares (2019), p. 300).

[219] Larenz (1927), p. 67.

[220] Niebaum (1977), pp. 57–58.

[221] NJW 1955, 1031. The decision, previously mentioned, addressed a case in which a lorry driver caused a traffic accident, blocking the flow of other vehicles. In response, these vehicles used the green strip (*Grünstreifen*) to bypass the blockage, damaging the land in the process. The Federal Republic of Germany, as the landowner, sued the party liable for the accident, seeking compensation for the material damages. The German court upheld the claim, affirming the existence of a causal link between the accident and the damages incurred.

[222] According to Larenz, the exclusion of imputation in these cases is grounded by the fact that a predominant degree of responsibility lies with the individual who acts intentionally. This solution would correspond to the "sense of justice" ("*Rechtsgefühl*"). In this context, the strongest form of responsibility, corresponding to intentional action, surpasses and eliminates the weaker form, which refers to attributing the harmful event to the cause that established the prior condition (Larenz (1955), p. 1012).

[223] Larenz (1958), p. 628.

"provocation" ("*Herausforderung*").[224] According to the author, the exclusion of objective attribution in these cases is based on the fact that the second tortfeasor was not "provoked" by the first event and, therefore, is the only one responsible for the harmful consequences.[225]

In jurisprudential terms, these ideas were adopted by the BGH[226] in the green strip case,[227] denying the attribution of damages to the initial perpetrator, since the impatient drivers would not have been "provoked" to act unlawfully. However, the criterion was further developed in the "pursuit cases" ("*Verfolgerfälle*").[228] The formulations used by the BGH (NJW 1971, 1980[229]) contain a normative expression that allows the judge to examine the decision to pursue in terms of its reasonableness: The pursuer or rescuer must feel "provoked" ("*herausgefordert*") to act "in the form and manner chosen" ("*in der gewählten Art und Weise*").[230] Although the "provocation formula" was initially developed by Larenz in the context of three-person case groups, the BGH has more recently stated that this criterion is not decisive in such cases.[231]

Similar to the theory of the scope of protection of the norm, the "provocation formula" has also faced criticism. Despite its general formulation, which suggests a broad range of potential applications, it is primarily used in certain case groups. In other categories, it is not applied or does not represent a particularly useful decision-making tool.[232] Rather than being considered a universal theory or an

[224] The provocation formula originates from a formulation by Kipp, which was later adopted by Larenz and accepted and further developed by jurisprudence (Steffen (1980), p. 137). In the *Lehrbuch des Pandektenrechts*, in the passage indicated by Steffen, it is stated that a person who has caused, through their own fault, a dangerous situation, must also bear the consequences of a free action carried out by the injured party, if this responsibility is justified by the circumstances (Windscheid and Kipp (1963), p. 64).

[225] Such a circumstance does not "interrupt," as was previously assumed, the causal chain itself, because, at the level of the purely causal connection, every cause produces its effect, and every effect subsequently becomes the cause of new effects (Larenz (1970), p. 87).

[226] BGHZ 58, 167. According to Weitenberg, causation, in the cases involving the green strip, should be denied, as the accident is considered only an external circumstance (*äußerer Umstand*), which lost its continuity once the accident site was bypassed (Weitenberg (2014), p. 769).

[227] Niebaum (1977), p. 58.

[228] Ristow (2003), pp. 137–138.

[229] This is the case, previously mentioned, decided on June 24, 1967, by the BGH, involving the operations supervisor of the Deutsche Bundesbahn, who was injured while pursuing a defaulting passenger.

[230] Niebaum (1980), p. 13; Strauch (1992), p. 1204.

[231] Courts failing to properly apply the "provocation criterion" and misjudging its implications are reprimanded by the BGH (Niebaum (1980), p. 11). Lange and Schiemann note the limited utility of this criterion in cases of intentional third-party intervention (Lange and Schiemann (2003), p. 145).

[232] Causer acts intentionally in violation of legal interests, as the issue of "being able to feel provoked" ("*Sich-herausgefordert-fühlen-Dürfen*") becomes irrelevant when the transgression is committed deliberately (Forst (2000), pp. 96–97). Deutsch observes that the criterion is limited to cases of "psychological causation" and, as a general principle for delimiting liability, its applicability is restricted (Deutsch (1996), p. 106).

abstract formula capable of resolving a variety of situations, this theoretical construct should be assessed based on its specific criteria, which show varying levels of effectiveness depending on the case group.

The "provocation formula" is subdivided into several criteria,[233] based on the analysis of the BGH decisions on the matter. Generally, it is required that the party who acted under the influence of the initial conduct must have felt "provoked" by that conduct. The motive of the rescuer or pursuer is also examined, as well as whether their conduct was proportional to the pursued objective.[234] Finally, it is also required that the risk increased by the escape or by the accident that gave rise to the rescue attempt has materialized in the injury caused.

4.5.3.1 Provocation

Larenz[235] asserts that when an individual participates in a rescue operation or assists in combating a fire caused by a third party and subsequently gets injured, that individual is considered "provoked" ("*herausgefordert*") and "sufficiently motivated" ("*hinreichend motiviert*") by the actions of the person who created the risky situation. According to German scholars, the attribution of responsibility is excluded if the damage is caused by an action of the injured party or a third party that was based on a free decision and not "provoked" by the event that established liability. In such cases, a new risk is created, which then materializes in the injury.[236] Larenz further explains that any additional damages caused by a third party's conduct, based on their free deliberation, cannot be attributed to the first perpetrator. This is the case if the third party's behavior, although made possible by the initial act, was not "provoked" by it, specifically, if the third party's actions did not serve to reduce or eliminate the initial harm but instead pursued a different objective.[237]

The term "provocation" is not sufficiently explained by German doctrine[238] and tends more to obscure[239] than to provide reliable guidelines in cases of "psychological causation." Schiemann,[240] citing German jurisprudence, states that there is "provocation" in cases of "occasioning" ("*Veranlassung*").[241] In contrast, the behavior that gave rise to the first cause would only constitute the external occasion

[233] Zhang (2016), pp. 62–66.

[234] Vieweg and Lorz (2022), p. 585.

[235] Larenz (1987), p. 452.

[236] Larenz (1987), p. 457.

[237] Larenz (1987), p. 450.

[238] Martens questions whether what the BGH referred to as "provocation" should more accurately be designated as speculation (Martens (1972), p. 743).

[239] Ristow (2003), p. 140.

[240] Schiemann (2017), p. 90.

[241] Traeger, highlighting the fragility of this distinction, asserts that the terms "*Ursache*" ("cause") and "*Bedingung*" ("condition"), "*Verursachung*" ("causation") and "*Veranlassung*" ("occasioning") are identical expressions (Traeger (1929), p. 39).

and merely the opportunity for the injured person to expose themselves to a risk unrelated to the accident. Görgens[242] understands "provocation" as a stronger factor than mere "occasioning" ("*Veranlassung*"). "Provocation" would be linked to a kind of "coercion" ("*Zwang*"),[243] without constituting a duty. According to the author, "mere occasioning"[244] ("*bloße Veranlassung*") consists of a mere external occasion for the act of a third party, without reaching the level of a coercive act.

Zimmermann[245] alludes to the fact that the term "provocation" refers to a certain degree of urgency, mediated by impulse. The issue that arises is whether it is appropriate to emphasize the intensity of the psychological influence and the spontaneity of the action.[246] Both in emergency cases and in pursuit situations, spontaneous interventions are also debated. In the latter, however, the specific risk increase is particularly clear, as acting with such urgency implies special dangers, which it is often not even possible to fully recognize. Zimmermann[247] points out that there is no reason to privilege the volunteer rescuer over an emergency services worker, as, if the risk materializes, it does not seem appropriate to leave these professionals to bear the damages.

According to Min Zhang,[248] "occasioning" refers to a causal connection of equal nature, while "provocation" involves a greater intensity of psychological influence. Consequently, the latter concept sets a higher standard than the former. In this context, "provocation" does not have to reach the same intensity as "Provokation" (also translated as provocation).[249] For the author, the psychological mediation should be stronger than "simple occasioning" but not attain the level of "Provokation."[250]

---

[242] Görgens (1977), p. 714.

[243] According to this position, if a pursuer risks their own interests to rescue someone from a dangerous situation, the resulting damage should be attributed to the pursued, provided that the condition they are responsible for carries significant weight and a demanding character, making the intervention reasonable and justifiable (Müller (2016), p. 126).

[244] On the distinction between cause, condition, and occasion, see Pirson and Ville (1935), p. 37.

[245] Niebaum (1980), pp. 12–13.

[246] Even in situations where the second causer has time to reflect on the most appropriate course of action, the liability of the first causer is recognized. This can be seen in cases like the mother who donates a kidney to her daughter after the latter becomes a victim of a medical error. Similarly, this principle applies to the case of a police officer who, not feeling "provoked" by the fugitive's actions, decides to pursue him anyway after carefully considering the risks and chances involved (Schwarz (1966), p. 163).

[247] Niebaum (1980), pp. 12–13.

[248] Zhang maintain that it is necessary to maintain the characteristic of "provocation," despite some conceptual imprecision. However, the example provided by the author, in which an individual begins a pursuit to greet someone they know, lacks convincing practical relevance. Although it presents an interesting academic scenario, it can be more effectively analyzed through the criteria that will be explored in the following sections (Zhang (2016), pp. 82–83).

[249] Although the two terms are often used as synonyms, the latter has a stronger connotation. The alteration and combination of words demonstrate the lack of technicality in the use of these expressions in German law. It is a hollow requirement, without practical relevance, of a purely rhetorical nature.

[250] Supporting this same position, see Weber (1995), p. 513.

The expression, on its own, without other defining criteria, lacks legal value for the purpose of delimiting liability.[251] Stürner[252] even goes so far as to say that the use of the "provocation formula" implies the existence of other underlying motives, such as the burden on public service. Similarly, Schiemann[253] emphasizes that the term "provocation" tends to obscure the evaluative judgment required by jurisprudence itself, rather than guide it. The term can also lead to misleading interpretations, as, in everyday language, it could suggest that the first perpetrator should incite or stimulate the second one to act in a certain way,[254] when it has already been seen that "psychologically mediated causation," within the scope of the investigation carried out in this work, does not cover situations where the first perpetrator acts intentionally, aiming at a certain result.

The idea of the individual "feeling provoked" ("*sich herausgefordert fühlen dürfen*")[255] refers to an excessive subjectivism, which should be replaced by more objective parameters,[256] such as the proportionality of the act committed by the second perpetrator. The subjective emphasis given by the requirement of "provocation" leads the interpreter toward more intuitive solutions based on equity criteria, which, although not entirely eliminable, as discretion in evaluations is always present, ought to be avoided in the process of objective imputation.[257]

Thus, although the expression is widely used by German doctrine[258] and replicated by the courts,[259] it seems inappropriate to apply the mentioned criterion due to its insufficient analytical precision. It is sufficient, at this initial evaluative stage, to conclude that the first perpetrator enabled or facilitated the emergence of damage by creating a risk situation.

---

[251] According to Niebaum, there is no need for a formula that only offers a description of the result, without revealing the truth of the relevant evaluative aspects (Niebaum (1977), p. 61).

[252] Stürner (1984), p. 308.

[253] Schiemann notes that the colloquial use of language in this context has no relevance (Schiemann (2017), p. 90).

[254] Oetker emphasizes that the term "provocation" should not be understood in the sense of a conscious causation, further stating that it is irrelevant whether the helper is obligated to intervene or acts voluntarily (Oetker (2019), p. 408).

[255] Forst (2000), pp. 96–97.

[256] As noted by Waldkirch, this criterion (*das Kriterium des 'Sich-herausgefordert-fühlen-Dürfens*) essentially consists of a reasonableness test, noting that several other criteria are used interchangeably without substantive differences (Waldkirch (2018), p. 383).

[257] In the case of police officers and rescuers, Hager asserts that it is not necessary for the individual to be "provoked" in order to perform their professional duties; it is sufficient for them to take action (Hager (2018), p. 708).

[258] Also using the expression, among others, see Stoll (1980), p. 423; Staake (2014), p. 241; Matthies (2009), p. 878; Jansen (2002), p. 523.

[259] BGHZ 132, 164; BGHZ 192, 261.

4.5.3.2 Justifiable Motives

A significant part of German doctrine confirms the criterion adopted by jurisprudence[260] that the intervening party must have had a justifiable motive[261] ("*billigenswerte Motive*") to act. In this sense, Medicus[262] refers to a decision of the BGH[263] in which it was established that there is no general mandate to prevent others from putting themselves in danger, nor a prohibition against assuming a risky position. However, it is possible to establish a duty of behavior aimed at preventing the occurrence of socially undesirable emergencies, which might otherwise place others in situations requiring hazardous interventions.[264]

This occurs, for example, when someone attempts to stop the passage of horses to prevent others from being harmed and sustains an injury themselves, or when, in a bus fire, a passenger tries to help a child exit the vehicle and is injured. The issue that arises is to what extent the intervention of a third party in a dangerous situation, caused by a first perpetrator but resulting in harm to the third party, is justifiable. Not every intervention by a second party in a risky situation will automatically result in the first causer's liability for the harm suffered by the individual.

In principle, justifiable actions are those required by law, such as a firefighter performing a rescue or a police officer pursuing a fleeing offender.[265] However, in many instances, individuals without a legal duty to act intervene and suffer harm. The question that arises in such cases is whether the first perpetrator should be held liable for the injuries sustained by the second causer. Consider the case of a passerby who witnesses a car accident and voluntarily attempts to rescue the victims trapped in the wreckage, injuring themselves in the process. Or consider the case of a mother who donates a kidney to her daughter, and the organ is lost due to a medical error or malpractice (*Nierenspende-Fall*).[266]

---

[260] BGHZ 132, 164.

[261] In addition to the common characteristics of an unlawful act, in cases of pursuit, the specific circumstances must be evaluated, particularly the fact that the pursuer felt "provoked" to act for justifiable reasons (Strauch (1992), p. 937).

[262] Medicus (2005), pp. 293–294.

[263] NJW 1986, 1865.

[264] Lange and Schiemann (2003), p. 132.

[265] Händel asserts that the public interest in police intervention should not be disregarded. In cases of pursuit, the officer is not only authorized to intervene, but also has a legal duty to do so (Händel (1976), p. 1204).

[266] NJW 1987, 710. See Sect. 5.2.1.1.

Some authors argue that justifiable motive should encompass not only legal duties but also ethical[267] and moral obligations.[268] Relying on moral judgments could lead to predetermined conclusions based on the intended outcome rather than an objective legal analysis.[269] Zimmermann[270] distinguishes between rescue cases, where socially desirable human behavior should be acknowledged by the legal system, and pursuit cases, which lack a comparable moral foundation. Even in the latter scenario, he argues that the pursued individual should not be exempt from the risks associated with the chase.

In many cases, it is not possible to clearly determine the motive behind the subsequent action. When the second behavior is morally neutral or even questionable, this criterion may lead to incoherent results. Situations where no specific motive can be identified are not uncommon, and self-endangerment arises from behaviors that appear unreasonable or are even undertaken for personal gain.[271] The BGH[272] has already recognized that, in cases of private pursuit, simple "street camaraderie" *("Kameradschaftlichkeit der Straße"),*[273] which does not constitute a moral obligation,[274] would justify the act and therefore establish the obligation of the pursued to provide compensation.[275]

Illustrative examples of self-interested motivation include a son who rescues his father, not to protect his life and physical integrity, but to secure the financial support on which he relies, and a mother who donates an organ to her daughter with the expectation of maintaining her standard of living, since the daughter derives significant income from her successful early musical career. Even in these situations, where the motive for the rescue does not stem from a noble intention, it does not seem possible to argue that the first perpetrator should not be held responsible for the damages suffered by the second causer. If the motive is considered as the mere intention to save, the criterion also seems to lose its practical utility, since in emergency cases any motive would be justifiable.[276]

---

267 Lange and Schiemann (2003), p. 132. Grüneberg refers to "legally or morally required actions" ("rechtlich oder sittlich gebotene Handlungen") (Grüneberg et al. (2020), p. 294). Oetker asserts it is irrelevant whether the helper is obligated to intervene or acts voluntarily (Oetker (2019), p. 405).

268 In cases of voluntary assistance, from the standpoint of the theory of adequacy, it can be argued that what is at least morally imperative is not entirely improbable (Schwarz (1966), p. 163).

269 Ristow (2003), p. 142.

270 Niebaum (1980), p. 13.

271 Hasselblatt (1996), p. 75.

272 NJW 1964, 1363.

273 Consider the scenario where a vehicle collides with a taxi and the negligent driver flees the scene. Another taxi driver, noticing the incident, initiates a pursuit.

274 Medicus (2005), p. 292.

275 In contrary, Weber notes that in the case of "street camaraderie," there is an appeal to the pursuer's sense of public spirit (Weber (1995), p. 513).

276 According to Theo Schwarz, if the moral quality of the rescuer's behavior is taken into account, it would be very difficult to deny the liability of the individual who caused the dangerous

Consequently, investigating whether a legal or moral duty exists to perform the act becomes unnecessary. The rescuer's or pursuer's conduct is justified when they act proportionally to neutralize or mitigate effects from a danger source created or maintained by the first wrongdoer. For this reason, the BGH's decision seems problematic when it considered compensable the damages suffered by a private pursuer who merely aimed to detain a third party that had caused an accident. The pursuit, in this case, aimed to identify the wrongdoer's license plate.[277]

Equally questionable is the idea that, in a case where an individual is struck by a vehicle while crossing against a red light in reliance on another's lead, the liability of the initial perpetrator is excluded on the ground that the victim, though arguably provoked, is deemed not to have acted in a justifiable manner.[278] This reasoning fails to explain why the case should be treated differently based on whether the injured party is an adult or a minor. The criteria underlying the so-called provocation formula do not apply here. In both scenarios, there is no justifiable motive, as outlined above, to support the victim's actions.[279]

4.5.3.3 Increased Risk

According to prevailing German doctrine, attributing damages to the first perpetrator requires that an increased risk has been established through the violation of a legal norm or duty of care.[280] The foundation of liability lies in the creation of a dangerous situation,[281] which makes the intervention of a second wrongdoer justifiable. This created reprehensible condition, dangerous from the perspective of general duties of care, constitutes the ground for damage attribution.[282] The second causer, therefore, shall only be held liable when the "increased risk situation" ("*gesteigerter Gefahrenzustand*"), created by them, materializes in the occurrence of damages.[283]

---

situation, as the interests of the injured party are easily overestimated in the balancing required by equity (Schwarz (1966), p. 163).

[277] BGH, NJW 1964, 1363.

[278] On the contrary, see Zhang (2016), p. 84.

[279] Even in the case of the minor, it is necessary that the second causer cannot independently assess the danger of their behavior correctly (Ristow (2003), p. 86).

[280] Bar (1980), p. 166.

[281] In Brazilian law, see Miranda (1984a, b, c), p. 194.

[282] Caemmerer (1970), pp. 290–291.

[283] Weber (1995), p. 513.

It is not enough that the occurrence of the injury has been verified as merely an increased risk, but that the "typical risk" (*typisches Risiko*)[284] of that particular situation effectively materialized.[285] If the second causer suffers injuries that could have occurred equally without the dangerous situation,[286] such damages cannot be attributed to the first perpetrator.[287] Even in the case of intentional acts committed by the second wrongdoer, the damages suffered by the first causer can be attributed to them if the "specific opportunity" ("*spezifische Gelegenheit*") for these intentional conducts arose through the initial act.[288] Thus, for example, if the pursuer's vehicle tire bursts during the escape while driving at the permitted speed, it cannot be stated that the injurious result stemmed from the increased risk created by the pursuit.

The idea of specific risk is opposed to that of "general life risk"[289] ("*allgemeines Lebensrisiko*"),[290] which, according to a significant part of German doctrine, serves a negative function in the delimitation of liability.[291] Deutsch[292] states that it is relatively easy to determine the "general life risk" as grounds for non-liability (*Nichthaftung*). In terms of the bases of liability, this general risk is related to fortuity,[293] meaning that no one should be held liable for accidental events, and the holder of the protected interest must, as a rule, bear the losses.[294] Even if there is a basis for liability, this is limited by the aspect of imputation. According to the author, the scope of damage limitation,[295] which does not lead to compensation, could be referred to as "general life risk."[296]

---

[284] In escape cases, Grüneberg highlights the necessity of concretizing the "typical risk of pursuit" ("*verfolgungstypisches Risiko*") (Grüneberg et al. (2020), p. 294). Strauch also refers to a "specific risk of pursuit" ("*spezifische Verfolgungsrisiken*") (Strauch (1992), p. 936).

[285] Pereira (2019), p. 464. Montijano further argues that the theory of objective imputation demands not only that the conduct increased the risk of the result, but also that the risk was reflected in the result (Montijano (2008), p. 91). Juarez Tavares similarly contends that imputation is based on the principle that the perpetrator's conduct, in addition to being causal, must have created a risk for the occurrence of the result (Tavares (2019), p. 297).

[286] Reinig (2015), p. 134.

[287] Oetker (2019), p. 408.

[288] Schiemann (2017), p. 95.

[289] Comes (1972), p. 2022.

[290] Von Caemmerer refers to a "own sphere of life" ("*eigener Lebensbereich*") (Caemmerer (1956), p. 15). In the 60s, Hermann Lange introduced the term "general life risk" ("*allgemeines Lebensrisiko*"), which has become widely used (Lange (1960), p. 53).

[291] Strauch (1992), p. 936.

[292] Deutsch (1993), p. 1043.

[293] According to Rümelin, as the domain of responsibility defined by risk expands, the sphere of fortuity correspondingly diminishes. Thus, risk and fortuity stand in opposition to one another (Rümelin (1896), pp. 42–43).

[294] Brox and Walker (2020), p. 376.

[295] General duties of care also serve as a tool for the "allocation of liability" ("*Zuweisung von Schadenslasten*"), either broadening or limiting the scope of liability (Jansen (2002), p. 534).

[296] Emphasizing the negative aspect of delimiting responsibility, it is argued that the term "general life risk" lacks any substantive criteria or characteristics from which legal

Intending to develop an autonomous concept of "general life risk," it is necessary to circumscribe the risk inherent to an individual. General risk, therefore, includes the dangers that one must bear, even where negligent interference by another occurs, as long as they can be attributed to the normal risk sphere of the individual.[297] This implies that, according to the grounds and extent of liability, there exists a risk zone for the holder of the protected interest that is not affected by the negligent intervention of third parties.[298] Given this premise, attributing such risk to the offender through a compensatory norm would contradict the coherence of the legal system as a whole.[299]

The attribution of the damage to the victim's sphere represents a specific form of protection for the individual exercising control over their actions within their area of responsibility. Everyone shapes their life in such a way that ensures personal security and enables them to meet the ordinary demands of daily life. The risks that normally accompany their existence belong to the sphere for which they are responsible.[300] The scope of this rule encompasses both fault-based liability and strict liability. For instance, if a person witnesses a harmless collision between two vehicles and suffers psychological damage,[301] the driver should not be held liable. The claim for compensation should be rejected because the "general risk of life" should be attributed to the sphere of responsibility of the injured party.[302]

---

consequences can be derived. It would therefore be nothing more than a broad conceptual grouping that encompasses various value judgments. Such a situation is the inevitable consequence of the lack of precise mathematical formulas for resolving issues of imputation (Ekkenga and Kuntz (2014), p. 80).

[297] Liability would be excluded, for instance, if the requested taxi arrives too late, resulting in the passenger missing the first flight; however, the subsequent flight ends in a crash (Oetker (2019), p. 417).

[298] Deutsch (1993), p. 1044; Strasser (2008), p. 86.

[299] Hübner (1972), p. 65.

[300] In contractual obligations, the general rule for risk distribution is set forth in in Art. 393 of the Civil Code (CC/02). However, this rule can be modified not only by party autonomy but also by statutory provisions (Fonseca (1958), p. 181). In this context, the legislator has provided a clearer delineation of risk spheres, making the criteria applied in the domain of "psychological causation" of limited relevance. Viewing the contract as a mechanism for risk distribution, the rule generally allocates performance risk to the debtor and the risk of use to the creditor, see Martins-Costa and Costa E Silva (2020), pp. 132 and 274. As noted by Catarina Monteiro Pires, the distribution of risks should be specifically defined within the contract. Relying on an abstract and rational criterion for risk allocation may result in equity, but at the expense of precision (Pires (2020), pp. 668–669).

[301] Judith Martins-Costa notes that few decisions make a distinction between "psychological damage" and "non-pecuniary damage." She references the pioneering opinion of Ruy Rosado de Aguiar, then a judge at the Court of Appeal of Rio Grande do Sul, who, before the Federal Constitution recognized the compensability of non-pecuniary damages, upheld a claim for compensation of psychological damage (Infringement Embargoes n. 183,001,056–2nd Civil Group—Novo Hamburgo, March 25, 1985) (Martins-Costa (2001), p. 192).

[302] Mädrich (1980), p. 109.

Jürgen Hübner[303] noted that the theories of adequacy and the scope of norm protection ultimately concern the attribution and distribution of losses. However, as they do not allow this circumstance to be clearly recognized and often even prevent fair regulation, risk theories are becoming increasingly prominent. This arises, according to the author, from the observation that the delimitation of risk areas, and not causation, constitutes the real problem of attribution.[304] The "general risk of life" should be analyzed according to case groups.[305] Two aspects must be distinguished: first, the increased risk of damage created by the tortfeasor's act in generating a dangerous situation; second, the injured party's own risk sphere. Damage allocation should be determined by balancing these spheres of risk in the specific case, while avoiding the formulation of generic rules for risk distribution.

When a party creates a risky situation through direct normative violation or breach of a duty of care, they must eliminate this increased risk or else become liable for losses to third parties, provided the typical risk has materialized in the resulting injury. Risk, therefore, may serve as an autonomous criterion of imputation, distinct from the theory of the scope of the violated norm,[306] with its own independent configuration.

According to Pontes de Miranda,[307] the party responsible for creating the risk is liable for it, as from this circumstance arises the duty to prevent harm. The individual who ignited a fire on a farm has the duty to extinguish it to prevent its spread to neighboring lands. Similarly, a merchant who discovers a contagious disease in their animals must promptly inform neighboring traders so they can also take measures to protect their livestock.

---

[303] Hübner (1972), p. 70.

[304] Wilburg (1941), p. 6.

[305] Risk areas, being flexible, should be defined on a case-by-case basis, criteria that have already been developed and those still to be explored by doctrine and jurisprudence (Comes (1972), p. 2025).

[306] Lange and Schiemann, when addressing the "general risk of life," argue that dangers that do not exceed what is typically accepted in everyday life, with the approval of the legal system, fall outside the scope of protection of violated behavioral norms. Therefore, a (negative) attribution criterion should be recognized (Lange and Schiemann (2003), p. 148). Ekkenga and Kuntz contend that the "general risk of life" should be understood as a distinct category, rather than as a component of the adequacy theory (Ekkenga (2014), p. 80). Hans Stoll also maintains that this criterion performs an independent function and cannot be framed within any limiting element of liability in the existing theories (Stoll (1968), pp. 26–27). Mädrich, in a dedicated study on the matter, reaffirms the autonomous nature of this criterion within theories of imputation (Mädrich (1980), pp. 89–91).

[307] Relevant are not only omissions that generate danger but also failures to act where, under the general duty of care, the individual was expected to avert the risk. Thus, a bystander who sees a bridge collapse and does not warn passersby commits an unlawful omission (Miranda (1984a, b, c), p. 194).

Although risk is enshrined in Art. 927, sole paragraph of the Civil Code of 2002 (CC/02)[308] as a basis for strict liability,[309] thereby displacing fault as the decisive criterion,[310] it is rarely explored by Brazilian doctrine as a criterion for objective imputation. Part of the authors, still tied to a naturalistic conception of causation, disregard the creation or elevation of danger as a legal factor of attribution. Judith Martins-Costa,[311] citing criminal doctrine, asserts that, according to the theory of objective attribution, damage must be attributed to the perpetrator if it results from an escalation of risk. It is necessary to determine whether the unlawful conduct increased the probability of producing the result compared to the normal risk.

It should also be verified whether the damage did not result from a "general risk of life,"[312] as the injuring party cannot be held liable for consequences that are normal to everyday life and do not result from the specific increase in the dangerous situation.[313] This rule derives from the fact that the individual themselves must answer for fortuitous events, so that the holder of the protected interest bears, as a rule, the losses arising from merely accidental episodes. This is a criterion delimiting the risk spheres of the parties, in concrete terms, which transits between the natural events of life and the typical dangers created by the first wrongdoer. Thus, the rescuer who, while attempting to save another, trips on the sidewalk and suffers a foot injury cannot demand from the first causer compensation for the damages suffered, as it is a risk that could fall upon the injured individual even if the first event had not occurred.

In the case of "psychologically mediated causation," it is crucial to verify whether the specific risk created by the first wrongdoer materialized or whether the damage resulted from the "general risk of life." The issue becomes more complex when it involves risks that are typically associated with a specific professional activity, such as in the case of firefighters and rescuers.[314] Generally, the damages suffered by these individuals in the performance of their professional

---

[308] Emphasizing the significance of risk as a factor in attribution, see Godoy (2010), pp. 32–33; Godoy (2015), p. 28; Carrá (2017), p. 224.

[309] Álvaro Villaça de Azevedo distinguishes between two categories of liability based on risk theory: pure and impure. The latter derives from the fault of a third party whose conduct is linked to the indemnifier's activity, whereas the former triggers compensation even when no fault can be attributed to any of the parties involved (Azevedo (1993), pp. 10–11).

[310] Lima (1963), pp. 347–351.

[311] Martins-Costa (2014), p. 7108.

[312] Not all risks should be avoided, as life in society necessarily involves inherent dangers. These "tolerated" risks are called "general risks of life" (Chamon Jr. (2005), p. 73).

[313] Reinig (2015), p. 174.

[314] Lange and Schiemann discuss a specific kind of "general risk of life" that applies to certain groups of people, such as police officers and rescue services. For example, a fugitive would not be held liable for the damages suffered by a police officer who slips on wet grass. Similarly, a firefighter who suffers a sprained ankle after extinguishing a fire cannot hold the person responsible for starting the fire liable for the injury (Lange and Schiemann (2003), p. 147). Stöhr also states that the risks borne by these professionals fall under the category of professional risks (Stöhr (2009), p. 164).

duties are considered part of the "general risk of life" of the profession, which must be accepted without any form of compensation.[315]

Risks that clearly exceed the normal level of a certain professional activity should be attributed to the perpetrator. The BGH decided accordingly on April 17, 2018.[316] One of the most violent incidents in German schools occurred in Ludwigshafen in 2010, when a former student entered the building armed with a knife and a loaded pistol,[317] killing a teacher by stabbing him five times.[318] The police were called to contain the attack (*Amoklauf*), and one of the officers, who entered the school with three other colleagues, subsequently suffered a psychiatric disorder as a result of the reaction to severe mental stress. The officer had to undergo medical treatment and was unable to work for almost a month.

The state, as the provider of benefits, legally pursued the former student, who was ordered by the *Landgericht* to pay 3053.77 euros. After an appeal, the *Oberlandesgericht* overturned the decision. Some argue that part of the training and profession of police officers and other rescue and aid agents involves facing situations of psychological stress, as well as processing the experiences resulting from them. According to this reasoning, psychiatric disorders resulting from traumatic events during missions would, in principle, be part of the general life risk of these professionals. The situation could be different, according to the German court, in the event of additional circumstances, such as in the case of a direct physical attack on the police.

The BGH[319] found the defendant liable for the harm to the police officer's mental health,[320] since the danger that materialized in the psychological injury cannot be classified as a "general risk of life."[321] Furthermore, the fact that a specific

[315] Oetker (2019), p. 418.

[316] BGHZ, VersR 2018, 829.

[317] The former student, who had Klinefelter's syndrome and personality disorders, intended to kill a teacher and a student (Luckey (2019), p. 397).

[318] Wündiger (2018), p. 408.

[319] BGHZ, VersR 2018, 829.

[320] Vieweg and Lorz (2022), p. 589.

[321] On December 8, 2020, the VI Senate of the BGH (NJW 2021, 925) issued a controversial decision that significantly broadened the scope of liability in cases involving occupational risks. The defendant, an 18-year-old, drank excessively at a bar and began vandalizing the premises. The police were called and issued a restraining order, which the young man failed to comply with. He resisted both verbally and physically during the subsequent attempt to detain him. One of the officers suffered an injury to his right thumb and developed a psychiatric condition that permanently incapacitated him from work. The state of Niedersachsen filed a lawsuit, seeking compensation for the costs of medical treatment and the loss of earnings due to the officer's incapacity. The *Oberlandesgericht* Celle (OLG Celle NJOZ 2020, 1557) restricted compensation to the physical injury to the officer's thumb, reasoning that, by choosing the profession, the officer had assumed its inherent risks. Furthermore, the attack was not aimed directly at the officer but resulted from the defendant's defensive actions. However, the BGH ruled that there is no justification for distinguishing between physical and psychological damages, asserting that psychological harm should also be attributed to the offender, even if an occupational risk is involved.

professional risk materialized does not prevent attribution[322] in cases like this.[323] The decisive criterion was that the perpetrator compelled the police officer to take part directly in the event and that the injured party was unable to mentally cope with the incident. It would not be relevant, therefore, for attribution purposes, that the professional was a direct victim of the attack. It was pointed out that, in the case of serious intentional crimes, which generally aim to spread fear and horror,[324] there is no reason to attribute the psychological effects of the event to the injured party.[325]

In Brazilian law, if the state bears the losses, it may subsequently claim compensation from the perpetrator. In the case of payment of social security amounts, Art. 120 of Law 8.213/91, amended in 2019, allows the Social Security (INSS) to file a regress action against those responsible in cases of negligence regarding safety and hygiene at work and in cases of domestic and family violence against women. Even before the introduction of this hypothesis through Law 13.846/2019, the Superior Court of Justice (STJ) had already admitted that the INSS has standing and interest to claim reimbursement of expenses resulting from the granting of social security benefits to the dependents of an insured murder victim.[326] This interpretation enables the state to pursue compensation for damages caused by third parties in other circumstances.[327]

---

[322] The matter remains unresolved in German jurisprudence. The *Oberlandesgericht* Koblenz (VersR 2011, 938 Rn. 43) held that for attribution purposes, it is irrelevant whether the occupational risk of the police officer materialized in the case of a professional who was attacked during an operation and sustained both physical and psychological injuries. The *Oberlandesgericht* Celle (VersR 2006, 1376, 1377), on the contrary, rejected liability for the psychological injury of a border guard who had been dispatched to an accident site following a train collision, partly because the occupational risk of the injured party had materialized. The *Landgericht* Duisburg (Urteil vom 28. September 2015–8 O 361/14, juris Rn. 35, 43) similarly refused to attribute psychological damages to the organizers in the case of a firefighter who suffered distress after a rescue operation at a mass event, reasoning that such distress was not covered by the protective purpose of the duty of care that had been violated.

[323] Krüger (2019), p. 478.

[324] In this case, there would not be the materialization of a normal operational risk, but rather a specific risk of attack (*Amoklaufgefahr*) (Wündiger (2018), p. 410).

[325] In *White v. Chief Constable of the South Yorkshire Police* [1999] 2 A.C. 455, stemming from the Hillsborough football stadium disaster, where the police were responsible for crowd control, resulting in 95 deaths, the House of Lords rejected the claim of police officers suffering psychiatric damages. Lord Steyn observed that, although the demand for justice in this case is substantial, it is not as significant as that for others who, under the law, are denied compensation. He concluded that the law concerning compensation for purely psychiatric damages is a patchwork of distinctions that are difficult to justify.

[326] "The individual responsible for the wrongful act resulting in the insured's death must compensate for the expenses associated with the payment of the social security benefit, even if it does not constitute a work-related accident. This is in accordance with Arts. 120 and 121 of Law No. 8213/91, in conjunction with Arts. 186 and 927 of the Civil Code" (STJ, REsp 1,431,150/RS, rel. Humberto Martins, j. 23.08.2016).

[327] In Germany, state laws generally allow state entities to seek financial compensation from third parties, perpetrators of wrongful acts, for the costs incurred from paying pensions or benefits to the insured. An example of this is § 72 of the *Landesbeamtengesetz* (State Civil Service Act) of the state of Rheinland-Pfalz.

At this point, attention should be drawn to the differences between the German and Brazilian tort law systems when assessing the applicability of the professional risk criterion in the latter. While in German law, in cases of non-pecuniary damages (*immaterieller Schaden*), monetary compensation can only be demanded in cases specified by law, by virtue of § 253 of the BGB,[328] Brazilian law has adopted a general clause.[329] In German law, the discussion primarily concerns mental and physical damages, as the violation of the body (*Körper*) and health (*Gesundheit*) has been contemplated by statutory law. By allowing professional risks to be attributed to the perpetrator, as part of the doctrine argues,[330] there is no risk of excessively expanding the scope of liability.[331]

The situation is different under Brazilian law. Arts. 186 and 927 of the CC/02 do not restrict the categories of compensable damages.[332] As a result, the failure to apply the professional risk criterion shifts an excessively broad sphere of risks to the initial perpetrator of the damage, leading to disproportionate and excessive liability. The application of the professional risk criterion in Brazilian law may operate effectively, as it limits liability in cases of certain professional activities, especially in the context of non-pecuniary damages.[333] Indeed, certain situations that might not be considered normal for an ordinary individual and would certainly be recognized as non-pecuniary damages, such as confronting a fire or a vehicle collision during a pursuit, are typical circumstances for those engaged in risky activities.

4.5.3.4 Proportionality

The doctrine highlights the importance of applying the criterion of proportionality (*Verhältnismäßigkeit*). In pursuit cases, for instance, there must be a reasonable relationship between the risks assumed and the objective of apprehending the

---

[328] "§ 253. Intangible damage. (1) Money may be demanded in compensation for any damage that is not a pecuniary loss only in the cases stipulated by law."

[329] Sanseverino (2010), p. 205.

[330] Schiemann argues that resorting to the so-called "professional risk" ("*Berufsrisiko*") cannot justify excluding the perpetrator's liability for creating a dangerous situation (Schiemann (2019), p. 104).

[331] In its decision of December 8, 2020, the BGH emphasized that there is no risk of an unlimited expansion of liability, even where attribution is accepted in cases of primary psychological injuries, where a professional risk materialize. This is so because the VI Senate has established in its jurisprudence that psychological damages, in this hypothesis, may only qualify as such under § 253 BGB if they result in a psychiatric illness (*Krankheitswert*), certified by a physician (NJW 2021, 925).

[332] It has been suggested, perhaps with some exaggeration, that the idea of compensating all damage, whether it affects the personality rights or the assets of the injured party, has become widely accepted (Theodoro Jr. (2008), p. 41).

[333] The use of the expression "non-pecuniary damages" has been preferred, due to the controversies surrounding the term "moral damage," as this has led to serious confusion, as well as the German expression "Schmerzensgeld" (Miranda (1984a, b, c) pp. 30–31).

fugitive.[334] This balance[335] applies to various scenarios: cases involving particularly high pursuit dangers, situations such as a police officer jumping from a four-meter window, and instances where the evader is accused of only a minor crime and has already been identified by name.[336] The legal system does not accept disproportionate action; therefore, such cases should typically be decided according to the rule of exemption from liability for third-party acts.[337]

The more serious the accusations against the suspect attempting to flee, the greater the risks the pursuer may take. The personal factors of the parties involved can also play a relevant role in examining proportionality.[338] Indeed, a police officer must assume greater risks than an ordinary individual.[339] Crucially, police officers are obliged to balance risks more carefully than non-professionals because their training and work involve regular danger assessment. It is reasonable to expect them to make prudent judgments, even in stressful situations.[340] This same level of consideration and evaluation cannot be reasonably expected of an ordinary individual when faced with a risky situation.[341]

It should not be overlooked that those operating within their institutional responsibilities can better assess their physical and technical abilities than non-professionals, due to their training and expertise. They can more accurately evaluate intervention dangers.[342] If pursuit risks become excessive, professionals should terminate the action; otherwise, resulting damages may no longer be attributable to the fugitive. More generally, it can be concluded that all parties operating within their institutional roles should be able, in dangerous situations, to act and assess with greater precision. This does not only apply to "professional

[334] Lange and Schiemann (2003), p. 134; Ekkenga (2014), p. 85; Grüneberg et al. (2020), p. 294. According to Larenz, the attribution can be excluded when the pursuer assumes a "disproportionate" ("*unverhältnismäßig*") risk (Larenz (1987), p. 455).

[335] Jörgens refers to the balance between the interest pursued by the action ("*Handlungsinteresse*") and the risk associated with it ("*Handlungsrisiko*") (Görgens (1977), p. 714).

[336] Oetker (2019), p. 408.

[337] Niebaum (1976), p. 1674.

[338] Zhang (2016), p. 87.

[339] Lange and Schiemann (2003), p. 135; Schiemann (2017), p. 91; Zhang (2016), p. 88. In contrast, Deutsch asserts that for the pursued individual, there is no difference between private and state pursuits, even though state intervention occurs more frequently (Deutsch (1967), p. 377).

[340] Facts that the pursuer was unaware of should not be considered in the balance of interests. For instance, in BGH JZ 67, 639, the police officer was unaware that the fugitive did not have a driving license. Therefore, the mere fact that someone continues to drive despite a stop order does not automatically justify the objective assessment that they have committed other offenses, depending on the circumstances.

[341] Ristow (2003), p. 125.

[342] According to Teichmann, the reasonableness of the action should not be determined based on the level of information available during the legal process, but grounded on the knowledge that the individual could have. For example, it may also be necessary to prosecute individuals who falsely raised suspicion of a crime (Teichmann (1996), p. 1178).

helpers" ("*Berufshelfer*"),[343] such as police officers and firefighters, but also to volunteer members of rescue services. The decisive factor is not whether someone is remunerated to perform in a certain way, but whether they have been trained to intervene in a particular risky situation.[344]

Regarding the subjective attribution, German jurisprudence[345] also deems it necessary for the fugitive to have perceived, or been able to recognize, that the pursuit would be initiated and that this would lead to an increase in the risky situation.[346] Proportionality must therefore be assessed between the pursued objective and the discernible risk.[347] However, it may occur that the fugitive escapes so quickly that they cannot observe whether the pursuer followed them. In this case, the fugitive imposes a particular potential danger on their pursuer, as the pursuer is deprived of the opportunity for a thorough consideration of the escape and should therefore anticipate pursuit.[348]

If the criterion of proportionality is not observed, the question arises as to whether there would be joint liability between the injurer and the injured party. It should be noted initially that the limit of objective attribution is drawn by the dangers to which the pursuer and the rescuer expose themselves in a disproportionate manner.[349] In these cases, the second wrongdoer is fully responsible for the damages suffered. However, if the action taken, compared to the pursued result, was not completely unreasonable but also did not fully meet the criterion of proportionality, it becomes possible to determine liability according to the risk spheres assumed by each party.[350]

Unlike German law,[351] fault is not relevant when determining the extent of joint responsibility for each party.[352] In Brazilian law, following Pontes de Miranda's perspective,[353] it has been established that it is not possible to address

[343] The professional qualifications of the pursuer should be considered in the balance (Zhang (2016), p. 87).

[344] Ristow (2003), p. 125.

[345] See BGH, NJW 1990, 2885.

[346] Kötz and Wagner (2006), p. 84; Lang (1983), p. 160; Larenz (1987), p. 455.

[347] Hübner (1972), p. 496; Niebaum (1976), p. 1673.

[348] Teichmann (1996), p. 1180.

[349] Oetker (2019), p. 408.

[350] The assessment of the form and nature of the state official's intervention during the pursuit, and any excess in favor of the pursued, arises at the stage of allocating damages (*Schadensverteilung*) (Hübner (1974), p. 501).

[351] Looschelders (2019), p. 235.

[352] In common law, liability was traditionally excluded where the injured party was at fault (Miranda (1984a, b, c), p. 195; Oetker (2019), p. 641).

[353] Miranda (1984a, b, c, p. 195). The understanding was consolidated in Statement no. 630 of the CJF: "Art. 945: Faults do not compensate. For the purposes of Art. 945 of the Civil Code, the following criteria should be observed: (i) there is a reduction in the quantum of damage compensation when, alongside the conduct of the offender, there is action or omission by the injured party which results in damage, or its aggravation, provided that (ii) both conducts

"compensation of faults" but rather concurrent causation.[354] Although Art. 945 of the CC/02[355] refers to gross negligence as a rule for damage attribution, national jurisprudence has established that the decisive consideration in comparing the behavior of the injurer and the victim is the extent to which the conduct or omission of each has contributed causally.[356]

Objections to the exclusion of fault[357] as a criterion for liability are not convincing. The assertion that this would excessively expand the reach of the so-called "victim's act" cannot be sustained. Indeed, as has already been noted,[358] mere factual causation should not be taken into account for the purpose of delimiting liability, for otherwise the victim's mere presence at the site of the event could already be treated as contributory. The inadequacy of the causal theories currently adopted in Brazilian law does not provide a conclusive argument, as this flaw impacts the entire scope of tort law rather than being limited to the area of damage attribution. Rather than introducing fault as a determining criterion, it would be preferable to adopt objective imputation criteria.

The argument that the protection system for legally incapacitated persons[359] would be compromised is likewise unconvincing.[360] According to Art. 928 of the CC/02, such persons are only liable for damages they cause if their legal guardians are not obligated to do so or do not have sufficient means. The sole paragraph[361] of

are related to the same fact, or the same basis for imputation, although they may be simultaneous or successive, the causal percentage of each one's action should be considered."

354 According to Art. 570 of the Portuguese Civil Code, when a culpable act of the injured party has contributed to the production or aggravation of damages, it is up to the court to determine, based on the degree of the faults of both parties and the consequences that resulted from them, whether the compensation should be fully granted, reduced, or even excluded.

355 "Art. 945. If the victim has negligently contributed to the damaging event, their compensation will be determined considering the degree of their fault in comparison with that of the author of the damage."

356 Guedes (2005), p. 343. Among others, also adopting this idea, see Miragem (2021), p. 195; Direito (2011), p. 406.

357 Daniel Dias systematically presents a series of criticisms to the prevailing interpretation in Brazilian law (Dias (2020a, b).

358 See Sect. 3.2.7.

359 It is argued that, in cases of concurrent victim incapacity, requiring the injured party to bear the consequences of their immaturity is said to conflict with the values of the Brazilian legal system (Dias (2020a, b), Sect. 3).

360 Pointing out the inconsistencies of this reasoning, Brandão Proença states that the non-imputable offender is less protected than the non-imputable injured party, victim of someone else's fault, despite the fact that, in one case and another, they may have acted with equally serious conduct (Proença (1997), p. 106).

361 José Fernando Simão reports that the rule in Article 928, sole paragraph, does not depart from foreign law. The Portuguese Civil Code of 1867 had already established that, in calculating compensation against a legally incapacitated person, the sustenance necessary for their survival should be taken into account (Art. 2.378) (Simão et al. (2021), pp. 433–434). In pre-codification Portuguese law, Coelho da Rocha stated that the damage caused by a madman or a minor under

the provision further establishes that compensation should be equitable and will not occur if it deprives the legally incapacitated or their dependents of the resources required for their maintenance and support.[362] The principles of German doctrine cannot be invoked at this point,[363] as the Brazilian tort system, particularly with respect to those lacking legal capacity, especially minors, is more protective than German law.[364] Fault, in the Brazilian legal system, constitutes a criterion of attribution of damages, but it should not be used, in these cases, as a criterion for determining their extent.[365]

The inclusion of the volitional element in assessing the extent of damages also contradicts the growing use of fault as a normative element of liability,[366] emphasizing the complex issue of its gradation. While not completely excluded from the Brazilian legal system,[367] as exemplified in Art. 944, sole paragraph, of the CC/02,[368] the subjective analysis of fault has been increasingly limited in favor of a more objective approach.[369] Although liability for negligence is theoretically the system's default rule, in practice strict liability finds frequent application.

---

seven years old would be considered accidental, unless negligence was demonstrated by the person supposed to supervise them (Rocha (1917), p. 79).

[362] The 2002 Civil Code replaced the previous regime of absolute non-liability of legally incapacitated persons with the possibility of subsidiary and mitigated liabilit (Simão (2008), p. 153).

[363] Looschelders argues that the idea that a young injured party should bear the disadvantageous consequences of their immaturity is incompatible with the principles of German tort law. The risks associated with immaturity should be attributed to the perpetrator. A contrary view would fail to uphold the essential protection of weaker individuals in legal relations (Looschelders (2019), p. 355).

[364] § 828(2) of the BGB stipulates that minors, aged between seven and ten, are liable for damages caused to others in motor vehicle accidents if they acted intentionally. The subsequent section of § 828 provides that minors under eighteen are liable for the damages they cause if they possess the necessary discernment to recognize their responsibility. In both cases, § 829 of the BGB stipulates that subsidiary liability does not apply to legally incapacitated persons.

[365] Miranda (1984a, b, c), p. 197.

[366] Observing that the traditional idea of "psychological fault" has gradually been replaced by the concept of "objective fault", see Lima (1963), p. 117. According to Orozimbo Nonato, "objective fault" disregards psychological and moral factors (Nonato (1929), p. 32).

[367] As noted by Bruno Carrá, although there is no longer room for the re-entry of the gradation of fault in the terms conceived in the past, modern dogmatics has carried out its own gradations, adjustments, and adaptations. Therefore, it can be concluded that fault stratifications are still being applied to some extent in practice (Carrá (2017), p. 225).

[368] Sanseverino observes that the distinction between degrees of fault and the criteria for their assessment has regained significance with the enactment of the Civil Code of 2002, due to the general clause on the reduction of compensation (Sanseverino (2010), p. 101).

[369] It is undeniable that the prevalence of the fault principle in tort liability has been somewhat compressed by the evolution of an "objectivist tendency" (Pires (2020), p. 635).

4.5.4 Models of Indirect and Negligent Causation

Starting from the criterion of self-responsibility, Forst[370] states that the initial wrongdoer is exempt from liability, since the causal link between their voluntary decision and the violation of a legally protected interest is "interrupted" by the intervention of the second causer. However, this rule of attribution is only justified, according to the author, if the voluntary acts of both perpetrators are qualitatively comparable[371] with respect to the degree of self-determination in their decisions. This means that the intervention of the second tortfeasor would only exclude the responsibility of the initial wrongdoer in the event that their action is based on an equally autonomous decision.[372] Otherwise, the harmful outcome does not seem to be a voluntary act of the second perpetrator and can still be considered a consequence of the previous act.

The definition of when the act of the second perpetrator should be considered autonomous, according to Forst,[373] is a matter of objective imputation and should not be analyzed solely from a scientific point of view. According to the author, if the second causer's intent is disturbed in any way, "psychological causation" does not apply. The objective of the investigation should focus primarily on the conditions that allow for the conclusion that the will of the second perpetrator was nullified in its autonomy.

For this purpose, the author uses the concept of "indirect perpetration" or "mediated perpetration" ("*mittelbare Täterschaft*"), originally developed in criminal law and codified in § 25 (1) of the StGB.[374] In this framework, the perpetrator does not directly commit the offensive acts but rather uses another person as an instrument[375] to achieve a specific objective. Indirect perpetration is characterized by the subordinate position of the direct author, whether due to factual or legal reasons, and by the dominant role of the person controlling the act, who fully understands the situation and has command over the entire event, directing and guiding it.[376]

---

370 Forst (2000), p. 128.

371 The criterion for direct or personal liability requires the correspondence between the volitional acts involved. Thus, cases are problematic only when the second individual acts autonomously. Otherwise, one merely observes the instrumentalization of one individual by another, who initiates a certain outcome (Barbosa (2019), p. 21).

372 According to Min Zhang, Forst's approach is based on the idea that if the will of the second wrongdoer is not freely formed, there can be no self-responsibility for the consequences of the damage. The losses cannot be attributed to the second causer if the first has restricted their freedom to such an extent that they can only be considered a mere instrument of the former (Zhang (2016), p. 77).

373 Forst (2000), p. 129.

374 The German Penal Code (*Strafgesetzbuch*—StGB) provides, in its § 25 (1): "Whoever commits an offence themselves or through another incurs a penalty as an offender."

375 Jescheck (1981), p. 895.

376 Forst (2000), p. 129.

Thus, criteria are identified to substantiate the liability of the first perpetrator for the result caused by both, despite the interference of the second wrongdoer. For this reason, the solution proposed by Forst[377] is referred to as the "model of indirect causation" ("*Modell der mittelbaren Verursachung*"). This proposal is categorized as an imputation criterion in the theory of the scope of protection of the norm. The author maintains that the norm protects the interest only where the second causer's freedom of determination is severely curtailed by the prior conduct, rendering the act imputable as voluntary to the first perpetrator. The analysis of the criterion is divided by Forst into evaluative parameters.

Firstly, it should be examined whether the second tortfeasor is obliged to act,[378] in which case the pressure of potential sanctions influences their decision-making process to the extent that their autonomy is relegated to a secondary role. According to the author, the duty to act may arise from a contractual or legal obligation. This applies to firefighters, who are legally required to intervene, to the point where their decision-making freedom is so constrained that the violation of legal interests should also be considered an act of will by the person in distress.[379]

The same reasoning, according to Forst,[380] applies to cases where the second causer, although not legally bound, is morally obliged to act,[381] as in the example already discussed in which the mother donates a kidney to her daughter.[382] The author argues that the breach of moral rules creates a subjective pressure on the individual to act, which is often comparable to that emanating from legal duties. In addition to legal and moral obligations, Forst also cites situations where the second causer is compelled to act for factual reasons. He gives, as an example, the case of the green side strip of the highway. According to the author, the decision-making freedom of impatient drivers would have been largely theoretical, as they had to slow down their vehicles to avoid further dangers and accidental damage.[383] The

[377] Forst (2000), p. 130.

[378] Forst notes that if the second wrongdoer acts in a non-autonomous manner, they should no longer bear the responsibility for the risk arising from their conduct, as it would be more appropriately attributed to the first causer. According to the author, this freedom would be excluded if the second wrongdoer were obligated to act, facing sanctions or adverse consequences (Barbosa (2020), p. 987).

[379] Forst (2000), pp. 131–132.

[380] Forst (2000), pp. 132–133.

[381] In rescue situations, there is often a legal or moral obligation to intervene (Zhang (2016), p. 77).

[382] Deutsch refers to the decision of the *Oberlandesgericht* Schleswig, later confirmed by the BGH, arguing that the mother's decision to donate her kidney should be highly valued from a moral perspective and, consequently, recognized and endorsed by the legal system (Medicus (2005), p. 293).

[383] If a third party (or the injured party themselves) intervenes in the situation, such interference may possess sufficiently intense independent characteristics that it becomes impossible to attribute it to the initial cause. The third party's contribution is less autonomous the greater the physical or psychological "coercion" ("*Zwang*") exerted by the original act. The decisive factor is the intensity of the influence the initial conduct exerts on the third party. An example of indirect

damages caused to the marginal lands should be attributed to the person responsible for the accident.

Legal, moral, or factual reasons should, according to the theory of indirect causation, be analyzed from an objective point of view. Only if the subjective viewpoint of the second causer differs significantly from the objective evaluation of the events should the former prevail. Thus, in an emergency assistance case, if there is no objective legal obligation to intervene, but the second causer believes it is their duty to provide help, objective attribution should, according to Forst,[384] depend on subjective judgment. The primacy of subjective assessment stems from the notion that the first wrongdoer's conduct restricted the second causer's freedom of determination to the point where the violation of protected interests is imputable as their voluntary act.

Next, Forst explores the permissions granted to the second causative individual to act. He[385] acknowledges that permission to act does not exert the same level of decision-making pressure as a duty to act, regardless of whether it is of a legal, moral, or factual nature, since rights can be exercised voluntarily and are not necessarily required to be enforced by the right holder. However, by establishing behavioral permissions, the legislator has indicated that such actions are either desired or, at the very least, accepted by the legal system. This legal appeal or tolerance, according to Forst, limits the free will of the second wrongdoer in the same way as a norm that imposes a duty. This hypothesis could be illustrated with the example of § 127 (1) of the StPO,[386] which authorizes anyone to arrest an individual caught in the act of committing a crime. This norm would have an appealing character (*Appellcharakter*), insofar as it exhorts individuals to ensure the public interest.[387]

The position of authority (*Autoritätsstellung*)[388] of the first wrongdoer is also taken into account for the purpose of assessing the decision-making autonomy of

---

physical "coercion" is illustrated by a driver who brakes to avoid colliding with a crashed car ahead, only to be struck by a car from behind. In such circumstances, the mandatory stop of the car becomes inevitable, meaning that the attribution of damages should fall on the initial cause (Görgens (1977), p. 713).

[384] Forst (2000), p. 134.

[385] Forst (2000), p. 135.

[386] The Strafprozessordnung (StPO) is the German Code of Criminal Procedure. The first part of § 127 stipulates that, if a person is caught in the act or pursued, any individual is authorized to detain them temporarily, even without a court order, if there is a reasonable suspicion of flight or if their identity cannot be immediately verified.

[387] Zhang (2016), p. 77.

[388] Although Ristow agrees with Forst's position, he argues that it requires further development. According to Ristow, there should be a relationship between the first and second causers that allows the former to influence and, consequently, control the latter's behavior. This is because the second perpetrator trusts the information provided by the first, perceiving them as an authority. Two decisive factors are essential for attributing the damage to the first wrongdoer. First, the initial causer must possess specific knowledge about the risks associated with the activity and must convey this information either incorrectly or incompletely. Second, there must be

the second causer. In Forst's view,[389] it should be questioned whether the latter is aware of the special knowledge (*Sonderwissen*) of the initial perpetrator or whether he is unaware of this circumstance. If the second causer knows that the initial perpetrator has this differentiated knowledge, which he does not possess, and acts based on this circumstance, his decision-making freedom is restricted. The second tortfeasor then becomes dependent on the behavior of the first one.[390] For Forst, it suffices that the second perpetrator believes that the first causer possesses this special knowledge, as this belief itself limits his freedom of determination.

Forst[391] also acknowledges the value of the proportionality of the act committed by the second causer, so that any excesses committed by him could not be attributed to the initial perpetrator. Even if the act of the first wrongdoer constitutes a *conditio sine qua non* for the subsequent act, if the second perpetrator exceeds the limits set by the first, it can no longer be considered an act of will of the initial causer. According to the author, this requirement of attribution serves solely to relieve the first causer of liability in cases where the risk assumed by the second perpetrator is grossly disproportionate to the threatened legal interest. Actions that, although disproportionate, do not exceed this threshold of unacceptability may give rise to the application of § 254 of the BGB.[392]

Although Forst's theoretical framework[393] gives central importance to the rule that the first causer's liability should only be excluded when the second perpetrator's free and comparable will intervenes in the causal chain, he acknowledges cases where attributing damages to the first perpetrator seems fair, even without any restriction of the second perpetrator's freedom. Forst complements the model

---

a relationship between the parties that enables the first perpetrator to "control" ("*in der Hand hält*") the conduct of the second. In the case of a child following the behavior of an adult, attribution of liability would be justified by the adult's role as a role model (Ristow (2003), p. 88–90).

[389] Forst (2000), pp. 137–138.

[390] Niebaum considers that a voluntary act is subordinate if it occurs within a sphere that is factually controlled by the initial perpetrator. According to the author, two groups can be differentiated. The first category includes cases where the ability of the initial perpetrator to influence the actions of the third party is based on a familial or close relationship between the parties. However, a relationship of subordination can suddenly arise between individuals who do not know each other. Such situations are referred to as "temporary subordination relationships" (*flüchtige Subordinationsverhältnisse*) (Niebaum (1977), p. 92).

[391] Forst (2000), pp. 139–140.

[392] "§ 254. Contributory Negligence. (1) Where fault on the part of the injured person contributed to the occurrence of the damage, liability in damages as well as the extent of compensation to be provided depend on the circumstances, in particular on the extent to which the damage was caused mainly by one or the other party." The doctrine has pointed out the deficiency in the wording of § 254 of the BGB, interpreting it, consequently, as a general principle of reduction applicable to all forms of liability, including cases where the injured party incurs in "own risk" (*Eigengefahren*), regardless of fault" (Proença 1997, p. 395).

[393] Forst (2000), pp. 143–144.

of "indirect causation" ("*mittelbare Verursachung*") with that of "negligent causation" ("*fahrlässige Verursachung*").[394]

For damage to be attributed to the first causer, the subjective quality of their conduct is assessed. If the behavior is negligent, specific criteria such as the violation of the duty of care, and the foreseeability and avoidability of the violation of the legal interest are used. According to Forst[395] would also be appropriate to allocate the risk of liability in cases of psychologically mediated causal courses, provided that both causers, evaluated from a value-based perspective, act autonomously.

When considering the causal sequence as a whole, for the effects to be attributed to the first causer, it is necessary for the condition established by them to occupy a prominent position relative to all other conditions necessary for the materialization of the result. Thus, the act of the first perpetrator only acquires this differentiated status if a specific misconduct is characterized, defined by the violation of rules of conduct imposed on participants in legal relations.[396]

The objective foreseeability of the violation of the legal interest is introduced as a second requirement, alongside the breach of a duty of care or the first wrongdoer's liability. This criterion, generally applicable to other cases of objective imputation, can also be used, according to Forst,[397] in cases of "psychological causation." Although the adequacy parameter[398] serves as a basic filter and is therefore inadequate on its own, it sets the minimum necessary conditions for objective imputation. Lastly, the author suggests that it should be examined whether the first perpetrator had the ability to control the causal process in order to prevent the injury from occurring. If all requirements are met, it should still be investigated, within the theory of the scope of the norm, whether the specific risk created by the first perpetrator materialized in the violation of the legal interest.[399]

The theories formulated by Forst, despite their undeniable merits, are not immune to criticism. The author's models initially fail, like previously analyzed theories, in their attempt to encompass all imaginable factual scenarios. As observed, "psychologically mediated causation" can be divided into various case groups, each requiring different combinations of objective imputation criteria. In the pursuit of developing a universal general theory, Forst created a model of indirect causation that is surpassed in its practical application by the model of negligent causation, which was intended to be exceptional and subsidiary, since the

[394] Barbosa (2019), p. 22.

[395] Forst (2000), pp. 144–145.

[396] Forst (2000), pp. 145–147.

[397] Forst (2000), pp. 148–150.

[398] Points of contact between the thesis outlined by Forst and the theory of adequacy are identified by Mafalda Miranda, such as the idea of probability, grounded in the notion of an optimal observer. However, she emphasizes the author's different perspective. She asserts that the dialogical process is not initiated from the result, but from the verification of a diligent action obligation that, in the practical case, was not observed (Barbosa (2020), p. 989).

[399] Zhang (2016), p. 78.

parties' intents can hardly be qualitatively comparable. The previous conduct influences, in some way, the subsequent behavior.

Although Forst establishes human freedom as the foundational principle of responsibility (from which other imputation criteria derive) and treats the influenced party's liability as exceptional, he overemphasizes this factor. He requires that, for the first perpetrator to be exonerated, the second party's action must result from a freedom of determination comparable to that of the first.

As seen, as a rule, the conduct of the first perpetrator will influence or affect the behavior of the second causer, with varying levels of influence,[400] making the task of comparing the degrees of autonomy of the conducts complex.[401] Forst's assertion that the breach of moral rules is usually comparable to the violation of legal duties appears exaggerated. As previously discussed, it is not always possible to identify the motives behind the second causer's actions. Assessing the moral reasons that drove their conduct would result in analyses that are predetermined by a conclusion sought in advance.[402]

Finally, the author reaches deeply problematic conclusions when applying the thesis that the second perpetrator is forced to act due to factual circumstances. In the case of the green side stripe, he suggests that the damages caused by the drivers should be attributed to the original perpetrator of the accident. This outcome, in addition to being firmly opposed by legal doctrine,[403] runs contrary to the foundational principle of his theory, which holds that the free act of the second wrongdoer excludes the initial causer's liability.

4.6 Summary

The legal phenomenon of "psychological causation" is characterized by a second perpetrator's voluntary act interfering in a causal chain initiated by a first wrongdoer. This complex concept raises fundamental issues, ranging from establishing causation to defining functional criteria for objective imputation. An example of this phenomenon is the case of the Bundesbahn inspector who pursued a passenger for fare evasion, suffering damages during the chase. In this situation, the passenger's initial action led to a voluntary response from the inspector, resulting in the damages.

The criterion of self-responsibility derives from the very idea of human freedom and decision-making autonomy, asserting that damages arising from a voluntary

[400] Winiger (2007), p. 253.

[401] The weaknesses inherent in Forst's approach cannot be ignored, particularly regarding the application of the theory of the scope of the norm, which becomes questionable as it presupposes the realization of a specific danger through the violation of legally protected interests (Zhang (2016), p. 78).

[402] Ristow (2003), p. 142.

[403] Larenz (1955), p. 1009.

decision should be attributed to the one who made such a decision. This criterion becomes particularly relevant in cases of suicide, where the victim's self-determination plays a decisive role in the attribution of liability.

Controllability refers to whether the injurious event remains within the perpetrator's sphere of influence. Merely initiating the causal chain is insufficient; it must be determined whether the perpetrator could effectively influence the development of subsequent events, although the mere fact that the causal course can no longer be controlled by the initial causer does not exclude their liability.

The "provocation formula," developed by German jurisprudence, presents significant insufficiencies. The term "provocation" lacks legal precision and leads to mistaken interpretations, implying that the first perpetrator must induce the subsequent one to act in a particular manner. The subjectivism inherent in the notion of "feeling provoked" leads to intuitive solutions based on equitable considerations, which should be avoided in the process of objective imputation. This formula proves applicable only in specific groups of cases, such as pursuit and rescue, and does not serve as a general model for all cases of "psychological causation."

Proportionality requires that the reaction of the second perpetrator be reasonable and appropriate to the situation created, preventing excesses that unnecessarily extend the liability of the first wrongdoer. An emblematic example occurs when a police officer, while pursuing a fugitive, decides to jump from a four-meter window. If the pursuit involves a dangerous criminal whose capture is crucial to preventing a serious risk to the community, it can be argued that the risk assumed by the police officer aligns with the intended objective. However, if the fugitive is accused of a minor offense and has already been identified by name, the officer's action becomes disproportionate, excluding imputation. This criterion ensures that the first tortfeasor is not held liable for exaggerated responses or for disproportionate risks voluntarily assumed by the second perpetrator.

The justifiable motive seeks to determine whether the action of the second perpetrator resulted from a necessary or socially accepted impulse in response to the situation created. This means that it is not enough for the conduct of the first tortfeasor to have created a scenario of danger; it is necessary that the second causer acted in a manner consistent with the context and in accordance with a justifiable purpose. The case of a fire on a bus illustrates this issue. If a passenger, while trying to help a child get out of the burning vehicle, injures himself in the process, his conduct can be considered justifiable, as it aimed at protecting a vulnerable third party. However, the criterion of the justifiable motive has been widely criticized in the doctrine. One of the main problems is that the moral evaluation of the motives that led the second causer to act can lead to arbitrary and inconsistent conclusions.

The criterion of increased risk, finally, examines whether the first perpetrator created or intensified a dangerous situation that effectively materialized in the final damage. It is not enough that his act was a mere antecedent condition; it is necessary that he introduced a relevant and foreseeable risk, which played a decisive role in the realization of the damage. An illustrative example would be that of a pursuer who has his tire burst during the escape of a criminal. If he was driving at the permitted speed and suffered the damage due to an unforeseeable external factor, liability cannot be attributed to the fugitive. However, if the increase in risk resulted directly from the reckless driving necessary to follow the escape, the solution should be to hold the first perpetrator responsible. The distinction between increased risk and generic life risk is essential to prevent an excessive expansion of liability, ensuring that only the damages related to the risk created by the first perpetrator are effectively attributed to him.

Seeking to overcome these limitations, Forst develops a theory based on two complementary models. The model of indirect causation starts from the principle of self-responsibility but argues that the imputation to the first perpetrator is justified when the freedom of the second one is reduced by legal, moral, or factual pressures, making him an instrument of the first. The model of negligent causation, applicable even when there is autonomy of the second causer, requires a violation of a duty of care by the first, the objective foreseeability of injury, and the possibility of its control, in addition to the materialization of the specific risk created. Although it has merits in valuing human freedom, the theory falls short by attempting to cover all factual hypotheses, when "psychological causation" requires differentiated analysis according to the group of cases.

Brazilian law can adopt the legal criteria developed by German scholarship and case law but must adapt them to fit the peculiarities of its legal system, particularly the general clause liability regime in the Brazilian Civil Code. This approach requires careful consideration, as while in German law the duties of care serve as a safety valve to the rigid legal typification, in Brazil they serve to better delineate the contours of legal attribution. The Brazilian system of the general clause of liability, unlike the German model of typification of protected legal interests, requires particular attention in the delimitation of imputation, rejecting its excessive expansion based solely on abstract constitutional principles.

References

Ahrens HJ, Spickhoff A (2022) Deliktsrecht: mit Wirtschaftsdeliktsrecht Großes Lehrbuch. C.H. Beck, München

Angelin KA (2012) Dano injusto como pressuposto do dever de indenizar. Dissertation (Mestrado), Faculdade de Direito, Universidade de São Paulo

Ataíde RPCM (2019) Responsabilidade civil por violação de deveres no tráfego. Almedina, Coimbra

Azevedo AV (1993) Proposta de classificação da responsabilidade objetiva: pura e impura. Revista dos Tribunais 82(698):7–11

Barbosa AMCNM (2019) Responsabilidade civil pelo financiamento de grupos terroristas. Revista IBERC 1:01–39

Barbosa AMCNM B (2020) Causalidade, imputação e responsabilidade por informações. Revista de direito da responsabilidade 2:971–1006

Barcelona M (2011) Trattato del danno e della responsabilità civile. Utet Giuridica, Torino

Benöhr HP (1999) Die Redaktion der Paragraphen 23 und 826 BGB. In: Zimmermann R (ed) Rechtsgeschichte und Privatrechtsdogmatik. C. F. Muller Verlag, Heidelberg

Bernsmann K (1982) Zum Verhältnis von Wissenschaftstheorie und Recht: Überlegungen zur sog. "psychischen Kausalität" im Strafrecht. Archiv Für Rechts- und Sozialphilosophie 68(4):536–555

Beviláqua C (1953) Theoria geral do direito civil, 6ª edn. (atual. por Achilles Bevilaqua) Livraria Francisco Alves, Rio de Janeiro

Bianca M (2010) Trattato della responsabilità civile: l'illecito, 2ª edn. t. 1. Giuffrè, Milano

Bitencourt CR (2021) Tratado de direito penal: Parte Geral, 27ª edn. Saraiva Educação, São Paulo

Brandão C (2004) Culpabilidade: sua análise na dogmática e no direito penal brasileiro. Ciências Penais: Revista da Associação Brasileira de Professores de Ciências Penais 1(1):171–184

Brito PLA, Silva MC, Barbosa CCN (2021) A responsabilidade civil dos influenciadores digitais pela publicidade ilícita por eles veiculada. Revista de direito da responsabilidade 7:341–380

Brox H, Walker WD (2020) Allgemeines Schuldrecht, 44ª edn. C.H. Beck, München

Bydlinski F (2007) Causation as a legal phenomenon. In: Tichý L (ed) Causation in law. IFEC, Beroun

Canaris CW (1983) Schutzgesetze-Verkehrspflichten-Schutzpflichten. In: Canaris CW, Diederischsen U (eds) Festschrift für Karl Larenz zum 80. Geburtstag am 23 April 1983. C. H. Beck'sche Verlagsbuchhandlung, München

Carnaúba DA, Reinig GHL (2016) Abuso de direito e responsabilidade por ato ilícito: críticas ao Enunciado 37 da 1.ª Jornada de Direito Civil. Revista de Direito Civil Contemporâneo 7 (3):63–94

Cándano-Pérez M, Guerra-Espinosa RA (2017) Aproximación analítica a la imputación en el ámbito de la responsabilidad extracontractual chilena. Entramado 13(2):128–142

Carrá BLC (2015) Responsabilidade civil sem dano: uma análise crítica: limites epistemológicos a uma responsabilidade civil preventiva ou por simples conduta. Atlas, São Paulo

Carrá BLC (2017) A doutrina da tripartição da culpa: uma visão contemporânea. Revista de Direito Civil Contemporâneo 13(4):199–229

Chamon Junior LA (2005) Imputação objetiva e risco no direito penal: do funcionalismo à teoria discursiva do delito. Mandamentos, Belo Horizonte

Chidester D (2003) Salvation and suicide: Jim Jones, The peoples Temple and Jonestown. Indiana University Press, Indiana

Comes H (1972) Zum Begriff des "gesteigerten Risikos" im Recht der unerlaubten Handlungen. Neue Juristische Wochenschrift 45:2022–2026

Cornacchia L (2011) Il problema della c.d. causalità psichica rispetto ai condizionamenti mentali. In: Canestrari S, Fornasari G (ed) Nuove esigenze di tutela nell'ambito dei reati contro la persona. Clueb, Bologna

Cunha LR (2022) Orlando Gomes e a responsabilidade civil. In: Monteiro Filho CE, Morsello MF, Rosenvald N(eds) Protagonistas da responsabilidade civil. Foco, Indaiatuba

Cvetković MS (2021) Psychological influence and causation in tort law. Зборник радова Правног факултета у Нишу 93:45–61

da Silva RP (2017) Dano reflexo ou por ricochete e lesão à saúde psíquica: os casos de "choque nervoso" (Schockschaden) no Direito Civil alemão. Civilistica.com 6(2):1–34

Dantas ST (1979) Programa e direito civil: aulas proferidas na Faculdade Nacional de Direito [1942–1945]: parte geral, vol 1. Editora Rio, Rio de Janeiro

da Silva RP (2019) Antijuridicidade na responsabilidade civil extracontratual: da amplitude conceitual aos mecanismos de identificação. In: Benetti G et al (orgs) Direito, cultura, método: leituras da obra de Judith Martins-Costa. LMJ Mundo Jurídico, Rio de Janeiro

Dencker F (1996) Kausalität und Gesamttat. Duncker and Humblot, Berlin

Deutsch E (1967) Zivilrecht. JuristenZeitung 22(20):639–643

Deutsch E (1972) Regreβverbot und Unterbrechung des Haftungszusammenhangs im Zivilrecht: Bemerkungen zum Urteil des VI. Zivilsenats des BGH v. 16.2.1972. JuristenZeitung 27(18): 551–553

Deutsch E (1993) Das "allgemeine Lebensrisiko" als negativer Zurechnungsgrund. Versicherungsrecht 44(25):1041–1088

Deutsch E (1996) Allgemeines Haftungsrecht, 2ª edn. Carl Heymanns Verlag KG, Köln, Berlin, Bonn, München

Deutsch E (2005) Die neuere Entwicklung der Rechtsprechung zum Haftungsrecht. JuristenZeitung 60(20):987–994

Deutsch E, Ahrens HJ (2014) Deliktsrecht: unerlaubte Handlungen, Schadensersatz, Schmerzensgeld, 6ª edn. Verlag Franz Vahlen, München

Dias D (2020a) A chamada "culpa da vítima" é mesmo um problema apenas de causalidade? Revista eletrônica Conjur. Coluna Direito Civil Atual, São Paulo. 20 jan 2020

Dias D (2020b) Mitigação de danos na responsabilidade civil. Thomson Reuters Brasil, São Paulo

Direito CAM, Cavalieri Filho S (2011) Comentários ao novo Código Civil: da responsabilidade civil, das preferências e privilégios creditórios, v. 13. Forense, Rio de Janeiro

Ekkenga J, Kuntz T (2014) Vor §249. In: Soergel HT, Siebert W (orgs) Soergel: kommentar zum Bürgerlichen Gesetzbuch: schuldrecht 1/2: §243–304, 13ª edn. v. 13. 3/2. W. Kohlhammer, Stuttgart

Engisch K (1931) Die Kausalität als Merkmal der strafrechtlichen Tatbestände. Verlag von J. C. B. Mohr (Paul Siebeck), Tübingen

Fischer M (2016) Der Schockschaden im deutschen Recht und im Common Law: eine rechtsvergleichende Untersuchung des deutschen, englischen, australischen und kanadischen Rechts. Duncker and Humblot, Berlin

Fischer W (1988) Ausservertragliche Haftung für Schockschäden Dritter: ein Beitrag zur dogmatischen Analyse der sog. Fernwirkungsschäden. Schulthess Polygraphischer Verlag, Zürich

Forst SP (2000) Grenzen deliktischer Haftung bei psychisch vermittelter haftungsbegründender Kausalität. VVF, München

Frada MAC (2010) Direto civil, responsabilidade civil: o método do caso. Almedina, Coimbra

Frada MAC (2015) Teoria da confiança e responsabilidade civil. Almedina, Coimbra

Frota PMC (2014) Responsabilidade por danos: imputação e nexo de causalidade. Juruá, Curitiba

Galluccio A (2014) Terremoto dell'Aquila e responsabilità penale: Nesso causale ed addebito di colpa nella sentenza "Grandi Rischi". Tribunale dell'Aquila 22 ottobre 2012 (dep. 19.01.2013), n. 380. Diritto Penale Contemporaneo 22(1):190–214.

Garcia B (1941) Causalidade material e psíquica. Revista Forense 39(90):593–607

Geigel R (2020) Der Haftpflichtprozess: mit Einschluss des materiellen Haftpflichtrechts, 28ª edn. C.H.Beck, München

Godoy CLB (2010) Responsabilidade civil pelo risco da atividade: uma cláusula geral no Código civil de 2002, 2ª edn. Saraiva, São Paulo

Godoy CLB (2015) Responsabilidade civil pelo risco da atividade e nexo de imputação da obrigação de indenizar: reflexões para um Colóquio Brasil-Portugal. Revista Jurídica luso-brasileira 1(1):21–43

Gomes O (1989) Tendências modernas na teoria da responsabilidade civil. In: Francesco JRP Di (org) Estudos em homenagem ao Professor Silvio Rodrigues. Saraiva, São Paulo

Görgens P (1977) Konkurrierende Zurechnungstatbestände im Rahmen der deliktsrechtlichen Haftung nach § 823 BGB. Juristische Schulung 17(11):709–714

Gottwald P (1979) Schadenszurechnung und Schadensschätzung. C. H. Beck'sche Verlags Buchhandlung, München

Greger R (2013) Haftungsrecht des Straβenrverkehrs: Handbuch und Kommentar, 5ª edn. De Gruyter, Berlin, Boston

Grüneberg C (2020) Vorb v § 249. In: Palandt O, et al Palandt: bürgerliches Gesetzbuch 79ª edn. C.H. Beck, München

Guedes GSC (2005) O problema do nexo causal na responsabilidade civil. Renovar, Rio de Janeiro

Guedes GSC (2011) Lucros cessantes: do bom-senso ao postulado normativo da razoabilidade. Ed. RT, São Paulo

Haberhausen R (1973) Kausalität und zwischenmenschlicher Bereich. Neue Juristische Wochenschrift 1307–1310

Hager J (2018) BGH, Urteil vom 17.04.2018—VI ZR 237/17: psychische Gesundheitsverletzung. Juristische Arbeitsblätter 9:706–708

Händel K (1976) Anmerkung zu BGH, Urt. v. 13.1.1976—VI ZR 41/75. Neue Juristische Wochenschrift 27:1204

Hart HLA, Honoré T (1985) Causation in the law, 2ª edn. Oxford University Press, Oxford

Hartmann A (2009) Unterlassungsansprüche im Internet: störerhaftung für nutzergenerierte Inhalte. Verlag C.H. Beck, München

Hasselblatt GN (1996) Die Grenzziehung zwischen verantwortlicher Fremd- und eigenverantwortlicher Selbstgefährdung im Deliktsrecht. DeutscherAnwaltVerlag, Bonn

Herldermann GB (2004) Schadensersatz für Schockschäden Dritter im Vergleich des deutschen Rechts gemäß § 823 I BGB zu Englischen bzw. irischen Recht: eine rechtsvergleichende Untersuchung über die Möglichkeiten einer angemessenen und juristisch begründbaren Haftungsbegrenzung. Verlag im Internet, Berlin

Hilgendorf E (1995) Der "gesetzmäßige Zusammenhang" im Sinne der modernen Kausallehre. Juristische Ausbildung 514–522

Hübner J (1972) Schadenszurechnung nach Risikosphären: eine Studie zur schadensgeneigten Arbeit selbständig Tätiger am Beispiel der privatrechtlichen Haftung des Seelotsen. In: Inaugural-Dissertation zur Erlangung des Grades eines Doktors der Rechte bei dem Fachbereich Rechtswissenschaft der Freien Universität, Berlin

Hübner J (1974) "Schadensverteilung" bei Schäden anläβlich der Verfolgung festzunehmender Personen durch Beamte – eine Wiederkehr der Culpa-Kompensation? Juristische Schulung 8:496–502

Jansen N (2002) §§ 249-253, 255. Das Problem der Rechtswidrigkeit bei § 823 Abs. 1 BGB. Archive für civilistische Praxis 202:517–554

Jansen N (2003) Die Struktur des Haftungsrechts: Geschichte, Theorie und Dogmatik außervertraglicher Ansprüche auf Schadenersatz. Mohr Siebeck, Tübingen

Jescheck HH (1981) Tratado de Derecho Penal. Bosch, Barcelona

Karczewski C (1992) Die Haftung für Shockschäden: eine rechtsvergleichende Untersuchung. Peter Lang, Frankfurt am Main

Kindermann CP (1984) Verkehrssicherungspflichten. Richard Boorberg Verlag, Stuttgart, München, Hannover

Kleindiek D (1997) Deliktshaftung und juristische Person: zugleich zur Eigenhaftung von Unternehmensleitern. Mohr Siebeck, Tübingen

Kleinschmidt J (2012) Causation. In: Basedow J et al (eds) The Max Planck encyclopedia of European private law, v. 1 Oxford University Press Oxford

Koller I (1979) Die Risikozurechnung bei Vertragsstörungen in Austauschverträgen: eine Untersuchung zur Rechtsfortbildung auf dem Gebiet der materiellen Leistungserschwerung, Zweckstörung sowie Schadensersatzhaftung bei Sach- und Dienstleistungen. C. H.Beck, München

Koriath H (1988) Kausalität, Bedingungstheorie und psychische Kausalität. Verlag Otto Schwartz & Co, Göttingen

Kötz H, Wagner G (2006) Deliktsrecht, 10ª edn. Wolters Kluers, München

Koziol H (2020) Österreichisches Haftpflichtrecht: Allgemeiner Teil. Jan Sramek Verlag KG, Wien

Krüger M (2019) Straftaten gegen das Leben. In: Laufhütte HW, Rissing-van-saan R, Tiedermann K (eds) Leipziger Kommentar: Strafgesetzbuch: §§ 211–231. Bd. 7, Teil 1. Walter de Gruyter, Berlin, Boston

Lang R (1983) Normzweck und duty of care: eine Untersuchung über die Grenzen der Zurechnung im deutschen und anglo-amerikanischen Deliktsrecht. C.H. Beck, München

Lange H (1960) Gutachten für den Verhandlungen des dreiundvierzigsten deutschen Juristentages. In: Ständigen Deputation des deutschen Juristentages (ed) Verhandlungen des dreiundvierzigsten Deutschen Juristentages, vol 1. Mohr (Paul Siebeck), Tübingen

Lange R, Schiemann G (2003) Schadensersatz, 3ª edn. Mohr Siebeck, Tübingen

Larenz K (1927) Hegels Zurechnungslehre und der Begriff der objektiven Zurechnung: ein Beitrag zur Rechtsphilosophie des kritischen Idealismus und zur Lehre von der "juristischen Kausalität". Inaugural-Dissertation zur Erlangung der Doktorwürde der Hohen Rechts- und Staatswissenschaftlichen Fakultät der Georg August-Universität zu Göttingen. Druck von Reinhold Berger, Lucka

Larenz K (1955) Tatzurechnung und "Unterbrechung des Kausalzusammenhanges". Neue Juristische Wochenschrift 8(28):1009–1013

Larenz K (1958) Anmerkung zum Urteil des BGH v 2.7.157. Neue Juristische Wochenschrift, 627–628

Larenz K (1963) Rechtwidrigkeit und Handlungsbegriff im Zivilrecht. In: von Caemmerer E, Nikisch A, Zweigert K (eds) Festschrift für Hans Dölle, vol. 1. J.C.B. Mohr (Paul Siebeck), Tübingen

Larenz K (1970) Zum heutigen Stand der Lehre von der objektiven Zurechnung im Schadensersatzrecht. In: Festschrift für Richard M. Honig: zum 80. Geburtstag. Verlag Otto Schwartz & Co, Göttingen

Larenz K (1987) Lehrbuch des Schuldrechts: Allgemeiner Teil, 14ª edn. vol 1. C. H. Beck'sche Verlagsbuchhandlung, München

Larenz K, Canaris CW (1994) Lehrbuch des Schuldrechts: Besonderer Teil, 13ª edn. vol 2, pt. 2. Beck, München

Larenz K (2019) Metodologia da ciência do direito, 8th edn. (Portuguese translation by José Lamego). Fundação Calouste Gulbenkian, Lisboa

Leitão AM (2009) Normas de proteção de danos puramente patrimoniais. Almedina, Coimbra

Leitermeier H (1968) Die Deliktsrechtliche Haftung des Verfolgten für Schäden bei der Verfolgung. Inaugural-Dissertation des Fachbereichs Rechtswissenschaft der Friedrich-Alexander-Universität Erlangen-Nürnberg

Leser HG, Klippel D (1983) Zu den Instrumenten des Rechtsgüterschutzes im Delikts- und Gefährdungshaftungsrecht. Archiv Für Die Civilistische Praxis 183(4/5):568–607

Lima A (1963) Culpa e risco. Ed.RT, São Paulo

Lima PB (2019) A causalidade virtual e o comportamento lícito alternativo na responsabilidade civil aquiliana: uma perspectiva integrada. O Direito 151(II):349–413

Looschelders D (2019) Die Mitverantwortlichkeit des Geschädigten im Privatrecht. Mohr Siebeck, Tübingen

Luckey J (2019) § 249. In: Prütting H, Wegen G, Weinrich G (eds) BGB Kommentar, 14ª edn. Luchterhand Verlag, Köln

Mädrich M (1980) Das Allgemeine Lebensrisiko: ein Beitrag zur Lehre von der Haftungsbegrenzung im Schadensersatzrecht. Duncker and Humblot, Berlin

Magadan GFM (2019) Responsabilidade civil extracontratual: causalidade jurídica: seleção das consequências do dano. Editora dos Editores, São Paulo

Magnus U (2020) § 830. In: Dannemann G, Schulze R (eds) German civil code: bürgerliches Gesetzbuch (BGB), v. 1. C.H. Beck; Nomos, München

Marinoni LG (2011) Tutela específica: arts. 461, CPC e 84, CDC, 2nd edn. Revista dos Tribunais, São Paulo

Marinho RS (2013) Princípio da autorresponsabilidade no direito penal. Dissertação (Mestrado)—Faculdade de Direito. Universidade de São Paulo

Markesinis BS, Unberath H (2002) The German law of torts: a comparative treatise, 4ª edn. Hart Publishing, Oxford, Portland

Marrey A (1968) Causalidade material e causalidade subjetiva. Revista Justitia 60:51–57

Martens KP (1972) Die Verfolgung des Unrechts. Neue Juristische Wochenschrift 17:740–746
Martins-Costa J (2001) Os danos à pessoa no direito brasileiro e a natureza de sua reparação. Revista da Faculdade de Direito da UFRGS 19:181–207.
Martins-Costa J (2007) Os avatares do abuso do direito e o rumo indicado pela boa-fé. In: Delgado ML, Alves JF (coords) Novo Código Civil—Questões controvertidas: Parte Geral do Código Civil. Método, São Paulo
Martins-Costa J (2014) Dano moral à brasileira. Revista do Instituto do Direito Brasileiro 3 (9):7073–7122
Martins-Costa J (2017) O árbitro e o cálculo do montante da indenização. In: Carmona CA, Lemes SF, Martins PB (eds) 20 anos da lei de arbitragem: homenagem a Petrônio R. Muniz. Atlas, São Paulo
Martins-Costa J (2018) A boa-fé no direito privado: critérios para a sua aplicação, 2ª edn. Saraiva Educação, São Paulo
Martins-Costa J, Costa E Silva P (2020) Crises e perturbações no cumprimento da prestação: estudo de direito comparado luso-brasileiro. Quartier Latin, São Paulo
Matthies KH (2009) Richterliche Mediation im Lichte der Amtshaftung. In: Ahrens HJ (ed) Medizin und Haftung: Festschrift für Erwin Deutsch zum 80. Geburtstag. Duncker and Humblot, Berlin
Medicus D (2005) Die psychisch vermittelte Kausalität im Zivilrecht. Juristische Schulung 289–296
Mello SBA (2010) A evolução do conceito de culpabilidade e a moderna doutrina alemã. Ciências penais: Revista da Associação Brasileira de Professores de Ciências Penais 7(12):261–291
Menezes Cordeiro A (2017) Da boa fé no direito civil. Almedina, Coimbra
Mertens HJ (1980) Verkehrspflichten und Deliktsrecht: Gedanken zu einer Dogmatik der Verkehrspflichtverletzung. Versicherungsrecht 31:397–408
Michelon C (2023) Direito privado, razão e justiça. Almedina, São Paulo
Miragem B (2021) Responsabilidade civil, 2ª edn. Forense, Rio de Janeiro
Miranda FC (1983) Tratado de direito privado, 4ª edn. 2ª tir, t. 1. RT, São Paulo
Miranda FC (1984a) Tratado de direito privado, 3ª edn. 2ª reimp, t. 22. RT, São Paulo
Miranda FC (1984b) Tratado de direito privado, 3ª edn. 2ªreimp, t. 26. RT, São Paulo
Miranda FC (1984c) Tratado de direito privado 3ª edn. 2ª reimp, t. 53. RT, São Paulo
Montijano M García-Ripoll (2008) Imputación objetiva, causa próxima, y alcance de los daños indemnizables. Editorial Comares, Granada
Moore R (2009) Understanding Jonestown and Peoples Temple. ABC-CLIO, Santa Barbara
Moraes MCB (2003) Danos à pessoa humana: uma leitura civil-constitucional dos danos morais. Renovar, Rio de Janeiro
Moro A, Invernizzi N (2017) A tragédia da talidomida: a luta pelos direitos das vítimas e por melhor regulação de medicamentos. História, Ciências, Saúde Manguinhosvol 24(3):603–622
Müller WP (2016) D. Kausalität. In: Jahnke J, Burmann M (eds) Handbuch des Personenschadensrecht. C.H. Beck, München
Munhoz LM (1943) Da causalidade subjetiva no Código Penal brasileiro. Emp. Gráfica da "Revista dos Tribunais", São Paulo
Niebaum G (1976) Die Verfolgungsfälle und ihre Wertungskriterien. Neue Juristische Wochenschrift 29:1673–1674
Niebaum G (1977) Die deliktische Haftung für fremde Willensbestätigung. Duncker and Humblot, Berlin
Nonato O (1929) Aspectos do modernismo jurídico e o elemento moral na culpa objetiva. Revista da Faculdade de Direito da Universidade de Minas Gerais 11:13–43
Noronha F (2013) Direito das obrigações, 4ª edn. Saraiva, São Paulo
Oetker H (2019) § 249. In: Oetker H, et al (orgs) Münchener Kommentar: Schuldrecht—Allgemeiner Teil I, 8ª edn. v. 2. C.H. Beck, München
Pereira RS (2019) O nexo de causalidade na responsabilidade delitual: fundamentos e limites do juízo de condicionalidade. Almedina, Coimbra
Pinto CA (1992) Teoria geral do direito civil, 3ª edn. 6ª reimp. Coimbra Editora, Coimbra

Pires CM (2020) Impossibilidade da prestação. Almedina, Coimbra
Pirson R, De Ville A (1935) Traité de la responsabilité civile extra-contractuelle, vol 2. E. Bruylant, Bruxelles
Proença JCB (1997) A conduta do lesado como pressuposto e critério de imputação do dano extracontratual. Almedina, Coimbra
Puppe I (2016) Strafrecht Allgemeiner Teil: im Spiegel der Rechtsprechung, 3ª edn. Nomos, Baden-Baden
Reale JM (2013) Instituições de direito penal, 4ª edn. Forense, Rio de Janeiro
Reinecke H (1960) Objektive Verantwortung im zivilen Deliktsrecht. Michael Triltsch Verlag, Düsseldorf
Reinig GHL (2015) O problema da causalidade na responsabilidade civil: a teoria do escopo da proteção da norma (Schutzzwecktheorie) e sua aplicabilidade no Direito Civil brasileiro. Tese (Doutorado)—Faculdade de Direito, Universidade de São Paulo
Renzikowski J (2011) Ist psychische Kausalität dem Begriff nach möglich? In: Paeffgen HU et al (orgs) Festschrift für Ingeborg Puppe zum 70. Geburtstag. Duncker and Humblot, Berlin
Renzikowski J (2020) É possível um conceito de causalidade psíquica? (Trad. Lucas Montenegro). Revista Direito GV 16(2):1–18
Ribas AJ (1905) Curso de direito civil brasileiro, 3rd edn. Jornal do Commercio, Rio de Janeiro
Risicato L (2007) La Causalità psichica tra determinazione e partecipazione. G. Giappichelli Editore, Torino
Fonseca AM (1958) Caso fortuito e teoria da imprevisão, 3rd edn. Forense, Rio de Janeiro
Ristow T (2003) Die psychische Kausalität im Deliktsrecht. Peter Lang, Frankfurt am Main
Rocha MA Coelho da (1917) Instituições de direito civil portuguez, 8th edn. Livraria Clássica, Lisboa
Rocha MP (2016) Reflexões sobre nexo causal, imputação objetiva e teoria do cotejo das esferas de risco na responsabilidade civil extracontratual. Revista de Direito Privado 67(17):213–238
Rodrigues Jr OL (2016) Nexo causal probabilístico: elementos para a crítica de um conceito. Revista de Direito Civil Contemporâneo 8(3):115–137
Rodrigues Jr OL, Peteffi da Silva R (2017) Daño reflejo o por rebote: pautas para un análisis de derecho comparado. Revista de Direito Civil Contemporâneo 7(3):207–240
Roppo V (2016) Diritto privato, 5th edn. Giappichelli Editore, Torino
Rother W (1965) Adäquanztheorie und Schadensverursachung durch mehrere. Neue Juristische Wochenschrift 5:177–183
Roxin C (2011) Probleme psychisch vermittelter Kausalität. In: Hellmann U, Schröder C (orgs) Festschrift für Hans Achenbach. C.F. Müller, Heidelberg
Roxin C (2013) Problemas de causalidade psiquicamente mediada. (Trad. Alaor Leite). Direito Penal 11(111):247–272
Roxin C (2015) Täterschaft und Tatherrschaft, 9ª edn. Walter de Gruyter, Berlin, Boston
Rümelin M (1896) Der Zufall im Recht. Akademische Verlagsbuchhandlung von J. C. B. Mohr, Freiburg i. B. und Leizpig
Safferling CJM (2008) Vorsatz und Schuld: Subjektive Täterelemente im deutschen und englischen Strafrecht. Mohr Siebeck, Tübingen
Sanseverino PTV (2010) Princípio da reparação integral: indenização no Código Civil. Saraiva, São Paulo
Scheller IJG (1805) Lateinisch-deutsches (und deutsch-lateinisches) Wörterbuch, 3ª edn. v. 2. Fritsch, Leipzig
Schiemann G (2017) § 249. In: J. von Staudingers Kommentar zum Bürgerlichen Gesetzbuch mit Einführungsgesetz und Nebengesetzen: § 249–254 (Schadensersatzrecht). Walter de Gruyter, Berlin
Schiemann G (2019) Anmerkung zu BGH, Urt. v. 17.4.2018—VI ZR 237/17. JuristenZeitung 74 (2):103–104

Schmidt JP (2009) Zivilrechtskodifikation in Brasilien: Strukturfragen und Regelungsprobleme in historisch-vergleichender Perspektive (Schriften zum ausländischen und internationalen Privatrecht, v. 226). Mohr Siebeck, Tübingen

Schwarz T (1966) Die Grenzen deliktischer Verantwortlichkeit für Gesundheitsbeschädigungen in den Fällen freiwilliger Hilfeleistung. JuristenZeitung 21(5/6):162–167

Serra APS (1959) Obrigação de indemnização (Colocação. Fontes. Conceito e espécies de dano. Nexo causal. Extensão do dever de indemnizar. Espécies de indenização). Direito de abstenção e de remoção. Boletim do Ministério da Justiça 84:5–301

Simão JF (2008) Responsabilidade civil do incapaz. Atlas, São Paulo

Simão JF (2021) Art. 403. In: Schreiber A, et al Código Civil Comentado: doutrina e jurisprudência, 3ª edn. Forense, Rio de Janeiro

Spickhoff A (1998) Gesetzesverstoβ und Haftung. Carl Heymanns Verlag KG, Köln, Berlin, Bonn, München

Staake M (2014) Gesetzliche Schulverhältnisse. Springer, Berlin, Heidelberg

Staffler L (2017) Presseinterview als fahrlässige Tötung: Der italienische Strafprozess gegen die Expertenkommission zum Erdbeben von L'Aquila(2009) Die Feststellung der psychischen Kausalität im Erdbebenfall. Zeitschrift Für Internationale Strafrechtsdogmatik (ZIS) 2:125–138

Steffen E (1980) Verkehrspflichten im Spannungsfeld von Bestandsschutz und Handlungsfreiheit. Versicherungsrecht 31:409–412

Steffen E (1989) §823 BGB. In: Dunz W, et al Das Bürgerliche Gesetzbuch: mit besonderer Berücksichtigung der Rechtsprechung des Reichgerichts und des Bundesgerichtshofes: §§ 812–831, 12ª edn. v. 2, t. 5. Walter de Gruyter, Berlin, New York

Steiner RC (2018) Reparação de danos: interesse positivo e interesse negativo. Quartier Latin, São Paulo

Stoco R (2007) Tratado de responsabilidade civil: doutrina e jurisprudência, 7ª edn. Ed. RT, São Paulo

Stöhr K (2009) Psychische Gesundheitsschäden und Regress. Neue Zeitschrift für Verkehrsrecht 161–166

Stoll H (1963) BGH, 30. 6. 1987—VI ZR 257/86. Unrechtstypen bei Verletzung absoluter Recht. Archive Für Civilistische Praxis 162:205–236

Stoll H (1968) Kausalzusammenhang und Normzweck im Deliktsrecht. J.C.B. Mohr (Paul Siebeck), Tübingen

Stoll H (1980) Rechtsfragen bei Hilfeleistungen in vermeintlicher Not. In: Ehmann H, Hefermehl W, Laufs A (eds) Privatautonomie, Eigentum und Verantwortung: Festgabe für Hermann Weitnauer zum 70. Geburtstag. Duncker and Humblot, Berlin

Stoll H (1993) Haftungsfolgen im bürgerlichen Recht: eine Darstellung auf rechtsvergleichender Grundlage. C.F. Müller Juristischer Verlag, Heidelberg

Strasser F (2008) Die Zurechnung von Retter-, Flucht- und Verfolgerverhalten im Strafrecht. Duncker & Humblot, Berlin

Strauch RG (1992) Die Haftung des Verfolgten für Schäden des Verfolgers aus § 823 Abs. 1 BGB: Zugleich Anmerkung zum Urteil des BGH vom 3.7.1990 (VI ZR 33/90) VersR 91, 111. Versicherungsrecht 22:932–937

Stürner R (1984) Zur Gerechtigkeit richterlicher Schadenszuweisung 297–308. Versicherungsrecht

Tavares J (2009) Teoria do crime culposo, 3ª edn. Lumen Juris, Rio de Janeiro

Tavares J (2019) Teoria do injusto penal, 4ª edn. Tirant lo Blanch, São Paulo

Teichmann A (1996) BGH, 12. 3. 1996—VI ZR 12/95. Haftung des Verfolgten und Mitverschulden des verfolgenden Polizeibeamten. JuristenZeitung 51(23):1178–1183

Teotônio PJF, Silva AAB (2014/2015) Tóxicos: ponderações sobre as exceções dualistas na Lei de Tóxicos. Revista Magister 11(63):5–63

Tepedino G (2019) O art. 931 do Código Civil e a antijuridicidade do dano injusto. Revista Brasileira de Direito Civil (Rbdcivil) 22:11–13

Thalheim E (1964) Möglichkeiten der Haftungsbegrenzung: ein Vergleich zwischen Adäquanz-, Schutzzweck- und Schutzbereichsstheorie. Thesis (doctoral), Universität Hamburg
Theodoro Júnior H (2008) Comentários ao novo Código Civil: dos atos jurídicos lícitos. Dos atos ilícitos. Da prescrição e da decadência. Da prova, 4th edn. Forense, Rio de Janeiro
Tolsada MY (1993) Responsabilidad civil contractual y extracontractual, vol 1. Reus, Madrid
Traeger L (1929) Der Kausalbegriff im Straf- und Zivilrecht: Zugleich ein Beitrag zur Auslegung des BGB. N. G. Elwert'sche Verlagsbuchhandlung, Marburg
Varela JMA (2000) Das obrigações em geral, 10ª edn. Almedina, Coimbra
Vieweg K, Lorz S (2022) Schadensersatzrecht. In: Stoffels M, Herresthal C, Magnus R (orgs) J. Von Staudingers Kommentar zum Bürgerlichen Gesetzbuch mit Einführungsgesetz und Nebengesetzen. Eckpfeiler des Zivilrechts. Otto Schmidt; De Gruyter, Berlin
Visintini G (2005) Trattato della responsabilità civile: fatti illeciti, inadempimento, danno risarcibile, 3ª edn. Cedam, Padova
von Buri M (1894) Beiträge zur Theorie des Strafrechts und zum Strafgesetzbuche: gesammelte Abhandlungen. Verlag von Veit & Comp, Leipzig
von Caemmerer E (1956) Das Problem des Kausalzusammenhangs im Privatrecht. Hans Ferdinand Schulz Verlag, Freiburg
von Caemmerer E (1968) Die absoluten Rechte in § 823 Abs. 1 BGB. In: Leser HG (ed) Ernst von Caemmerer—Gesammelte Schriften: rechtsvergleichung und Schuldrecht, vol v. J.C.B. Mohr (Paul Siebeck), Tübingen, p 1
von Caemmerer E (1970) Die Bedeutung des Schutzbereichs einer Rechtsnorm für die Geltendmachung von Schadensersatzansprüchen aus Verkehrsunfällen. Deutsches Autorecht 283–292
von Bar C (1980) Verkehrspflichten: richterliche Gefahrsteuerungsgebote in deutschen Deliktsrecht. Carl Heymanns Verlag KG, Berlin, Bonn, München
von Bar C (1988) Entwicklungen und Entwicklungstendenzen im Recht der Verkehrs(sicherungs) pflichten. Juristische Schulung 169–174
Voss K (2007) Die Verkehrspflichten: eine dogmatische Kategorie des deutschen Haftungsrechts und ihre europäische Zukunft. Mohr Siebeck, Tübingen
Waldkirch C (2018) Zufall und Zurechnung im Haftungsrecht. Mohr Siebeck, Tübingen
Weber R (1995) Verfolgungsfälle: objektive und subjektive Zurechnung. In: Deutsch E, Klingmüller E, Kullmann HJ (eds) Festschrift für Erich Steffen zum 65. Geburtstag am 28. Maio 1995: der Schadensersatz und seine Deckung. Walter de Gruyter, Berlin, New York
Weitenberg M (2014) Der Begriff der Kausalität in der haftungsrechtlichen Rechtsprechung der Unionsgericht: Zugleich ein Beitrag zur Kohärenz der EU-Haftungssystem. Nomos, Baden-Baden
Wilburg W (1941) Die Elemente des Schadensrechts. N.G. Elwert'sche Verlagsbuchhandlung, Marburg
Windscheid B, Kipp T (1963) Lehrbuch des Pandektenrechts, 9ª edn. v. 2. Scientia Verlag, Aalen
Winiger B (2007) Damage caused by psychological influence: comparative report. In: Winiger B, et al (orgs) Digest of European tort law: essential cases on natural causation. Springer, Wien, New York
Wündiger M (2018) Psychische Gesundheitsverletzung und Zurechnung bei einem Amoklauf. Juris 408–410
Zhang M (2016) Aktiv psychische Kausalität im Deliktsrecht. Duncker and Humblot, Berlin
Zimmermann R (1980) Herausforderungsformel und Haftung für fremde Willensbetätigung nach § 823 I BGB. JuristenZeitung 35(1):10–16
Zimmermann R (2010) Derecho romano, derecho contemporáneo, derecho europeo: la tradición del derecho civil en la actualidad. (Trad. Javier M. Rodríguez Olmos). Universidad Externado de Colombia, Bogotá

Chapter 5
Application of Theoretical Models to Practical Cases

5.1 Introduction

It was established in Sect. 2.3 that the causal theories currently adopted in Brazilian law cannot address all the intricate issues that emerge from social reality,[1] particularly in cases involving damages caused by psychological influence. Accordingly, the theory of adequate causation, after assessing the existence of natural causation, should, in certain groups of cases, be complemented by other criteria of objective imputation.

Subsequently, in Sect. 4.5, the criteria adopted by German doctrine and jurisprudence regarding cases of "psychologically mediated causation" were critically examined. It was concluded that not all the proposed criteria are useful for determining the liability of the initial wrongdoer, especially when considering the framework of Brazilian law. Others, however, when combined with the investigation of the adequacy of the cause in its negative formulation, effectively establish limits to liability in cases of "psychological causation." Particularly relevant at this point are the purpose of the norm's protection, the materialization of the created risk,[2] the proportionality of the act committed, the self-responsibility

[1] A change of perspective is necessary regarding liability, which is governed not by ontological data, natural or psychological issues, but by imputation criteria. These criteria reflect choices made within each society, even if such choices partially integrate those data into their imputation rules. Objective imputation rules, therefore, reflect the dogmatic constructions through which a given society expresses its models for attributing liability (Machado (2008), p. 327). For a discussion on the distinction between the ontological and legal nexus, see Nespoli and Amaral (Nespoli and Acczm 2022), p. 21.

[2] As discussed in Section 4.5.3.3, the risk-based criterion may be applied as an autonomous ground for liability, independently of the adequacy theory, the protective scope of the infringed norm, or the provocation formula.

C. Dantas Bisneto, *Psychological Causation in Tort Law*,
https://doi.org/10.1007/978-3-032-03825-8_5

of the second causer, the controllability of the causal course, and the position of authority of the initial wrongdoer, considering the possibility of recognizing concurrent causation (Art. 945 of the CC/02).

It is essential to move forward by critically examining the practical cases decided by German and Brazilian courts and proposing solutions that align with national law, in accordance with the criteria already analyzed. To this end, the categorization of case groups plays a fundamental role, classifying them according to the factual and legal similarities found and identifying the appropriate imputation criteria to be employed.

5.2 Classification

Various classifications have been proposed to better systematize the matter[3] and facilitate the resolution of cases through the application of coherent imputation criteria. The detailed analysis of situations faced by the courts reveals the complexity and variety of existing scenarios, facilitating the selection of objective imputational parameters that prove functional in practice. The study of cases[4] demonstrates the different and comprehensive forms of "psychological causation."[5]

Winiger[6] categorizes cases according to different levels of psychological influence, observing that it is challenging to establish a universal rule regarding the degree of psychological pressure necessary for attributing damage to the individual in foreign legal contexts.

Initially, he points to situations of minimal influence (*slightest influence*), which include cases of simple excitement (*simple excitement*), such as when someone observes a traffic accident, crosses the street to help the victims, and is hit by another vehicle. At the same level of influence, the author refers to the case of mere temptation (*simple temptation*), which would occur, for example, when a boy plays with pieces of glass he found in the school garden. Still at the level of minimal influence, he mentions the case of seduction (*seduction*). In an Italian case,[7] a marriage proposal was used to obtain consent for the performance of sexual activities. After the bride had two miscarriages, her partner was ordered to compensate for the damages due to his refusal to marry.

---

[3] The debate surrounding "psychological causation" remains underdeveloped, such that it is not yet possible to rely on undisputed knowledge or coherent theoretical frameworks (Koriath (1988), p. 141).

[4] By emphasizing the importance of case studies, see Dantas (2001), p. 39.

[5] As a matter of methodological delimitation, this work will not examine the hypotheses of contractual liability, although the criteria developed below may prove relevant, depending on the characteristics of that context.

[6] Winiger (2007), p. 253.

[7] *Court of Cassation*, 08.07.1993, n. 7493.

In the class of slight influence (*slight influence*), certain forms of imitation (*imitation*)[8] are found. Austrian jurisprudence[9] dismissed the liability of two twelve-year-old boys who entered a warehouse and set fire to some clothes there, subsequently extinguishing the flames. A third child, who was also playing in the space, repeated the act of the others, set fire to a piece of clothing, but was unable to extinguish the flames, causing them to spread throughout the environment and completely burn the warehouse. Winiger cites, as a particular hypothesis of slight influence, the attempt to escape a sanction, as in the mentioned case[10] of the operations supervisor of the *Deutsche Bundesbahn* who fell off the ladder.[11]

A form of stronger influence consists of explicit incitement to commit a dangerous or illegal act, such as in the case of someone who encourages a drunk friend to take a car ride, resulting in an accident.[12] Also mentioned in this category is the hypothesis of incitement to breach a contract.[13]

In the group of strongest influence, individuals who acted on someone's orders to carry out a certain dangerous activity[14] are included. The same classification includes the case of explicit provocation. For instance, in a Hungarian case mentioned by Winiger, a waiter challenged a customer, stating that he would not be able to drink all the alcohol stock in just one session, inducing the consumer, with such conduct, to ingest a lethal dose of alcohol.[15] Another form of strong influence is intimidation, as in the case of the union that threatened to disaffiliate an employer if he did not terminate the contract of a worker who joined another association.[16]

A final and particular group mentioned by Winiger, which is not necessarily linked to the strength of the influence, concerns incorrect or insufficient information,[17] especially in situations of breach of the duty to inform[18] on the part of

---

[8] Considering imitation as a form of influence, it is worth noting that the role model may either be unaware of their position of leadership in relation to the follower or, conversely, consciously recognize that their opinions, suggestions, or ideas serve as guidance to others. On this point, see Weimann (1994), p. 54.

[9] JB1 1986, 589.

[10] BGHZ 57,25.

[11] Winiger (2007), p. 254.

[12] As already stated in Section 4.2, cases characterized by the intentional, malicious act of the first perpetrator, are not covered by the scope of this work.

[13] On the subject, in Brazilian law, see Lima (2015), pp. 310–311; Rodrigues Jr (Rodrigues 2004); Azevedo (1998); Penteado (2007), pp. 121–122.

[14] Barbosa (AMCNM 2020), p. 984.

[15] LB. P. törv. II 20.220/1960.

[16] Winiger (2007), p. 255.

[17] Barbosa (AMCNM 2020), pp. 971–1006.

[18] It is underestimated, especially in cases involving liability for misinformation, omission, or breach of the duty to provide adequate information. These situations raise the question of how the injured party would have acted if properly informed. According to Ahrens and Spickhoff, German case law has resolved this issue through rules on the burden of proof, adopting the presumption that the victim would have acted in accordance with the information that should have been provided (Ahrens and Spickhoff (2022), p. 63).

physicians. The issue here lies in whether the medical professional provided sufficient information to the patient about the risks and possible harmful consequences of the intervention. Additionally, at this point, the liability of financial intermediaries, auditors, and investors who favor the creation of psychological frameworks conducive to investment, but which later prove to be partially or entirely false, can be discussed.[19]

In these cases, the psychological influence would not be based on a form of pressure but on omission, since the patient did not receive all the necessary information for informed consent.[20] Winiger[21] suggests that it could be argued that this is not a question of psychological influence, as there is no influence in its strict sense, but a form of abstention. Thus, it could be referred to as an "influence by lack of influence." Only in rare cases is the influence explicit, such as when a physician exerts psychological pressure on a patient, forcing them to accept the proposed medical treatment.

Lange and Schiemann[22] present a different systematization, dividing the instances of "psychological causation" into two main groups. In the first category, there are cases where the damage is caused by a free act of the injured person (*freie Handlungen des Verletzten*). This is the case, for example, in emergency aid situations (*Nothilfefälle*), where assistance is provided to someone in danger who has not caused their own emergency situation through fault (e.g., someone who tries to stop the passage of horses in order to protect others from harm and becomes injured).[23] Alternatively, in a bus fire, a passenger tries to help a woman get out and sustains injury.[24] This group also includes situations of escape (*Fluchtfälle*), such as the well-known case of the injured supervisor of the *Bundesbahn*. The remaining cases are treated in a separate category (*Selbstschädigung des Verletzten, Verhalten des Verletzten und Folgeschäden*).

---

[19] Given the specificities of the financial system and the corporate sector, where particular regulatory frameworks apply, these cases will not be examined in this study. The criteria discussed in Section 5.2.1.2, which refer to interventions grounded in the authority position of the initial actor, such as self-responsibility and the materialization of a typical risk created, appear, at first glance, to offer useful guidance in addressing the complex issues that arise in such contexts.

[20] It is necessary to demonstrate that an ordinary individual would have refused the treatment if properly informed. According to Kfouri, compensation should be denied when another individual, equipped with the same information and placed under the same circumstances, would have agreed to undergo the therapy. The insufficient fulfillment of the duty to obtain informed consent from the patient must be duly proven (Kfouri Neto (2019), p. 16). Daisy Gogliano contends that informed consent, on its own, does not constitute ground for excluding or limiting liability, nor does it operate as a mechanism for transferring treatment risks to the patient. (Gogliano (2021), pp. 149–150).

[21] Winiger (2007), pp. 255–256.

[22] Lange and Schiemann (2003), p. 131.

[23] RGZ 50, 219.

[24] RGZ 164,125.

In a second category, Lange and Schiemann[25] address third-party interventions (*Eingriffe Dritter*),[26] which can cause or increase the damage, raising the question of whether, and under what conditions, the individual who facilitated the third party's conduct should be held liable for the injuries inflicted.[27] For example, they assert that an individual who damages a pasture fence is responsible for the loss of the cows,[28] even if the cows were taken by a third party.[29] Similarly, they reference a decision from the BGH that attributed liability to a driver who left the car parked without the required security measures (e.g., door open or without the lock), after it was stolen and used by a criminal on the run. The careless owner was held liable for the attempted murder committed by the fugitive against the pursuing police officer.[30]

Min Zhang[31] divides "psychological causation" based on the intention of the first perpetrator. If they acted intentionally, it is referred to as "intentionally mediated causation" ("*absichtlich vermittelte Kausalität*").[32] This occurs, as already mentioned, in cases of deception (*Täuschung*),[33] threat (*Drohung*), and incitement (*Anstiftung*). If there is no intention on the part of the first wrongdoer, there is a form of "unintentionally mediated causation" ("*unabsichtlich vermittelte Kausalität*"). The manifestation of this kind of causation is characterized by the fact that an intentional act by the initial perpetrator is not necessary for the occurrence of the damaging result. It can be passive, when the act of the second causer is merely reflexive (e.g., chain car accidents and nervous shock), or active, when the damage results from the voluntary conduct of that individual.[34]

The taxonomy proposed by Till Ristow is adopted, with minor modifications, based on the distinction between damages resulting from the behavior of

---

[25] Lange and Schiemann (2003), p. 142.

[26] After analyzing the adequacy theory and the theory of the protective scope of the violated norm, Thomas Raiser questions whether a two-stage system of liability limitation is sufficient to resolve all cases in a satisfactory manner. He argues that, in situations involving deficient third-party intervention, the theory of the norm's protective scope does not offer a reliable criterion. Consequently, in cases of errors caused by third parties, the courts tend to adopt convincing attribution parameters without relying on overarching general theories (Raiser (1963), p. 465).

[27] Oetker (2019), p. 404. On the issue of liability arising from the interference of a third party's voluntary conduct, see Niebaum (1977).

[28] Ebel (1980).

[29] BGH JZ 1979, 33.

[30] BGH NJW 1971, 459.

[31] Zhang (2016), p. 14.

[32] As seen, this group of cases is not analyzed in the present work.

[33] This is illustrated by a Greek case in which an illiterate woman was persuaded by a businessman to invest in a plot of land, despite the seller's awareness that no building permit would ever be granted. The court grounded its decision on the concept of adequate causation, considering the businessman's influence to be a *conditio sine qua non* for the woman's conduct (*Athens Court of Appeal* 4172/1982, NoV, 822–825).

[34] Medicus asserts that "active psychological causation" represents a narrower form of "psychologically mediated causation" (Medicus (2005), p. 291).

the second causer (where the second causer of damage and the injured party coincide) and those resulting from the actions of a third party (where the second causer of damage and the injured party are different individuals). This framework acknowledges various issues within the same category, thereby justifying the application of distinct attribution criteria.

According to Ristow,[35] the first category is subdivided into the following: (a) intervention for assistance (*Dazwischentreten zur Hilfeleistung*); (b) intervention due to the authority position of the first causer (*Dazwischentreten bei Autoritätsstellung des Erstverursachers*); (c) mandatory intervention of the second causer (*Dazwischentreten bei Eingriffspflichten des Zweitverursachers*); (d) and intervention due to the specific duty of danger control of the first causer (*Dazwischentreten bei gegenständlichen Gefahrenkontrollpflichten des Erstverursachers).*

Regarding situations involving a third party, Ristow[36] presents the following classification: (a) intervention due to the omission of a safety provision by the first causer (*Dazwischentreten bei Unterlassung einer hinreichenden Sicherheitsvorkehrung durch den Erstverursacher*); (b) intervention due to interference in preexisting safety measures (*Dazwischentreten bei Beeinträchtigung einer bestehenden Sicherungsvorkehrung durch den Erstverursacher*); and (c) intervention in cases that correspond to two-person relationships (*Dazwischentreten bei Konstellation, die den Zwei-Personen-Verhältnissen entsprechen*).

5.2.1 *Cases Where the Second Causer Harms Their Own Interests*

In the analysis of damages caused by psychological influence, it is very common to distinguish between cases that involve only two individuals (*Zweipersonenverhältnissen*) and those where there is interference from a third party (*Dreipersonenverhältnissen*).[37] In the first scenario, the initial tortfeasor establishes a cause in the external environment (primary cause), which the second subject uses as an opportunity for their own causal contribution (secondary cause). Consequently, the second wrongdoer suffers damages, for which they demand compensation from the primary perpetrator.[38] The issue that arises in this group of cases is whether the first tortfeasor is liable for the damages incurred to the detriment of the second causer. Assuming such liability, it should be questioned whether there should be a proportional allocation of the damages[39] (§ 254 of the BGB and Art. 945 of CC/02).

---

[35] Ristow (2003), p. 45.

[36] Ristow (2003), p. 145.

[37] Forst (2000), pp. 31–35; Zimmermann (1980), p. 14.

[38] Ristow (2003), p. 45.

[39] Looschelders (2019), p. 479.

5.2.1.1 Cases of Assistance and Pursuit

The assistance situations are characterized by the imminent violation of a legal interest or its actual occurrence, where the second causer acts to prevent the realization of the damage or its worsening. The second perpetrator intends to prevent or reduce the injury but ultimately suffers harm themselves.[40] In certain cases, the second causer is obliged to intervene[41] due to their professional position, as there is a risk to public order, leading to the emergence of damage as a consequence. Unlike the following category, where the first tortfeasor holds authority over the second, in the cases discussed, it is the second causer who occupies a superior position in relation to the first.[42]

Decisions regarding cases of attempted rescue and salvage[43] (*Rettungs- und Nothilfeversuche*)[44] are frequently encountered in German jurisprudence,[45] with the prevailing position recognizing that compensation should be granted to rescuers sustaining harm.[46] A paradigmatic decision is that of the OLG Stuttgart (*Tankstellenfall*)[47] on November 24, 1964. In this case, a drunk driver, while transporting two work colleagues, collided with a parked lorry, causing his own vehicle to catch fire. A young man, at his parents' petrol station, ran with a fire extinguisher and, along with a passerby, rescued the driver and the two passengers from the burning vehicle. During the rescue, this young man suffered severe burns, rendering him unable to work for two weeks. The defendant's insurer paid compensation for material damages but denied liability for non-pecuniary damages.

The *Landgericht* did not accept the victim's claim, so the plaintiff appealed. The *Oberlandesgericht,* however, held that the plaintiff was entitled to compensation for the non-pecuniary harm suffered, pursuant to §§ 823 (1 and 2)[48] and

---

[40] In *Gibney v. State*, decided in 1983, a child fell from a bridge into a canal. The state, as defendant, had failed to implement adequate safety measures, and the parents had not breached their duty of supervision. The father jumped into the canal in an attempt to rescue his son, but both drowned. The court awarded five thousand dollars in compensation, holding that the state's failure to comply with safety obligations constituted the causal factor in both deaths (Nökel (1968), p. 7).

[41] Fuchs et al. (2017), p. 88.

[42] Ristow (2003), p. 91.

[43] In Germany, rescue cases are treated as a matter of causation, so that reasonable attempts to prevent damage do not "interrupt" the causal chain (Youngs (2014), p. 502).

[44] Oetker (2019) p. 405.

[45] In Austria, a rescuer who is injured during a rescue operation is entitled to compensation from the third party who negligently created the dangerous situation (Koziol and Koziol (2012), p. 551).

[46] Zhang (2016), p. 47.

[47] OLG Stuttgart NJW 1965, 112.

[48] The OLG Stuttgart examines both legal bases jointly, without engaging in a detailed analysis of the distinction between the two relevant paragraphs of the BGB. According to Till Ristow, this

847[49] of the BGB. It was observed that the conclusion that the accident caused by the defendant was not an adequate cause of the injury suffered by the plaintiff was incorrect. Although the adequate cause does not include conditions that, according to general human experience, are completely irrelevant to the occurrence of the damage,[50] it could not be accepted that, in the case analyzed, the bodily injuries experienced by the victim were unrelated to what would be normal and objectively expected as a result of the accident.

Even though the injury was caused by another act of the plaintiff's free decision, namely his intervention to rescue the defendant and the passengers, such a circumstance does not exclude, in itself, according to the German court, the adequate causal link between the wrongful act and its consequences.[51] It could not be asserted that, when there is independent and voluntary intervention by a third party, the causal adequacy can only be recognized if this interference was aimed at preventing a public danger[52] or in the performance of a legal obligation. The court decision mentions a judgment of the BGH,[53] in which it was established that, after a sufficiently serious traffic accident, it is not uncommon for other drivers to attempt to assist individuals in danger, regardless of any legal duty. According to the court, the act was justified, and the rescuer's conduct can be considered of high moral standard.[54]

The decision further rejected the conclusion that the harm suffered by the injured party is not a consequence attributable to the defendant's wrongful act.

---

approach supports the thesis that attribution in this area could be treated uniformly under tort law provisions (Ristow (2003), p. 51).

[49] Paragraph 847 of the BGB was repealed by the Second Act to Amend the Law of Torts, dated July 19, 2002. Regarding the series of reforms introduced in the BGB over the past decade, António Menezes Cordeiro noted that the 2001/2002 reform of the BGB was received as the most significant legal-scientific, legislative, and civil innovation of the past hundred years (Cordeiro (2004), p. 76). The idea of a comprehensive reform of the law of obligations appears to be attributable to then-Minister of Justice Hans-Jochen Vogel, who initially presented the proposal to the Federal Parliament in 1978 and later to the 52nd Deutscher Juristentag (Congress of the Association of German Jurists) (Zimermann (Zimmermann 2017), p. 348; Zimmermann (2008), p. 31).

[50] As previously discussed, under Traeger's formula, a condition is considered causally adequate if it does not insignificantly increase the objective possibility of a result of the same type as the one that occurred (Traeger (1929), p. 159; Schack (1986), p. 305).

[51] In a case decided by the OLG Celle (RGZ 50, 223), a farmer repeatedly drove his large and noisy tractor toward a group of horse riders in an attempt to intimidate them into revealing their names. Some horses, which were not being ridden, ran off. One of the riders followed and attempted to catch a loose horse by the reins while trotting along a main road. The horse slipped and fell, causing a serious fracture to the rider's arm. The German court recognized the farmer's liability for the injury (Lang (1983), p. 157).

[52] OLG Stuttgart NJW 1965, 112.

[53] NJW 1964, 1363.

[54] Regarding the discussion on liability in cases of attempted suicide followed by rescue, see Zimmermann (1979).

The Stuttgart Court considered this a misinterpretation of Larenz's position,[55] which suggests that even if there is adequate causation between the rescue and the wrongful act, such causation should be treated as an insignificant factor in relation to the rescue and the resulting harm, thereby excluding it from attribution to the initial conduct. The decision of the *Landgericht* held that, although the driver may, in any case, be held liable for negligence in relation to the injuries suffered by the plaintiff, the latter would have full responsibility for his intentional conduct.

The German court noted that, as argued by the plaintiff in his appeal, Larenz was merely defending the point of view according to which, even when several individuals caused the damage, since one after the other provided conditions for the eventual consequence, the intervening party can be considered the author, thereby rendering the acts of the remaining parties insignificant. According to the court, the *Landgericht* failed to realize that Larenz, when referring to the decisions of the *Reichsgericht* in RGZ 164,125, expressly stated that the free act of a third party does not exclude the attribution of liability to the one who caused the adequate cause.[56]

In Brazil, the Court of Justice of Minas Gerais[57] rejected the liability of the local sanitation company in a case where two individuals were passing through the Bandeirantes neighborhood on August 7, 2006, when they witnessed an accident involving a woman's vehicle caused by a sewer breakage. The strong impact caused the car to lose control and catch fire. The driver, a retired fire brigade major, and the passenger managed, in a brave act, to rescue the victim. Following the incident, they filed a claim against COPASA (Sanitation Company of Minas Gerais), seeking compensation for non-pecuniary damages in the amount of R$ 20,000.00 for each. At the first instance, the claims were dismissed.

---

[55] Larenz argues that, although attributing liability for the act (possibly combined with objectified negligence) is generally sufficient, liability may, in exceptional cases, be excluded if the outcome is attributable to the intentional conduct of another individual acting with a high degree of culpability. Even in the presence of adequate causation, imputation can be denied because, alongside the liability of the intentional wrongdoer, the original causer's liability becomes insignificant (Larenz (1955), p. 1012).

[56] This case resembles the one decided by the LG Berlin on October 29, 1998 (LG Berlin NJW 99, 2906). In that case, the plaintiff sued the defendant for a traffic accident that occurred on August 12, 1996. The plaintiff was driving on W-Strasse when the defendant, a ten-year-old child, rode his bicycle into the road a few meters ahead of the vehicle, emerging from between parked cars. The plaintiff swerved to avoid hitting the child, colliding with a parked car. He subsequently filed a claim against the minor and the child's parents, seeking 5176.24 DM in material damages. The *Amtsgericht* Berlin ruled entirely in favor of the plaintiff, holding that he had done everything possible to protect the child's life and that the parents were responsible for covering the material damages. The court did not find contributory negligence, as the defendants' assertion of speeding was unsubstantiated. On appeal, the judgment was upheld, with the court affirming that the first defendant's argument was unfounded. As Ristow aptly notes, unlike the case before the OLG Stuttgart, the plaintiff here acted preventively to avoid imminent harm. Prior to the child's actions, the plaintiff had not suffered any damage (Ristow (2003), p. 46).

[57] TJMG, ApCív 1.0024.09.580833–3/001, rel. Wander Marotta, j. 11.01.2011.

The claimants appealed, arguing that they put their lives at extreme risk, considering that the rescue was both dangerous and prolonged, as the victim was trapped by one foot on the pedals. They also contended that it was proven that the sewer breakage was the cause of the accident. The appeal was dismissed on the grounds that the causal link between the alleged omission of the public service provider and the event that allegedly caused damage to the plaintiffs was not demonstrated. It was emphasized that, in such cases, it is necessary to establish that the injury suffered resulted directly from the malfunction of a public administration service.

In rescue cases, there is no difficulty in demonstrating the natural causation, since, hypothetically, removing the initial accident would mean there would have been no rescue attempt. The adequacy of the cause is also present in these cases, since, given a dangerous situation, it is not beyond all probability that drivers or passersby, noticing the existence of a disaster, would assist the victims, even if it meant risking their own lives.

The negligence of the accident causer creates a risk not only for the occupants of the other vehicle but also for passersby, which materializes when, in an attempt to rescue, the third party sustains injuries. The harm to the private rescuer does not fall within the general risk of life, except in exceptional cases—such as when a pedestrian, while rendering assistance, trips on the pavement and incurs injury. This kind of damage may arise irrespective of the initial accident and cannot be traced to a risk specifically created by the first wrongdoer.

The criteria of "provocation" and justifiable motive, though recurrent in German jurisprudence and legal doctrine, fail to clarify the basis of imputation. Instead, they introduce unnecessary complexity and impede the formulation of coherent interpretative parameters, rendering them of limited legal significance. The two parameters lead the interpreter to unnecessary subjectivism, it being sufficient for imputation purposes that the first wrongdoer has enabled or favored the occurrence of the damage by creating a risk situation.

The proportionality[58] of the rescue or pursuit act should also be investigated. If an excessive disproportion between the risk assumed by the second causer and the intended objective is detected, the latter will be fully liable for the damages suffered. Otherwise, the losses may be distributed in proportion to each party's contribution to the harmful event (Art. 945 of the CC/02).

Regarding the criterion of self-responsibility, it is important to recognize that the decision to carry out the rescue, made by the passerby, is not sufficient by itself to exclude the liability of the accident causer, since this, combined with the urgency of the situation, limited the free will of the second perpetrator.[59] Exclusion of imputation is justified solely when the harmful outcome can be traced

[58] The proportionality criterion is applicable only in cases where an empirically identifiable causal relationship exists between the means and the objective. The objective represents the intended result, while the means consist of concrete measures directed toward achieving it (Sanseverino (2010), p. 108).

[59] Forst (2000), p. 135.

to the rescuer's fault at its highest degree,[60] as the act of the original causer then becomes negligible compared to the harmful consequences.[61]

The decision rendered by the Court of Justice of the State of Minas Gerais, mentioned above, should be subject to criticism. The local sanitation company, by not carrying out the necessary maintenance on the sewer, created a risk of injury to third parties, which materialized in the accident involving a woman's vehicle and the subsequent rescue attempt. The actions of the rescuers were proportional, considering that they exposed themselves to a specific risk situation, which materialized,[62] aiming to save the life of the driver, who was trapped by one foot on the pedals. The argument mentioned in the decision, that the direct causal link between the injury suffered and the malfunction was not evident, should not prevail, as it is based on a strictly naturalistic conception of causation, which fails to adequately distribute risks between the parties.

It is also classified as an intervention for the provision of aid,[63] as in the mentioned case of kidney donation (*Nierenspendefall*),[64] involving a thirteen-year-old girl who, on 06.12.76, suffered an accident during sports practice and, under suspicion of having injured her spleen, was referred by a doctor to the hospital. The medical professional, standing in for the chief surgeon, examined the injured girl and decided to perform surgery to open the abdominal cavity. When he found injuries to the left kidney, he removed it. The following day, the teenager was transferred to the university hospital due to acute kidney failure. It turns out she had been born without a right kidney.[65]

On March 31, 1976, the child's mother decided to donate one of her kidneys to her daughter. Subsequently, she brought an action against the doctor who performed the surgery,[66] seeking compensation for non-pecuniary and material damages. It was proven that the removal of the girl's organ resulted from negligent medical action during treatment and that, had the correct procedures been followed, the kidney could have been saved.[67]

---

[60] It is also possible to consider the hypothesis that the rescuer intentionally aims to harm himself, as in a case of attempted suicide. In this situation, the liability of the initial wrongdoer who caused the accident would no longer apply.

[61] Larenz (1955), p. 1012.

[62] According to Fernando Pantaleón Prieto, the death of an individual in an air accident cannot be attributed to someone who, either intentionally or negligently, caused the victim to miss a previous flight (or a train, in the case of an individual who fears flying) and thereby compelled them to board the aircraft that crashed (Prieto (1990), p. 1567). In a similar example, it is stated that an individual who advises his friend, perfectly capable and aware, crossing a brittle ice lake, one will not be held accountable for the accidental death of a colleague (Machado (2008), p. 317).

[63] Zhang (2016), p. 47; Niebaum (2003), p. 51.

[64] NJW 1987, 710.

[65] Stoll (1988), p. 150.

[66] Magnus (2000), p. 67.

[67] Markesinis and Unberath (2019), p. 660.

The BGH confirmed the surgeon's liability[68] due to the kidney transplant. It was asserted that the removal of the teenager's only kidney constituted a culpable error in treatment, which not only harmed her body and health but also forced relatives to put their own physical integrity at risk in an attempt to save the victim.[69] The causal link between the removal of the kidney and the donation made by the mother, which is beyond doubt, is not interrupted by the mother's voluntary decision. This decision was based on the fact that the medical error created a dangerous situation, which directly influenced the mother's decision to act, making the rescue attempt (*Rettungshandlung*)[70] possible. Without this error, the act of saving the victim would not have occurred.

It was correctly noted that there is no duty to protect others from injuring themselves and, conversely, no general prohibition against inducing another to act according to their own will. Social interaction, which inherently involves frequent encounters between individuals, allows one person to influence another in various ways without incurring liability. However, the individual who creates a dangerous situation, which requires urgent action from the rescuer, must be held liable for any injury inflicted on the rescuer.[71] The BGH emphasized that it cannot be maintained that the mother did not suffer compensable damage simply because

[68] Neuefeind (2001), p. 67.

[69] In Anglo-American law, under the rescue doctrine, efforts to protect the personal safety of another do not supersede the liability for the original negligence that exposed them to harm. It has been recognized, ever since the case involving a crowd rushing to save a balloonist, that a rescue attempt does not constitute an abnormal event, regardless of whether the rescue was considered "foreseeable." The rule is not confined to spontaneous or instinctive actions; it also applies when there is sufficient time to deliberate on the course of action. Moreover, whether the individual injured in the rescue attempt is the rescuer, the rescued party, or a bystander, the original tortfeasor remains liable (Prosser and Keeton (1984), pp. 307–308). It is also argued that, in rescue and emergency situations, the test of foreseeability may have limited relevance. In *The Oropesa* (1943), the ship of the same name collided with the *Manchester Regiment*, causing severe damage. The captain of the latter vessel launched a lifeboat intending to consult the captain of the *Oropesa* on measures to save his crew. However, the lifeboat capsized, resulting in significant loss of life. Although the sequence of events was not easily foreseeable, the captain's actions were reasonable under the circumstances and did not break the causal chain (Deakin and Adams (2019), p. 227).

[70] Musielak (2013), p. 245.

[71] A notable example from case law is the decision of the Sala Primera del Tribunal Supremo, rendered on March 10, 1983. In that case, a claim was filed on behalf of a minor who sustained severe burns when his clothes caught fire as he tried to assist his nine-year-old friend, whose clothing had also ignited. The children, including the minor's four-year-old brother, were attempting to operate a model aeroplane stored by their father in a storage unit. The father was found liable under Art. 1.903-II of the Spanish Civil Code. In addressing causation, the decision emphasized that once a fire is caused by one individual's actions, any measures taken by others to prevent or mitigate the disaster's consequences, even at the risk of their own physical safety, are considered arising from the initial negligent act, and their effects are included among the resulting harm (Prieto (1990), p. 1576).

she consented to the kidney transplant. Even the postponement[72] in making the decision does not exclude the doctor's liability, as affirmed by the German court.[73]

Also, in the case of kidney donation, the natural causation is present, according to the technique of hypothetical elimination, as well as the adequate cause, since the damage did not result from extraordinary or anomalous circumstances. It can also be affirmed that the organ transplant became necessary due to the unlawful risk created by the surgeon, which resulted in the removal of the mother's kidney. The mother's altruistic act must be considered equally proportional, given the minor's life-threatening situation. Finally, it should be emphasized that the criterion of self-determination does not exclude the professional's liability, considering that the medical error substantially limited the mother's decision-making capacity, even though she had sufficient time to carefully consider her choice.

Another scenario addressed is that of pursuit carried out by a private pursuer[74] (*Privatverfolger*). In a case decided by the BGH,[75] a driver was operating his vehicle under the influence of alcohol when, at an intersection, due to failing to yield the right of way, he collided with another car, which was thrown into a house, causing significant damage.[76] The defendant fled at high speed, pursued by the victim's stepson, who was following closely behind. The fugitive, in an attempt to escape, maintained a speed of 100 km/h, while the pursuer, however, kept a distance of approximately three hundred meters. After the chase crossed two communities, the two vehicles collided at a road construction site.

Although the *Landgericht* Köln rejected the plaintiff's claim, the appellate court (*Berufungsgericht*) decided that he was entitled to compensation in his own name, as the defendant, by fleeing, ultimately influenced the behavior of the pursuer.[77] The court recognized the plaintiff's contributory negligence, limiting the compensation to three-quarters of the total damage. The BGH asserted that the attribution of the consequences is not excluded due to the intervention of a third party, even if

---

[72] The BGH decision refers to various precedents in Anglo-American law, especially regarding the *rescue doctrine*. See *Urbanski v. Patel*, Manitoba Queen's Beach, 25 January 1978; *Sirianni v. Anna*, 21 December 1967; *Moore v. Shah*, 30 December 1982 and *Ornelas v. Fry*, Court of Appeals of Arizona, 06 May 1986.

[73] Deutsch (1983), p. 205.

[74] According to Arndt Teichmann, a systematic distinction arises when a private individual feels "provoked" ("*herausgefordert*"), as opposed to situations where state officials are engaged in the performance of a public law function (Teichmann (1996), p. 1181).

[75] NJW 1964, 1363.

[76] The case's distinctiveness lies in the fact that the second causer does not intervene to prevent or mitigate the harm (Ristow (2003), p. 62).

[77] In pursuit cases, such as the instance of a young man jumping from a window, Schiemann contends that liability should not be attributed to the fugitive, since the decisive factor is the lawfulness of the defendant's conduct, not the idea of "professional risk" ("*Berufsrisiko*"). From this perspective, it would be inappropriate to hold the defendant civilly liable in situations of escape (Schiemann (2019), p. 104). On the contrary, it has been argued that while escaping is not, in itself, deemed unlawful, the specific risk created by the fugitive cannot be transferred to the pursuer (Jansen (2002), p. 523).

based on their free decision.[78] This conclusion remains valid even if the third party acts negligently. The *Bundesgerichtshof* (BGH), therefore, affirmed the liability of the original accident wrongdoer, while declining to consider the stepson's negligence, which did not form part of the appeal.

As in cases of rescue, it is possible, under Brazilian law, to establish the liability of the fleeing wrongdoer for the damages caused to the pursuer. Without the flight, the pursuit would not have occurred and, consequently, the injury (natural causation). The filter of adequacy is also generally present, since upon witnessing the commission of an unlawful act, it cannot be considered abnormal for the injured party or a third party to pursue the perpetrator.

The flight, after the commission of an unlawful act, represents the creation of an unpermitted risk, which may lead to damage. As in the cases of rescue, in certain circumstances, it is possible to consider the occurrence of a "general life risk", which may exclude the first perpetrator's liability. Consider the example of a pursuit, where the vehicle, traveling within the speed limit, falls into a hole in the road, causing it to collide with a post. In this case, the damage did not result from the materialization of the specific risk of flight; it is a danger to which all drivers are exposed.

Of particular importance in this case is the proportionality of the act carried out by the pursuer. It is necessary to assess, through the comparison of the risk spheres, in concrete terms, the causal contribution of each of the perpetrators to the production of the harmful event. In the case under analysis, the BGH correctly decided to reduce the compensation due by a quarter, as the individual pursuing the perpetrator, although to a lesser degree, contributed to the occurrence of the harmful event since, even without specific training for such an action, he undertook a high-speed pursuit, thus putting his physical integrity at risk. Therefore, Art. 945, which addresses concurrent causation, is applicable in this case.

The intervention of the pursuer or rescuer, as already stated, can also be obligatory, as in the case of police officers and firefighters.

In its judgment of February 3, 1967, the BGH[79] addressed the case[80] involving two police officers, while patrolling, noticed an unusual noise coming from

[78] The BGH examined the relationship between the risk and its objective, as well as the fugitive's knowledge (or the possibility of such knowledge) of the pursuit (Schäfer (Schäfer and Ott 1995), p. 217). According to one perspective, only actual knowledge of the pursuit would give rise to a duty to avoid compelling the pursuer to face increased risks. For the BGH, however, "the necessity to know" ("*Kennen-müssen*") suffices on the fugitive's part (Lange and Schiemann (2003), pp. 135–136).

[79] VersR 1967, 580.

[80] In another similar case, decided on July 03, 1990, the BGH (NJW 1990, 2885) reached a different conclusion despite comparable factual circumstances. In that matter, two police officers pursued a suspicious vehicle along a forest road. The vehicle, which had a defective rear light and emitted a loud noise, was travelling at high speed on a snow-covered road. The police car skidded and collided with a row of trees. Subsequent investigations revealed that the pursued driver had consumed alcohol and lacked a valid driver's license. The BGH dismissed the police officer's claim for compensation, relying on the "provocation formula" ("*Herausforderungsformel*"), which requires that the fugitive reprehensibly "provoked"

a vehicle that was traveling on the road. The vehicle was also being driven without proper lighting, leading to a police pursuit. Even after being ordered to stop, the driver fled at high speed.[81] During the chase, the patrol car collided, resulting in bodily injuries to the officers.[82] Upon detaining the driver, it was revealed that he did not possess a valid driving license.[83] The BGH decided that the driver was liable for three-quarters of the damages caused to the police officers, finding a direct causal link between the flight and the injuries sustained by the officers.[84] Due to the officers' lack of skill during the pursuit, the BGH[85] acknowledged their contributory negligence (*Mitverschulden*), applying § 254 of the BGB.[86]

Another group of cases helps to illustrate the situations of mandatory intervention by the second causer. In a case decided by the BGH[87] on January 13, 1976, the defendant, then 19 years old, was sentenced to serve three weekends in detention. After attending the establishment for the first two weekends, he did not appear for the last one. On the morning of September 27, 1970, two police officers, armed with an arrest warrant, appeared at his apartment. The defendant, who was not yet fully dressed, asked if he could use the bathroom, receiving permission to do so. One of the officers, upon entering the adjacent room, noticed that the young man had jumped out of the window.[88] In an attempt to detain him, the officer jumped from the neighboring window, four meters down, fracturing his right foot. The claim for damages was rejected by both the *Landgericht* and the *Oberlandgericht.*

("*herausgefordert*") the pursuer's risky reaction for tortious liability to be established (Schur (2001), p. 310) or a detailed analysis of the decision, see Lange (1990).

[81] Strauch (1992), p. 933.

[82] According to Martens, it is not improbable that disregarding traffic rules might result in a police chase, and that the ensuing traffic risks could lead to an accident causing bodily injury or property damage (Martens (1972), p. 741).

[83] Zhang (2016), p. 13.

[84] Deutsch and Ahrens (2014), p. 31.

[85] In the most recent case of a police pursuit, decided by the BGH (NJW 2012, 1951) on January 31, 2012, a driver evaded a traffic control checkpoint, injuring an officer. Shortly thereafter, four police vehicles joined the pursuit, ultimately forcing the fugitive's car to stop by pressing it from behind and the sides. As a result, all four police cars were damaged. The BGH upheld the claim for compensation, holding that the officers' deliberate actions were not disproportionate to the objective of apprehending the fugitive, as his continued flight posed a significant danger to other road users.

[86] Teichmann (1996), p. 1180. It is therefore possible, in principle, to attribute liability for damages to the pursuer in pursuit cases, at least partially (Beurskens (2017), pp. 153–154).

[87] NJW 1976, 568.

[88] A comparable case is discussed by Erwin Deutsch. In this instance, a police officer jumped from a height of approximately 1.50 meters while pursuing a suspect, injuring himself in the process. The state initiated legal proceedings to recover expenses and obtain reimbursement for payments made to the officer during his disability. Both the *Landgericht* and the *Oberlandesgericht* dismissed the claim. However, the BGH held the defendant liable, reasoning that the increased risk materialized as a direct consequence of the pursuit and that the incident was not unrelated to the increased danger (Deutsch (1975), p. 375). In the NJW 1996, 1533 decision, the BGH addressed a case involving escape through a window.

The BGH upheld the outcome of the lower courts but clarified that liability for the violation of legal interests may be dismissed if adequate causation is absent. It emphasized that, once adequate causation is confirmed, it should be examined whether the damaging result (bodily harm), caused by the defendant's behavior, can be objectively attributed to him.[89] Such an assessment should be addressed based on evaluative considerations. The basis of liability in these cases is that the fugitive created an increased risk of injury,[90] insofar as he has foreseen and avoided his pursuit and the danger associated with it. The fact that the police officer, through his own decision, assumed the risk of injury does not prevent the recognition of causal attribution.[91]

In the group of pursuit cases,[92] the BGH decided that it is not legally justified to hold the pursued fully liable for all injuries negligently caused to the legal interests of the pursuer. The limitation of liability, based on evaluative criteria as defended by Larenz,[93] is expressed in the fact that the BGH only recognizes objective attribution in the case of the pursuer having been "provoked" to act (provocation formula).[94]

In the context of Brazilian law, there has been insufficient discussion about the wrongdoer's liability in cases of mandatory intervention, especially in pursuit cases. In almost all instances, liability is sought from the state entity to which the injured or deceased police officer or firefighter belonged. This is primarily due to the difficulty in identifying the fugitive and the common occurrence of their lacking sufficient assets to cover potential damages. However, lawsuits filed against the state tend to have a prolonged duration due to the procedural privileges granted to it, such as extended deadlines[95] and the mandatory appellate review, in addition to the inherent challenges involved in enforcing judgments against public entities.

---

[89] Niebaum (1976), p. 1673.

[90] The contribution of the pursued individual to the harmful event lies in having initiated the pursuit. However, the individual does not directly cause the damage by obstructing the pursuer, resisting apprehension, or engaging in any other harmful conduct (Leitermeier (1968), p. 1).

[91] In earlier criminal doctrine, these cases were referred to as an "interruption" ("*Unterbrechung*") or "break" ("*Abbruch*") of the causal chain. The theory of the "*Regreßverbot*" led to the same result (Hübner (1974), p. 496). According to the "prohibition of regression" ("*Regreßverbot*") thesis, defended by Reinhard Frank but not widely accepted in the doctrine, the assessment of causation should exclude conditions eliminated through third-party intervention or chance (Baumann and Weber (1985), p. 222).

[92] In a similar case (NJW 1971, 1982) that occurred on September 17, 1966, the defendant, a 16-year-old girl, secretly left her parents' home and tried to solicit a ride along a road with two other minors. The girls were detained near the federal highway and taken into police custody. When the defendant left the vehicle, she fled, leading the police chief to pursue her. While crossing a wet, freshly cut lawn, he slipped, fell, and injured his left thigh, leaving him temporarily unable to work (Weber (1995), p. 507).

[93] Larenz (1976), pp. 10–11.

[94] Händel (1976), p. 1204.

[95] For a discussion on the foundations that differentiate procedural rules applicable to the state, see Cunha (2009), p. 31.

In a rare case where the state claimed compensation for material damages resulting from a police pursuit, the Court of Justice of the State of Rio Grande do Sul[96] held the pursued individual liable for the damages suffered by the state entity due to his escape. During the pursuit, the patrol car collided with the fugitive's vehicle. He contended that he was not at fault for the damaging event, asserting that upon realizing that the car pursuing him was a police vehicle, he immediately complied with the stop orders. However, while braking, he claimed to have been struck by the patrol car, arguing that the police vehicle had been driven recklessly.

The Court of Justice stated that, by disobeying the stop order and deciding to flee at high speed, the fugitive attracted to himself the liability for the damages caused as a result of the accident. It was also noted that, in such a situation, it could not be demanded that the police maintain a safe distance in relation to the pursued vehicle, as it would hinder operations and cause severe social repercussions. As an additional basis, it was argued that the patrol car's driving cannot be evaluated from the perspective of an amateur driver, nor should it be expected that, in such circumstances, the vehicle operate at normal traffic speed.

In cases of rescue and pursuit conducted by professionals, it is possible to identify the presence of natural causation and the adequacy of cause. Without the escape or the creation of risk, the pursuit or rescue would not be carried out and, consequently, neither would the injury. The adequacy filter is also present, as it cannot be considered abnormal for the professional to pursue the perpetrator or attempt to carry out the rescue upon identifying the commission of an offense. On the contrary, it is a duty imposed on the professional.

However, in these cases, where there is an obligation to intervene, it is necessary to consider, as a general risk to the rescuer's or pursuer's life, the professional risk to which they are subjected due to their occupational activities. The firefighter[97] who suffers burns as a result of a fire caused accidentally or intentionally by a third party cannot seek to hold that third party liable for the damages suffered. Similarly, the police officer who suffers injuries during a pursuit will not be compensated by

---

[96] TJRS, ApCív 70077580389, rel. Pedro Luiz Pozza, j. 18.09.2008.

[97] In a case decided on May 4, 1993 (BGH NJW 1993, 2234), a farmer caused a fire by burning waste during a windstorm. After the volunteer fire brigade extinguished the fire, a firefighter, while unrolling hoses after the work was completed, twisted his left foot, which had been previously injured. Although there was an adequate causal link between the defendant's conduct and the injury, and the farmer's negligent behavior was evident, given that he could foresee that causing a fire would expose individuals to the risk of injury, the attribution was denied. The firefighter's injury did not result from the increased risk of injury (*gesteigertes Verletzungsrisiko*) associated with the farmer's initial act. Instead, the volunteer firefighter twisted his ankle after the firefighting operation had concluded, meaning he was not, at that moment, in a high-risk or stressful situation related to the nature of the task. Emmerich, commenting on the decision, argues that the BGH distinguishes between damage arising from the increased risk caused by the initial conduct and the mere materialization of general life risks. Although the BGH does not explicitly use this terminology in its decision, the interpretation can be inferred. Any damage not arising from the increased risk should be considered part of the general risk of life (Emmerich (2018), p. 172).

the individual who initiated the escape. Liability will only be attributed if the damage sustained during professional exercise does not relate to the risks inherent in the activity, such as in the case where the individual who set the house on fire waits for the arrival of the firefighter and violently assaults them.

5.2.1.2 Cases of Intervention by the Position of Authority of the First Wrongdoer

This category is characterized by the fact that the first perpetrator holds a position of authority in relation to the second causer, influencing their conduct through their own actions.[98] Unlike the first group of cases analyzed, the action of the second causer is not motivated by a risk created by the initial wrongdoer but rather by reliance[99] on their authority, which manifests in conduct that leads to a specific injury.[100] While the second causer is, in principle, free to choose their course of action, it is reasonable for them to follow the guidance of someone in a position of authority, given that person's specialized knowledge on the matter.[101] It is not a matter of a direct order or threat directed at the second causer, as such scenarios would fall under "intentionally mediated causation" ("*absichtlich vermittelte Kausalität*"), which, as previously stated, is beyond the scope of this work.

A common example of this category, previously mentioned, is the case of an adult who, despite the pedestrian light being red, crosses the street, leading a child, who was waiting for the green light, to follow shortly after, resulting in the child being struck by a vehicle.[102] Another variation of this illustrative scenario involves a "reckless young man" ("*forscher junger Mann*"), who suddenly crosses on a red light, leading other pedestrians to act in the same way, resulting in a collision between two vehicles.[103] Although widely debated in legal doctrine, these cases have not yet been decided by the German courts.[104]

---

[98] The Court of Justice of the European Union (CJEU) determined that the false information provided to a civil servant, who anticipated receiving a full pension, caused his early retirement. Similarly, Finnish courts found a causal link between the dissemination of false financial information about a company and investments made by a third party. In a Spanish case, newspaper articles describing certain individuals as terrorists were deemed the cause of their executions a few days later (Winiger (2007), p. 255).

[99] Carneiro da Frada posits that the diminished emphasis on reliance in tort liability is entirely justified, given that such liability does not depend on any pre-existing relationship between the offender and the victim. Instead, it is primarily grounded in the unlawfulness of the infringement of legal interests and the presence of fault, rather than the frustration of subjective expectations. He also maintains that reliance-based liability transcends the traditional dichotomy between tort and contractual liability (Frada (2015), pp. 285–287).

[100] Ristow (2003), p. 76.

[101] Forst (2000), pp. 137–139.

[102] Medicus (2005), p. 291.

[103] Dunz (1966), p. 135.

[104] Ristow (2003), p. 84.

It has been stated that the mere bad example of the first perpetrator would not be enough to attribute liability to him for the actions of other pedestrians. This is because, although the example set by someone who disregards general duties of care may produce an "imitation effect" ("*Nachahmungseffekt*"), this sole circumstance would not seem sufficient to significantly affect the risk assessment made by other pedestrians.[105] It should be considered, however, that the behavior of the initial offender creates a dangerous situation, as experience shows, encouraging other pedestrians, who tend to be less attentive after seeing the first pedestrian cross the street, to adopt a "herd behavior" ("*Herdenreaktion*").[106] If the individual imitating the original offender is a minor, the situation becomes even more problematic, as the child or teenager may feel encouraged to follow the adult without hesitation.[107]

In instances where the second causer holds a position of authority over the victim (cases of intervention resulting from the first wrongdoer's position of authority), the attribution criteria outlined in Sect. 5.2.1.1 are not entirely applicable. In this group of cases, in addition to verifying natural causation, causal adequacy, and the materialization of a specific risk, the relationship between the parties involved must also be considered.

The individual in a superior position should seem to the victim as someone possessing special knowledge about the circumstances related to the decision-making process of the second causer. This perceived authority of the first perpetrator must appear credible to the injured party, even though the former should bear the risks due to the second subject's inability to understand. Contrary to what some German scholars[108] argue, the first wrongdoer does not have to actually possess differentiated knowledge about the matter but only has to present themselves as someone who does, as long as the victim reasonably perceives them in that manner under ordinary experience standards.[109]

---

[105] Ristow (2003), p. 85.

[106] Dunz (1966), p. 135. Also on the "herd behaviour" or "herd reaction" ("*Herdenreaktion*"), see Zimmermann (1980), p. 13.

[107] Niebaum, in analyzing the case decided by the BGH (NJW 1963, 101) on October 23, 1962, refers to a relationship of subordination (*Subordinationsverhältnis)* between the adult and the child. In that case, the defendant, a toy store attendant, had sold a sharp dart to a ten-year-old child. Although she had warned the child about its proper use, he subsequently threw the dart and struck the plaintiff, a playmate, in the left eye, which had to be surgically removed. The BGH focused primarily on the inadequacy of the warning given by the attendant to prevent the negligent act. According to Niebaum, however, this reasoning does not resolve the issue from the standpoint of imputation. The decisive factor lies in the relationship of subordination characterizing the defendant's position in relation to the child. Although no familial relationship existed between them, the seller was in a position to exert a significant influence over the child's careful behavior (Niebaum (1977), p. 95).

[108] Niebaum (2003), pp. 88–89.

[109] Whether the attribution of liability should depend on a comparison of the parties' respective levels of knowledge has been questioned. The central issue, according to Puppe, is whether the injured party is sufficiently aware of the risk to make a responsible decision regarding their own conduct, regardless of the other party's level of awareness (Puppe (2017), p. 517).

The relationship between the parties should be such that the actual influence of the first perpetrator projects onto the behavior of the second, diminishing or annihilating the voluntariness of their act. This trust relationship can be facilitated by the existence of a prior relationship, such as in family and work groups, or it can be established suddenly (transitory subordination relationships),[110] as in the case of a minor who follows an adult across the street against a red light. The superior position of the first wrongdoer must be intense enough to exert a sort of "control" over the second party; otherwise, it merely constitutes a bad example.[111]

The criterion of self-responsibility acquires, in this group of cases, special relevance. As a rule, liability attaches to individuals for their own conduct, and the allocation of damages to third parties is exceptional.[112] It is not possible to hold individuals liable for any advice or information provided,[113] or for risks that the injured party decided to assume, even if encouraged by another individual, as long as the autonomy of their will has been preserved.[114]

In the case of the traffic light, the adult who crosses the street, disregarding the general duties of care, and is followed by another adult is not liable for the damages caused to the latter. There is no relationship of superiority or ascendancy between the parties; the first adult does not possess special knowledge compared to the second, so no subordination relationship is established. As already asserted, a mere bad example is not sufficient to establish attribution. Regarding the minor who follows the adult, despite the presence of natural causation, as well as the adequacy of the cause—since it is not an extraordinary condition for a minor to follow an adult—the liability should fall on the parents, whose duty of protection was violated, thus absorbing the sphere of risk created. Even if the adult's liability were acknowledged, given the creation or increase of an impermissible risk, and due to the position of authority of the former, the causal contribution should be evaluated with regard to the concurrence of each of the wrongdoers in causing the damage (Art. 945, CC/02).[115]

[110] Niebaum (1977), p. 92.

[111] Schiemann (2017), p. 92.

[112] Self-responsibility is based on the principle that each person is responsible for their own actions and choices, exercising their autonomy in the free development of their personality. As a consequence, individuals must also bear the consequences of their conduct, and such responsibility cannot be attributed to third parties (Marinho (2013), p. 47).

[113] Discomforts that, although potentially detrimental to social harmony or even to the mental health of others, do not give rise to liability. Likewise, claims grounded in trivialities, occasional indolence, or in a self-victimizing refusal to exercise responsibility and diligence in safeguarding one's own interests are not afforded legal recognition (Martins-Costa (2014), p. 7089).

[114] On the concept of individual legal autonomy in Brazilian, see Borges (2007), p. 243.

[115] In such cases, the assessment should focus on whether the adult was aware of the presence of a minor waiting for the signal to change in order to cross the street. If not, liability is excluded due to the absence of fault. It would be unreasonable to expect an adult to investigate, each time they cross a pedestrian crossing, whether any legally incapacitated individuals are nearby.

In another case decided by the BGH,[116] a petrol station attendant incorrectly changed the oil of a customer's car, causing damage to the vehicle's engine shortly afterward. As the car was still under warranty, the buyer reported the issue to the seller, who, in turn, claimed that the damages resulted from inadequate maintenance. The vehicle owner presented this information to the attendant, who, however, denied having made any mistake whatsoever. Based on this, the claim was dismissed. It was proven during the proceedings that the negligent oil change was the cause of the damages. The car owner subsequently sued the attendant, seeking compensation for the losses resulting from the previous lawsuit.

In the case analyzed, the second individual trusts the information[117] provided by the first party, who possesses special knowledge about the situation. The first and true cause of the damages incurred by the vehicle owner, concerning the costs of the lawsuit, lies in the false information provided by the service provider, making the psychological component in the course of events linked to this fact.[118] Although the damage was based on the car owner's free decision to initiate a legal dispute, such a circumstance does not have the power to exonerate the liability of the party who provided incorrect information.

The authoritative position of the petrol station attendant can be used as an argument due to the "special knowledge" ("*Sonderwissen*") he possessed—-knowledge that the customer lacked regarding the negligent oil change. Based on life experiences, the customer could have trusted the information provided by the "specialist" ("*Fachmann*"), just as the service provider could have reasonably presumed that the car owner would base his future behavior on the information given to him.[119] If an excessive disproportion between the seriousness of the service provider's fault and the extent of the damage is demonstrated, a fair reduction of the compensation is applicable under the terms of Art. 944, sole paragraph, of the CC/02.

The liability of medical professionals for false or incomplete information provided can also be considered in this context.[120] Take the example of a health

---

[116] NJW 1971, 134.

[117] A distinction has been drawn between advice, recommendation, and information. Advice involves making another person aware of what is considered preferable or more advantageous in a given situation, and therefore necessarily contains a value judgment. A recommendation is regarded as a subtype of advice: It conveys favorable qualities of a person or object with the aim of influencing behavior. The difference between the two lies in degree, with advice implying a more emphatic exhortation than a recommendation. Information, in the strict sense, consists in presenting a given factual circumstance, whether relating to persons, things, or other relations. Pure information is limited to the communication of objective facts, without any form of behavioral suggestion (Monteiro (1989)), pp. 14–15).

[118] Ristow (2003), pp. 80–81.

[119] Ristow (2003), p. 83.

[120] A case decided by the BGH (NJW 1970, 511) involved a physician who prescribed an arsenic-based solution for the treatment of warts, which is a recognized method when administered over a short period. However, the prescription enabled the patient to obtain larger quantities from the pharmacy, leading to prolonged use and, ultimately, arsenic poisoning. The BGH held the

professional who, upon completing the diagnosis, recommends a certain drug, informing the patient that this medication is safe and effective in combating the disease. However, according to the most recent medical research, frequently disclosed by the media, the drug has not proven efficacy and poses health risks—circumstances not properly communicated to the patient. The latter, after consuming the drug for a certain period, has their health affected.

In times of a pandemic, this debate becomes of great importance. Even after the disclosure of various studies about the inefficiency of certain drugs, such as hydroxychloroquine, for treating COVID-19, many doctors continued to prescribe these drugs, often causing even more serious injuries to the physical integrity of the patients.[121] The second party (the patient), by trusting the information of the first wrongdoer (the doctor), is harmed by the act of following this guidance.

In the relationship between doctor and patient, it is easy to ascertain the existence of a party who holds special knowledge and assumes a position of superiority. In most cases, the bond of trust[122] is so strong that the patient bases their behavior almost "blindly" on the information provided by the professional. The injured party's decision is, in this sense, greatly influenced by the information provided. Should the doctor prescribe drugs that have been proven to have no efficacy in combating the disease, such as COVID-19, liability is imposed if any damage to health is produced, given the materialization of the risk resulting from the medical error. Due to the information deficit, the doctor transfers to themselves a sphere of risk, which, in theory, should be borne by the patient.[123] Exceptionally, the lack of information does not lead to liability if the risk not explained by the professional does not materialize, or if the explanations are irrelevant to the patient's decision-making.[124]

---

physician liable, emphasizing the inherent risks associated with the treatment. The case can also be understood on broader grounds, considering the physician's specialized knowledge in health-related matters and the structurally weaker position of the patient in that relationship (Ristow (2003), pp. 77–79).

[121] A case reported in the press concerned a 50-year-old man from Campinas who, following medical advice, took the so-called Covid kit, which included azithromycin, hydroxychloroquine, and ivermectin. He was later diagnosed with drug-induced hepatitis by a physician at the Hospital das Clínicas of Unicamp and was placed on the liver transplant waiting list (Teixeira (2021).

[122] The notion of trust constitutes an inherent condition of social life, grounded in the normative expectations that individuals reciprocally establish within a shared community. Although initially associated with traffic relations, it has progressively extended to encompass a wide range of social interactions. It is based on the premise that each person occupies a functional role within the collective order and that, accordingly, individuals may reasonably rely on one another to fulfill their respective responsibilities with due care (Mascarenhas Jr. (2008), pp. 118–119). It has been maintained that, as a general rule, there is no legal duty to meet the reliance unilaterally placed by another. From this perspective, liability grounded in reliance must be distinguished from that which arises from the violation of duties to act. As a consequence, duties to inform do not fall within the domain of reliance-based liability (Frada (2015), pp. 902–903).

[123] Barbosa (AMCNM 2021), p. 233.

[124] If, hypothetically, the physician had acted in an alternative and lawful manner (*rechtsmäßiges Alternativverhalten*), by properly informing the patient of the risks involved, the relevant question

The issue becomes more complex when it comes to analyzing the liability of the doctor and the digital influencer. Imagine the case of a professional who, even after the disclosure of various studies, posts on social media[125] urging his followers to undergo preventive treatment against COVID-19 using hydroxychloroquine and ivermectin. Subsequently, one of these followers, after using these drugs, develops severe hepatic damage.

It is important to distinguish between the simple opinion[126] expressed by the doctor on social media, which clearly indicates that the treatment has not yet been scientifically proven or that there are studies to the contrary, and posts that recommend, based on false information or without due warnings, the indicated procedure.[127] By neglecting medical rules regarding advertising[128] and the duties of care inherent to the profession, the specialist creates or increases the risk of a health injury to the follower. However, it is difficult to affirm the existence of a special relationship in which the doctor has the follower's behavior under "control," not preventing them from making a free and autonomous decision, unless the social media user is already a patient of the influencer or the professional is acting on behalf of the state.

The criterion of self-responsibility[129] once again plays a decisive role in the assessment of imputation. In most cases, the follower can and should inform themselves, in the best possible way, about the risks of the treatment by scheduling a medical consultation and seeking information through reliable media sources. If it is proven that the medical information shared on social media influenced the follower's behavior, restricting their freedom to decide, the risk spheres of the parties should be compared in order to determine to what extent each one's

would be whether the patient would still have consented to the treatment (Gödicke 2008, p. 103). The burden of proof for this counterfactual scenario rests with the physician (Katzenmeier 2002, p. 369).

[125] Regarding medical advertising on social media, defined by the Federal Council of Medicine (CFM) as including websites, blogs, Facebook, Twitter, Instagram, YouTube, WhatsApp, and similar platforms, Resolution No. 2.126/2015 introduced certain regulatory changes. Nonetheless, the prevailing view in the literature is that, despite the adjustments brought by this resolution, the new digital environment remains only partially regulated (Mildemberger and Pereira (Mildemberger and Lemos Pereira 2020), p. 416).

[126] It has been noted that, when not linked to a consumer relationship, statements made by influencers are to be regarded as exercises of freedom of expression (Ody and D'Aquino (2021), p. 15).

[127] A distinction must be drawn between those who simply express a personal opinion and those who are, from the outset, aware that their statements are likely to influence a significant number of people. According to part of the doctrine, the decisive criterion does not lie in an objective classification separating information, advice and recommendation, but rather in the identification of distinct spheres of risk (Barbosa (AMCNM 2020), p. 1005).

[128] Resolution No. 1.974/2011 of the Federal Council of Medicine (CFM) provides in Art. 3, Section f, that it is forbidden for physicians to advertise any method or technique not accepted by the scientific community.

[129] Emphasizing the importance of the key concept of self-responsibility, based on the free and conscious conduct of the individual, see Proença (1997), p. 831.

behavior contributed to the damage (Art. 945 of the CC/02).[130] However, the doctor's liability should not serve as a form of censorship or punishment for the incorrectness of the posted content.

The influence of public authorities on the behavior of individuals belonging to a certain community is also a topic of discussion. Speeches, interviews, attitudes, or advertising campaigns can motivate the behavior of social group members, resulting in the occurrence of damages. The extent to which injuries caused to the population, who act of their own decision but are influenced by the behavior of the authority, can be attributed to the latter is a matter of debate.

In Italy, on April 6, 2009, at 03:32, the city of L'Aquila was shaken by an earthquake of magnitude 6.7 on the Richter scale, resulting in the death of 309 people, a further 1600 injured, and over 100,000 homeless, who were forced to evacuate the historic center. The main shock occurred in the context of a series of seismic tremors that had been ongoing for several months[131] (since June 2008) and which, before April 6, had recorded an earthquake of magnitude 4.1 on March 30, 2009. Following this catastrophic event, the *Procura della Repubblica di L'Aquila* launched various investigations aiming to determine the causes and identify those potentially responsible. The investigation focused on the meeting held on March 31, 2009, intended to provide the citizens of Abruzzo with all the information available about the seismic activities of the previous weeks.[132]

On this date, a few days before the seismic event, the members of the *Commissione Nazionale per la Prevenzione dei Grandi Rischi* met to assess the risks of a new shock. After the meeting, the local media began to broadcast the statements of its members, recorded during and after the meeting. Enzo Boschi, one of the six experts consulted, when asked if the current seismic swarm could be the precursor of a larger earthquake, like the one that occurred in 1703,[133] replied that it was unlikely that a similar shock would occur in a short period, but that he could not rule out this possibility. Meanwhile, interviewed by the local television network before the start of the meeting, Bernardo de Bernardinis announced that the situation remained favorable,[134] reassuring the population.

In the following days, many individuals who had been living and sleeping on the streets due to the tremors decided to return to their homes, where they became victims of the earthquake that occurred just six days after the meeting and the media campaign. The Public Prosecutor's Office of L'Aquila criminally charged Bernardo de Bernardinis and the six experts who participated in the meeting,

[130] It has been reaffirmed that the mere existence of an intervening act between the influencer's conduct and the resulting harm does not exclude liability. What must be considered, under this view, is the significance of each party's contribution to the harmful event and the proper delimitation of their respective spheres of risk (Barbosa (AMCNM 2020), p. 1005).

[131] Cocco et al. (2015), p. 46.

[132] Billi (2017), p. 11.

[133] The 1703 earthquake in the Abruzzo region resulted in approximately six thousand deaths and over four thousand people injured or seriously injured (Gatti (1976), pp. 914–915).

[134] O'Mathúna and Beriain (2019), p. 216.

arguing that some of the victims changed their minds as a result of the ambiguous public statements. In 2012, the local court convicted the defendants, as participants in an alleged negligent communication campaign, to six years in prison for manslaughter.[135] In particular, the seven defendants were found guilty of negligence for providing inaccurate, incomplete, and contradictory information to citizens.[136]

In 2014, the Court of Appeal of L'Aquila acquitted the six scientists, emphasizing that, based on the scientific knowledge available in 2009, earthquakes were unforeseeable. However, regarding the conduct of Bernardo de Bernardinis, the court argued that his public statement was scientifically incorrect and seriously negligent, considering its possible and foreseeable effects on the behavior of citizens.[137] It was assumed that his conduct indeed affected the behavior of some of the victims.[138] Finally, in 2015, the Italian Court of Cassation[139] confirmed the decision of the Court of Appeal.

The speeches and behavior of public authorities can also be scrutinized in relation to the current pandemic. Despite certain health precautions being recommended by health organizations and specialized scientific bodies, such as wearing masks and avoiding gatherings, several prominent public officials, including executive leaders, acted in a completely contrary manner. They promoted and encouraged large gatherings and adopted risky health-related practices by attending public and private events without proper protective equipment. Additionally, they downplayed the importance of these measures in official statements or media interviews and even recommended the preventive use of drugs without any proven efficacy.

The spread of false information or fake news[140] by certain authorities also has the potential to cause serious harm to the population.[141] A different situation may

[135] *Judgement n.* 380/12, issued in the context of criminal proceedings n. 448/II R.G.Dib.

[136] O'Mathúna and Beriain (2019), pp. 216–217.

[137] In analyzing the L'Aquila case, it has been argued that the dissemination of information lacking scientific support may, and indeed should, give rise to personal liability on the part of the individual responsible for such conduct (Divino et al. (2022), p. 314).

[138] In its judgment, the Court of Cassation addressed the issue of "psychological causation," noting that it arises under conditions that differ significantly from traditional forms of causation involving physical or naturalistic phenomena. In such cases, the court held that causation must be established on the basis of consolidated and verifiable maxims of experience, which are capable of identifying the relevant conditioning behaviors (*Judgement n.* 3317/14, issued in the context of criminal proceedings n. 2583/13 R. G. App, on the date of 10 November 2014). For a detailed discussion on the application of the maxims of experience in this case, see Palavera (2017), pp. 180–184.

[139] *Judgement* n. 12478/16, of 19.11.15.

[140] Since 2017, when then-President Donald Trump accused CNN of disseminating fake news, the expression has become a cultural phenomenon in the United States. In his first year in office, Trump used the term more than 400 times. Its widespread use led political scientists and analysts to examine the impact of fake news on American democracy (Higdon (2020), p. 1).

[141] Several American news outlets reported a sharp increase in accidental poisonings in the United States during April 2020, attributed to the misuse of disinfectants and bleach. The spike followed

also occur in which a public authority accuses a news platform, whether official or independent, of spreading fake news when the information is accurate, thereby negatively influencing public behavior. This can happen when a leader or another government official publicly dismisses certain medical or scientific research or even denies its existence, as well as falsely asserting the existence of a contradictory study.

The January 6, 2021, Capitol attack has been widely discussed as a critical moment in U.S. political history. Supporters of then-President Donald Trump stormed the U.S. Capitol while congress was in the process of certifying Joe Biden's victory in the 2020 presidential election. This event followed months of unsubstantiated claims by Trump regarding widespread electoral fraud, claims that were never proven. The violent mob injured over 140 officers from both the Capitol and Metropolitan Police forces. Tragically, three individuals died in the days after the attack, and four additional security officers who had defended the Capitol later died by suicide in the following months.[142]

A similar event occurred in Brazil on January 8, 2023, when extremists stormed the plenary of the STF, the National Congress, and the Planalto Palace, rejecting Jair Bolsonaro's defeat in the 2022 presidential election. The financial damage, just in terms of damaged artworks, was estimated at R$ 8 million. High-value cultural items, such as the piece "As Mulatas" by the artist Di Cavalcanti and the clock by Balthazar Martinot, Louis XIV's watchmaker, were vandalized.[143] Similar to former President Donald Trump, Bolsonaro and his allies frequently questioned the integrity and credibility of the Brazilian electoral process, suggesting a conspiracy by the judiciary, particularly the TSE, to ensure his opponent's victory.

Consequently, the question has arisen as to whether these public agents could be held liable for these behaviors, which influence the conduct of many others, causing damage to third parties and even to public funds.

It is important to note that the attempt to always hold a third party responsible for one's own actions subverts the logic that, as a rule, every individual should bear the damages resulting from their decisions.[144] However, the false premise has emerged that every harm must be compensated and that there is always

President Trump's widely criticized statement on 23 April of that year, suggesting that scientists investigate whether injecting such substances into the human body could serve as a treatment for COVID-19. The National Poison Data System, part of the American Association of Poison Control Centers (AAPCC), which compiles data from poison control centers nationwide, recorded a 122% increase in reports related to disinfectants and a 77% increase related to bleach. The precise impact of Trump's statement on this surge in cases remains unclear (Perez (2020).

[142] Tortella (2022).

[143] Sousa (2023).

[144] According to the rule of *casum sentit dominus*, it is the owner of the affected property, or, in cases involving physical or moral harm, the victim themselves who must bear the resulting loss, unless a specific criterion justifies its attribution to another party (Pereira (2001), p. 300). Within the law of obligations, this rule also holds particular significance. As a general principle, patrimonial losses are assumed by the injured party, and no alternative solution is justified in the absence of a legally recognized basis (Pires (2020), p. 762).

a "responsible party"[145] to whom life's misfortunes should be attributed.[146] As Judith Martins-Costa[147] aptly puts it, this represents a true "victimization that denies self-responsibility," which, in conjunction with other factors, has led liability to an unlimited expansion movement.[148] While the importance of protecting victims' rights is acknowledged, a superficial understanding of the principles of tort law may lead to its distortion, threatening its integrity as an independent legal framework.

This reasoning applies to public authorities in relation to conduct and speeches made during pandemic times, as well as to the spread of fake news. It is not overlooked that the governing authority, as a representative[149] and personification of the state, exerts a greater influence over individuals, but such a circumstance does not necessarily result in indiscriminate liability for state entities or their agents. The aspects and particularities of the specific case[150] must be carefully analyzed in order to investigate whether the requirements of liability are effectively present. Even if the acts contradict the recommendations of the scientific community, individual liability will not always be the satisfactory response to these cases. The typical instruments of criminal law and administrative sanctions, in addition to the use of class actions,[151] may prove more appropriate to reprimand these unlawful conducts.

---

[145] The focus has moved away from identifying a person at fault and toward establishing liability based on risk as an imputational criterion (Godoy (2010), p. 32).

[146] David (2018), p. 97. It has been noted that, at times, Brazilian doctrine and jurisprudence seem to treat liability as a universal solution for any kind of frustration (Carnaúba (2018), p. 224).

[147] The unrestricted recognition of liability for trivial matters ultimately prejudices the community itself, which has to bear the resulting costs (Martins-Costa (2014), pp. 7089–7090).

[148] Attention has been drawn to the growing emphasis in Brazilian law on the so-called flexibilization of the elements and prerequisites of tort law, such as causation and fault, as well as the recognition of so-called new damages. According to this view, such developments revive and expand a discourse present in Brazilian and French legal doctrine between the 1930s and 1950s, which acknowledged the impact of industrial transformations on production relations and the allocation of risk within frameworks governed by tort liability (Rodrigues Jr. (Rodrigues 2016), p. 132).

[149] Miranda (1983), p. 413.

[150] Given the uncertainty that characterizes pandemic contexts, described by the authors as the "instability of instability," it has been observed that, within the law of obligations, the possible configurations of cases are virtually unlimited (Martins-Costa and Costa E Silva (2020), p. 29–34). In matters of tort liability as well, the pandemic has given rise to a myriad of situations and legal questions, each of which must be assessed taking into account the specific circumstances.

[151] Judicial decisions that increase compensation awarded for "collective non-pecuniary damage," without expressly acknowledging the punitive or deterrent character of such awards, raise concern from a doctrinal standpoint. In discussing the notion of "social damage," Antonio Junqueira de Azevedo warns that such decisions are doctrinally unsound when courts surreptitiously increase compensation awards without expressly acknowledging that such increases serve a punitive or deterrent function (Azevedo (2009), p. 378). It has been argued that "collective non-pecuniary" damage can only be legitimately construed as a civil penalty if supported by legislative reform, establishing minimum objective and subjective criteria for its application as a punitive sanction

Thus, the fact that a government authority does not wear a protective mask during public events will seldom serve as a basis for holding the authority liable for material and non-pecuniary damages in an individual lawsuit, should someone claim, after not using the mandatory accessory and contracting the virus, to have been influenced by the conduct of the public official. As already stated, the mere bad example (*schlechtes Beispiel*) is not sufficient to establish liability. Similarly, speeches with clearly political or ideological tones do not, as a rule, meet the criteria for objective imputation, as they do not diminish the injured party's freedom of decision, thereby applying the criterion of self-responsibility.

However, the situation differs when the state authority, or a technical member of their team, transmits official information about the disease, indicating treatments or arguing against the necessity of important sanitary precautions, or when false information is disseminated. In this case, the state authority acts in a condition of superiority, as it is credible that they have "special knowledge" on the subject, thus interfering with the free and autonomous will of the injured party. Similarly, information provided by a political representative regarding the electoral process, when asserting the existence of fraud or manipulation of results, may be considered plausible, as it is being disclosed by individuals in public office who are duty-bound to ensure the proper functioning of elections. The manner in which the information is transmitted, whether through public announcements or official communication channels, gives the news a sense of authority and reliability.

The challenge here, as in the cases that preceded it, lies in proving natural causation. It is inherently difficult to provide conclusive evidence that the information provided was a *conditio sine qua non* of the harmful event. Proving that an individual acted in a certain way because of a particular speech, or that someone stopped wearing a mask after witnessing a public authority engaging in the same conduct, is not a simple task. However, when evaluating the evidence in the case, it will be up to the judge to assess the plausibility of the allegations based on the rules of experience, remaining attentive to the specificities and particularities of the characterization of "psychological causation" at this initial stage.[152]

Cases of riots, fights, or acts of vandalism, where it is not possible to identify the actual person responsible for the damage, although the individual who initiated the events that led to the harm can be determined, can also be analyzed from the perspective of "psychologically mediated causation." Doctrine and jurisprudence remain divided on this matter. Those who defend the joint liability of the group members, by invoking alternative causation, base their arguments on principles

(Rosenvald (2018), p. 122). For an analysis of the punitive function attributed to "collective non-pecuniary damage," see Teixeira Neto (2014), pp. 206–216.

[152] On the relationship between natural causation and damages caused by psychological influence, see Sect. 4.3.

such as solidarity, full reparation, and human dignity,[153] or through analogous reasoning, particularly referencing Art. 938 of the Civil Code of 2002.[154]

The Court of Justice of São Paulo[155] decided that, during the 2013 protests against the increase in public transport fares, one of the participants, who was caught attacking the City Hall, should be held liable for all the damages caused to the building, even though it was acknowledged that a group of people vandalized public property. The court stated that liability is not confined to part of the damages but encompasses their full extent, in accordance with Art. 942 of the Civil Code.

It could be inquired, in this sense, whether the individual who starts a riot[156] or a fight can be held liable for damages suffered by third parties, even if it is unknown who actually caused a specific injury.[157] Consider, for example, an individual who initiates a series of provocations between rival fans, or even physically or verbally assaults members of an organized fan group,[158] resulting in widespread confusion and causing damage to third parties. Upon performing the first act, the leader of this group is followed by their supporters, leading to the commission of various other criminal acts and causing damage that was not initially planned by the group's leadership.

The criteria developed in this work also prove effective in these cases, solving part of the so-called alternative causation cases, which are not expressly provided

[153] Mulholland (2009), p. 220.

[154] Art. 938 of the Brazilian Civil Code does not apply to situations involving the liability of group members. The provision originates from the Roman *actio de effusis et dejectis*, which addressed harm caused by objects thrown or spilled from buildings. In contrast, the *damnum in turba datum* (D. 47, 8) concerns damage caused by crowds (Moraes (2017), p. 163).

[155] TJSP, ApCív 1015707–41.2014.8.26.0053, rel. Heloísa Martins Mimessi, j. 14.05.2018.

[156] In situations involving incitement, understood as intentionally mediated causation, the controversy appears to be less pronounced. As previously noted, the conduct of the initial actor may represent a strong psychological influence and, as such, be sufficient to establish causation (Zhang (2016), p. 36).

[157] In the *Messerstecherei* case (BGHZ 103, 197), the victim was fatally stabbed during a fight involving several individuals. The deceased's son brought a compensation claim against one of the participants, alleging the loss of maintenance support. The defendant had already been convicted for participation in the criminal offence of brawl (*Schlägerei)* in connection with the incident. He argued, however, that he had not delivered the fatal stab, claiming that his involvement had been limited to punches and kicks. The BGH held that Section 227 of the StGB constitutes a protective norm within the meaning of Section 823 II of the BGB, as it is designed to safeguard specific individuals against the infringement of a legally protected interest. The court nevertheless allowed the defendant to prove that his participation in the brawl did not contribute, either directly or indirectly, physically or psychologically, to the victim's death.

[158] The Fan Statute (Law No. 10.671/2003) establishes, in Art. 19, that the entities responsible for organizing the competition, together with their officials, are jointly and strictly liable with the home club and its managers for damages caused to spectators as a result of security failures in stadiums. Additionally, Art. 39-B of the same statute provides for the strict and joint civil liability of organized supporter groups for damages caused by any of their members or affiliates at the venue, in its vicinity, or along the routes to and from the event.

for in the CC/02.[159] Those who hold a prominent position or leadership in movements, associations, or organized fan groups, and who, in some way, promote the gathering of people, must take the precautions expected by the general duties of care,[160] as they create a situation of risk, which can result in damages.

It is also important to assess whether the actions of the leader actually created the specific risk situation, which subsequently materialized.[161] It cannot be said that a small gathering of people protesting for peace creates a real danger of acts of vandalism or violence occurring. The occurrence of acts of this nature cannot be attributed to the liability sphere of the organizer, as it constitutes "a general risk of life".[162]

The same reasoning applies to cases where a group member is identified as having initiated acts of vandalism or, for example, a fight between fan groups. This is not simply a case of a bad example being followed by others, but rather the creation of a high-risk situation where the initial perpetrator, in factual terms, assumes a position of leadership or command and should be held responsible for all resulting damages, even though he may later file a regressive action against the actual perpetrators of the harm. In this context, a comparison should be made between the risk created by the initial wrongdoer and the risk sphere of the injured party. In many cases, an initial provocation or assault triggers a disproportionate response from the other party.[163]

The same solution does not seem to be applicable to the aforementioned case, decided by the Court of Justice of the State of São Paulo,[164] in which an individual was caught vandalizing the City Hall building during a series of protests that took

[159] Despite the absence of an express legal provision, Brazilian courts have applied the theory by relying on constitutional principles and analogical reasoning: "In such cases, where it is not possible to precisely determine causation among the potential wrongdoers, the application of the theory of alternative causation has been deemed appropriate, considering the value of human dignity and the principles of full consumer reparation, solidarity, and good faith. Although not expressly regulated, this theory finds support in Arts. 938 and 942, sole paragraph, of the Civil Code, and has been adopted in analogous decisions [. . .]" (TJRJ, ApCív 0327063–65.2013.8.19.0001, rel. Marcos Alcino de Azevedo Torres, j. 12.06.2019).

[160] The Superior Court of Justice (STJ) has recognized that, in cases involving fights among fans, the hosting entity is subject to a general duty to ensure the safety of spectators both inside and around the stadium, before, during, and after the match (STJ, REsp 1924527/PR, rel. Nancy Andrighi, j. 15.06.2021).

[161] According to Juarez Tavares, there is no imputation when the individual, even if failing to reduce the risk to the protected legal interest, has not increased it either. This applies to situations in which a general risk of daily life has materialized (Tavares (2019), p. 300).

[162] It has been argued that the mere causation of disapproved conduct is not sufficient for imputation, since an unlawful act may have causal effects on a result either in a foreseeable manner or, alternatively, through mere variation in the general risks of life (Jakobs (2014), p. 94).

[163] In German law, it has been asserted that the distribution of damages (*Schadensverteilung*) should be carried out by weighing the risk areas (Hübner (1972), p. 70).

[164] The decision was upheld based on the theory of alternative causation. According to the court, joint liability among members of a group is applicable when it can be established that the damage was caused by one of them, even if it is not possible to determine, with the required degree of certainty, which individual was in fact responsible (TJSP, ApCív 1015707–41.2014.8.26.0053, rel. Heloísa Martins Mimessi, j. 14.05.2018).

place in 2013 against the increase in public transport fares. The São Paulo Court held the defendant liable for all the damages caused to the building, applying the theory of alternative causation to the case. Even while acknowledging the participation of another individual, it was incorrectly stated that the case should be resolved based on Art. 942 of the Civil Code. The fact is that this is not a case of joint responsibility, as it cannot be assumed that all participants were responsible for the full extent of the vandalism to the public property, but rather a case of uncertain authorship, as the other participants were unidentified.

Similarly, it is not possible to apply the risk theory to attribute liability for all the damage to the defendant. Without demonstrating that he initiated the acts of vandalism or occupied a position of command or leadership over the others, it is not possible to assert that mere participation in the movement to vandalize the building led to or increased the risk that the entire building would be affected by violent acts. In a context where hundreds of people were destroying public property in an intense wave of protests, it would be not legally grounded to assert that the isolated act[165] of the perpetrator led to an escalated dangerous situation, which caused all the damages. Thus, he should only be held liable for the damages directly attributed to him.

Lastly, the liability of "*digital influencers*" has raised concerns, as they employ their persuasive capacity to shape trends and encourage the purchase of products and services,[166] resulting in substantial financial gains. The activity carried out by influencers, however, can cause damage when the product or behavior they promote proves dangerous to those who follow them on social networks.[167] Despite discussions usually revolving around the issue of the influencer's liability in cases

---

[165] The existence of a subjective link among the individuals who caused the damage was addressed in the decision, in which the Court of Justice of the State of São Paulo held that the absence of any prior connection among those involved, the lack of evidence of a jointly devised plan, or even the fact that others were identified and held responsible by the municipality, does not preclude the recognition of the defendant's liability for the harm resulting from the group's conduct (TJSP, ApCív 1015707–41.2014.8.26.0053, rel. Heloísa Martins Mimessi, j. 14.05.2018).

[166] Several celebrities and digital influencers have reportedly been involved in the cryptocurrency market, either promoting brands or endorsing investment products. Recently, actress and influencer Kim Kardashian was fined a substantial amount by the U.S. Securities and Exchange Commission (SEC) for promoting an obscure cryptocurrency without disclosing that she had received financial compensation for her endorsement. In Brazil, data from the Brazilian Association of Financial and Capital Market Entities (Anbima) revealed that, in the first half of 2022, influencers mentioned cryptocurrencies more frequently than stocks—12,349 mentions compared to 11,591 in the monitored profiles (Marins (2023).

[167] Recently, it was reported that Portuguese authorities have started investigating a group of at least 22 Brazilian influencers suspected of committing fraud and promoting illegal immigration to Portugal. According to investigators, it was particularly striking that the influencers openly flaunted their wealth online, posting images of new homes and travels, giving the impression that social mobility in Portugal is easily attainable (Amato (2022).

of product advertising, it is also possible to consider a situation where the influencer promotes a risky activity, causing harm to third parties.[168]

In a recent decision, the Court of Justice of the State of São Paulo[169] held a digital influencer liable for having published several posts on her social networks, in which she reported being poorly served by employees of a commercial establishment, especially by the plaintiff, whose image and name were expressly disclosed without authorization. The defendant urged her over 90,000 followers on Instagram to visit the company's profile and express their dissatisfaction with the incident. The influencer's request, however, led to the virtual lynching of the plaintiff, who was described as a "terrible employee, terrible human being." The employee received numerous derogatory comments on her social media, with many demanding her dismissal from her position.[170]

Regarding digital influencers in general, there is a prevailing trend in legal doctrine supporting strict liability,[171] particularly when they promote products that subsequently prove defective for consumption. Even in instances where the matter does not directly concern the supply of goods or services, Art. 29 of the Consumer Protection Code (CDC)[172] is often invoked to impose liability on the influencer. Despite this approach, which cannot be endorsed,[173] it remains important to recognize that the criteria for objective imputation can prove useful in resolving these conflicts.

---

[168] A scenario is presented in which an influencer promotes, even without being commissioned by anyone, a risky practice that subsequently leads to harm. When a third party's absolute right (such as life, physical integrity, or property) is violated, it raises the question of how much of the damage can be attributed to the influencer, given that the immediate cause of the injury is the victim's own behavior. It is argued that adhering to a traditional approach to causation would fail to adequately resolve this issue (Barbosa (AMCNM 2020), pp. 1003–1004).

[169] TJSP, ApCív 1100867–48.2018.8.26.0100, rel. César Peixoto, j. 30.11.2021.

[170] The Court of Justice of São Paulo (TJSP) decided that the public exposure of the plaintiff's image and name by the defendant clearly exceeded the limits of reasonableness and common sense, regardless of whether the service at the commercial establishment was indeed unsatisfactory. Without addressing the causal link between the conduct and the damage, the court found a clear violation of the plaintiff's personality rights, particularly their honor, privacy, and image, and reasoned that the non-pecuniary harm suffered was both "presumed and intuitive" given the factual circumstances. Consequently, the court increased the compensation for moral damages from five thousand reais to 25 thousand reais.

[171] Brito et al. (2019), p. 16; Sampaio and Miranda (2021), p. 281. Efing et al. (2019), p. 83.

[172] "Art. 29 of the CDC. For the purposes of this Chapter and the next, all determinable or indeterminable persons exposed to the practices provided for herein are considered consumers."

[173] Under this reasoning, all actors, celebrities, and media outlets involved in any form of advertising activity may be considered participants. However, the STJ has rightly decided that the responsibility for the quality of a product or service lies with its supplier, as defined in Art. 3 of Law no. 8.078/1990, and does not extend to a broadcaster that airs the advertisement through a presenter during a television program. This type of promotion, often referred to as "stage advertising," was addressed in REsp 1,157,228/RS(STJ, REsp 1,157,228/RS, rel. Aldir Passarinho Junior, j. 27.04.2011). Regarding Portuguese law, Mafalda Miranda Barbosa argues that such a solution fails to address the attribution of liability to digital influencers (Barbosa (AMCNM 2020), p 1004).

A primary criterion for avoiding the liability of digital influencers lies in imposing the duty to inform followers that the message contains advertising content.[174] When influencers comply with this duty of care—by labeling their posts or providing clear and explicit disclosures that unmistakably indicate advertising content—they should, as a rule, be exempt from liability, except where they also act as suppliers of the product or service, in which case the CDC applies. The attempt to subsume all influencer conduct under consumer law ought not to prevail. In such cases, circumventing private law rules through subterfuges like the improper and uncritical application of theories such as the "dialogue of sources" ("*Dialog der Quellen*")[175] is unacceptable, even when the primary aim is victim protection.

Many behaviors presented on social networks do not contain the necessary elements for liability. As a rule, the influencer's initial conduct does not have the effect of nullifying or diminishing the injured party's freedom of action,[176] unless the messages are directed at a specific vulnerable audience, such as minors.[177] It cannot be claimed that, generally, a special relationship is established between the individuals, where one, due to their specialized knowledge, exerts any form of "control" over the behavior of the other. On the contrary, in a hyperconnected society,[178] people are exposed to various external influences, particularly virtual ones, making many of the risks they face "general risks" of modern life.

5.2.1.3 Cases of Intervention Due to the Duty to Control a Source of Danger

In this other group of cases, the initial wrongdoer exercises control over a dangerous source and fail to take adequate protective measures, thereby violating a duty of care.[179] The second causer suffers harm through their own actions, which are connected to this source of danger. In these scenarios, the basis for attributing liability to the first wrongdoer theoretically lies in the fact that they created a situation of risk for the second causer. The injured party is generally less capable

---

[174] On the need to indicate the advertising nature of the post, in German law, cf. Fritz (2021).

[175] The "theory of dialogue of sources" was developed by Erik Jayme in the context of private international law (Jayme (1996), p. 259), under assumptions that differ from the way it is employed in Brazilian law (Carnaúba (2018), p. 228. Cláudia Lima Marques defends its application in Brazilian law to resolve hard cases (Benjamin and Marques (2018), p. 29). For a critique of the method, see Souza (2019), p. 231.

[176] Zimmermann highlights the importance of the criterion of self-responsibility as a counterbalance to every individual's freedom of conduct (Zimmermann (1980), p. 13).

[177] The injured party's intervening conduct does not exclude the influencer's liability for the harm caused. This view is shared by Ristow, in Germany (Ristow (2003), p. 165), and by Mafalda Miranda, in Portugal (Barbosa (AMCNM 2020), p. 1005).

[178] Magrani (2019), pp. 20–21.

[179] The evolution of general duties of care has been recognized as a response to dangerous situations. Their adoption in Portuguese legal doctrine and case law has been commended, although differences with the German tort system have also been noted (Cordeiro (2017), pp. 834–835).

of assessing the danger of their conduct than the first tortfeasor, who bears the obligation to safeguard against the risks posed.[180]

Unlike cases of intervention by the authority of the first wrongdoer, the initial perpetrator not only provides a "purely psychological contribution" ("*rein psychischer Beitrag*") to the realization of the harmful event, as in the case of the doctor who advises the patient to undergo a certain treatment, but also a "physical component" ("*physische Komponente*"), by making the dangerous substance available to the second causer.[181]

In the first case,[182] which occurred on October 11, 1982, two minors (the defendant was 14 years old and the plaintiff 15 years old), students of the eighth grade of a secondary school attempted to build a rocket for their gliders. According to the previously agreed plan, the defendant prepared a mixture of sulfur and potassium permanganate, filling a sealed tube. While he went to wash his hands, the plaintiff clamped the tube in a vice and hammered a thinner pipe from the top to make the ignition. After the third strike, there was an explosion. A 6-cm-long metal shard penetrated the victim's left eye.[183]

The plaintiff claimed that the defendant acted negligently in making the mixture, as if equal quantities of sulfur and potassium permanganate had been added, the accident would not have occurred. He also argued that he was entitled to rely on the defendant not prepare an explosive substance and, admitting his contributory negligence (§ 254 of the BGB), claimed non-pecuniary damages. The *Landgericht* rejected the plaintiff's claim, but the *Oberlandesgericht*, however, overturned the decision, holding the defendant liable for half of the damages.

The *Berufungsgericht* considered that, in the acquisition and mixing of chemical products, as well as in the joint decision to manufacture the propellant, the defendant made a significant causal contribution to the occurrence of the bodily injury suffered by the plaintiff, even though it was the latter, and not the former, who struck the hammer blow that caused the explosion. The liability of the defendant would be reasonable, since the fitting of the two tubes corresponded to the plan drawn up by both. The defendant would have also acted negligently (slight negligence), as 14-year-olds can recognize the dangers involved in handling chemical products (§ 828 of the BGB[184]).

---

[180] Ristow (2003), p. 126.

[181] Ristow (2003), p. 126–127.

[182] Zhang (2016), pp. 66–67. The case has been described as "a counterpart to provocation cases" ("*Gewissermaßen ein Gegenstück zu den Herausforderungsfällen*") (Medicus (2004), p. 454). Although it might be argued that the injured party felt partially provoked by the other's participation in the joint plan, no justifiable reason can be found for this reaction. Instead, it should be regarded as a poor example provided by the initial participant (Schiemann (2017), p. 92).

[183] Schellhammer (2014), p. 20.

[184] Under § 828 of the BGB, liability arises if the minor has the discernment necessary to understand responsibility. In other words, when the child is capable, according to their individual development, of recognizing the danger of their actions. Minors under the age of seven cannot be

The BGH,[185] on the contrary, held that the injury suffered by the plaintiff could not be attributed to the defendant. It was affirmed that there is no doubt the defendant would be liable for the consequences of an explosion if, and to the extent that, third parties were harmed. It is discussed, however, whether the defendant must bear part of the damages suffered by the plaintiff, who was also involved in the dangerous adjustment. In this group of cases, the peculiarity lies in the fact that the injury did not arise from a more or less accidental contact with the danger zone defined by the young individuals, but rather stemmed from the plaintiff's own decision to participate in the dangerous experiment.

It was established that, in such cases, the principle becomes relevant that there is no general mandate prohibiting individuals from putting themselves in a dangerous situation.[186] If the defendant's role in sharing liability for the damage suffered by the injured party is confined to mere participation in the harmful event, there is, according to the VI Senate, no necessary causal link between the outcome and the breach of a behavioral norm by the wrongdoer, which would justify distinguishing this case from one in which the victim independently engages in a dangerous activity. According to the BGH, the mere fact that the injured party was encouraged to engage in risky behavior, having planned and carried out the propellant construction together with his colleague, is not sufficient by itself to make the latter liable for the damages, provided that the defendant did not assume a role of authority or leadership in executing the project.[187]

The defendant provided the chemical products from his stock, in addition to mixing and pouring them into the tube. Thus, the defendant's role was not limited to merely ensuring that the injured party acted, but rather contributed to creating the dangerous situation. However, according to the BGH, even this involvement of the defendant in the preparation and execution of the experiment is not sufficient to absolve the plaintiff from the consequences of the risk he created for himself, as the dangers introduced by the defendant's participation did not create an additional risk for the victim. The chemical combination could have easily been carried out by the plaintiff alone, without relying on the defendant's special knowledge or skills.

In this situation, according to the German court, the danger to each party was such that its materialization would represent a "general life risk", not entitling them to compensation (*entschädigungsloses allgemeines Lebensrisiko*).[188] The plaintiff would then have violated the principle of prohibition of contradictory behavior

---

held liable. Between seven and ten years old, liability for damages in car or railway accidents is excluded unless the harm was caused intentionally (Sprau (2020), p. 1491).

[185] NJW 1986, 1865.

[186] Feurer (2010), p. 401; Waldkirch (2018), p. 378.

[187] The BGH, in the decision, found that the defendant did not act as an "expert" ("*Experte*") or "spokesperson" ("*Wortführer*") for the plaintiff. Lange and Schiemann observe that, in some cases, the initial actor assumes the role of an "opinion leader" ("*Meinungsführer*") in relation to the injured party (Lange and Schiemann (2003), p. 136).

[188] Medicus (2004), p. 454. Although focusing on psychological injuries, Geigel maintains that, at a primary level, the general risks of life must first be delineated (Geigel (2020), p. 10).

(*venire contra factum proprium*),[189] a partial figure of good faith (§ 242 of the BGB[190]), by trying to partially transfer the financial consequences of his bodily injury to the defendant, even though it was he himself who, by free decision and his own negligence, put himself in a dangerous situation.

The BGH's decision is correct. There is no doubt that the factual causation between the behavior of the first young man and the harmful result is established, as, hypothetically eliminating the initial event, the harmful occurrence would not have happened. Adequate causation can also be affirmed, since the delivery of the explosive material to the victim does not constitute an improbable condition for the harmful result, especially considering that the first wrongdoer incorrectly prepared the mixture of the compounds.

However, the damages suffered should not be attributed to the defendant. Although the young student created the specific risk of the explosion by preparing a mixture of sulfur and potassium permanganate with the improper arrangement of the components, it must be recognized that the injured party was actively involved in the setup, clearly consenting to and engaging in the risky activity, thus accepting the inherent risks of the venture. The first perpetrator did not assume any leadership role in this case, nor can it be argued that he exercised control over the situation due to special knowledge. Through his participation, the victim voluntarily assumed the risks associated with the activity (self-responsibility), meaning that the harmful event merely represented the materialization of a "general life risk" for both parties.

The reference by the BGH, in the commented decision, to the violation of the principle of prohibition of contradictory behavior (*venire contra factum proprium*) is unnecessary, given that the aforementioned objective imputation criteria are sufficient to resolve the case.[191] The use of partial figures of good faith in a merely rhetorical manner[192] should be avoided to prevent trivializing the concept,

---

[189] The expression *venire contra factum proprium* refers to the exercise of a legal position that contradicts previously assumed behavior. Menezes Cordeiro notes that such conduct is universally deemed inadmissible by the doctrine that acknowledges it (Cordeiro (2017), p. 742).

[190] Section 242 of the BGB is widely recognized as a leading example of a general clause (Martins-Costa (2018), p. 135). Clóvis do Couto e Silva, however, emphasizes that Section 242 of the BGB does not confer extraordinary legislative powers upon the judge. Instead, it serves as a reinforcement to Section 157 of the BGB, which sets forth the traditional rule of interpreting legal transactions in good faith (Couto E Silva (2014), p. 34). In Brazilian law, good faith was already enshrined in the Commercial Code of 1850, Art. 131, which provided for interpretation in good faith. Additionally, Teixeira de Freitas' Draft included provisions on good faith in general terms (Tomasevicius (Tomasevicius Filho 2020), p. 154).

[191] It is noted that good faith is used in place of certain legal institutions that have not been successful in their practical application, due to the lack of dogmatic development (Tomasevicius (2010), p. 93).

[192] Doctrine indicates that good faith is often used merely as a rhetorical figure in Brazilian law (Schmidt (2009), p. 507). Schmidt also observes that the belief that all disputes can be resolved solely on the basis of principles or general clauses is widely accepted in Brazil (Schmidt (2016), p. 431). On the potential pitfalls of improperly applying the general clause of good faith in Brazilian law, see Martins-Costa (2018), p. 257.

particularly when other decision-making parameters are adequate for addressing the practical issues.

In the second case referenced by the doctrine, an adult gives a minor, aged 15 years old at the time, two chemical products (potassium chlorate and red phosphorus) which, if mixed, can detonate. The young man, upon adding the substances, causes an explosion, injuring himself.[193] In this scenario, therefore, there is, on one side, a first individual who is superior in knowledge and may also hold a certain position of authority, and, on the other, a minor.[194]

The BGH[195] held the adult liable for civil reparation, based on § 823 of the BGB. According to the German court, the responsibility arises from the uncontrolled delivery of a dangerously large amount of potassium chlorate to a young person of only 15 years. The transfer of the material can generally be considered an adequate cause of this type of accident. The aptitude of potassium chlorate to produce dangerous explosives was recognized in professional circles, so this substance should not have been made available to minors.

As stated, the recognition of causal adequacy is not sufficient for the purpose of attributing liability. However, by transferring the product for experiments without any safeguards, the first perpetrator unlawfully created a typical source of danger[196] (*typische Gefahrenquelle*), breaching his duty of care (*Verhaltenspflicht*), given that the young man had no knowledge of chemistry and had not demonstrated caution.

The adult acted negligently, as he should have anticipated the possibility of the minor using the products to create dangerous compounds. It is not certain whether the first causer knew about the explosive power of the mixture, but it was intellectually possible (*geistig möglich*) for him to inform himself about the properties of the substances.[197] The BGH's solution for objective attribution was based on the criterion of adequacy, yet the court did not address the violation of a general duty of care (*Verkehrspflicht*), although it recognized the establishment of a source of danger by the first causer.[198]

---

[193] This scenario, which might initially appear to fall under the previous category (intervention based on the authority of the first wrongdoer), does not align with that framework. As noted earlier, these cases are distinguished by the transfer of a physical component to the second party, such as making a dangerous substance available, irrespective of whether the first party holds a position of authority. The adult's specialized knowledge relative to the young person strengthens the grounds for imputation.

[194] Niebaum (2003), p. 127–128.

[195] VersR 73, 30.

[196] Chapter 4, Art. 4:101 of the Draft Common Frame of Reference (DCFR), provides that a person causes legally relevant damage if the harm can be regarded as a consequence of that person's conduct or of a source of danger for which they are responsible.

[197] Niebaum (2003), p. 128.

[198] Discussing the risks faced by companies operating in the Internet domain, Stelzner argues that those who take risks must also bear responsibility for the resulting dangers, as they typically control and profit from these activities. Beyond tangible assets, the operation of a company itself is considered a source of danger (*Gefahrenquelle*). Consequently, Internet providers can pose

In Brazilian law, cases involving the sale of dangerous products are more readily resolved through the application of the CDC.[199] In a case decided by the Court of Justice of the State of Minas Gerais,[200] it was determined that a merchant who sold ten bombs to a minor—five priced at R$ 1.00 each and five priced at R$ 0.80 each—was held liable. While handling the explosive, the minor, accompanied by other children, had part of his left-hand finger amputated and suffered burns on the remaining part of his hand. The decision was based on Art. 14 of the CDC, which establishes the strict liability of the service provider in cases where insufficient or inadequate information about its use and risks is provided.

In another case, decided on March 12, 1968, the BGH[201] also used the criterion of adequacy as a parameter for attributing liability, without addressing the issue of "psychological causation" and failing to develop other restrictive criteria for objective imputation.[202]

According to the facts reported in the case decided by the German court, a couple decided to paint the walls of their apartment and hired a professional. During the work activities, the professional, due to a mix-up with his beer bottle, accidentally ingested a quantity of caustic soda solution, which had been stored by the homeowners in a similar container. The chemical, used by the defendants as a cleaning agent, had been placed in a beer bottle and stored behind the toilet.[203] During the process, a colleague of the professional moved the bottle into the apartment's corridor. The bottle was marked with a label that read: "Caution, danger to life."

The BGH, based on the theory of adequacy, considered that the careless conduct of the painter did not prevent the characterization of adequate causation, as the conduct of the hired professional was foreseeable. Therefore, according to the court, it was not possible to assert an "interruption of the causal chain"

---

genuine threats to third parties' legal interests and must therefore observe relevant safety duties (Stelzner (2011), p. 126).

199 The assessment of causation under the Consumer Defence Code (CDC) lies outside the scope of this work. Excluding supplier liability for products and services based on risk allocation criteria proves more complex, given that the inherent dangers in the use of such goods typically rest with the suppliers. In exceptional circumstances, causation is dismissed due to an external fortuitous event or the victim's exclusive act. Although the CDC does not explicitly address fortuitous events or force majeure as grounds for excluding liability, legal doctrine has acknowledged their applicability in consumer relationships (Marques (2010), p. 383). The CDC expressly establishes a range of conduct obligations for suppliers (Art. 6), further limiting the scenarios in which liability may be excluded. Consequently, the materialization of risk as a criterion for attributing liability becomes significantly less useful in this context.

200 TJMG, ApCív 0021128–34.2018.8.13.0026, rel. Antônio Bispo, j. 10.02.2022. A comparable case was decided by the Court of Justice of São Paulo (TJSP). However, the court neither referred to the CDC nor offered additional analysis regarding causation (TJSP, ApCív 0003589–22.2014.8.26.0030, rel. Jair de Souza, j. 10.11.2022).

201 NJW 1968, 1182.

202 Forst (2000), p. 63.

203 Fuchs et al. (2017), p. 111.

("*Unterbrechung des Kausalzusammenhangs*"), so causation should be affirmed. The BGH did not examine whether the defendants violated the "duty to avoid danger" ("*Gefahrvermeidungspflicht*"), limiting itself to analyzing the adequacy of the cause.[204]

The solution found by the German court deserves criticism. The causal link between the conduct and the damage is characterized according to the formula of hypothetical elimination. It is debatable, however, whether the storage of caustic soda in a properly labeled container constitutes an adequate cause of the damages suffered by the painter, even from the standpoint of an experienced observer. Even if it is argued, using the theory of causal adequacy in its negative aspect, or from the perspective of an ideal, optimal, or extremely perceptive observer, that the harmful result was not highly improbable, the injury should not have been attributed to the owners of the property.

The criterion used by the BGH concerns the interruption of the causal chain. As has been asserted several times, this criterion refers to a naturalistic sense of causation. This approach disregards the fact that the attribution of damages is determined through the use of evaluative parameters that limit liability. Moreover, no violation of general duties of care occurred on the part of the contractors, since the bottle was marked with very clear words warning about the dangers of handling its contents. The worker assumed the risks of his behavior (self-responsibility), as he decided to ingest an alcoholic beverage during the performance of his work. Ultimately, as there was no breach of a duty of care, it cannot be concluded that the damage occurred due to a specific risk created by the couple, but rather resulted from an ordinary life risk.

5.2.1.4 Cases of Self-Harm

Complex issues may arise when the resulting damage occurs because the second perpetrator, influenced by the conduct of the first causer, consciously and intentionally harms themselves or their interests.[205] There are numerous examples of self-destructive reactions by the injured party following the occurrence of the initial harmful event, such as in cases of *revenge porn,*[206] *bullying,* and the occurrence of environmental and financial disasters.[207] Under the impact of the

---

[204] Forst (2000), p. 63.

[205] The Munich Regional Court ordered a convicted criminal to pay damages resulting from a suicide attempt. In this case, the victim's decision was influenced by the blindness in one eye and the experience of intense pain (LG Munich VersR 19955, 398, m. Anm. Wille 447).

[206] Revenge porn, also known as non-consensual pornography, refers to the distribution of explicit sexual content without the consent of the person depicted, often driven by a desire for retaliation against a former partner (Twerski et al. (2021), p. 873).

[207] The perpetration of financial scams may also lead victims to suicide, raising the question of whether the perpetrator is liable solely for the economic losses suffered or also for the damages resulting from the victims' deaths. One notable example is the largest financial fraud in

initial harm, the victim may prematurely cease commercial activities, take their own life,[208] or even refuse a necessary medical procedure, such as a blood transfusion, for religious reasons.[209]

On August 24, 2014, the Fukushima District Court[210] decided a case in which the relatives of a survivor of the nuclear accident, who later took their own life, sought compensation for loss and damage from the company responsible for the plant.[211]

According to reported facts, the victim lived with her husband and their two children in the municipality of Kawamata, in the Yamakiya district, northwest of the reactor, when, on March 11, 2011, the power source of the Fukushima I nuclear plant, owned by the TEPCO company (*Tokyo Electric Power*), collapsed due to a tsunami caused by an earthquake. On 15 March, the family fled the area, returning on the 20th of the same month. On 22 April, it was announced that the district would become part of the so-called planned evacuation zone, which led them to move to an apartment in the city of Fukushima. On 30 June, the victim, Hamako Watanabe, and her husband spent the night at their house in Yamakiya. The following morning, the victim took her own life in front of the house.[212]

The deceased's husband and their children always believed that the suicide was predominantly caused by the fact that she was forced to abandon her home.[213]

U.S. history, committed by Bernie Madoff, who used funds from new investors to pay returns to earlier ones as part of a so-called "business strategy." The pyramid scheme eventually collapsed, and at least two victims died by suicide as a result of the fraud (Portela (2022).

[208] In Roman law, although mere "temperamental defects" of slaves were not covered by the term *vitium*, many of these traits were considered significant enough by buyers that they would typically request specific guarantees from the seller. The *aediles curules*, therefore, required sellers to declare a certain number of such "defects." Slaves who were prone to suicide, for instance, had to be identified, as a previous suicide attempt indicated a disregard for life and was interpreted as a sign of potential danger to others, based on the assumption that someone who had acted violently toward themselves might do the same to others (Zimmermann (1996), p. 314).

[209] Looschelders (2019), p. 487.

[210] Hanrei Jihō 2237 (2014) 7.

[211] In Japan, according to Goodman, plaintiffs do not necessarily expect to prevail in court but often aim to draw public attention to an issue, hoping to generate social consensus in support of their position. This approach, he notes, may be changing as a result of the earthquake and tsunami that struck the eastern region of the country, followed by the Fukushima nuclear disaster. These events triggered a wave of lawsuits filed by local residents seeking to prevent the reopening of older nuclear facilities on safety grounds (Goodman (2012), p. 387). Japanese contracts also typically include a clause stating that, in case of disagreement, both parties agree to meet in good faith and attempt to resolve the dispute (GILSON, Ronald. Value creation by business lawyers: legal skills and asset pricing. *The Yale Law Journal*, v. 94. n. 2, p. 244–313, 1984, p. 307–308).

[212] Bälz (2015), p. 271.

[213] Natural disasters and their consequences often lead to psychological distress among affected individuals, though such reactions do not necessarily correspond to the development of a mental disorder. In Fukushima, the combination of the earthquake, the tsunami, and the nuclear accident resulted in the mandatory evacuation of residents from nearby areas. Many were forced to relocate under extreme stress, due to family separation, displacement from their homes, and the need to adjust to unfamiliar conditions. Studies indicate an immediate increase in suicide rates following

In May 2012, the surviving spouse demanded compensation from TEPCO,[214] seeking reimbursement for the loss of income caused by the death, as well as for the suffering experienced due to the tragedy that affected the family. The Fukushima District Court partially upheld the claim, attributing 80% of the damages to the defendant company, recognizing a causal link between the stress of the evacuation and the suicide, and ordered the defendant to pay 49,093,629 yen[215] (approximately 357,675 euros).[216]

TEPCO sought to challenge causation, referring to the victim's prior psychological issues as indicative of her emotional fragility. The Japanese court, however, stated that the operator of a reactor is responsible for damages that have an adequate causal relationship (*sōtō inga kankei*) with the nuclear fission process. It was also defined that scientific proof excluding all doubts is not necessary, but a high degree of probability (*kōdo no gaizen-sei*) that, taking into account all circumstances and general experience, a certain fact caused the harmful result.[217]

According to the court, suicide is not provoked by a single cause. On the contrary, several factors, such as the environment, preexisting mental disorders, and character inclinations, can contribute to the execution of the extreme act. After a detailed analysis of the evidence, the court concluded that it was not proven that the victim suffered from depression, according to the precise medical definition. Such a circumstance, however, would not be decisive for proving causation. In order to establish causation, the court relied on the "stress-vulnerability" model (*sutoresu zeikai-sei riron*), as is usual in cases of work accident insurance. According to this interpretation, psychological issues originate from the interaction between the individual's disposition (vulnerability) and external stress factores.[218]

The Fukushima District Court identified various stress factors caused by the reactor issue, such as anxiety about fleeing the accident area, displacement, and the lack of prospects for return. It would be reasonable to assume that the victim's sudden and intense exposure to a series of such events would lead her to a state of mental

the Fukushima nuclear accident, particularly among men, in areas that underwent full or partial evacuation. After a temporary decline, delayed increases in suicide rates were recorded, with variations depending on sex, age, and location (Orui et al. (2018), pp. 353 and 361).

[214] Numerous lawsuits were filed against TEPCO, alleging a causal link between the nuclear accident and suicides. In June 2013, the company, for the first time, admitted that the disaster had played a crucial role in the suicide of a farmer in 2011, who had been prohibited from selling his agricultural products due to concerns about radioactive contamination (Feldman (2014), p. 141).

[215] Feldman (2015), p. 146.

[216] In a similar case, the Fukushima District Court ordered TEPCO to pay 15.2 million yen (approximately US$142,000) to the family of a 102-year-old man who took his own life after being forced to leave his home because of the nuclear disaster. The man, who had never lived outside his hometown, was found hanged in his room on April 12, 2011, one day after learning that the government was about to issue an evacuation order for the village (Sturmer (2018).

[217] Bälz (2015), pp. 272–273.

[218] Bälz (2015), p. 273.

disturbance[219] that could culminate in her suicide. Her greater susceptibility to stress only aggravated the condition created by the nuclear catastrophe. According to the Japanese Court, what really led the deceased to commit the extreme act of taking her own life was despair about her future. Using the theory of adequate causation, it was concluded that, in tragedies of this magnitude, it is not unforeseeable that some people become mentally debilitated to the point of committing suicide.[220]

The debated issue is relevant, especially in cases of major tragedies,[221] such as the ones that struck the cities of Brumadinho and Mariana,[222] Data from a survey conducted by UFMG demonstrate the prevalence of suicidal behavior in the population affected by the rupture of the Fundão dam, compared to the general population. Once again, factors such as the abandonment of the place of residence, resettlement difficulties, and discrimination suffered prove decisive in increasing the rate.[223] Unlike the Japanese case, the Brazilian courts have not yet addressed whether the damages that the victim caused to themselves, whose actions were influenced by the behavior of the first wrongdoer, can be attributed to them.

In the case of *White v. Lawrence*,[224] Barbara White, administrator of the estate of her late husband, Earl R. White, sued Dr. William H. Lawrence after Earl White committed suicide. Earl White was 55 years old at the time of his death. He was addicted to alcohol and suffered from severe depression, which is why he started consulting the defendant, an osteopathic physician with a family practice covering a variety of illnesses, including bronchitis, hypertension, and back problems. The doctor was aware of the deceased's issues with alcohol. After identifying in 1990 that Earl's liver and pancreas were damaged by excessive alcohol use, the defendant referred him to another doctor, although he continued to treat him until his death on July 4, 1993.[225]

---

[219] In an English case cited by Lüer (Pigney v. Pointer's Transport Ltd. (1957) 1 W.L.R. 1121), an individual who had not sustained head injuries as a result of an accident developed a nervous disorder that ultimately led to suicide eighteen months later. The court upheld the widow's claim for compensation for the damages resulting from her husband's death. The German Federal Court (BGH) also addressed this issue, although it did not render a definitive ruling. Nonetheless, it can be inferred that the reasoning the German court is likely to adopt is that the wrongdoer should be held liable for damages if the physical and mental consequences of the accident constitute a significant contributory cause of the suicide (NJW 1958, 1579) (Lüer (1969), p. 144).

[220] Bälz (2015), pp. 273–274.

[221] Regarding the suicide attempt following a minor incident, in this case, a car accident, see OLG Nürnberg ZfS 2000, 58.

[222] Shortly after the tragedy, the populations of Bento Rodrigues and Paracatu de Baixo, as well as other areas directly affected by the mud, were relocated to the urban area of Mariana, where they were received, registered by the health and social assistance teams of the municipality, and provided with initial orientation (Pessoa (2017), p. 103).

[223] Studies reveal that the population affected by the Mariana disaster, like that of Fukushima, can be classified as being at special risk due to the displacement from their place of residence, the challenges of resettlement, and the discrimination suffered as a result of the shift from rural to urban areas (Prismma (2018), p. 59).

[224] *White v. Lawerence*, 975 S.W. 2d 525 (Tenn. 1998).

[225] Rapp (2020), p. 297–298.

In May or June of 1993, the defendant prescribed Disulfiram, commonly known as Antabuse, to the deceased in an effort to discourage him from consuming alcohol. The doctor instructed Barbara White to crush the medication and discreetly[226] mix it into the patient's food. On July 14, Earl White went alone to the emergency room of Valley Regional Hospital, complaining of pain. He was diagnosed with heat exhaustion and discharged. Four hours later, Earl took his own life, shooting himself in the head with a pistol. The plaintiff attached to the case the statement of Dr. Smith, who concluded that the defendant could have foreseen that secretly prescribing and administering Antabuse to an alcoholic and depressive patient could cause serious physical harm and lead to the patient's suicide.[227]

It was highlighted in the trial[228] that, although, as a rule, an independent intervening cause interrupts the chain of causation,[229] the victim's behavior cannot be considered a supervening cause as long as it was foreseeable and the original offender's conduct constitutes a substantial factor in causing the harm. It was reported that suicide will constitute an intervening cause if it is an intentional, considered, and deliberate act by someone with the capacity for autonomous decision-making. The act of taking one's own life is not necessarily an act of intervention. The circumstance that the deceased was not suffering from mental illness or lacked rational capacity does not lead to the conclusion that suicide was an unforeseeable event.[230]

Another significant case was decided by the Court of Justice of Rio Grande do Sul[231] on August 28, 2019. The claim concerned a compensation request made by the mother of a minor against her ex-boyfriend. According to the claim, the man, being older, had a strong influence over the young girl. The relationship lasted until early 2011, when the minor discovered she was pregnant. The defendant, upon learning of the pregnancy, allegedly pressured the teenager to have an abortion, providing the necessary medication. She, succumbing to the defendant's pressure, ingested a high dose of the medication in question, successfully terminating the pregnancy. Overcome with distress, the minor left home in March 2012, heading to Florianópolis, where she took her own life. The defendant argued that there was no causal link between his conduct and the suicide of the deceased.

---

[226] Schwartz et al. (2010), p. 350.

[227] Rapp (2020), p. 298.

[228] A commonly adopted approach by courts, skeptical of legal claims concerning professional malpractice resulting in suicide, is to require the claimant to prove that the act would not have occurred but for the negligent action of the mental health specialist (Stefan (2016), p. 293).

[229] The defendant cited Tennessee law, which holds that suicide, committed by an individual who understands the nature of their act, is, as a matter of law, an independent, intervening, and proximate cause of death. The court rejected this argument, asserting that the case should be distinguished from the scenarios proposed by the defendant (Patterson (2021).

[230] Suicide, once regarded as a sin, viewed as a weakness, and treated in law as a circumstance that excluded liability, is now evaluated by juries alongside other factors, particularly regarding its foreseeability (Rapp (2020), p. 298).

[231] TJRS, ApCív 0121086–64.2019.21.7000, rel. José André Pereira Gailhard, j. 28.08.2019.

The court decided that the first-degree dismissal sentence should be upheld, as the plaintiff failed to demonstrate that the defendant had coerced her daughter into having the abortion through psychological violence. It was also stated that it would not be possible to hold the defendant liable for the young girl's suicide,[232] since the event resulted from circumstances that were not clarified and there was no causal link between his conduct and the harmful event. The decision, however, fails to specify the causal theory adopted, as well as the criteria for attributing liability that led to the final decision.

The Regional Court of the 3rd Region[233] also decided that there was no causal link between the suicide of the insured, who was suffering from depression, and the denial of a social security benefit. The court followed the understanding that the denial or cessation of a social security benefit, when supported by medical expertise, even if done administratively, does not constitute an unlawful act and therefore does not lead to the liability of the INSS for non-pecuniary damages, even if the insured is subsequently granted or reinstated the benefit by judicial decision. It was highlighted that the disability benefit was judicially granted to the insured when a provisional urgent protection was granted on July 13, 2017, with the suicide occurring on October 28, 2017.

In the religious context,[234] an example often discussed is that of an individual who, after being assaulted by a third party, refuses a blood transfusion, leading to death.[235] German legal doctrine discusses whether the injured party's actions would absolve the first wrongdoer, who created the risk situation, from liability. It has been argued that, in such a case, an "atypical causal course" ("*atypischer*

---

[232] In another case, decided by the Court of Justice of Goiás, an employee of *Banco do Brasil* was accused of theft by the financial institution, which allegedly caused him significant distress, culminating in his suicide. The deceased's ex-partner and daughter filed a lawsuit for non-pecuniary damages against the institution. The bank defended itself by arguing that it acted within its rights in suspending the employee from his duties, as there were solid indications of his involvement in the illicit acts committed. The TJGO merely stated that it was not proven that the deceased's reputation had been tarnished due to his suspension. While acknowledging that comments and speculations may have arisen in this regard, it was noted that at no point was it demonstrated that they may have originated from the legal representatives of the institution (TJGO, ApCív 0290350-50.2008.8.09.0129, rel. Fernando de Castro Mesquita, j. 31.01.2012).

[233] TRF3, ApCív 5010873–21.2019.4.03.6100, rel. Antônio Carlos Cedenho, j. 04.09.2020.

[234] The ascetic behavior of leaders and members of certain confessional segments and certain religious practices cannot be considered unlawful, as it derives from the exercise of private autonomy and religious freedom. The practice of these activities by third parties, performed voluntarily, generally constitutes a free decision to put oneself in danger. Aware of the risks involved, the victim must bear the consequences of their own actions. As Luís Greco rightly points out, the result should not be attributed to the first wrongdoer; otherwise, the author would paternalistically be transformed into the guardian of the integrity of an adult individual, which would contradict what is conventionally called the "principle of self-responsibility" (Greco (2014), p. 72). Every individual's capacity for self-determination must be ensured, as the individual bears the primary or preferential responsibility for organizing their life and legal assets (Péña (2010).

[235] Lasson (2009), p. 359. In German jurisprudence, see BGH NStZ, 94, 394.

Kausalverlauf") is characterized. Even though, as previously stated,[236] the unusual nature of the event does not inherently bar imputation, it remains possible to exclude attribution where the danger created by the wrongdoer does not culminate in the expected result. It is argued that the causal process would no longer be under the control of the wrongdoer, and the victim would be held responsible for the risk she exposed herself to,[237] unless her decision-making capacity was diminished.[238]

Finally, it should be noted that, recently, a 22-year-old student from Minas Gerais committed suicide after becoming the target of fake news spread by celebrity news profiles. Starting on December 18, 2023, these profiles shared screenshots of a fabricated conversation between the victim and comedian Whindersson Nunes, suggesting that they were flirting on Instagram and culminating in a request for a personal meeting. Following the release and widespread attention of the false messages, the student posted a lengthy message on her social media, revealing that she was suffering attacks after the spread of fake news. The young woman's mother even recorded a video requesting the removal of the material from social media and informing the public that the student was suffering from depression. Despite all the repercussions, one of the individuals responsible for the "Choquei" profile ridiculed the young woman's reaction in the post where she cried for help. On December 22, 2023, it was reported that the student had committed suicide.[239]

In the group of cases currently being analyzed, once natural causation is established, the first criterion to be observed is the adequacy of the cause, which, as already seen, constitutes a prior legal parameter for attribution.[240] Events like natural or human disasters, the execution of revenge porn[241] as well as aggravated forms of bullying and the dissemination of false news, are not entirely indifferent to the occurrence of the harmful event. Others, however, although reprehensible from

[236] Wessels et al. (2017), pp. 88–93.

[237] Bernd (2019), p. 445.

[238] Zieschang (2020), p. 272.

[239] Borges (2024).

[240] In certain cases, the unlawfulness itself can be dismissed in advance, even if damage has occurred, as in the case where a strict teacher demands a certain intellectual performance from a student, and the student, failing to achieve the reasonable, yet severe, goals set, commits suicide or self-harm.

[241] Marco Mattia argues that there is no doubt that a crime such as the illicit dissemination of sexually explicit images or videos can constitute a risk situation where the most serious consequence is, in abstract, foreseeable. According to the author, since death results from the victim's behavior, it must be demonstrated that there was a significant, if not total, reduction in the victim's capacity for self-determination in order to eliminate the insurmountable nature of the suicidal act. The author suggests that various factors be considered, such as the type of dissemination carried out, the nature and intensity of the relationship between the perpetrator and the victim, in addition to the personal, physical, and mental characteristics of the offended party (Mattia (2019), p. 65.). Recognizing the contribution of revenge porn to the suicides of women, see TJRJ, ApCív 0000445-89.2015.8.19.0033, rel. Emílio Ribeiro, j. 22.08.2017.

an ethical and social point of view, are inadequate to cause damage. Thus, for example, the acts of provocation, or even insult, by a club's supporter are generally indifferent to the perpetration of self-harm by the defeated party. Similarly, taunts or mockeries, which are normal among groups of friends, should not be considered, as a rule, as the cause of damage inflicted upon oneself by the affected individual.

At a second stage, it is essential to verify whether the intensity of the initial facts compromises, to some extent, the freedom of action of the injured party, creating a typical risk that ultimately materializes. Depending on the magnitude of the events, these cannot be considered as "general risks of life," part of the victim's risk sphere, so the consequences of the danger must be assumed by the one who originated it. The situation is different when an individual is victimized by a great tragedy, such as Brumadinho, compared to a case where a bride, seeing her relationship come to an end on the night of her wedding, takes her own life. Breakups, under normal conditions, are an ordinary aspect of human life; suicide, however, cannot be understood as the realization of an increased risk of death attributable to the mere end of a relationship.[242]

Also, in this group of cases, the impossibility of controlling the course of events is not a relevant criterion for attributing damages. Once the risk situation has been created by the first wrongdoer, little or nothing can be done to prevent the materialization of self-harm by the victim. Once the act of aggression had occurred, the wrongdoer had no means to alter or prevent the victim's decision, grounded in religious beliefs, to refuse a blood transfusion. This, however, does not serve as a basis for excluding liability, as the mere occurrence of the harmful result does not constitute a typical event of the danger generated by the wrongdoer's behavior. After the initial act, the wrongdoer exercises no influence over subsequent events.[243]

The act of the first wrongdoer need not result in a psychiatric illness so severe as to wholly compromise the victim's capacity for decision-making. If the typical risk created materializes, at least part of the damages must be attributed to the initial wrongdoer, given the impairment of the victim's ability to decide freely. Severe and extraordinary events, such as a dam failure or a nuclear disaster, cannot be considered normal life events, and the initial perpetrator must be held liable for the injuries caused.

Similarly, it cannot be said that there is no internal connection between the abortion performed by a young woman, under pressure from her ex-boyfriend, and her subsequent suicide,[244] if it is proven that the initial act had a strong psychological influence on the victim's behavior. Even if not all damages are attributed to

---

[242] In some cases of relationship termination, it seems correct to affirm that causal adequacy is not present.

[243] Leitermeier (1968), p. 54.

[244] TJRS, ApCív 0121086–64.2019.21.7000, rel. José André Pereira Gailhard, j. 28.08.2019.

the defendant, given that the young woman may have preserved part of her deliberative autonomy, the risk spheres assumed by the parties, considering the peculiarities of the specific case, must be balanced to proceed with the allocation of damages. It is important to emphasize, once again, that the circumstance of the extreme act constituting an apparently voluntary decision by the victim does not exclude legal attribution.[245]

In the case of the denial of a social benefit,[246] the simple refusal of coverage, based on insurance and supported by medical expertise, does not meet the requirements for a state entity's liability. Initially, it should be noted that there is no unlawful act in the cessation of the benefit, as long as it is properly justified. Its interruption, in accordance with legal rules, constitutes an ordinary risk for the recipient, and the decision can be contested in the appropriate forum, including through judicial measures. It cannot be asserted that the victim's suicide, due to the denial of the social benefit, which was adequately justified, even in the case of serious illness, could be a consequence of an increase in the specific risk posed by the act of the authority.

Another factor that should be taken into consideration when attributing damages concerns the special sensitivity or medical or psychological predisposition of the offended.[247] In general, due to the risk sphere created by the offender,[248] they must assume responsibility for the damages caused as a result of the establishment of this source of danger.[249] This follows from the corollary of the rule of full compensation whereby, as a general principle, the offender must compensate the victim for all losses sustained, even if a latent vulnerability

---

[245] Forst (2000), p. 46.

[246] TRF3, ApCív 5010873-21.2019.4.03.6100, rel. Antônio Carlos Cedenho, j. 04.09.2020. See Section 4.3.1.5.

[247] Nils Jansen states that, already in Roman law, the rule was that the perpetrator was liable for the injury, regardless of the victim's vulnerability (Jansen (2007), p. 12).

[248] Pirson (1964), p. 22.

[249] Caemmerer (1956), p. 18; Barbosa (2020), cit., p. 1005. The issue is controversial in Portuguese doctrine. Antunes Varela provides the example of an individual who assaults another with a slap. The latter, suffering from a serious heart condition, dies. The author questions whether the victim's illness should be considered when judging the adequacy of the cause, stating that there are divergences among authors on this point (Varela (2000), p. 892). Maria de Lurdes Pereira holds that compensation should be granted even in cases of special significance of the injured interests (Pereira (2022), pp. 312–313). German jurisprudence typically applies the English rule of the "eggshell skull rule," arguing that the particular vulnerability of the individual does not exempt the liable party from liability (Wagner (2021), p. 898). The term "thin skull" or "eggshell skull" originates from illustrations in English cases where the plaintiff dies as a result of the defendant's negligence, whereas a normal individual would only suffer a minor blow to the head (Best (Best and Barnes 2007), p. 256). On the contrary, Larenz asserts that the perpetrator should only be held responsible if he knew or should have known about the pre-existing illness (Larenz and Canaris (1994), pp. 378–379). In Brazilian law, part of the doctrine, based on the unpredictability of the situation, has rejected liability (Schreiber (2013), p. 73).

renders the extent of the damage greater than would ordinarily be foresee.[250] Only in cases where the vulnerability is extremely atypical and profound can the exclusion of attribution be considered.[251] Thus, in the case of the student who took her own life due to the irresponsible spread of fake news, the attribution of damages to the one who disseminated the false conversations should not be dismissed, especially since they knew about the delicate situation of the victim's mental health and had made derogatory comments on the young woman's personal profile.

Looschelders[252] argument should be rejected in asserting that the same criteria for "provocation" cases should be applied to cases of suicide or self-harm. It makes no sense to require that the victim feel "provoked" to take her own life, regardless of the meaning attributed to this term. It is also not relevant to assess whether the motive behind the act was justifiable, since there is, evidently, no legal or moral duty to commit suicide. However, it is possible, under Art. 945 of the CC/02, to balance the risk spheres of the parties to determine the allocation of the damages. In the case of Fukushima, given TEPCO's causal contribution in creating a high-risk situation, the district court acted correctly in partially accepting the claim for compensation and attributing 80% of the damages to the defendant company.[253]

5.2.2 *Cases of Damages Caused to Third Parties*

In this group of cases, which involves at least three persons, the second causer and the injured party are different individuals.[254] The causal contexts involving three persons (*Dreipersonenverhältnisse*) refer to situations where the first perpetrator establishes an initial cause, and a second causer then intervenes, harming not himself but a third party—unlike the cases discussed so far. Thus, the party seeking compensation is not the second intervener but another individual harmed by the unfolding of the second cause.[255]

[250] In the case of *Vosburg v. Putney*, a teenage student kicked another in the leg. Unexpectedly, the kick exacerbated a pre-existing condition to such an extent that the victim was crippled. The defendant argued that he could only be held liable for the damages that could be expected from a simple kick. The court, however, rejected this position, stating that the perpetrator is obligated to compensate for the damages, even to a magnitude that could not have been foreseen. Goldberg and Zipursky assert that this rule may seem, at first glance, contrary to the principle of proximate cause. The principle rests on the notion that no wrong is committed by a careless individual if the harm suffered by the victim stems only from a succession of exceptional or chance events (Goldberg and Zipursky (2010), p. 347).

[251] In this case, Mafalda Miranda defends that the injured party assumes special duties toward themselves (Barbosa (2020), pp. 995–996).

[252] Looschelders (2019), p. 487.

[253] Feldman (2015), p. 146.

[254] Forst (2000), p. 32.

[255] Niebaum (2003), p. 145.

The relationships in these cases are more complex than those involving only two individuals. The focus remains on the link between the first causer and the injured party, as the claim for compensation is directed solely against the original perpetrator. This analysis of "psychological causation" remains independent of both the injured party's claim against the second causer and any obligations between the first and second individuals.[256]

The issue of the attribution of damages to the initial perpetrator is especially important when the second causer cannot be held liable or identified,[257] or does not have the financial resources to compensate the injured party. In these cases, the victim can sue the first perpetrator. However, the affirmation of liability does not imply that they should always bear the losses permanently. If the second causer is held liable and identified, part of the compensation may be recovered.[258]

It is also possible that, in practice, the issue of the first perpetrator's liability does not arise in the relationship between three individuals. This occurs when the first cannot be identified -[259] for example, when a driver uses high beams, impairing the vision of an oncoming motorist who then collides with another vehicle. In this case, it is relatively easy for the first perpetrator to escape detection. It is even conceivable that they do not realize the harmful effects of their actions. Although the contribution of the initial perpetrator may be more significant than the actions of the one who directly caused the damage, the injury is compensated without their involvement.[260]

5.2.2.1 Cases of Omission of Safety Precautions

The cases discussed here are characterized by the fact that the first wrongdoer did not take sufficient safety precautions for a risk they created.[261] The second causer performs an action that harms a third party. If the initial wrongdoer had taken the necessary precautions, the damage would have been avoided. In this group of cases, it may happen that the second wrongdoer causes the injury intentionally and with punitive intent, a circumstance that is relevant for liability purposes. The issue that arises is whether the first perpetrator is also liable for the damages caused to third parties. As already stated, this third party will usually bring an action against the initial perpetrator when the second perpetrator cannot be identified or where the first perpetrator is in a stronger financial position than the second.[262]

---

[256] Zhang (2016), p. 50.

[257] Rother (1965), p. 28.

[258] Niebaum (1977), p. 22.

[259] Rutkowsky (1952), p. 606.

[260] Niebaum (1977), p. 22.

[261] Rui Ataíde provides the example of a driver who, while parking, forgets the key in the ignition, allowing an unqualified third party to set the vehicle in motion, thereby committing several harmful violations. He then references the case decided by the BGH on December 15, 1970 (NJW 1971, 459) (Ataíde (2019), p. 642).

[262] Niebaum (2003), pp. 146–147.

Perhaps the most typical and discussed case of this category is the already mentioned[263] "green strip case" ("*Grünstreifenfall*").[264] Two decisions are usually referenced by the doctrine in relation to this group of cases.[265] In the first case, decided by the *Landgericht* Düsseldorf,[266] a truck caused a traffic accident, which resulted in the road being blocked. Given the traffic jam of about 3 km in length, many drivers decided to use the adjacent green strip, destroying approximately 400 m of area belonging to the federal road administration (*Bundesstraßenverwaltung*). The German court decided that the causal link between the driver's negligent act and the damage was not "interrupted,"[267] since the accident constituted a condition for the destruction of the strip and was also considered an adequate cause[268] of the damages.

According to the court, the behavior of the impatient drivers was not beyond all probability (*außerhalb aller Wahrscheinlichkeit*), so the possibility of its occurrence could not reasonably be considered improbable according to life experience. It was asserted that, even though the drivers who used the green strip to bypass the traffic obstacle were not in an emergency situation and therefore acted not only intentionally but also unlawfully, such a circumstance would not exclude the adequacy of the cause.[269]

The *Landgericht* Düsseldorf also grounded its decision by stating that the defendant's fault extended to the damages caused to the side strip, emphasizing that discipline in road traffic, especially in long-distance circulation, would be extremely deficient. According to the German court's understanding, the driver involved in the accident should assume that some road users would not behave appropriately in the event of such an incident, resulting in the deterioration of the side strip. The conduct of the drivers would be not only purely objective but also subjectively foreseeable for the accident causer. According to the *Landgericht*, the first wrongdoer would be

---

[263] See Sect. 2.2.

[264] In the "green strip case," the question revolves around whether the party who negligently caused a traffic accident, resulting in the closure of the road, is also responsible for all damages caused by subsequent drivers who bypassed the site. It is asserted that the careless driving behavior of the party responsible for the accident and the inherent impulse to act certainly extend to the closure of the road. At this point, however, the earlier behavior would be considered complete, with no further consequences arising from it (Roth-Stielow (1971), p. 181).

[265] In addition to these two cases, Forst also addresses other scenarios similar to the "green strip case." In one of them, a driver causes a traffic accident, resulting in serious injuries to another driver. The ambulance driver can only reach the accident site by passing through the green side lane, thereby damaging it (Forst (2000), p. 40).

[266] LG Düsseldorf NJW 1955, 1031.

[267] It is highly improbable that adequacy would be denied in such a case. Additionally, the term "interruption of the causal chain" ("*Unterbrechung des Ursachenzusammenhangs*") should not be employed in contemporary doctrine, since causation itself cannot be interrupted; what may occur is the exclusion of legal imputation (Ristow (2003), p. 148).

[268] Musielak (2013), p. 244; Caemmerer (1970), p. 290; Esser and Schmidt (1993), p. 221; Oetker (2019), p. 405.

[269] Zhang (2016), pp. 123–124.

responsible for compensating the third party for the damages caused by the interveners, even in the hypothesis of intentional and illegal interference by these individuals, provided that the intervention was covered by the adequacy of the cause.

This decision of the Düsseldorf court was criticized by Larenz, Hermann Lange, and von Caemmerer.[270] Larenz[271] stated that the outcome of the decision seems astonishing. He raises the issue of whether the driver may justly be held liable for consequences arising from actions undertaken by others, entirely of their own volition, without his participation and at a stage where prevention was no longer within his power. The assumption, according to Larenz,[272] is that the court misunderstood the concept of causation in the sense of the dominant doctrine.[273] Lange,[274] in turn, asserts that the danger of unruly behavior by other drivers constitutes a "general traffic risk" ("*allgemeines Verkehrsrisiko*"), which should be assumed by the federal road administration.

In 1972, the BGH[275] decided a similar case: A NATO vehicle caused an accident while trying to overtake a lorry, colliding with a Renault car. This resulted in the road being blocked, forming a long queue of vehicles waiting for the police to arrive. Impatient drivers, who could not later be identified, used the cycle path and pedestrian crossing to continue their journey. When the traffic police arrived at the scene, after about fifteen minutes, they found that significant damage had been caused to the side roads. Based on the NATO troops statute, the owner of the crossing and cycle path claimed compensation from the Federal Republic of Germany for the losses incurred.

The *Berufungsgericht* examined whether the causal chain had been "broken" due to the intentional behavior of the drivers. The answer was negative, considering that the drivers' actions were motivated by the traffic jam caused by the accident, without any unusual reaction (*ungewöhnliche Reaktion*). The court recognized that establishing an adequate causal link between the conduct and the harmful event does not always conclusively determine whether the damage is attributable to the offender.

The German court investigated whether the damage was within the scope of protection of the violated norm (§ 7 StVG[276]), responding affirmatively. In its view,

[270] The truck driver, by colliding with the vehicle ahead, can be said to have breached his duty of care (*Sorgfaltspflicht*) toward other road users. However, this does not imply a breach of any duty toward the Federal Road Administration (*Bundesstraßenverwaltung*), the proprietor of the damaged road shoulder (Caemmerer (von 1956), p. 15).

[271] Larenz (1955), p. 1009.

[272] Larenz (1955), p. 1009.

[273] Larenz had not yet addressed the criterion of provocation (*Kriterium der Herausforderung*) in this article (Ristow (2003), p. 148).

[274] Lange (1960), p. 53.

[275] NJW 1972, 904.

[276] Under § 7, first part, of the Road Traffic Act (StVG)—a statute comparable to the Brazilian Traffic Code (CTB)—if, in the course of operating a vehicle, a person is killed or another's bodily integrity or health is impaired, the vehicle's owner is bound to compensate for the damage thereby caused.

there is not a mere external coincidence but an internal connection[277] between the accident, the resulting road closure, and the damages suffered by the claimant. Thus, even from an evaluative standpoint, the damage remained attributable to the lorry's owner and driver.

The BGH[278] affirmed that the *Berufungsgericht* acted correctly in considering the causal relationship between the behavior of the vehicle driver who caused the collision and the damage to the cycle paths and pavements[279] to be adequate. According to the BGH, it can even be assumed that the driver should foresee that an accident he causes in traffic will lead to such reactions from the drivers following behind. Thus, if adequate causation is not to be excluded, the resolution of the case would depend on whether such consequences can or cannot be attributed to the initial perpetrator,[280] even though they were produced by a "free decision" ("*freier Entschluss*") of a third party.[281]

Contrary to the decision of the lower court, the BGH held that attribution cannot be excluded merely because the impatient drivers acted intentionally. Liability cannot be excluded solely due to the intervention of a third party.[282] Only if the first circumstance is completely irrelevant to the occurrence of the second event can it be stated that the causal connection was "interrupted." According to the BGH, it is irrelevant, for the purposes of holding the first wrongdoer responsible, whether the

[277] Also invoking the necessity to verify of the internal connection between the events, see Cvetković (2021), p. 57.

[278] Kramer supports the BGH decision (Kramer (1976), p. 344). Also supporting the decision, see Ekkenga (2014), p. 88; Oetker (2019), pp. 404–405.

[279] At this point, the BGH refers to the LG Düsseldorf NJW 1955, 1031 decision, which also acknowledged this causal adequacy.

[280] According to Grüneberg (2020, p. 296), the road owner is not covered by the protective scope of the traffic regulation. By contrast, Kötz and Wagner maintain that there is no doubt that the directly infringed legal interest—namely, the property of the injured party's vehicle—falls within the protective purpose of the regulation (Kötz and Wagner (2006), p. 83).

[281] Regarding the subsequent intervention of a third party, Huber provides the example of a person injured in an accident who is admitted to a hospital. This patient then gets into an argument with their bed neighbor and is beaten to death. In this case, according to the author, the "specific risk" ("*spezifisches Risiko*") of the unlawful conduct does not materialize, as the fight could have occurred on a bus or in a bar (Huber (1973), p. 324).

[282] According to Larenz, as cited in the BGH decision, the liability of the first perpetrator for subsequent consequences ceases where a new and "unprovoked decision" ("*nicht herausgeforderter Entschluss*") by the injured party or a third party generates independent risks that are exclusively imputable to that decision, and thus fall within the sphere of responsibility of those actors. The author emphasizes that such a circumstance does not "interrupt," as previously believed, the causal connection itself. Larenz further argues that the imputation (*Zurechnung*) of consequences to the sphere of responsibility of the first perpetrator comes to an end where the liability of another party arises from an independent and unprovoked decision (Larenz (1970), p. 87).

third party acted lawfully or unlawfully.[283] In the case discussed, the drivers freely crossed the cycle path and the pedestrian path, so the accident was merely an external circumstance.[284]

The "green strip case" unequivocally demonstrates that merely examining natural causation and causal adequacy is not sufficient in determining liability in cases of "psychological causation." Indeed, without the occurrence of the initial accident (hypothetical elimination), the cars would not have bypassed the area and damaged the side lane. Similarly, the behavior of impatient drivers was not beyond all probability (causal adequacy). On the contrary, it was highly probable, considering the ordinary experience of events in vehicle traffic, that drivers would invade the pavement and cycle path.

However, it does not seem proper to attribute the damages suffered by the owners of the side lands to the individual who caused the accident. The BGH's decision in the "green strip case" is problematic: although it placed the damage within the protective scope of the violated norm, it nonetheless excluded imputation due to the absence of any "provocation" by the original causer. To argue that the material criterion of the risk created by the individual who caused the accident was not met in that case,[285] as the protected legal interest did not consist in the wealth of the owners of the marginal lands but in the physical safety of other drivers and the protection of road traffic.[286] The drivers individually assumed the risk of passing through the side lane, thereby being responsible for the damages caused.

The possibility of undisciplined behavior by other drivers is part of the "general traffic risk" (*allgemeines Verkehrsrisiko*), which must be assumed by the owner of the affected areas.[287] A different solution should be applied if the driver causing the accident had damaged the roadside property or had created a situation in traffic in which other drivers could only have avoided the damages by reacting extraordinarily quickly, as in the case of a driver who abruptly maneuvers his vehicle to the side lane to avoid an imminent collision.[288]

It should also be questioned whether, after the initial collision, the liable party could have taken traffic-required measures to prevent the damages to the owners of

[283] The irrelevance of the unlawfulness of the third party's interference, as well as whether the act was intentional or foreseeable, is also argued (Esser and Schmidt (1993), p. 221). In contrast, see Rother (1965), p. 179.

[284] Deutsch (1972), p. 553.

[285] It is acknowledged that there will be cases in which it will be difficult to determine whether the damage resulting from a violation of a legal interest materializes a specific risk or relates to the general risk of the affected individual's life (Huber (1969), p. 681).

[286] The duty of care to avoid causing the accident cannot be considered significant in relation to the damages caused to the neighboring land, as such a duty is not intended to prevent damage to the side strips, but rather to preserve road safety and avoid danger to road users (Zhang (2016), p. 155).

[287] In contrast, Wolf argues that the possibility of undisciplined road users using the side strip as an escape would, in any event, have been increased by the individual responsible for the collision (Wolf (1962), p. 31).

[288] Lange (1960), p. 53.

the marginal lands.[289] In this specific case, the driver only had the duty to protect the accident site but could not quickly clear the traffic nor prevent the other drivers from acting imprudently.[290]

Another case of intentional intervention by third parties was decided by the BGH[291] on October 2, 1979. An association organized an event for the demonstration of air shows (*Flugveranstaltungsfall*). About 50,000 people participated in the event, and some spectators, looking for a quiet place to eat, invaded a neighboring property, causing severe damage to the fence. The BGH held the association liable for compensating the owner of the destroyed fence, stating that the organizer did not take all necessary safety measures,[292] thus violating duties of care.[293] The general duty of care, according to the German court, also extended to dangers that could arise through the unauthorized and intentional intervention of third parties, so the organizing association could not rely solely on the mere presence of firefighters.[294]

According to the BGH, the association should be held liable because there was an evident possibility of intentional harm by third parties.[295] A gathering of individuals of this magnitude entails the risk of such attacks on another person's property. Therefore, the application of the "provocation formula" would not be necessary, as this criterion would only apply to groups of cases involving the relationship of two individuals (*Zweipersonenverhältnisse*), that is, in cases where the second perpetrator causes damage to themselves. According to Till Ristow, intentional damage to property would be covered by the scope of protection of the violated norm.[296]

The same question arises, for example, if someone organizes a festive event and the guests intentionally damage neighboring land by throwing objects, scratching the walls of the adjacent property, or even trespassing. This raises the issue of whether the behavior of third parties (guests) can exempt the organizer from liability for the resulting damage.

The natural and adequate causation is present, as it is not an improbable consequence of holding a large-scale event that neighboring properties may be invaded or damaged by guests or participants. However, the organizers failed to

[289] According to von Caemmerer, the driver of the vehicle who negligently collided with the car in front violated a duty of care toward other road users, and it cannot be said that there was a breach of duty toward the owner of the neighboring land. The damages caused to the side strip fall outside the scope of protection of the duty violated in this case (Caemmerer (von 1956), p. 15).

[290] Niebaum (2003), p. 89.

[291] NJW 1980, 223.

[292] Zhang (2016), p. 130.

[293] Lange and Schiemann (2003), pp. 142–143.

[294] The BGH has made the perpetrator's responsibility dependent on whether they have taken all necessary measures to neutralize the source of danger (Bar (1980), p. 194). Eike Schmidt, commenting on the case of the traffic accident, argues that taking the required measures only reduces the risk, not completely eliminating it. Therefore, the original perpetrator should be held responsible until the danger is removed (Schmidt (1970), p. 398).

[295] Forst (2000), pp. 198–199.

[296] Niebaum (2003), p. 158.

implement the necessary measures to contain the harm, violating general duties of care and increasing the risk of damage materializing. The risk increased by the omission of the event organizers materialized, and they should be held liable for the harm. The damages suffered by the neighbors are closely connected with the disregard for the duties imposed, in this case, by legal regulations, and do not represent a mere external circumstance.

The German doctrine also cites[297] the case decided by the BGH[298] on December 19, 1989. In 1987, the plaintiff, her husband, and their three children lived in one of the seven apartments in the defendant's house when, returning from a party around 1:30 in the morning, she fell into a light well (*Lichtschacht*). An unknown individual had removed the left front grid, one of a total of six grids, each measuring 39 cm x 69 cm, which protected the place. The plaintiff was unable to see the unprotected light well due to the defective exterior lighting of the building. As a result of the fall, she became permanently unable to work.

The *Berufungsgericht* found that the defendant negligently violated the required duty of care. The plaintiff fell into the well because the left front grid was completely displaced or removed, causing it to no longer provide support. This could only be explained by the intentional removal of the protection, which required minimal effort, as the grid weighed only 5.18 kg. The court emphasized that, as the owner and landlord of the property, the defendant had a duty to securely fasten the grids or take other precautions to prevent their deliberate removal by third parties. This was especially important because numerous residents, visitors, and other authorized individuals who needed to enter or exit the house had to walk over the 1.20-meter-deep well.

The BGH upheld the reasoning of the decision rendered by the *Berufungsgericht*, emphasizing that, according to widely recognized legal principles, anyone who creates or maintains sources of danger (*Gefahrenquellen*)[299] must take the necessary precautions to protect others,[300] in accordance with the circumstances. However, as the "legitimate expectations of safety" ("*berechtigte Verkehrserwartungen*") are not aimed at protecting against all conceivable dangers,[301] the safety duty would be limited to adopting measures that were reasonable in the general circumstances and that a reasonable and prudent individual would consider necessary and sufficient to protect the physical integrity of others.[302]

---

[297] Wilhelmi (2009), p. 154; Niebaum (2003), pp. 159–164; Dörner (2002), p. 120.

[298] NJW 1990, 1236.

[299] There is no fundamental prohibition on putting another individual in danger. What is crucial is that the precautions deemed necessary and sufficient by a prudent and reasonably cautious individual to safeguard others from potential harm are duly observed (Thüß (2012), p. 85).

[300] Mayr (2015), p. 137.

[301] A mere theoretical possibility of danger does not give rise to safety obligations. Rather, there must be concrete evidence of a risk for the individual responsible for ensuring safety (Fuchs et al. (2017), p. 107).

[302] According to Spindler, in principle, the individual who controls the source of danger has safety duties if experience demonstrates that improper conduct by third parties is foreseeable (Spindler (2011), p. 30).

The BGH stated that it is irrelevant whether the provisions of the state of *Niedersachsen's* construction regulations specifically mandate protection for the cover grids, as they only set general requirements for light well linings. According to the court, these duties under construction laws are not decisive, as the civil prohibition against endangering public safety is, by its nature, often more comprehensive than the duties imposed by state construction regulations. This leads to the conclusion that a pit must be protected against unauthorized removal, potentially more rigorously than what is required under the construction laws.[303]

In Brazilian law, various scenarios of accidents can be considered where the state, although responsible for the maintenance of public roads, fails to meet its duty adequately, resulting in non-pecuniary and physical damage to passersby or residents. Once the action of a third party interfering with the measures taken by the state is proven, the question arises whether this third party should be held liable for the injuries suffered or if the responsibility lies solely with the intervening third party. It is common in cases where the state exercises, in some way, its duty to maintain public roads but does so inadequately, allowing third parties to remove or damage manhole covers or other protections, thereby causing harm to pedestrians and drivers.

In a case decided by the 3rd Civil Court of the District of Feira de Santana/BA,[304] the plaintiff recounted an accident that occurred on April 09, 1999, when his bicycle collided with an open "storm drain" (manhole), causing him to be violently thrown to the ground, resulting in quadriplegia. He subsequently sued the local water and sanitation company. The defendant company was ordered to pay compensation for non-pecuniary and material damages. One of the grounds for the decision was that a concessionaire company cannot place inspection wells with covers that can be easily removed, thus exposing users to the risk of falls and accidents. In a similar case, where an individual fell into an open manhole in a shopping center parking lot, the Court of Justice of the State of São Paulo[305] held

[303] Deutsch presents a controversial example: A landowner digs a hole but fails to secure it. A third party then pushes a passerby into the excavation, causing them to break their leg (Deutsch (1996), p. 108). Ristow observes that, according to Deutsch, the intention behind the second perpetrator's actions excludes the negligence of the first act. The deliberate intervention of the second perpetrator would "break" the causal chain, as long as the first party neither created the specific risk nor had the duty to prevent the subsequent act (Ristow (2003), p. 165). The scope of the duty of care of the first causer is primarily concerned with the need to protect public safety. This duty is sufficiently satisfied if the first perpetrator is only required to take precautions against the risk of accidents arising from the dug pit. However, if a second perpetrator exploits the situation created by the excavation with the intent to deliberately harm a third party, the original causer cannot be held liable for failing to foresee or prevent this possibility (Forst (2000), p. 202). Von Bar confirms that the first perpetrator negligently violated a safety duty. However, he contends that whether this duty also extends to protecting passersby from criminals remains an unanswered question. The answer would likely be no, as such a danger does not appear sufficiently obvious to ground liability. Liability would only arise if such an act could have been anticipated or if the excavation of the well had "provoked" the offender (Bar (von 1980), p. 166).

[304] TJBA, Proc. no. 0011644–11.2002.8.05.0080, j. 25.03.2019.

[305] TJSP, ApCív 0025551–43.2004.26.0001, rel. José Luiz Mônaco da Silva, j. 12.08.2015.

that it would not be reasonable to attribute exclusive fault to a third party, even if the cover had been removed by a passerby prior to the accident.

In another case, however, decided by the Court of Justice of Santa Catarina,[306] the defendants were held responsible for the removal of an iron manhole cover located on a public road, which had been replaced with stones, causing a motorcyclist to fall. The municipality was not held liable, as it did not contribute to the harmful event. The court's decision included a passage in which it was emphasized that the protective grid remained in place due to the defendants' actions, as it was made of iron and was quite heavy. The court also noted that there was no obligation for the municipality to install seals that would prevent the grid from being removed by human force, considering that the opening needed to be made quickly in emergencies, such as during floods.

In cases of omission of safety precautions, the first party must be held liable for the damages caused to the victim, even if there is intervention by a second causer who removes the protective equipment. This is because the individual who creates or originates the danger, even without fault,[307] becomes responsible for taking preventive measures aimed at protecting other individuals, including from the interference of third parties. It is a duty of care to safeguard the place that poses a risk to passersby, such as in the case of manholes, by installing safeguarding devices against the interference of third parties.

However, it cannot be conceived that the equipment provides protection against all possible dangers, but only against those from which protection is expected according to the legitimate expectations of safety. For this reason, the decision made by the Court of Justice of Santa Catarina (TJSC) in the aforementioned case[308] seems correct, as the protective grid was made of iron and was heavy, making it difficult for third parties to act. The absence of a seal is justified by the need to handle the object in cases of emergency.

It is concluded that the interference of a third party, as a rule, does not "interrupt" the causal link existing between the creation of a source of danger and the materialization of the damage, since whoever originates the risk has the duty to eliminate it or reduce the chances of its realization using proportional and reasonable means. It is clearly assured to the initial causer the right to sue the party who removed the existing protection, giving rise to the occurrence of the damage.

5.2.2.2 Cases of Interference with Preexisting Safety Measures

This group of cases is distinguished by the fact that the first party interferes with a preexisting safety measure. The second causer exploits the weakened safety condition and damages the legal interest that was previously protected. The

[306] TJSC, ApCív 201000836255, rel. João Henrique Blasi, j. 15.05.2012.

[307] Miranda (1984), p. 194.

[308] TJSC, CivApp 201000836255, rel. João Henrique Blasi, j. 15.05.2012.

owner of the property is a third party who demands compensation from the first party for the losses incurred, since the second causer is unknown. Also in this category, the second perpetrator will cause the damage intentionally.[309]

In a case decided by the BGH,[310] on October 3, 1978, a military-armored vehicle destroyed part of a pasture fence that enclosed a farmer's cattle, resulting in the escape of the animals that had been confined. Some of these were never found, as they were allegedly stolen and slaughtered by unknown individuals.[311] The BGH held the owner of the armored vehicle liable.[312]

Although the "provocation criterion" ("*Kriterium der Herausforderung*") was discussed in this decision, it was not the determining factor for attributing the damages to the defendant. As already stated, the BGH established that this formula should only be used in cases of a two-person relationship (*Zweipersonenverhältnis*), in which the first wrongdoer, through reprehensible conduct, must have provided the injured party (second individual) with a justifiable motive, at least to some extent. As a result, the provocation formula could only be applied when the intervening party injures themselves. For this reason, the German court emphasized that the indicated criterion would not have been applicable in this case, as it involves a free decision of a third party, but not of the intervener themselves.[313]

Setting aside the provocation criterion, the BGH primarily relies on the basis of the violation of duty by the one who caused the destruction of the fence, further grounding liability under the aspect of increased danger. Certainly, the risk of theft increases when the cattle graze freely, without any form of protection. It is more probable that an "opportunistic thief" ("*Gelegenheitsdieb*") would appropriate cattle that roam in open areas or enter their stable than those that graze in fenced lands.[314] Liability will generally result, according to the BGH, from the fact that a third party's unlawful act was not prevented or was even facilitated.[315]

Hans Stoll[316] maintains that the attribution of losses stemming from the stolen cows to the individual responsible for damaging the fence is open to debate. He points out the challenge of determining liability for subsequent harm that arises from the increased risk faced by the injured party due to the initial event but only materializes through the intentional or even criminal actions of third parties. The decisive factor, according to the author, lies in determining whether the risk of intervention remains within the injurer's control. Thus, the solution becomes more

---

[309] Ristow (2003), pp. 172–173.

[310] NJW 1979, 712.

[311] Traditionally, legal doctrine questions whether there is a causal link between the violation of property and the loss of cows. The issue lies in whether the claimed loss falls within the scope of protection of the violated norm, thus being an element of imputation (Zimmermann and Kleinschmidt (2007), pp. 594–595).

[312] Flume (2019), pp. 1313–1314; Greger (1985), p. 31.

[313] Ristow (2003), pp. 173–174.

[314] Zhang (2016), p. 130.

[315] Dunz (1989), p. 136.

[316] Stoll (1993), pp. 406–407.

evident if the wrongdoer, after forcibly entering the locked room of a motor yacht, takes some objects and leaves the door open upon departure, enabling other offenders to seize additional items from the yacht.[317]

The case of the pasture fence differs from the case of the yacht room, decided by the *Landgericht* Lübeck, due to the "lesser degree of unlawfulness" in the first conduct, combined with the fact that the risk of a subsequent theft would not be as evident in this scenario. A fence is not a serious obstacle to the criminal actions of thieves. Thus, this case corresponds more closely to a "double-offence" (*Doppeldelikte*),[318] in which the wrongdoer acts unlawfully[319] against different legal interests of the same individual.[320]

In such cases, Stoll[321] observes that when the first wrongdoer is also considered liable for the consequential damages,[322] all the prerequisites for the establishment of liability must be fulfilled regarding subsequent violations. A decisive aspect in these situations is evaluating to what extent the initial perpetrator can be expected to take precautions against undue interference.

[317] The Landgericht Lübeck decided that, under the circumstances described above, there would be an adequate causal connection between the first and second theft (LG Lübeck *VersR* 1976, 104).

[318] The investigation undertaken by M. L. Müller provides the example of someone rolling a stone block down a mountainside, unforeseeably killing a dog. Although, according to the dominant doctrine, this individual would not be responsible for the animal's death, the solution would differ if the owner of both the dog and the stone block were the same. In this case, the subjective foreseeability of subsequent consequences would not be necessary. However, such liability would be internally unfounded, as the possible identity of the protected person could not justify extending liability (Sourlas (1974), p. 85).

[319] According to Stoll, the causal sequence of violations should not obscure the fact that the behavior of the first perpetrator endangers, from the outset, various legal goods and is therefore unlawful for two reasons. This, in the words of the German author, is an "ideal competition" ("*Idealkonkurrenz*") of various offenses against the same individual, but not the reinforcement of the primary offense through subsequent violations (Stoll (1968), p. 30).

[320] Hans Stoll's proposal does not provide a reliable criterion for solving practical cases, as there is no clear way to distinguish a "double-offense" scenario from a case where the second injury should be considered a subsequent injury to the first (Reinig (2015), p. 218).

[321] In these cases, the first violation would consist of a "casual passing station" ("*zufällige Durchgangsstation*") in the causal course between the initial damage and the subsequent injuries (Stoll (1993), p. 407). These cases are treated by Esser and Schmidt as "successive double violations" ("*hintereinandergeschaltene Doppelverletzung*"), where the transgression of one right or legal interest also affects another protected interest. According to the authors, it would be sufficient for the subsequent violation to still be covered by unlawfulness (Esser and Schmidt (1993), p. 214).

[322] The issue of whether the concept of "consequent damage" is exclusively logical-causal or should be understood in a normative-evaluative sense is problematic. Lange and Schiemann emphasize that the cases, referred to as "*Doppeldelikte*" in German doctrine, in which the transgression of a second legal good can be considered both independent and a consequence of the first violation, are critical (Lange and Schiemann (2003), p. 68). The issue of "*Doppeldelikte*" is also mentioned by Gotzler (1977), p. 43.

The author cites a case decided by the *Court of Appeal* of England,[323] in which, during plumbing and sewage works carried out by the defendant, a pipe was damaged, causing water to leak into the foundations of the house, rendering it uninhabitable. The plaintiffs abandoned the residence, and some homeless people trespassed onto the property. The owners initially managed to expel the invaders. However, a few months later, the homeless returned to the property and caused significant damage, burning wooden items and ripping out the installations.

The court rejected the claim for damages caused by the invaders. Lord Denning stated that, regardless of possible legal considerations of liability limitation, the issue ultimately rested on a matter of judicial policy.[324] The court considered it inappropriate to hold the defendant liable for the damages caused by the homeless, as the claimants could have protected themselves against these losses by taking out insurance.[325]

The two cases cited (pasture fence and property invasion) require different solutions. In both scenarios, natural causation is evident, as without the occurrence of the initial injuries, the subsequent events, according to normal rules of experience, would not have materialized. Similarly, the adequacy of the cause can be affirmed, as the initial events cannot be considered entirely irrelevant to the occurrence of consequential damages.

However, in the case of the pasture fence, the function of the barrier was precisely to protect against potential thefts and losses of the animals, so the destruction of the safeguard significantly increased the risk of livestock loss.[326] It is irrelevant whether the cows were stolen or drowned in a nearby river.[327] Similarly, the initial offender would not be exonerated if the animals were struck by a high-speed vehicle. What matters is that the offender created a high-risk situation, which should have been prevented by the presence of the fence but materialized due to its destruction, this danger falling within the protective scope of the rule (safeguarding against the loss of animals).

In contrast, the invasion of the residence should not be interpreted as resulting from the specific risk originating from the flooding; rather, it reflects a general risk to life.

---

[323] *Lamb. v. Camden London Borough Council*, [1981] Q.B. 625.

[324] The case is stated as a relevant example of the significant influence of judicial policy considerations in determining issues of causal intervention. The decision makes clear that there was no good reason or motive to transfer the costs to the state, as the plaintiffs should have adequately insured the property or protected it in some other way against the risks of invasion. The responsibility to secure the property against risks should fall on the owners (Hodgson (2008), p. 262).

[325] This outcome arises from the principle that, under most circumstances, an individual should not be held liable for another's conduct, unless the former bears some moral responsibility to protect the latter (Cane and Atiyah (2013), p. 127).

[326] The analysis examines whether the vehicle occupants could have taken measures to prevent the animals from escaping, such as repairing the fence or creating an obstacle to the cattle's passage. It is emphasized that the driver of the armored vehicle failed to take any safety measures, thus violating a duty of care, even though such measures appeared both possible and reasonable (Zhang (2016), p. 155).

[327] Zimmermann (1980), p. 15.

The provision requiring safety measures during plumbing and sewage works is intended to prevent structural damage to houses, not to mitigate the risk of future invasions by homeless individuals. Schiemann,[328] when comparing the case of the green strip and the pasture fence, makes similar considerations, stating that the distinction between them is justified, as traffic jams on the highway are frequent and not necessarily caused by culpable accidents. Therefore, the increased temptation to violate traffic rules in moments of congestion is not an exclusive consequence of such conditions. By contrast, in the case of cattle theft, the increased risk directly results from the removal of the pasture fence, as it enables the animals to escape.

It should be emphasized that the criterion of controllability does not constitute a decisive factor in the attribution or exclusion of liability. In both the case of property invasion and the theft of cows by a third party, the unfolding of events is no longer controllable by the initial wrongdoer. Nevertheless, the solutions are different in the two cases. In the first, it was stated that there is no liability on the part of the individual in charge of the plumbing and sewage services. In the second scenario, the damages were attributed to the individual who destroyed the fence.[329] The determining criterion for liability in these cases is the materialization of the specific risk created by the initial wrongdoer, due to their failure to exercise the duties of care required by the situation.

Another case of intentional third-party intervention was decided by the BGH[330] on December 19, 1996, resulting from an accident involving a vehicle transporting money. A car driver caused a traffic accident, colliding with the cash transporter while trying to overtake in the opposite lane.[331] The driver and the passenger of the transport vehicle left the armored car and received medical treatment on-site. The vehicle's doors were damaged. It was then taken to the police station. The next day, it was discovered that two money boxes, containing approximately 256,570.50 German marks, had disappeared.[332]

The plaintiffs, two insurance companies, claimed that the money was stolen by third parties at the accident site. The defendant argued that the funds were only taken after the police had taken custody of the transport vehicle.[333] According to the BGH, the accident perpetrator's liability for the loss of the two money boxes should be affirmed if the amount was stolen on the street. By contrast, such attribution could not be established if the loss occurred after the custody of the vehicle had been transferred to the police authorities. The German court held that the consequences of the damage cannot be attributed to the first wrongdoer if the risk of injury from the initial behavior did not materialize and the connection between the acts of the first and second individuals proved to be merely external and accidental.

328 Schiemann (2017), p. 95.

329 BGH JZ 1979, 33.

330 NJW 1997, 865.

331 Fuchs et al. (2017), p. 102.

332 Schlechtriem and Schmidt-Kessel (2005), p. 156.

333 Fuchs et al. (2017), p. 102.

In the opinion of the BGH, theft and robbery are normal consequences of an accident involving the transport of valuable objects, provided that the facts are beyond the victim's control. The court pointed out that such a causal sequence is not uncommon. On the contrary, it is even more frequent that third parties will have access to the cargo if a vehicle transporting valuables loses its technical and personnel safeguards in a traffic accident,[334] becoming unprotected and freely accessible to outsiders. It can be concluded, as Min Zhang does,[335] that the BGH applied the theory of adequacy to the case, since its decision was based on the assessment of whether the damage in question could be considered common or uncommon, given the circumstances of the specific case. At no point was the criterion of provocation (*Kriterium der Herausforderung*) invoked or discussed.

In this specific case, it was decided that the accident perpetrator should be held responsible.[336] As a result of the attempt to pass another vehicle in violation of traffic rules, and the damages caused to the transport vehicle, the safeguard[337] that this car offered as a "special vehicle" ("*Spezialfahrzeug*") to the two money bags was lost. Furthermore, the accident rendered the driver and the passenger unable to perform their guard duties in relation to the lost funds due to the injuries sustained. Only with the elimination of the twofold security of the cargo was it possible for the money to be stolen at the accident site.[338]

Cargo theft following vehicle collisions is frequent in Brazil, particularly in cases involving freight trucks. In a case judged by the Court of Justice of the State of Pernambuco,[339] the insurer, subrogated to the rights of the insured, sought compensation for the losses resulting from a road collision, which led to the looting of the cargo by locals after the truck overturned. The court decided, without further analysis, that the causal link between the accident perpetrator's conduct and the

---

[334] A case closely resembling the scenario of eliminating the safeguards of the injured party is that of a victim who is negligently injured by a first aggressor and subsequently attacked and robbed by a third party, precisely because they are physically incapacitated due to the previous injury. The same question may arise when the first perpetrator negligently injures someone, who is then robbed by a third party while lying unconscious. In Koziol's view, in both cases, the first party could not be held liable for the robbery, as the intentional infliction of harm goes beyond the fault of the original offender, which was only related to the first injury (Koziol (2012), p. 288). It is also argued that a driver who hits a pedestrian cannot be held responsible for the theft of the victim's wallet while they are injured and lying on the ground (Rogers et al. (1998), p. 229). The question concerns the perpetrator exploiting the situation created by the first perpetrator. This becomes particularly clear in the example where an individual, unconscious due to an accident, is robbed on their way to the hospital. Another commonly reported case involves the assault committed against a cashier or night watchman, which the aggressor only dares to carry out because the victim has a physical disability caused by the first wrongdoer (Friese (1968), p. 245).

[335] Zhang (2016), p. 127.

[336] Brüggemeier (2006), p. 344.

[337] Mayr (2015), p. 292.

[338] Niebaum (2003), p. 179.

[339] TJPE, ApCív 0001981–27.2014.8.17.0260, rel. José Viana Ulisses Filho, j. 24.05.2017.

damage extended only to the harm suffered by the vehicle involved in the collision. Since third parties looted the cargo, liability for the stolen goods could not be attributed to the initial perpetrator.

By contrast, the Court of Justice of the State of Santa Catarina[340] held the accident perpetrator liable for the theft of the cargo by unauthorized individuals. Applying the theory of adequate causation and citing the doctrine of Fernando Noronha, the court asserted that a causal relationship is established whenever the damage cannot be regarded as an extraordinary consequence unrelated to the act attributed to the responsible party. Immediately thereafter, however, it was stated that, since the cargo had been dumped, the most direct and determining cause of the damaging event (the theft of goods) was the accident itself.

In cases of theft following car accidents, the specific circumstances must be assessed. If a doctor, after providing first aid to a patient on the side of the road, leaves his belongings on a barrier and they are taken by a passerby, he cannot demand compensation for the loss from the collision perpetrator,[341] as the accident did not create the risk of theft. In this case, a general risk of life materialized, to which the professional would also be subject in other situations.

The assessment should differ in cases of cargo theft following the overturning of a truck due to a prior negligent collision. In such instances, it is not reasonable to argue that the actions of unknown individuals "interrupted" the causal chain between the initial conduct and the harmful result. Even less persuasive is the claim that the loss of goods resulted from the materialization of a general risk inherent to the activity. By causing the truck to overturn, the negligent driver intensified the specific risk of cargo loss, eliminating its existing safeguards, which justifies attributing liability to him.[342] To avoid disproportionate solutions, such as minor negligence by the driver leading to the theft of an exceptionally valuable cargo, the application of Art. 944, sole paragraph, of the Civil Code (CC/02) is appropriate.

The same reasoning applies to a vehicle transporting valuables that is struck and, shortly thereafter, a sum of money is taken by passersby due to the absence of protection. The removal of existing security measures increases the specific risk of furtive actions by third parties at the accident site, but not in secured locations, such as a police station.[343] If the theft occurs within the police station itself, there is no

[340] TJSC, EI 2010.064444–9, rel. Ronei Danielli, j. 13.12.2012.

[341] BGH NJW 1997, 865.

[342] This does not mean that the carrier should be exempt from responsibility to the contractor for any damages caused. The collision, and the subsequent theft of the goods, fall within the risks assumed by the service provider, as outlined in the safety clause inherent to the transport contract. The collision of the vehicle is merely an internal fortuity, which does not relieve the carrier from initially bearing the expenses incurred by the owner of the lost cargo. As concluded in Sect. 4.2, in cases involving three parties, even if the second party's (carrier's) liability is recognized, the injured party (recipient of the cargo) may still sue the first party (causer of the accident). However, if the carrier compensates the injured party, they may subsequently seek recourse from the causer of the accident.

[343] BGH NJW 1997, 865.

basis for attributing liability to the perpetrator of the accident, as the risk initially created was subsequently neutralized when the vehicle was taken to the station.

It should not be overlooked that, as already stated (see Sect. 3.2.5), the scope of the rule can also be investigated under its modal perspective.[344] Not all forms of violations and damages fall within the protective sphere of the norm.[345] The liability of the accident perpetrator is limited to situations where the theft occurs on the street. If the monetary values are misappropriated at the police station or another secured location, there is no basis to assert an internal connection between the consequences of the initial act and the subsequent losses. In this case, the specific risk generated by the first wrongdoer cannot be said to have materialized.

5.2.2.3 Cases that Correspond to Two-person Relationships

Till Ristow[346] identifies hypotheses that closely resemble situations involving two individuals. With a slight change in the factual circumstances, cases involving only two individuals can be transformed into scenarios with three individuals.[347] According to the author, the same criteria should be applied to this group of cases as to the hypotheses already analyzed, as there is no fundamental difference, in terms of liability, whether the injured party is the second wrongdoer himself or a third party.[348]

---

[344] The case of Kegeljung, decided by LG Hannover (Recht 1910, 36), involved a business owner who allowed a boy, who collected bowling pins, to work at night, contrary to child protection regulations. The young man was injured due to the unruly behavior of the players and sued the owner. The violated regulations were intended to protect young people from health damage due to overexertion, but not from injuries that had no material and internal connection (*sachlich-innere*) with night work (Lange (1960), p. 40). Sourlas, providing more details of the case, reports that the 13-year-old boy was hired to work after eight o'clock at night, but was injured by a ball thrown before this time (Sourlas (1974), p. 20).

[345] A claim for compensation is only justified if the law intended to prevent damage to the legal interest in the exact way it occurred. This congruence between the purpose of the norm and the type of damage is necessary for characterizing liability (Wolf (1962), p. 22).

[346] Niebaum (2003), pp. 183–187.

[347] The Oberlandesgericht Düsseldorf (OLG Düsseldorf *NJW* 1978, 2036) decided a case where two horsemen were caring for two horses for the same woman. One day, one of the horsemen decided to take the animal along a path that was not entirely safe, and was subsequently followed by the second horseman. The first horseman's horse fell into a ditch. When attempting to assist his companion, the second horseman saw his own animal escape and get hit by a locomotive. The Düsseldorf court rejected the compensation claim against the first professional, as the risky action of the first horseman was merely considered a bad example for his colleague (Schiemann (2017), p. 92). For a critical analysis of the decision, see Mohrenfels (von 1979), pp. 775–778.

[348] In a rescue case (LG Hannover *VersR* 1986, 48), a motorcyclist had an accident and was seriously injured, leading the police to request the use of a rescue helicopter. However, when the helicopter landed in a pasture, 72 cows belonging to a farmer panicked, resulting in many of the animals having to be slaughtered. The *Landgericht* denied the motorcyclist's liability, as it did not find gross negligence on the part of the first wrongdoer in this case. Min Zhang criticizes the court's position. According to the author, the LG Hannover did not exclude the causal connection, stating that the rescue operation was not merely due to the operation of the motorcycle, but rather to the probable and possible injuries of the

A relevant example is the case decided by *Oberlandesgericht* Frankfurt in 1981, 786, where a physician provided first aid to an injured individual who had caused a traffic accident. While assisting the victim, the professional hung his valuable watch on a railing. The object was ultimately stolen by a passerby.[349] The German court correctly rejected the claim for compensation.[350]

Although it is possible to affirm natural causation, as the theft would not have occurred without the negligently caused accident, and the adequacy of the cause, since the occurrence of the damage was not beyond all probability, it is not appropriate to conclude that the initial incident created or increased the specific risk of the rescuer's property being lost, but rather that it constituted a general risk of life, making the doctor responsible for the loss. The loss of the property could have occurred in various other circumstances and should not be classified as the materialization of a specific rescue-related risk, but rather as a general risk to which everyone is exposed. Traffic regulations are designed to safeguard the physical and property integrity of drivers and pedestrians, not to encompass events lacking an internal connection[351] to the accident.

Cases of medical treatment, as already discussed, can also be regarded as instances of rescue,[352] as a patient's health and life would be at considerable risk if the professional failed to provide the necessary assistance. It is quite common for a patient to initially receive negligent medical treatment, suffer harm as a result, and then turn to a second specialist who subsequently causes further injury.[353]

In the decision of June 3, 1921,[354] the *Reichsgericht* addressed the case of a patient who, after receiving treatment for pain following a fall from a first doctor who diagnosed only rheumatism in the knee, was later attended by a second physician who identified a dislocation in the right hip joint and attempted, without success, to resolve the issue.[355] According to the Court of the Reich, it was possible to establish an adequate causal relationship between the incorrect treatment by the first doctor and the physical harm suffered by the patient. Such a causal link would

victim. Furthermore, the driver's slight negligence could not be dismissed, even though gross negligence was not established. The author argues that attributing liability to the initial perpetrator for the damages suffered by the farmer seemed reasonable (Zhang (2016), pp. 108–109).

[349] Lange and Schiemann (2003), p. 145; Forst (2000), p. 41.

[350] Finke (2006), p. 145.

[351] Lange (1960), p. 53.

[352] Grünenberg (2020), p. 294; Ekkenga and Kuntz (2014), p. 86. On the contrary, Esser and Schmidt classify cases of "psychological causation" into three groups: a) persecution cases (*Verfolgungsfälle*); b) green strip cases (*Grünstreifenfälle*); and c) hospital cases (*Krankenhausfälle*) (Esser and Schmidt (1993), pp. 219–222).

[353] German jurisprudence generally extends liability for damages caused by incorrect medical treatment, similar to the approach typically seen in the United States. In contrast, English jurisprudence holds that liability is only applicable in cases involving intentional torts (Lüer (1969), p. 152).

[354] RGZ 102, 230.

[355] The patient in the hospital received inadequate treatment, though not grossly incompetent (Hart and Honoré (1985), p. 492).

only be dismissed if the second physician had grossly disregarded medical standards and expertise.[356]

In the decision issued on September 20, 1988, the BGH[357] followed the same approach as the *Reichsgericht*. In this case, after an initial incorrect treatment, the patient experienced a locking of the middle finger, preventing flexion at an angle of 50 degrees. The second doctor performed corrective surgery but accidentally severed the claimant's tendons, requiring four additional operations.

According to the BGH, the attribution of the first medical professional's liability was based on the adequacy of the cause,[358] since the abnormal condition of the finger, as well as the subsequent corrective operations, was presented as an effect caused by the initial treatment.[359] The risk of a second operation was also not considered unusual. The second doctor, still according to the German court, should only be held liable if the subsequent harm did not have an internal causal connection with the initial act of treatment.[360]

Another case widely discussed by German doctrine is that of the diverticulum,[361] where an individual, after a traffic accident caused by another driver, had to be hospitalized and undergo abdominal surgery. During the operation, a diverticulum, unrelated to the accident, was discovered in the small intestine and removed by the surgeon based on the presumed consent of the patient. Due to surgical complications, the patient died.[362] The surviving wife demanded the payment of a pension by the responsible party. Although the BGH[363] recognized the natural causation of the events, it rejected the liability[364] of the individual who caused the accident on the grounds that an adequate causal link between the

---

[356] In the case of gross negligence, the act of the second doctor would be considered a *novus actus interveniens* (Giesen (1988), p. 187). German courts apply the same principle to errors committed by lawyers (Hart and Honoré (1985), p. 492).

[357] NJW 1989, 767.

[358] Deutsch and Spickhoff (2014), p. 416.

[359] The prevailing view is that the risk of negligent medical treatment qualifies as one of the specific risks encompassed by the initial medical tortious act. The BGH affirmed the liability of the accident causer when the victim, due to the injury, was vaccinated with a lethal dose of tetanus as a preventive measure for future cases (*Tetanusfall* or *Impfschadenfall*). Lüer also cites the case where a traffic accident victim accidentally had their right leg amputated, even though only their left limb had been affected, and the case of the dentist who, while treating the patient's pain, extracted the wrong tooth (Lüer (1969), p. 153).

[360] Lange and Schiemann, referring to the analyzed case, also assert that the first doctor could be held liable for subsequent damages caused by another professional (Lange and Schiemann (2003), p. 145).

[361] Zimmermann (1980), p. 14.

[362] Huber (1969), p. 677.

[363] NJW 57, 1475.

[364] Larenz (1987), p. 450.

collision and the victim's death as a result of the medical procedure was not established.[365]

Larenz[366] correctly argues that the decision was justified, but the basis used by the BGH is not convincing. The court's assertion that the consequence should not be beyond any internal connection with the injury derived from the accident already shows that adequacy is not the decisive criterion for resolving the case. From the perspective of the theory of adequacy, the BGH should have questioned only whether performing a new surgical intervention (removal of the diverticulum) during the operation necessitated by the accident constituted an unforeseeable and extraordinary result, even for an "optimal observer" ("*optimaler Beobachter*"). The answer, according to Larenz, would have been debatable, leading to legal uncertainty.

While in the first two cases (knee rheumatism and locking of the finger), the specific risk created by the medical error materialized, as the patient had to undergo a new treatment, which may not have been successful. In the case of the diverticulum, the first professional should not be held liable for the consequences caused by the second intervention, since the discovery of the abdominal issue and the need for surgery cannot be considered the materialization of the risks arising from the traffic accident, there being only an external connection between the events.[367] The discovery of the intestinal disease presented itself as the materialization of a "general life risk", not related to the initial accident.

In support of the present arguments, reference may be made to the "cerebral arteriosclerosis case" ("*Hirnarteriosklerose-Fall*") (BGH JZ 1969, 702). Due to an accident, the victim, who worked as a barrier guard (*Schrankenwärter*), had to undergo medical examinations. During these examinations, it was discovered that he had cerebral arteriosclerosis, so his retirement was brought forward, as the disease prevented him from continuing to work normally. The party sought compensation due to the reduction of his monthly income, which would not have occurred if the accident had not taken place. The BGH found the cause to be appropriate but, using the theory of the scope of the norm, decided that the prohibition of bodily harm is not intended to protect the individual against the discovery of diseases that had remained hidden until then.[368]

The reasoning of the BGH clearly shows that the formula of adequacy can be varied as desired ("[...] *man mag die Adäquanzformel variieren wie man will*

[365] For an analysis of the case from the perspective of the theory of equivalence of conditions, see Fuchs et al. (2017), pp. 396–397.

[366] Larenz (1970), pp. 86–87.

[367] Killinger (2009), p. 282; Gründel (2000), p. 233.

[368] The peculiarity of the case lies in the fact that the subsequent intervention causing the damage is lawful. According to Reinig, this is not a new intervention in the victim's legal sphere, but merely a reflection of an already-established harmful interference in their assets. Therefore, the real reason for denying compensation would be the criterion of the legitimacy of the compensatory claim. The victim's subjective interest would not be considered legitimate (Reinig (2018), p. 289).

[. . .]"),[369] thereby necessitating additional criteria for imputation in order to limit the liability of the first perpetrator. The theory of adequacy, applied in isolation, both in Germany and in Brazil, cannot safely resolve a series of cases, so other criteria, such as the analysis of the materialization of the typical or specific risk of the activity, as well as the scope of the violated norm, may be used as ways of establishing imputation. It is important to note that the legal parameters for the attribution of responsibility are not intended to broaden liability but, on the contrary, to limit the sphere of compensable injuries.

5.3 Summary

The analysis of "psychologically mediated causation" in Brazilian law requires an approach that surpasses the isolated application of traditional causal theories. Although natural causal connection and adequate causation are necessary prerequisites, they are not sufficient to solve complex cases where one party, through their conduct, psychologically influences the behavior of another, who then causes harm to themselves or others.

To solve this issue, it is necessary to incorporate complementary criteria of objective imputation, which allow not only the existence of a causal link to be assessed but also the very normative justification of liability. Criteria such as the purpose of protection of the norm, the materialization of the specific risk, the proportionality of the act committed, the self-responsibility of the second causer, and the position of authority of the initial perpetrator should be applied in a combined way, allowing more refined solutions.

The German jurisprudential experience offers important parameters for the development of this approach in Brazilian law. The systematization of cases into categories, according to their common characteristics, allows for identifying which imputation criteria are most relevant for each type of situation. This classification, far from being merely academic, has crucial practical importance in guiding judicial decisions.

The increasing complexity of social relations makes this refinement of causal analysis even more relevant. Phenomena such as the spread of fake news, the role of digital influencers, and the psychological impact of major environmental disasters show how psychologically mediated causation assumes new dimensions in contemporary society, demanding adequate criteria for its legal evaluation.

In the first category of injury to one's own interests by the second causer, the cases of rescue and pursuit have as central criteria the proportionality of the act and the materialization of the specific risk. The rescuer who injures himself while trying to save someone must have acted proportionally to the danger faced, because if he assumes moderate risk to save a life, the initial causer's liability is grounded,

[369] Huber (1969), p. 677.

but if he exposes himself to extreme risk for interests of reduced legal value, his compensation may be reduced or excluded. The damage must result from the risk created by the initial situation, since injuries from circumstances unrelated to the rescue, such as tripping on the pavement, constitute a "general life risk" and do not give rise to liability. For professionals such as police officers and firefighters, the criterion of professional risk is also applied, excluding the imputation of typical damages inherent to the activity, such as burns during firefighting.

In cases of intervention by a position of authority, the criteria for the existence of special knowledge of the first perpetrator and the impairment of the decision-making autonomy of the second party are essential. A doctor who recommends inappropriate treatment with hydroxychloroquine for COVID-19 can be held liable if they established a trust relationship that effectively reduced the patient's freedom of choice. By contrast, a mere digital influencer who opines about treatments does not, as a rule, create a position of authority sufficient to compromise the autonomy of their followers, unless directed at a particularly vulnerable audience.

For situations involving intervention due to the duty of danger control, the central factors are the violation of duties of care and the creation of a specific risk that materializes in harm. An adult who hands over explosive chemicals to a minor under the age of 15, who subsequently injures himself by mixing them, is liable for the damage as they created a specific risk by making a dangerous substance available to an individual without adequate maturity. The case differs when two teenagers together decide to conduct dangerous experiments, as the victim's voluntary participation in the risky arrangement attracts the risks to himself. In the case of the couple who stored caustic soda in a bottle with a danger warning, there was no violation of general duties of care when the painter ingested the product by mistake, as the container was labeled and the damage resulted from a general risk assumed by the worker when consuming a drink during work.

In cases of self-harm, including suicides after disasters or due to fake news, the fundamental elements are the degree of impairment of the victim's autonomy and the materialization of the specific risk. In the case of Fukushima, the company was held liable for the suicide of a resident, as the nuclear disaster and forced evacuation created a situation of intense stress that compromised her decision-making capacity. The victim's predisposition or prior vulnerability does not necessarily exclude imputation, as in the case of the student who committed suicide after being targeted by fake news, with the aggressor aware of her emotional fragility.

In the second category of damages caused to third parties, the main criteria for cases of omission of safety precautions are the violation of duties of care and the legitimate expectations of protection. The organizer of an event with 50,000 people who does not provide adequate safety is liable for the damages caused by spectators who invade and damage neighboring properties, as the risk of such attacks is foreseeable at events of this magnitude. On the contrary, damages caused by the undisciplined behavior of drivers who use the side lane to bypass an accident are not attributable to the cause of the collision, as they constitute a "general risk of traffic."

For interference with preexisting safety measures, the essential factors are the purpose of the safeguard that was removed and the connection between the risk and the damage. In the case of the military vehicle that destroyed a pasture fence, allowing the theft of animals, there was liability, as the function of the fence was precisely to protect against this specific risk. Similarly, in the case of the armored transport vehicle that was hit and had money stolen shortly after the accident, the perpetrator was liable for the damages, as he eliminated the double protection (physical and human) designed to prevent exactly this type of loss.

In cases of subsequent medical treatment, the situation is analyzed where a first doctor acts negligently, causing harm to the patient and requiring consultation with a second specialist who subsequently causes additional injuries. Essential are the criteria of the internal connection between events and the materialization of the specific risk. For example, when the first doctor fails to identify a hip dislocation, misdiagnosing it as rheumatism, he is liable for the damages of the subsequent unsuccessful treatment, as this was necessary due to the initial error. Conversely, if during surgery necessary after a traffic accident, a preexisting unrelated disease is discovered and treated, such as diverticulitis, any complications are not attributable to the cause of the collision, as they represent the materialization of a risk unrelated to the initial event.

In all groups, the analysis of the parties' risk sphere allows the extent of liability to be calibrated. The appropriate combination of these criteria, according to the peculiarities of each case, is fundamental to achieving balanced solutions in a matter as complex as psychologically mediated causation.

References

Ahrens HJ, Spickhoff A (2022) Deliktsrecht: mit Wirtschaftsdeliktsrecht Großes Lehrbuch. C. H. Beck, München

Amato G (2022) Influenciadores brasileiros são investigados em Portugal por auxílio à imigração ilegal: páginas e perfis nas redes sociais que incentivam mudança para o país viraram um filão. O Globo. https://oglobo.globo.com/blogs/portugal-giro/post/2022/07/influenciadores-brasileiros-sao-investigados-em-portugal-por-auxilio-a-imigracao-ilegal.ghtml. Acesso em 16 nov 2022

Ataíde RPCM (2019) Responsabilidade civil por violação de deveres no tráfego. Almedina, Coimbra

Azevedo AV (2009) Proposta de classificação da responsabilidade objetiva: pura e impura. Revista dos Tribunais 82(698):7–11

Bälz M, Kawamura H (2015) Schadenersatz bei Suizid eines Nuklearopfers: Zur Entscheidung des Distriktgerichts Fukushima vom 26. Zeitschrift Für Japanisches Recht 39 (August 2014):261–288

Barbosa AMCNM (2020) Causalidade, imputação e responsabilidade por informações. Revista de Direito da Responsabilidade 2:971–1006

Barbosa AMCNM (2021) Responsabilidade civil médica. Causalidade fundamentadora e causalidade preenchedora da responsabilidade. Imputação objetiva. In: Dias Pereira AG, et al (coords) Responsabilidade civil em saúde: diálogo com o Prof. Doutor Jorge Sinde Monteiro. Instituto jurídico, Coimbra

Baumann J, Weber U (1985) Strafrecht, 9ª edn. Gieseking, Bielefeld

Bernd H (2019) Strafrecht: allgemeiner Teil, 6ª edn. W. Kohlhammer, Stuttgart

Best A, Barnes DW (2007) Basic tort law: cases, statues, and problems. Aspen Publishers, New York

Beurskens M (2017) Privatrechtliche Selbsthilfe: rechte, Pflichten und Verantwortlichkeit bei digitalen Zugangsbeschränkungs- und Selbstdurchsetzungsbefugnissen. Tübingen

Billi M (2017) La causalità psichica nei reati colposi: il caso del processo alla Comissione Grandi Rischi. Aracne editricie, Roma

Borges RCB (2007) Direitos de personalidade e autonomia privada, 2ª edn. Saraiva, São Paulo

Borges LF (2024) Comentários nas redes sociais podem ter influenciado na morte de Jéssica Canedo, que foi atacada na internet, diz delegado. G1 (globo.com). https://g1.globo.com/mg/triangulo-mineiro/noticia/2023/12/28/comentarios-nas-redes-sociais-podem-ter-influenciado-na-morte-de-estudante-mineira-atacada-na-internet-diz-delegado.ghtml. Acesso em 05 jan 2024

Brito PLA, Silva MC, Barbosa CCN (2019) Publicidade ilícita e influenciadores digitais: novas tendências da responsabilidade civil. Revista IBERC 2(2):1–21

Brüggemeier G (2006) Haftungsrecht. Struktur, Prinzipen, Schutzbereich: ein Beitrag zur Europäisierung des Privatrechts. Springer, Berlin; Heidelberg; New York

Cane P, Atiyah P (2013) Atiyah's accidents, compensation and the law. Cambridge University Press, Cambridge

Carnaúba DA (2018) Para que serve o art. 931 do Código Civil? Considerações críticas sobre um dispositivo inútil. Revista de Direito Civil Contemporâneo 22(7):203–239

Cocco M, et al (2015) The L'Aquila trial. In: Peppoloni S, di CG Geoethics: the role and responsibility of geoscientists. Geological Society, London

Cordeiro A (2004) Da modernização do Direito Civil: aspectos gerais, v. 1. Almedina, Coimbra

Cordeiro A (2017) Tratado de Direito Civil: direito das obrigações: gestão de negócios, enriquecimento sem causa, responsabilidade civil, v. Almedina, Coimbra. 8

Couto E Silva C (2014) O princípio da boa-fé no Direito brasileiro e português. In: Fradera VMJ (org) O direito privado na visão de Clóvis do Couto e Silva, 2ª. Livraria do Advogado, Porto Alegre

Cvetković MS (2021) Psychological influence and causation in tort law. Зборник радова Правног факултета у Нишу 93:45–61

Dantas ST (2001) Palavras de um professor, 2ª edn. Forense, Rio de Janeiro

David TB (2018) Da culpa ao nexo causal: o caráter valorativo do juízo de causalidade e as (de) limitações da responsabilidade objetiva. Revista de Direito Civil Contemporâneo 17(5):87–104

Deakin S, Adams Z (2019) Markesinis and Deakin's tort law, 8ª edn. Oxford University Press, Oxford

Deutsch E (1972) Regreβverbot und Unterbrechung des Haftungszusammenhangs im Zivilrecht: bemerkungen zum Urteil des VI. Zivilsenats des BGH v. 16.2. 1972. JuristenZeitung 27(18):551–553

Deutsch E (1975) Bürgerliches Recht. Scheckrecht JuristenZeitung 30(11/12)

Deutsch E (1983) Arztrecht und Arztneimittelrecht: eine zusammenfassende Darstellung mit Fallbeispielen und Texten. Springer, Berlin; Heidelberg

Deutsch E (1996) Allgemeines Haftungsrecht, 2ª edn. Carl Heymanns Verlag KG, Köln, Berlin; Bonn, München

Deutsch E, Ahrens HJ (2014) Deliktsrecht: unerlaubte Handlungen, Schadensersatz, Schmerzensgeld, 6ª edn. Verlag Franz Vahlen, München

Deutsch E, Spickhoff A (2014) Medizinrecht: arztrecht, Arzneimittelrecht, Medizinprodukterecht und Transfusionsrecht, 7ª edn. Springer, Berlin; Heidelberg

Divino SBS, Oliveira JC, Alves IDC (2022) Fake News, letramento informacional e saúde: a liberdade de expressão em dois níveis e a responsabilidade pelo discurso de autoridades públicas. Revista Direitos Sociais E Políticas Públicas (Unifafibe) 10(3):282–332

Dörner H (2002) Schuldrecht 2: gesetzliche Schuldverhältnisse, 5ª edn. C.F. Müller Verlag, Heidelberg
Dunz W (1966) Fremde Unrechtshandlungen in der Kausalkette. Neue Juristische Wochenschrift 4:134–137
Dunz W (1989) Das Bürgerliche Gesetzbuch mit besonderer Berücksichtigung der Rechtsprechung des Reichsgerichts und des Bundesgerichtshofes: kommentar, Bd. 2, Teil 5. Walter de Gruyter, Berlin, New York, pp 812–831
Ebel F (1980) Ein "adäquater". Kuhdiebstahl Juristische Schulung 20:865–867
Efing AC, Freitas COA, Gasparatto APG (2019) Responsabilidade civil dos influenciadores digitais. Revista Jurídica Cesumar 19(1):65–87
Ekkenga J, Kuntz T (2014) Vor §249. Soergel HT, Siebert W (orgs) Soergel: kommentar zum Bürgerlichen Gesetzbuch: schuldrecht 1/2: §243–304, 13ª edn. v. 3/2. W. Kohlhammer, Stuttgart).
Emmerich V (2018) BGB - Schuldrecht: besonderer Teil, 15ª edn. C.F. Müller, Heidelberg
Esser J, Schmidt E (1993) Schuldrecht: allgemeiner Teil, 7ª, vol 1, t. 2. C. F. Müller Juristischer Verlag, Heidelberg
Feldman EA (2014) No alternative: resolving disputes in Japanese style. In Zekoll J, Bälz M, Amelung I () Formalisation and flexibilisation in dispute resolution. Brill Nijhoff, Leiden; Boston
Feldman EA (2015) Compensating the victims of Japan's 3-11 Fukushima disaster. Asian-Pacific Law Policy J 16(2):127–157
Feurer H (2010) Amtshaftung und Staatskirchenrecht. Peter Lang, Frankfurt am Main
Finke T (2006) Die Minderung der Schadensersatzpflicht in Europa: zu den Chancen für die Aufnahme einer allgemeinen Reduktionsklausel in ein europäisches Schadensrecht. Universitätsverlag, Göttingen
Flume JW (2019) § 249 BGB. Bamberger HG Kommentarzum Bürgerlichen Gesetzbuch, 4ª edn. C.H.Beck, München
Forst SP (2000) Grenzen deliktischer Haftung bei psychisch vermittelter haftungsbegründender Kausalität. VVF, München
Frada MAC (2015) Teoria da confiança e responsabilidade civil. Almedina, Coimbra
Friese U (1968) Haftungsbegrenzung für Folgeschäden aus unerlaubter Handlung, insbesondere bei § 823 Abs. 1 BGB. Inaugural-Dissertation des Juristischen Fakultät der Friedrich-Alexander-Universität Erlangen-Nürnberg
Fritz KN (2021) BGH diz que nem toda postagem de produtos por influenciadores digitais é publicidade. Migalhas, 14 set 2021. Coluna German Report. https://www.migalhas.com.br/coluna/german-report/351584/bgh–toda-postagem-de-produtos-por-influenciadores-e-publicidade. Acesso em 25 set 2021
Fuchs M, Pauker W, Baumgärtner A (2017) Delikts- und Schadensersatz, 9ª edn. Springer, Berlin; Heidelberg
Gatti I (1976) Il p. Vincenzo Coronelli dei Frati minori conventuali negli anni del generalato (1701–1707), v. 2. Università Gregoriana Editricie, Roma
Geigel R (2020) Der Haftpflichtprozess: mit Einschluss des materiellen Haftpflichtrechts, 28ª edn. C.H.Beck, München
Giesen D (1988) International medical malpractice law: a comparative law study of civil liability arising from medical care. J.C.B. Mohr (Paul Siebeck), Tübingen; Martinus Nijhoff Publishers, Dordrecht; Boston; London
Godoy CLB (2010) Responsabilidade civil pelo risco da atividade: uma cláusula geral no Código civil de 2002, 2ª edn. Saraiva, São Paulo
Gödicke P (2008) Formularerklärungen in der Medizin: rechtliche Kontrollmaßstäbe für Einwilligungen in der medizinischen Heilbehandlung und Forschung. Mohr Siebeck, Tübingen

Gogliano D (2021) Consentimento esclarecido: ilusão de exclusão de responsabilidade. In Simão JF, Pavinatto T. Liber Amicorum Teresa Ancona Lopez: estudos sobre responsabilidade civil. Almedina, São Paulo>

Goldberg JCP, Zipursky BC (2010) Torts. Oxford University Press, New York

Goodman CF (2012) The rule of law in Japan: a comparative analysis, 3ª edn. Kluwer Law International B. V., Alphen aan den Rijn

Gotzler M (1977) Rechtsmäβiges Alternativverhalten im haftungsbegründenden Zurechnungszusammenhang. Beck, München

Greco L (2014) Um panorama da teoria da imputação objetiva, 4ª edn. Ed. RT, São Paulo

Greger R (1985) Zivilrechtliche Haftung im Straβerverkehr: grosskommentar zu §§ 7-20 Strassenverkehrsgesetz u. zum Haftpflichtgesetz unter Berücks. D. Delikts-, Vertrags- u. Versicherungsrechts sowie d. Schadens-regress. Walter de Gruyter, Berlin; New York

Gründel M (2000) Psychotherapeutisches Haftungsrecht: die zivilrechtliche Haftung des Psychologischen Psychotherapeuten bei Verletzung seiner Berufspflichten. Springer, Berlin; Heidelberg

Grüneberg C (2020) Vorb v § 249. In: Palandt O, et al Palandt: bürgerliches Gesetzbuch, 79ª. C.H. Beck, München

Händel K (1976) Anmerkung zu BGH, Urt. v. 13.1.1976 - VI ZR 41/75. Neue Juristische Wochenschrift 27:1204

Hart HLA, Honoré T (1985) Causation in the law, 2ª edn. Oxford University Press, Oxford

Higdon N (2020) The anatomy of fake news: a critical news literacy education. University of California Press, Oakland

Hodgson D (2008) The law of intervening causation. Routledge, London, New York

Huber U (1969) Normzwecktheorie und Adäquanztheorie: zugleich eine Besprechung des Urteils des BGH v. 7.6.1968. Juristenzeitung 24(21):677–683

Huber U (1973) Verschulden, Gefährdung und Adäquanz. Soell H, Mueller K (orgs) Rechtswissenschaft und Gesetzgebung: festschrift für Eduard Wahl zum 70. Geburtstag am 29. März 1973). Winter, Heidelberg

Hübner J (1972) Schadenszurechnung nach Risikosphären: eine Studie zur schadensgeneigten Arbeit selbständig Tätiger am Beispiel der privatrechtlichen Haftung des Seelotsen. Inaugural-Dissertation zur Erlangung des Grades eines Doktors der Rechte bei dem Fachbereich Rechtswissenschaft der Freien Universität Berlin

Hübner J (1974) "Schadensverteilung" bei Schäden anläβlich der Verfolgung festzunehmender Personen durch Beamte - eine Wiederkehr der Culpa-Kompensation? Juristische Schulung 8:496–502

Jakobs G (2014) A imputação objetiva no direito penal, 5ª edn. Trad. André Luís Callegari. Ed. RT, São Paulo

Jansen N (2002) §§ 249–253, 255. Das Problem der Rechtswidrigkeit bei § 823 Abs. 1 BGB. Archive Für Civilistische Praxis 202:517–554

Jansen N (2007) Damage caused by psychological influence: Germany. In: Winiger B, et al (orgs) Digest of European tort law: essential cases on natural causation. Springer, Wien, New York

Jayme E (1996) Identité Culturelle et Intégration: le droit international privé postmoderne. Cours général de droit international privé. Martinus Nijhoff Publishers, Haia. Recueil des Cours, t. 251

Katzenmeier C (2002) Arzthaftung. Mohr Siebeck, Tübingen

Kfouri Neto M (2019) A quantificação do dano na ausência de consentimento livre e esclarecido do paciente. Revista IBERC 2(1):01–21

Killinger E (2009) Die Besonderheiten der Arzthaftung im medizinischen Notfall. Springer, Berlin; Heidelberg

Koriath H (1988) Kausalität, Bedingungstheorie und psychische Kausalität. Verlag Otto Schwartz & Co, Göttingen

Kötz H, Wagner G (2006) Deliktsrecht, 10ª edn. Wolters Kluers, München

Koziol H, Trad. Fiona Salter Townshend (2012) Basic questions of tort law from a Germanic perspective. Jan Sramek Verlag, Wien

Koziol H, Koziol G (2012) Ansprüche des geschädigten Retters bei Selbstgefährdung eines Bergsteigers: lösungsansätze im österreichischen, deutschen und japanischen Recht. Rabels Zeitschrift Für Ausländisches Und Internationales Privatrecht 76:540–561

Kramer EA (1976) Schutzgesetze und adäquate Kausalität. JuristenZeitung 31(11/12):338–346

Lang R (1983) Normzweck und duty of care: eine Untersuchung über die Grenzen der Zurechnung im deutschen und anglo-amerikanischen Deliktsrecht. C.H. Beck'sche Verlagsbuchhandlung, München

Lange H (1960) Gutachten für den Verhandlungen des dreiundvierzigsten deutschen Juristentages deutschen Juristentag. Ständigen Deputation des deutschen Juristentages. Verhandlungen des dreiundvierzigsten Deutschen Juristentages, vol 1. J.C.B.Mohr (Paul Siebeck), Tübingen

Lange H (1990) Anmerkung zu BGH, Urt. v. 3.7.1990 - VI ZR 33/90 (Celle). Neue Zeitschrift Für Verkehrsrecht 11:425–427

Lange H, Schiemann G (2003) Schadensersatz, 3ª edn. Mohr Siebeck, Tübingen

Larenz K (1955) Tatzurechnung und "Unterbrechung des Kausalzusammenhanges". Neue Juristische Wochenschrift 8(28):1009–1013

Larenz K (1970) Zum heutigen Stand der Lehre von der objektiven Zurechnung im Schadensersatzrecht. In: Festschrift für Richard M. Honig: zum 80. Geburtstag. Verlag Otto Schwartz & Co, Göttingen

Larenz K (1987) Lehrbuch des Schuldrechts: allgemeiner Teil, 14ª, vol v, 1. C. H. Beck'sche Verlagsbuchhandlung, München

Larenz K, Canaris CW (1994) Lehrbuch des Schuldrechts: besonderer Teil, 13ª. v. 2, t. 2, Beck, München

Lasson M (2009) Eigenverantwortliche Selbstgefährdung und einverständliche Fremdgefährdung: Überblick über einen nach wie vor aktuellen Streiten in der Strafrechtsdogmatik. Zeitschrift Für Das Juristische Studium 4:359–368

Leitermeier H (1968) Die Deliktsrechtliche Haftung des Verfolgten für Schäden bei der Verfolgung. Inaugural-Dissertation des Fachbereichs Rechtswissenschaft der Friedrich-Alexander-Universität Erlangen-Nürnberg

Lima A (2015) A interferência de terceiros na violação do contrato. Revista de Direito Civil Contemporâneo 5(2):307–325

Looschelders D (2019) Die Mitverantwortlichkeit des Geschädigten im Privatrecht. Mohr Siebeck, Tübingen

Lüer HJ (1969) Die Begrenzung der Haftung bei fahrlässig begangen unerlaubten Handlungen: eine rechtvergleichende Studie zum deutschen, englischen und amerikanischen Zivilrecht. Verlag C. F. Müller, Karlsruhe

Machado MRA (2008) A definição da conduta típica: entre a superação da causalidade e a construção de teoria normativas para a imputação objetiva. In: Garcia B. Instituições de Direito Penal, 7ª edn. v. 1, t. 1. (coord. Maíra Rocha Machado e Denise Garcia). Saraiva, São Paulo

Magnus U (2000) Causation in German tort law. In Koziol H et al (orgs) Unification of tort law: causation. Kluwer Law International, The Hague

Magrani E (2019) Entre dados e robôs: ética e privacidade na era da hiperconectividade, 2ª edn. Arquipélago Editorial, Porto Alegre

Marinho RS (2013) Princípio da autorresponsabilidade no direito penal. Dissertação (Mestrado) - Faculdade de Direito, Universidade de São Paulo

Marins LG (2023) Celebridades invadem o mercado de criptomoedas. Infomoney. https://www.infomoney.com.br/mercados/celebridades-invadem-o-mercado-de-criptomoedas/. Acesso em 16 jan 2023

Markesinis BS, Unberath H (2019) Markesinis's German law of torts: a comparative treatise, 5ª edn. Hart Publishing, Chicago

Marques CL (2010) Artigo 12. In: Marques CL, Benjamin AH, Miragem B Comentários ao Código de Defesa do Consumidor, 3ª. Editora RT, São Paulo

Martens KP (1972) Die Verfolgung des Unrechts. Neue Juristische Wochenschrift 17:740–746

Martins-Costa J (2014) Dano moral à brasileira. Revista Do Instituto Do Direito Brasileiro 3(9):7073–7122

Martins-Costa J (2018) A boa-fé no direito privado: critérios para a sua aplicação, 2ª edn. Saraiva Educação, São Paulo

Martins-Costa J, Costa E Silva P (2020) Crises e perturbações no cumprimento da prestação: estudo de direito comparado luso-brasileiro. Quartier Latin, São Paulo

Mattia M (2019) "Revenge porn" e suicidio della vittima: il problema della divergenza tra 'voluto' e 'realizzato' rispetto all'imputazione oggettiva degli eventi psichici. La legislazione penale:1–71

Mayr L (2015) Der verwerflich handelnde Geschädigte: rechtsschutzversagung wegen rechts- oder sittenwidrig Verhaltens im deutschen und englischen Deliktsrecht. Mohr Siebeck, Tübingen

Medicus D (2004) Bürgerliches Recht: eine nach Anspruchsgrundlagen geordnete Darstellung zur Examensvorbereitung, 20ª edn. Carl Heymanns Verlag, Köln; Berlin; München

Medicus D (2005) Die psychisch vermittelte Kausalität im Zivilrecht. Juristische Schulung 289–296

Mildemberger CS, Lemos Pereira PMF (2020) Publicidade médica nas mídias sociais: proposta de um modelo contemporâneo no Brasil. In Kfouri Neto M, Nogaroli R () Debates contemporâneos em direito médico e da saúde. Thomson Reuters, São Paulo

Miranda FC (1983) Tratado de direito privado, 4ª, edn. 2ª tir, t. 1. RT, São Paulo

Miranda FC (1984) Tratado de direito privado, 3ª, edn. 2ª reimp, t. 26. RT, São Paulo

von MPW (1979) Zivilrechtliche Haftung für durchgehende Pferde. Juristische Schulung 775–778

Monteiro JFS (1989) Responsabilidade por conselhos, recomendações ou informações. Almedina, Coimbra

Moraes RDFD (2017) A causalidade alternativa e a responsabilidade civil dos múltiplos ofensores. LiberArs, São Paulo

Mulholland CS (2009) A responsabilidade civil por presunção de causalidade. GZ, Rio de Janeiro

Musielak HJ (2013) Kausalzusammenhang und Schadenszurechnung im Zivilrecht. Juristische Arbeitsblätter 241–248

Nespoli ALB, Acczm A (2022) Nexo de causalidade e juízo de equidade: da certeza à mera possibilidade. Civilistica.com 11(2):1–22

Neuefeind W (2001) Arzthaftungsrecht: ein Überblick für Rechtsanwender, Ärzte und Patienten, 3ª edn. Tectum Verlag, Marburg

Niebaum G (1976) Die Verfolgungsfälle und ihre Wertungskriterien. Neue Juristische Wochenschrift 29:1673–1674

Niebaum G (1977) Die deliktische Haftung für fremde Willensbestätigung. Duncker & Humblot, Berlin

Niebaum G (2003) Die deliktische Haftung für fremde Willensbestätigung. Duncker & Humblot, Berlin

Nökel D (1968) Die Rechtsstellung des Nothelfers: Anglo-amerikanisches im Vergleich zum deutschen Recht. Inaugural-Dissertation zur Erlangung der juristischen Doktorwürde der Hohen Rechts- und Staatswissenschaftlichen Fakultät der Albert-Ludwigs-Universität zu Freiburg

Ody LFW, D'Aquino LS (2021) A responsabilidade dos influenciadores: uma análise a partir do Fyre Festival, a maior festa que jamais aconteceu. Civilistica.com 10(3):1–18

Oetker H (2019) § 249. In: Oetker H, et al (orgs) Münchener Kommentar: schuldrecht - Allgemeiner Teil I, 8ª. vol 2. C. H. Beck, München

O'Mathúna DP, Beriain IM (eds) (2019) Ethics and law for chemical, biological, radiological, nuclear and explosive crises. Springer, Cham

Orui M, et al (2018) Suicide rates in evacuation areas after the Fukushima Daiichi nuclear disaster: a 5-year follow-up study in Fukushima Prefecture. Crisis 39(5):353–363

Palavera R (2017) Scienza e senso comune nel diritto penale: il ricorso problematico a massime di esperienza circa la ricostruzione della fattispecie tipica. Edizioni ETS, Pisa

Pantaleón Prieto AF (1990) Causalidad e imputación objetiva: criterios de imputácion. In Centenario del Código Civil (1889–1989). Editorial Centro de Estudios Ramon Areces, Madrid
Patterson R (2021) Drugs in litigation: damage awards involving prescription and nonprescription drugs. LexisNexis, New York
Penteado LC (2007) Efeitos contratuais perante terceiros. Quartier Latin, São Paulo
Pereira ML (2001) Conceito de prestação e destino da contraprestação. Almedina, Coimbra
Pereira ML (2022) Direito da responsabilidade civil: a obrigação de indemnizar. Imprensa FDUL, Lisboa
Perez M (2020) Accidental poisonings from bleach and disinfectants continued to rise in April. Forbes. https://www.forbes.com/sites/mattperez/2020/05/12/accidental-poisonings-from-bleach-and-disinfectants-continued-to-rise-in-april/?sh=79bf9ef67b25. Acesso em 07 jul 2021
Pessoa CV (2017) Lama, luto e luta: a vivência dos atingidos pelo desastre da Samarco e a organização popular no Movimento dos Atingidos por Barragens (MAB) como estratégia de enfrentamento. Dissertação (Mestrado) - Faculdade de Psicologia, Pontifícia Universidade Católica de São Paulo
Pirson R (1964) Droit belge de la responsabilité civile, 6ª edn. Librairie Dalloz, Paris
Pires CM (2020) Impossibilidade da prestação. Almedina, Coimbra
Portela J (2022) Morre Bernie Madoff, autor do maior crime financeiro da história. Metrópoles. https://www.metropoles.com/mundo/morre-bernie-madoff-autor-do-maior-crime-financeiro-da-historia. Acesso em 28 jan
Neves MCL et al (orgs) 2018 Prismma: pesquisa sobre a saúde mental das famílias atingidas pelo rompimento da barragem de Fundão em Mariana. Corpus, Belo Horizonte
Proença JCB (1997) A conduta do lesado como pressuposto e critério de imputação do dano extracontratual. Almedina, Coimbra
Prosser W, Keeton W (1984) On Torts, 5ª edn. West Publishing Company, St. Paul
Puppe I (2017) Die psychische Kausalität und das Recht auf die eigene Entscheidung. Juristische Rundschau 10:513–522
Raiser T (1963) Adäquanztheorie und Haftung nach dem Schutzzweck der verletzten Norm. JuristenZeitung 18(15):462–466
Rapp GC (2020) Tort law in focus. Wolters Kluwer, New York
Reinig GHL (2015) O problema da causalidade na responsabilidade civil: a teoria do escopo da proteção da norma (Schutzzwecktheorie) e sua aplicabilidade no Direito Civil brasileiro. Tese (Doutorado) - Faculdade de Direito, Universidade de São Paulo
Reinig GHL (2018) O escopo de proteção da norma como critério limitativo da responsabilidade civil por ato ilícito: algumas contribuições ao Direito Civil brasileiro a partir do Direito Civil alemão. Revista de Direito Civil Contemporâneo 14:237–309
Ristow T (2003) Die psychische Kausalität im Deliktsrecht. Peter Lang, Frankfurt am Main
Rodrigues Jr OL (2004) A doutrina do terceiro cúmplice: autonomia da vontade, o princípio res inter alios acta, função social do contrato e a interferência alheia na execução dos negócios jurídicos. Revista Dos Tribunais 821:80–98
Rodrigues Jr OL (2016) Nexo causal probabilístico: elementos para a crítica de um conceito. Revista de Direito Civil Contemporâneo 8(3):115–137
Rogers WV, Winfield PH, Jolowicz JA (1998) Winfield and Jolowicz on tort, 15ª edn. Sweet and Maxwell, London
Rosenvald N (2018) O dano moral coletivo como uma pena civil. Rosenvald N, Teixeira Neto F (coords) Dano moral coletivo. Foco, Indaiatuba
Roth-Stielow K (1971) Die Reichweite eines bestimmten Verhaltens als äuβerst Haftungsgrenze. Neue Juristische Wochenschrift 5:180–182
Rother W (1965) Adäquanztheorie und Schadensverursachung durch mehrere. Neue Juristische Wochenschrift 5:177–183
Rutkowsky H (1952) Die psychisch vermittelte Kausalität: zugleich ein Beitrag zur Frage der Sozialadäquanz. Neue Juristische Wochenschrift 606–608

Sampaio MA, Miranda TB (2021) A responsabilidade civil dos influenciadores digitais diante do Código de Defesa do Consumidor. Revista de Direito Do Consumidor 30(133):175–204

Sanseverino PTV (2010) Princípio da reparação integral: indenização no Código Civil. Saraiva, São Paulo

Schiemann G (2017) § 249. In Schadensersatzrecht J. von Staudingers Kommentar zum Bürgerlichen Gesetzbuch mit Einführungsgesetz und Nebengesetzen. Walter de Gruyter, Berlin, 249–254

Schiemann G (2019) Anmerkung zu BGH, Urt. v. 17.4.2018 - VI ZR 237/17. JuristenZeitung 74 (2):103–104

Schlechtriem P, Schmidt-Kessel M (2005) Schuldrecht: allgemeiner Teil, 6ª edn. Mohr Siebeck, Tübingen

Schack H (1986) Der Schutzzweck als Mittel der Haftungsbegrenzung im Vertragsrecht. JuristenZeitung 41(7):305–314

Schäfer HB, Ott C (1995) Lehrbuch der ökomischen Analyse des Zivilrechts, 2ª edn. Springer, Berlin; Heidelberg

Schellhammer K (2014) Schuldrecht nach Anspruchsgrundlagen, 9ª edn. C. F. Müller, Heidelberg; München, Landsberg, Frechen, Hamburg

Schmidt E (1970) Kompensation der Pflichtwidrigkeit durch nachfolgendes pflichtgemäßes Verhalten? Versicherungsrecht 17(A)

Schmidt JP (2009) Zivilrechtskodifikation in Brasilien: strukturfragen und Regelungsprobleme in historisch-vergleichender Perspektive (Schriften zum ausländischen und internationalen Privatrecht, v. 226). Mohr Siebeck, Tübingen

Schmidt JP (2016) Alegação de invalidade como comportamento contraditório proibido?—comentários ao Acórdão do REsp 1.461.301/MT. Revista de Direito Civil Contemporâneo 7 (3):419–437

Schreiber A (2013) Novos paradigmas da responsabilidade civil: da erosão dos filtros da reparação à diluição dos danos, 5ª edn. Atlas, São Paulo

Schur W (2001) Leistung und Sorgfalt: zugleich ein Beitrag zur Lehre von der Pflicht im Bürgerlichen Recht. Mohr Siebeck, Tübingen

Schwartz VE, Kelly K, Partlett DF (2010) Prosser, Wade and Schwartz's torts: cases and materials, 12ª edn. Foundation Press, New York

Sourlas P (1974) Adäquanztheorie und Normzwecklehre bei der Begründung der Haftung nach § 823 Abs. 1 BGB. Duncker & Humblot, Berlin

Sousa D (2023) Ataques em Brasília: prejuízo passará de R$ 8 milhões apenas em obras de arte do Palácio do Planalto. Istoédinheiro. https://www.istoedinheiro.com.br/ataques-em-brasilia-prejuizo-passara-de-r-8-milhoes-apenas-em-obras-de-arte-do-palacio-do-planalto/. Acesso em 16 jan 2023

Souza FS (2019) Diálogo das fontes: fundamentos, experiência jurisprudencial e crítica metodológica. Dissertação (Mestrado) - Faculdade de Direito, Universidade de São Paulo

Spindler G (2011) Haftung im IT-Bereich. Lorenz E (org) Karlsruher Forum 2010: haftung und Versicherung im IT-Bereich. Verlag Versicherungswirtschaft, Karlsruhe

Sprau H (2020) §§ 827, 828. Palandt O, et al Palandt: bürgerliches Gesetzbuch, 79ª edn. C.H. Beck, München

Stefan S (2016) Rational suicide, irrational laws: examining current approaches to suicide in policy and law. Oxford University Press, New York

Stelzner M (2011) Urheberrechtliche Medienrisiken im Internet: schadensersatz und Versicherbarkeit. Verlag Versicherungswirtschaft, Karlsruhe

Stoll H (1968) Kausalzusammenhang und Normzweck im Deliktsrecht. J. C. B. Mohr (Paul Siebeck), Tübingen

Stoll H (1988) Zum Schadensersatz wegen Körperverletzung durch "Herausgeforderte Organspende". JuristenZeitung 43(3):150–155

Stoll H (1993) Haftungsfolgen im bürgerlichen Recht: eine Darstellung auf rechtsvergleichender Grundlage. C. F. Müller Juristischer Verlag, Heidelberg

Strauch RG (1992) Die Haftung des Verfolgten für Schäden des Verfolgers aus § 823 Abs. 1 BGB: zugleich Anmerkung zum Urteil des BGH vom 3 July 1990 (VI ZR 33/90) VersR 91, 111. Versicherungsrecht 22:932–937

Sturmer J (2018) Threat of forced evacuation from Fukushima pushed 102yo to take his own life, judge rules. ABC News. https://www.abc.net.au/news/2018-02-21/102-yo-man-takes-life-of-being-evicted-from-home-near-fukushima/9469816. Acesso em 16 jul 2021

Tavares J (2019) Teoria do injusto penal, 4ª edn. Tirant lo Blanch, São Paulo

Teichmann A (1996) BGH, 12. 3. 1996 – VI ZR 12/95. Haftung des Verfolgten und Mitverschulden des verfolgenden Polizeibeamten. JuristenZeitung 51(23):1178–1183

Teixeira P (2021) Hepatite medicamentosa: entenda a intoxicação pelo 'kit Covid' que levou paciente à fila do transplante. G1. https://g1.globo.com/sp/campinas-regiao/noticia/2021/03/25/hepatite-medicamentosa-entenda-intoxicacao-pelo-kit-covid-que-levou-paciente-de-campinas-a-fila-do-transplante.ghtml. Acesso em 07 jul 2021

Teixeira Neto F (2014) Dano moral coletivo: a configuração e a reparação do dano extrapatrimonial por lesão aos interesses difusos. Juruá, Curitiba

Thüß J (2012) Rechtsfragen des Critical Incident Reporting in der Medizin: unter besonderer Berücksichtigung krankenhausinterner Fehlermeldesysteme. Springer, Berlin; Heidelberg

Tomasevicius Filho E (2020) O princípio da boa-fé no Direito Civil. Almedina, São Paulo

Tortella T (2022) Invasão do Capitólio completa um ano: relembre o ataque à democracia dos EUA. CNN Brasil. https://www.cnnbrasil.com.br/internacional/invasao-ao-capitolio-completa-um-ano-relembre-o-ataque-a-democracia-dos-eua/. Acesso em 16 jan 2022

Traeger L (1929) Der Kausalbegriff im Straf- und Zivilrecht: zugleich ein Beitrag zur Auslegung des BGB. N. G. Elwert'sche Verlagsbuchhandlung, Marburg

Twerski AD, et al (2021) Torts: cases and materials. Wolters Kluwer, New York

Varela JMA (2000) Das obrigações em geral, 10ª edn. Almedina, Coimbra

von CE (1956) Das Problem des Kausalzusammenhangs im Privatrecht. Hans Ferdinand Schulz Verlag, Freiburg

von CE (1970) Die Bedeutung des Schutzbereichs einer Rechtsnorm für die Geltendmachung von Schadensersatzansprüchen aus Verkehrsunfällen. Deutsches Autorecht 283–292

von BC (1980) Verkehrspflichten: richterliche Gefahrsteuerungsgebote in deutschen Deliktsrecht. Carl Heymanns Verlag KG, Köln; Berlin; Bonn; München

Wagner G (2021) Deliktshaftung für berufstypische Risiken. Neue Juristische Wochenschrift 74 (6):897–900

Waldkirch C (2018) Zufall und Zurechnung im Haftungsrecht. Mohr Siebeck, Tübingen

Weber R (1995) Verfolgungsfälle: objektive und subjektive Zurechnung. In Deutsch E, Klingmüller E, Kullmann HJ (eds) Festschrift für Erich Steffen zum 65. Geburtstag am 28. Maio 1995: der Schadensersatz und seine Deckung. Walter de Gruyter, Berlin; New York

Weimann G (1994) The influentials: people who influence people. State University of New York Press, Albany

Wessels J, Beulke W, Satzger H (2017) Strafrecht: allgemeiner Teil: die Straftat und ihr Aufbau, 47ª edn. C.F.Müller, Heidelberg

Wilhelmi R (2009) Risikoschutz durch Privatrecht: eine Untersuchung zur negatorischen und deliktischen Haftung unter besonderer Berücksichtigung von Umweltschäden. Mohr Siebeck, Tübingen

Winiger B (2007) Damage caused by psychological influence: comparative report. Winiger B, et al (orgs) Digest of European tort law: essential cases on natural causation. Springer, Wien; New York

Wolf JG (1962) Der Normzweck im Deliktsrecht: ein Diskussionsbeitrag. Verlag Otto Schwartz & Co, Göttingen

Youngs R (2014) English, French & German comparative law, 3ª edn. Routledge, London; New York

Zhang M (2016) Aktiv psychische Kausalität im Deliktsrecht. Duncker & Humblot, Berlin

Zieschang F (2020) Kausalität und objektive Zurechnung. Hilgendorf E, Kudlich H, Valerius B (eds) Handbuch des Strafrechts: strafrecht Allgemeiner Teil, vol 2. t. 1. C.F.Müller, Heidelberg

Zimmermann R (1979) Der Selbstmord als Gefährdungssachverhalt: aufwendungs- oder Schaden? Zeitschrift Für Das Gesamte Familienrecht 2:103–110

Zimmermann R (1980) Schadensverteilung" bei Schäden anläßlich der Verfolgung festzunehmender Personen durch Beamte - eine Wiederkehr der Culpa-Kompensation? Juristische Schulung 8:496–502

Zimmermann R, Trad. Esther Arroyo i Amayuelas (2008) El nuevo derecho alemán de obligaciones: un análisis desde la historia y el derecho comparado. Bosch, Barcelona

Zimmermann R (2017) O Código Civil alemão e o desenvolvimento do Direito Privado na Alemanha. Revista de Direito Civil Contemporâneo 12(4):317–358. Trad. Otavio Luiz Rodrigues Junior et al

Zimmermann R, Kleinschmidt J (2007) Damage caused by psychological influence: Germany. In: Winiger B, et al (orgs) Digest of European tort law: essential cases on natural causation. Springer, Wien; New York

Chapter 6
Conclusion

The main conclusion is that the so-called "psychological causation" constitutes an autonomous legal issue, requiring the application of specific criteria for legal attribution. The case groups analyzed have their own legal contours, distinguishing them from traditional scenarios where a certain behavior causes, according to natural laws, particular damage. In "psychologically mediated causation," the injury arises indirectly, facilitated by the conduct of a first perpetrator who influences or enables the actions of a second tortfeasor, causing harm to a third party or to themselves. This is evident in the case of digital influencers and public authorities who, through speeches, posts, and behaviors, motivate the actions of others, raising the question of the liability of these individuals for the damages suffered by the victims.

Having established the central outcome and developed the analysis from both theoretical and practical perspectives, the following conclusions can be drawn:

1. It is possible to identify, in Roman law from the Republican era, discussions involving the theme of "psychological causation," such as the case of an enslaved person who, persuaded by a third party to escape from their owner, was still considered a fugitive (*fugitivus*). The distinction between the expressions "to kill" ("*occidere*") and "to cause death" ("*causam mortis praestare*") highlights the initial emphasis on physical contact (*corpore corpori*) between the perpetrator and the victim in establishing liability. In Justinian law, there was a significant expansion of liability for indirect damages, a trend that became more pronounced in the Middle Ages.
2. The causal theories commonly applied by Brazilian doctrine and jurisprudence are inadequate to resolve the complex issues arising from the analysis of cases involving damages caused by psychological influence.
3. The theory of equivalence of conditions fails to satisfactorily delimit the liability of the first perpetrator, who influences or favors the conduct of a third party, thus expanding liability. It should only be considered as an initial

C. Dantas Bisneto, *Psychological Causation in Tort Law*,
https://doi.org/10.1007/978-3-032-03825-8_6

stage in causal investigation (natural causation). Thus, for example, in rescue cases, it would suffice to prove that the first perpetrator negligently caused a traffic accident to hold them liable for the damages suffered by the rescuer.

4. The hypotheses of damages caused by psychological influence cannot be resolved by using the theory of direct or immediate damage and the "subtheory of necessary causation." In addition to lacking a precise definition and well-established limits, these theories fail to explain why the act of the second causer does not necessarily exempt the first perpetrator from liability, as it would, in theory, constitute an "interruption" of the causal chain. In cases of thefts resulting from the overturning of cargo transport vehicles, the appropriation of products and goods by third parties should, according to this theory, be considered an interruptive cause of the causal chain, thereby exempting the perpetrator who caused the collision from liability.
5. The criterion of causal adequacy, in its negative formulation, remains valid as an initial filter for attributing liability. However, it cannot resolve, on its own, the problem of "psychological causation," considering that, in many cases, the adequacy of the cause is affirmed, even though the attribution is ultimately dismissed through the application of another complementary attribution criterion, such as the non-realization of a specific risk created by the first perpetrator. In this context, the behavior of a person who hires a professional to paint their apartment and forgets a bottle of beer containing caustic soda inside the residence, whose contents are ingested by the service provider, while not irrelevant to the occurrence of the damage, cannot be concluded to have resulted from the creation of a typical risk by the contractor.
6. There are no obstacles to applying the theory of the scope of the violated norm or its criteria, such as the materialization of the specific risk created or increased, in Brazilian law, since it is compatible with tort legal regimes composed of general liability clauses. However, it should not be used as an exclusive, autonomous attribution criterion. This was the decision of the Court of Justice of the State of São Paulo, which affirmed that the fact of a driver being parked on the channelization marks of a highway did not contribute to the occurrence of an accident. In this case, the driver, when skidding on the wet track, hit the car parked in an improper place. The Court concluded that the violated norm did not aim to prevent accidents but to direct the flow of vehicles.
7. Brazilian courts have not yet managed to demarcate the distinctive boundaries between the theories of direct and immediate damage and that of causal adequacy, indifferently applying the thesis that seems more convenient based on mere equity judgments. This culminates in the inconsistent treatment of the matter, making it difficult to recognize attribution criteria, including in cases of damages caused by psychological influence. There are numerous decisions that address the two theories indistinctly as synonyms or reveal the irrelevance of the distinction between their theoretical criteria.
8. Cases of "psychologically mediated causation" should be resolved based on the establishment of case groups that present similar factual circumstances and

allow the use of analogous criteria, thereby facilitating the control parameters of judicial decisions. It is not possible to adopt a universally valid general theory applicable to all groups of cases, given the peculiarities of each one. For example, cases involving state liability for acts committed by a fugitive can be identified, as they reveal patterns that help establish more precise attribution criteria.

9. The resolution of cases involving damage caused by psychological influence in Brazilian law begins with the examination of the theory of equivalence of conditions. Next, causal adequacy must be assessed in its negative formulation, serving as a prima facie filter in the attribution of liability. Finally, other objective attribution criteria should be applied complementarily, depending on the group of cases analyzed.
10. The concept of "psychological causation" is characterized by the voluntary intervention of the second causer, who performs an act influenced by the behavior of the first perpetrator or whose action is facilitated by the latter's conduct. Not covered by the notion of "psychologically mediated causation," for the purposes of this work, are hypotheses in which the emotional component (voluntary decision) of the second causer is absent, as in cases of chain accidents and reflex damages. Finally, hypotheses in which the first perpetrator acts intentionally or maliciously are also not included within the scope of this study.
11. "Psychological causation" is not a peculiarly German legal issue; rather, it is recognized in a number of European legal systems, although in some jurisdictions it has not yet been systematically addressed.
12. The theory of equivalence of conditions should be applied in the context of damages caused by psychological influence, without, however, relying on natural, statistical, or probabilistic laws, but rather on rules of experience. There is no deterministic connection between the Fukushima nuclear accident and the suicides that occurred after the disaster, although it can be argued that it is possible to establish a causal link between the two events through empirical principles.
13. General duties of care apply in Brazilian law, particularly in cases of damages caused by psychological influence, as they help address situations of risk that have been created or increased, making the decision on the liability of the first perpetrator easier and more rational. Applying this concept serves to avoid relying on less defined concepts, from a dogmatic perspective, such as unjust damage, while also preventing the reference, for the purpose of establishing unlawfulness, to implicit constitutional principles.
14. The criterion of self-responsibility, centered on the possibility of the second causer acting freely according to his will, acquires special relevance in cases of "psychological causation." However, it cannot be concluded that the voluntary intervention of this perpetrator "interrupts" the causal chain between the act of the first wrongdoer and the damage, thereby exempting him from any responsibility. It should also not be asserted that the criterion of self-responsibility is decisive in attributing liability, as it must be balanced with other parameters

unrelated to the perpetrator's will. The mere bad example, even when practiced by public authorities, cannot generally be considered a situation generating risks to third parties, leading to their liability.

15. The controllability of the course of the causal event cannot, in isolation, justify the exoneration of the first perpetrator's liability. It is not the fact that the causal process can no longer be controlled by the first wrongdoer that excludes his responsibility for the damages caused, but rather the materialization of a risk created or increased due to the violation of a legal norm or a general duty of care. In many cases of "indirect causation," where the harmful result only occurs after the interference of other causes, the first perpetrator has no influence over subsequent events.
16. The "provocation formula," although widely used in German jurisprudence for the resolution of cases, is not effective in establishing attribution, since many of the criteria used in its application fail to objectively delimit the scope of responsibility of the perpetrator creating the dangerous situation. The concept of "provocation" ("*Herausforderung*") lacks significant legal value, as it often obscures the true evaluative judgment made by the judge, leading to ambiguous interpretations. Additionally, it can be seen as a requirement for the first perpetrator to incite or stimulate the second to act in a particular manner.
17. The criterion of justifiable motive also does not achieve satisfactory results, as it is often impossible to identify the motive behind the second conduct, particularly in cases of rescue and pursuit. Furthermore, in situations where the motive for intervention is unreasonable or where the action was undertaken for the benefit of the agent themselves, it cannot be categorically ruled out that damages should be attributed to the first perpetrator. The requirement of a moral or legal duty to act should not be imposed; it is sufficient that the first perpetrator has created or exacerbated a source of danger.
18. The most relevant criterion for the purpose of attributing liability in cases of damages caused by psychological influence consists of verifying the materialization of a typical risk created or increased by the first perpetrator due to the violation of a legal norm or the breach of a general duty of care. If the second causer suffers injuries that could have occurred equally without the dangerous situation, such damages cannot be attributed to the first perpetrator, as they are covered by the "general risk of life", as in the case of the doctor who, after providing first aid to a patient on the roadside, leaves his belongings on the parapet, which are taken by a passer-by. This risk is a matter of chance, and therefore, no one should be held liable for events that occur accidentally. In the case of professionals, such as firefighters or first responders, occupational risks are generally considered part of their inherent life risk, encompassing typical situations associated with those engaged in high-risk activities.
19. The act of the second causer must be proportional to the intended objective. The risks assumed by this second perpetrator must be reasonable in comparison to the pursued outcome. If the individual acts in a completely disproportionate manner, they are fully responsible for the damages suffered. If the action undertaken was not completely unreasonable but also did not fully meet the criterion of

proportionality, it becomes possible to allocate the liability according to the spheres of risks assumed by each party, analyzing to what extent each party's behavior causally contributed to the harmful outcome (art. 945 of the CC/02).

20. The models of indirect causality and negligence proposed by Forst cannot be fully accepted. The first model, which suggests that the liability of the first perpetrator should only be excluded when the free and comparable will of the second perpetrator intervenes in the causal course (with the second perpetrator being seen as an indirect or mediate author), must be rejected, as the wills of the parties are rarely qualitatively comparable. The model, initially conceived as general, is surpassed in practical application by the model of negligent causality, which was intended to be exceptional and subsidiary.
21. The position of authority of the first wrongdoer, indicated by Forst as a criterion for attribution, holds significant relevance in certain case groups. It is crucial to assess whether the first perpetrator's position of superiority is sufficient to establish a form of "control" over the second causer, rather than merely setting a bad example. This perceived ascendancy of the first wrongdoer must be credible to the injured party. The first perpetrator does not need to possess specialized knowledge on the matter but only needs to position themselves as someone who does, with the victim perceiving them as such based on ordinary experience standards.
22. This study adopts, with certain modifications, Till Ristow's classification, distinguishing between damages resulting from the conduct of a second perpetrator (where the second cause of damage and the injured party coincide) and those arising from the conduct of a third party (where the second cause of damage and the injured party are different people). Within the same group, different problems are recognized, which require the use of different attribution criteria.
23. In cases of rescue and pursuit, after applying the theories of equivalence of conditions and adequate causation, it is necessary to determine whether the damage suffered by the rescuer or pursuer falls within the "general risk of life" or whether it results from the realization of a specific risk created by the first wrongdoer. The act of the second perpetrator must be proportional to the created risk; otherwise, the liability of the first individual will be completely excluded, or the damages will be distributed according to each party's contribution to the harmful event (art. 945 of the CC/02). The criterion of self-responsibility must also be observed, since, if the harmful result can be attributed to fault, in its highest degree, or to intent on the part of the rescuer/pursuer, the attribution must be excluded due to the absence of an internal connection between the events.
24. In cases of intervention by the position of authority of the first wrongdoer, the individual in a position of superiority must appear to the victim as someone who possesses special knowledge about the circumstances that are important in the decision-making process of the second causer. The relationship between the perpetrator and the injured party must be established in such a way that the influence of the first wrongdoer diminishes or minimizes the voluntariness of the latter's behavior. As a rule, everyone should be responsible for their own

actions, with the attribution of damages to third parties being the exception. A mere bad example is not sufficient to establish liability. This group of cases includes instances of improper behaviors by public authorities and doctors during the COVID-19 pandemic, the irresponsible actions of certain digital influencers, the speeches of government agents who discredited the electoral process, culminating in the invasion of the National Congress, and the occurrence of collective riots, where the responsibility of the movement leaders is debated.

25. In cases of intervention involving the duty to control a source of danger, in addition to the psychological contribution, the first perpetrator also provides a physical component to the victim by supplying a certain dangerous substance. Furthermore, in this group of cases, it should be examined whether the first individual, occupying a prominent position and supposedly possessing special knowledge, created a specific risk situation for the injured party—a circumstance exacerbated by the delivery of potentially harmful material and the neglect of duties of care. This is exemplified in the case where two minors attempted to build a rocket, with the first one preparing an explosive mixture and the second one activating the device, thereby injuring himself.
26. In the group of self-harm cases, it is necessary to assess whether the intensity of the initial facts justifies the act performed by the victim, considering to what extent the freedom of action of the injured party was compromised. The impact of large-scale events affects the power of self-determination of the person affected in the face of the risk created by the perpetrator of the unlawful act, which materializes. Depending on the intensity of the events, these cannot be considered a mere "general risk of life." The act of the second causer, by itself, however, does not "interrupt" the causal chain, making it possible to assess the liability of the first perpetrator. The medical predisposition or psychological state of the injured party does not preclude the attribution of damages, except in cases where the vulnerability is extremely atypical, becoming part of the general risk of the victim's life. Cases were analyzed, among others, of suicides caused by the Fukushima nuclear disaster and the Brumadinho dam, as well as cases of self-harm due to acts of bullying and revenge porn.
27. In cases of omission of safety precautions, it is essential to investigate whether the specific risk created by the first perpetrator has indeed materialized, while also assessing whether the violation of a general duty of care has infringed a legally protected interest, according to the scope of the norm applicable to the specific case. The losses suffered by the injured party must have a close connection with the disregard for the duties of care imposed, not representing a mere external circumstance. The fact that there has been third-party interference, by itself, does not "interrupt" the causal link between the behavior of the first perpetrator and the injurious event. A paradigmatic example is the "green strip case," where impatient drivers decide to use the side lane due to a traffic jam caused by an accident, thereby causing damage to adjacent properties.
28. When interference with pre-existing safety measures is identified, it is important to note the function performed by the protection mechanism. The removal

of the safety apparatus can create or increase the specific risk of a certain injurious event. However, if the violated general duty of care does not aim to prevent a certain risk, even if the protection measure is eliminated, the damaging event should be considered a "general risk of life", and the attribution of damages is not appropriate. The controllability criterion is not a decisive factor in determining or excluding liability. Cases involving the destruction of pasture fences by vehicles, resulting in the escape and subsequent theft of animals by third parties, were investigated, as well as the occurrence of a negligent accident between a car and a cargo transport truck, where, due to the overturning of the second vehicle, the goods were taken by passers-by.

29. Finally, in cases resembling two-person case groups, the same criteria should be applied as in the cases already analyzed, since there is no fundamental difference, in terms of liability, whether the injured party is the second perpetrator or a third party.

MIX
Papier aus verantwortungsvollen Quellen
Paper from responsible sources
FSC® C105338
FSC
www.fsc.org

If you have any concerns about our products,
you can contact us on
ProductSafety@springernature.com

In case Publisher is established outside the EU,
the EU authorized representative is:
Springer Nature Customer Service Center GmbH
Europaplatz 3, 69115 Heidelberg, Germany

Printed by Libri Plureos GmbH
in Hamburg, Germany